A THEORY OF BIOETHICS

This volume offers a carefully argued, compelling theory of bioethics while eliciting practical implications for a wide array of issues including medical assistance-in-dying, the right to health care, abortion, animal research, and the definition of death. The authors' dual value theory features mid-level principles, a distinctive model of moral status, a subjective account of well-being, and a cosmopolitan view of global justice. In addition to ethical theory, the book investigates the nature of harm and autonomous action, personal identity theory, and the "non-identity problem" associated with many procreative decisions. Readers new to particular topics will benefit from helpful introductions; specialists will appreciate in-depth theoretical explorations and a novel take on various practical issues; and all readers will benefit from the book's original synoptic vision of bioethics. This title is also available as Open Access on Cambridge Core.

DAVID DEGRAZIA is Elton Professor of Philosophy at George Washington University. In addition to several books, including *Taking Animals Seriously* (1996), *Human Identity and Bioethics* (2005), and *Creation Ethics* (2012), he has written numerous book chapters and journal articles on applied ethics, moral philosophy, and the philosophy of mind and cognitive sciences.

JOSEPH MILLUM is a bioethicist at the US National Institutes of Health. He is author of *The Moral Foundations of Parenthood* (2018) and coeditor of *Global Health Priority-setting* (2020). His research, which has appeared in journals including *The BMJ* and *Ethics,* focuses on consent, international research ethics, priority-setting for health care and research, and parenting.

T0381880

A THEORY OF BIOETHICS

DAVID DEGRAZIA

George Washington University

JOSEPH MILLUM

National Institutes of Health

CAMBRIDGE
UNIVERSITY PRESS

CAMBRIDGE
UNIVERSITY PRESS

University Printing House, Cambridge CB2 8BS, United Kingdom

One Liberty Plaza, 20th Floor, New York, NY 10006, USA

477 Williamstown Road, Port Melbourne, VIC 3207, Australia

314–321, 3rd Floor, Plot 3, Splendor Forum, Jasola District Centre, New Delhi – 110025, India

103 Penang Road, #05–06/07, Visioncrest Commercial, Singapore 238467

Cambridge University Press is part of the University of Cambridge.

It furthers the University's mission by disseminating knowledge in the pursuit of education, learning, and research at the highest international levels of excellence.

www.cambridge.org
Information on this title: www.cambridge.org/9781316515839
DOI: 10.1017/9781009026710

First published 2021

A catalogue record for this publication is available from the British Library.

Library of Congress Cataloging-in-Publication Data
NAMES: DeGrazia, David, author. | Millum, Joseph, author.
TITLE: A theory of bioethics / David DeGrazia, George Washington University, Washington DC, Joseph Millum, National Institutes of Health, Bethesda.
DESCRIPTION: Cambridge ; New York, NY : Cambridge University Press, 2021. | Includes bibliographical references and index.
IDENTIFIERS: LCCN 2021019754 | ISBN 9781316515839 (hardback) | ISBN 9781009011747 (paperback) | ISBN 9781009026710 (epub)
SUBJECTS: LCSH: Bioethics. | BISAC: PHILOSOPHY / Ethics & Moral Philosophy | PHILOSOPHY / Ethics & Moral Philosophy
CLASSIFICATION: LCC QH332 .D44 2021 | DDC 174.2–dc23
LC record available at https://lccn.loc.gov/2021019754

ISBN 978-1-316-51583-9 Hardback
ISBN 978-1-009-01174-7 Paperback

For Ellen O'Connor de Grazia and Danny Millum

Contents

Figures

Acknowledgments

In working on this book we have accumulated many debts of gratitude. David thanks Kathleen and Zoe for their love and support. He also thanks the Department of Philosophy at George Washington University and the Department of Bioethics at the National Institutes of Health (NIH), where he held a part-time position during work on this project, for their collegial, supportive work environments. Joe likewise thanks the Clinical Center Department of Bioethics at NIH for its encouragement and intellectually vibrant work environment.

Both of us are grateful to various people. Almost all chapters of *A Theory of Bioethics* were workshopped in the Department of Bioethics, greatly improving the argumentation, scholarship, and presentation of our ideas. Each of the following individuals helpfully commented on one or more draft chapters: Bernardo Aguilera, Jake Earl, Sophie Gibert, Frank Miller, Annette Rid, Ben Schwan, Robert Steel, Camila Strassle, Alex Voorhoeve, David Wasserman, and Dave Wendler. We are exceptionally grateful to David Benatar, who read the entire book for Cambridge University Press and provided us with a remarkable amount of helpful feedback. We also thank David Elliot for the cover design, Stephanie Sakson for copyediting, and Hilary Gaskin of Cambridge University Press for editorial oversight of this project. Meanwhile, we acknowledge a special debt to Christine Grady, Chief of the Department of Bioethics, for her extraordinary moral support for this project and for making it possible to publish the book in an open-access format.

Disclaimer: Work on this project was supported, in part, by intramural funds from the Clinical Center of NIH. The views we express in this book are our own and do not represent the views of the NIH, the Department of Health and Human Services, or any other US government agency.

CHAPTER I

Introduction

1.1 Why This Book?

Bioethics is a young discipline. It has been recognized as a distinct area of scholarly investigation only since the late 1960s or early 1970s. The term "bioethics" apparently came into use in the early 1970s, with recognition of the discipline in the United States closely tied to institutional support through the founding of the Hastings Center in Hastings-on-Hudson, New York, in 1969 and the Kennedy Institute of Ethics at Georgetown University in Washington, DC, in 1971.[1] The Centre for Bioethics at the Clinical Research Institute of Montreal was established in 1976 as the first Canadian center focused on bioethics.[2] Driving discussions in the 1970s were such topics as the determination of human death, the ethics of birth control and abortion, fair allocation of kidney dialysis machines, the permissibility of forgoing life support for impaired newborns, and the rights of human research subjects. These debates took place in the press, in medical journals, and in new specialist academic journals, including the *Hastings Center Report* in the United States (from 1971) and the *Journal of Medical Ethics* in the United Kingdom (from 1975).[3] By the end of the decade the young discipline had its own encyclopedia.[4]

As we use the term, "bioethics" refers to the study of ethical issues that arise in medicine, in such allied fields as nursing, pharmacy, and public health, and in the life sciences. A theory of bioethics is a general framework for illuminating and ultimately addressing ethical issues that arise in

---

[1] See Warren Reich, "The Word 'Bioethics': Its Birth and the Legacies of Those Who Shaped It," *Kennedy Institute of Ethics Journal* 4 (1994): 319–335; and Robert Martensen, "The History of Bioethics: An Essay Review," *Journal of the History of Medicine* 56 (2001): 168–175.

[2] John Williams, "The Influence of American Bioethics in Canada," *Journal International de Bioéthique* 20 (4) 2009: 95–105.

[3] For a history of bioethics in the United Kingdom, see Ruth Chadwick and Duncan Wilson, "The Emergence and Development of Bioethics in the UK," *Medical Law Review* 26 (2018): 183–201.

[4] Warren Reich (ed.), *The Encyclopedia of Bioethics* (New York: Macmillan, 1978).

bioethics. Is euthanasia, or medical mercy killing, ever justified? Do people have a moral right to health care? Is it permissible to involve animals in experiments that seriously harm them in order to benefit humanity? A theory of bioethics will offer a set of ethical guidelines – and perhaps an explicit method for deploying them – to help people address such questions in a manner that (according to the theory) is likely to yield justified or correct answers.

There are a variety of bioethical theories already on offer. Some are tailored to the content of bioethics or, more specifically, medical ethics. Examples include the principle-based approach to bioethics associated with Tom Beauchamp and James Childress,[5] Tristram Engelhardt's libertarian bioethics,[6] and Robert Veatch's contract-based theory of medical ethics.[7] Some theories employed in bioethics are *ethical* theories – theories offering guidelines for addressing ethical questions in general rather than bioethical issues in particular. Examples of ethical theories that have been put to work in bioethics are utilitarianism,[8] Kantian ethics,[9] a rules-based common morality theory,[10] and virtue ethics.[11] Other theoretical approaches to bioethics are distinguished less by the content of their central ethical norms than by their methods for investigating ethical questions. Examples include casuistry, a type of case-based reasoning in historical context;[12] feminist ethics, which interrogates mainstream ethical thinking and theories with an eye toward exposing gendered and oppression-supporting assumptions;[13] and narrative bioethics, which views the exploration of stories as a means to ethical insight.[14]

Despite the richness of current offerings in bioethical theory, we perceive a substantial gap in the literature. A satisfying bioethical theory, in

[5] Tom Beauchamp and James Childress, *Principles of Biomedical Ethics*, 8th ed. (New York: Oxford University Press, 2019; first published 1979).
[6] H. Tristram Engelhardt, Jr., *The Foundations of Bioethics* (New York: Oxford University Press, 1986).
[7] Robert Veatch, *A Theory of Medical Ethics* (New York: Basic, 1981).
[8] See, e.g., R. M. Hare, "A Utilitarian Approach," in Helga Kuhse and Peter Singer (eds.), *A Companion to Bioethics*, 2nd ed. (Oxford: Blackwell, 2009), 85–90.
[9] See, e.g., Onora O'Neill, *Autonomy and Trust in Bioethics* (Cambridge: Cambridge University Press, 2002).
[10] Bernard Gert, Charles Culver, and K. Danner Clouser, *Bioethics* (New York: Oxford University Press, 1997).
[11] See, e.g., Justin Oakley, "Virtue Ethics and Bioethics," in Daniel Russell (ed.), *The Cambridge Companion to Virtue Ethics* (Cambridge: Cambridge University Press, 2013), 197–220.
[12] See, e.g., John Arras, "Getting Down to Cases: The Revival of Casuistry in Bioethics," *Journal of Medicine and Philosophy* 16 (1991): 29–51.
[13] See, e.g., Susan Wolf (ed.), *Feminism and Bioethics* (New York: Oxford University Press, 1996).
[14] See, e.g., Hilde Lindemann Nelson (ed.), *Stories and Their Limits* (New York: Routledge, 1997).

our estimation, would achieve several aims. First, it would provide a high-quality discussion of ethical theory and methodology in ethics, recommending an approach that holds up well under critical scrutiny. Second, an adequate bioethical theory would avoid the narrowness of normative vision that one finds in some theories – with excessive focus on, for example, hypothetical agreement in contract theories, on liberty in libertarianism, and on moral rules in the rules-based common morality approach. Third, a fully adequate contribution to bioethical theory would probe and integrate areas of philosophical theory that are relevant to ethics but tend to receive little coverage in the bioethical theory literature. These include the nature of harm, the nature of well-being, models of moral status, personal identity theory, and the "nonidentity problem." We are not aware of any previous book on bioethical theory that achieves all three aims. In pursuing them, we think we have arrived at a normative vision of bioethics that is wider in scope, but is also more progressive than many works in bioethical theory. For example, our theory treats nonhuman animals with the moral seriousness they deserve and accepts extensive institutional and individual obligations to the global poor.

This book is intended for several overlapping audiences. It is intended for upper-level undergraduate and graduate classes in bioethics, applied ethics, or ethical theory. It is intended for scholars from any discipline who are interested in these areas. Most generally, this book is intended for readers – ranging from those with little theoretical background to specialists – who are interested in bioethical theory or a vision of normative bioethics that covers a broad array of important issues.

Some limitations are inevitable for a book that attempts to cover so much ground. In particular, we acknowledge geographical restrictions in the scope of many discussions of specific issues in the book. Our theory is intended to be universal – correct (or incorrect) everywhere. But its application must be sensitive to context. We lack the expertise to speak to the contexts in which many health care practitioners operate. We therefore mostly draw our examples from the Anglophone high-income countries with which we are most familiar: Canada, the United Kingdom, and the United States. In addition, although our book discusses the relationship between our theory and other broad types of ethical theory, it does not offer a thorough introduction to ethical theory. Finally, while we have made every effort to achieve accessibility while seeking philosophical depth and precision, our book is unlikely to be suitable for high school students and perhaps for lower-level undergraduates.

1.2   Plan for the Book

Each of the nine chapters that follow this introduction engages theoretical issues. Each of Chapters 4–10 also includes two or three substantial applications of the theoretical material developed in the chapter to concrete issues of bioethical interest.

Chapter 2 presents our methodology for bioethics. A methodology, although theoretical, is not itself a theory. A theory of bioethics features *substantive* norms, or action-guides, such as "Respect the informed, voluntary choices of autonomous decision-makers" and "Do not deceive patients or prospective research participants." These norms have ethical content. A methodology for bioethics, by contrast, is a structured *process* for arriving at such norms. One methodology, sometimes called "deductivism," recommends starting with (purportedly) self-evident or rationally provable general ethical principles and then, in view of relevant facts, deriving specific conclusions about right conduct. A second methodology, featuring a type of inductive reasoning, involves carefully examining a variety of specific cases, intuitively judging the right answer in each case, and then generalizing on the basis of these specific judgments to more general principles, which can then be applied to new cases. Our methodology is distinct from each of these.

The method we embrace has been called both "reflective equilibrium" and "the coherence model of ethical justification." It is neither purely deductive (justifying specific moral judgments on the basis of general principles) nor purely inductive (justifying general norms on the basis of confident judgments about specific cases). Instead, it provisionally accepts "considered moral judgments" – judgments taken to be especially reliable in virtue of their inherent plausibility, stability, and low likelihood of being motivated by biases – at any level of generality. Some considered judgments will be very general. For example, the principle of nonmaleficence – which states that it is wrong to harm others in the absence of special justifying circumstances – is a very general considered judgment. Others will be judgments about a specific case. For example, the judgment that the act of running a particular dog fight is wrongful is a specific considered judgment about a particular case. Still others will be of intermediate generality. For example, the judgment that rape is wrong is a considered judgment of intermediate generality. According to the method of reflective equilibrium, a moral judgment is justified if it is part of an overall view of ethics that we could accept, upon reflection, on the basis of its incorporation of considered judgments, its overall plausibility and coherence, and various other theoretical virtues such as simplicity, comprehensiveness, and explanatory power. The discussion of Chapter 2 explains how the critical tools of this method entail that what we intuitively believe about an ethical issue may sometimes have to be rejected. For instance, this will be the case with intuitive judgments that seem prejudiced or misinformed and fail to cohere with judgments that persist in reflective equilibrium. The methodology is therefore capable of generating radical and surprising conclusions, even though it starts with our existing moral beliefs.

Chapter 3 presents an overview of the ethical theory that emerges from our application of the method of reflective equilibrium. Our theory acknowledges two fundamental and irreducible values: well-being and respect for rights-holders (or "respect" for short). Accordingly, we refer to it as our *dual value theory*. Some prominent alternative ethical theories are grounded in a single value. For example, utilitarianism may be understood as being grounded in utility or well-being alone. Kantian ethics may be regarded as grounded entirely in respect for persons. Bernard Gert's rule-based common morality approach appears to be grounded entirely in nonmaleficence, insofar as all of its ten rules require the avoidance of some kind of harm.[15] Other theories are pluralistic. For example, W. D. Ross's theory of prima facie duties features multiple moral obligations that are treated as irreducible to any more basic norm[16] while William Frankena's ethical theory features two ultimate principles, beneficence and justice.[17]

The two fundamental values in our theory, well-being and respect for rights-holders, inform the theory's scope – that is, who has moral status. Our answer is: all beings who have a welfare have moral status. This means all sentient beings – beings who are capable of having pleasant or unpleasant experiences. All sentient beings are entitled to a form of equal moral consideration. We understand such equal consideration in consequentialist terms, meaning that the well-being of some sentient beings may be traded off for the well-being of others. Both equal consideration and the permissibility of consequentialist trade-offs are important in considering obligations of nonmaleficence as they apply to nonhuman animals. Equal consideration entails a moral prohibition against many of the harms that humans have traditionally felt entitled to impose on animals. The prerogative of trade-offs permits sacrifices of some animals' well-being for the greater good.

---

[15] See Bernard Gert, *Morality* (New York: Oxford University Press, 1988).
[16] W. D. Ross, *The Right and the Good* (Oxford: Oxford University Press, 1930).
[17] William Frankena, *Ethics* (Englewood Cliffs, NJ: Prentice-Hall, 1963).

In our theory, in addition to having obligations of nonmaleficence, and sometimes beneficence, to sentient beings, moral agents have distinct obligations to rights-holders. Rights, as we understand them, protect individuals from consequentialist trading-off of their interests for the greater good. These protections are not absolute and so may sometimes be overridden when the consequences of doing so are sufficiently important. In our theory, those who have full-strength rights are individuals with *narrative capacity*: the capacity to form narrative identities or temporally structured mental stories about their own lives. Beings who lack this narrative capacity, but still have some significant self-awareness over time, have rights of partial strength. This group likely includes animals such as dogs and monkeys. While rights-holders, in our approach, enjoy special protections in connection with obligations of nonmaleficence, they also have entitlements related to the principles of distributive justice.

Chapter 4 examines the principle of nonmaleficence, which states a prohibition on causing harm to others in the absence of justifying circumstances. The chapter begins with a type of theoretical exploration that is generally lacking in other books on bioethical theory: an investigation of the nature of harm. After surveying several leading accounts of the nature of harm, and noting challenges to each, it defends a counterfactual account: you harm someone if and only if you make them worse off than they would have been in the absence of your intervention. Next we specify nonmaleficence into several general moral rules corresponding to ways in which individuals can be harmed.

Following these foundational reflections, the chapter explores three areas of practical ethical concern in which rules concerning harm figure prominently: (1) the ethics of torture (an important, instructive issue even if not squarely within bioethics), (2) the limits of permissible risk in pediatric research, and (3) the ethics of medical assistance-in-dying. We find that nonmaleficence supports a right not to be tortured that should never, in practice, be overridden, and children's right to adequate protection, which allows children to be exposed to some net risks for the sake of valuable scientific knowledge, while placing a ceiling on this risk. In exploring medical assistance-in-dying we find a conflict, in some circumstances, between two rules: "Do not cause pain, suffering, or other experiential harm" and "Do not kill." We argue for the permissibility of physician-assisted suicide and euthanasia in some cases but also for an array of safeguards to protect against error and abuse. We find that death is not always a harm. Perhaps surprisingly, whether or not death is a harm for an autonomous individual, given their circumstances, is partly determined by their values.

Chapter 5 analyzes autonomy. The concept of autonomy has played a pivotal role in bioethics. Recognition of the importance of patient autonomy – in relation to informed consent, patient rights, and the value of people making their own decisions about medical care – has transformed medical practice and clinical research, distinguishing contemporary medical ethics from the far more paternalistic medical ethics that preceded it. According to our analysis, an agent, A, performs a particular action autonomously if and only if (1) A performs the action (a) intentionally, (b) with sufficient understanding, and (c) sufficiently freely of controlling influences, and (2) A decided, or could have decided, whether to perform the action in light of A's values.

The importance of autonomy, we argue, may be understood both in its contribution to individual well-being and in terms of the intrinsic moral importance of an individual's sovereignty over their own life. We discuss how autonomy grounds certain rights and then construct a taxonomy of ways in which someone's autonomy can be interfered with. The chapter briefly explores two justifications for interfering with someone's autonomous actions: paternalistic justifications and the prevention of harm to others. Autonomous individuals have the power to waive some of their rights by giving consent. Because this is a crucial concept for bioethics, we identify necessary and sufficient conditions for valid consent. Our analysis of valid consent departs from most others in the literature in the way it understands the condition of comprehension.

When someone lacks competence to make their own decisions, someone else must decide for them. This brings us to the topic of surrogate decision-making, where we introduce and defend a novel "reasonable subject" standard. The chapter's final two sections take up practical applications of our theoretical reflections: the right to refuse medical treatment and the ethics of direct-to-consumer advertising of pharmaceuticals.

Chapter 6 explores both distributive justice and beneficence – which we believe to be more closely related than is generally appreciated. Justice involves giving individuals what they are due. *Distributive justice* governs the distribution of valuable resources (e.g., income), the distribution of burdens (e.g., taxes), and the granting of certain legal rights (e.g., the right to marry). Beneficence concerns agents' duties to benefit other individuals. The *imperfect duty of beneficence* is a duty to contribute substantially, relative to one's ability, to assist individuals in need over the course of one's life. We consider it an advance over much prominent work in bioethical theory that our theory unequivocally supports such a duty. The *perfect duty of beneficence* or *duty of rescue* is a duty agents have to provide large benefits to others when they can do so at relatively low cost to themselves. There are, in addition, *special duties of beneficence* that attach to agents in virtue of their roles and relationships, such as the special duties of clinicians to their patients or parents to their children.

The chapter highlights two crucial distinctions: (1) between the ideal and the nonideal and (2) between how institutions should be arranged and how individuals should act. *Ideal theory* concerns the organization of just social and international institutions. It tells us how individuals ought to act against a background of just institutions and on the assumption that other people will act rightly. *Nonideal theory* concerns what ought to be done when the institutional background is not just and other people cannot be relied upon to act as they should. Most saliently, we understand nonideal theory to address what particular actors – both states and persons – should do in the world as it is now.

Regarding institutions, domestically, we defend a relatively generic *liberal egalitarian* view about distributive justice: unchosen differences in individual advantage within a society are prima facie unjust. Justifications for differences in individual advantage might include a great gain in overall well-being, the need for such differences to secure a fundamental right, or the fact that the inequality results from voluntary, informed decisions. Globally, we endorse a form of *cosmopolitanism*: similar principles of justice apply internationally as apply domestically. Regarding individuals' obligations in our nonideal world, we defend extensive duties of beneficence, albeit consistent with considerable leeway for people to prioritize their own projects.

The practical consequences of our theoretical views for institutional arrangements and the obligations of individuals are far-reaching. Among other implications, we argue that national governments should ensure that all their residents have access to affordable health care and that the international community ought to amend the global intellectual property regime that governs pharmaceutical patents.

As discussed in Chapters 4–6, morality generates obligations related to nonmaleficence, autonomy, distributive justice, and beneficence. But to whom are these obligations owed? Who has rights that correspond to such obligations? To address these questions is to engage the concept of *moral status*. Chapter 7 examines moral status in depth.

The discussion begins with the concept of moral status, formally unpacking its elements before commenting on its usefulness. It proceeds to a sketch of our account of moral status. Our account embraces equal consequentialist consideration for all sentient beings while ascribing the stronger protection of rights to those with narrative capacity (full-strength rights) and to those with nontrivial temporal self-awareness that falls short of narrative capacity (partial-strength rights). This account of moral status is neutral with respect to species in the sense that membership in *Homo sapiens* is, in itself, neither necessary nor sufficient for moral status or rights.

The final three sections explore ethical implications for research involving human embryos, rodents, and great apes. We defend a very liberal position with respect to embryo research, a relatively restrictive approach to rodent research (one that accords equal consequentialist consideration to rodents' interests while permitting their use on utilitarian grounds), and a prohibition of invasive, nontherapeutic research involving great apes.

Chapter 8 explores the nature of individual well-being. The chapter examines subjective value theories, which understand well-being in terms of the experiences or judgmental authority of the individual subject, and more objective theories, which understand individual well-being partly in terms of factors that are independent of the subject's experiences or authority. We then sketch our preferred approach, a type of subjective theory.

According to our theory, both enjoyment (positively experienced mental states) and the satisfaction of narrative-relevant desires (desires whose satisfaction makes a difference to one's life story) are prudentially good for an individual. Suffering and the frustration of narrative-relevant desires are prudentially bad for an individual. Critically, in our view, contact with reality – as contrasted with illusion or delusion – plays an amplifying role. Enjoyment is better for someone when they are taking pleasure in something real. Likewise, the fulfillment of desires is prudentially better when those desires are informed and rational. Enjoyment and desire-satisfaction are unified in a single coherent account of well-being in that both reflect the lived, self-caring perspective of a conscious subject. The chapter's final three sections address three areas of practical concern: (1) the relationship between disability and well-being, (2) decision-making for impaired newborns, and (3) decision-making for patients in irreversibly unconscious states.

The topic of Chapter 9 is *personal identity theory*. Two concepts of personal identity are important for bioethics, but need to be kept distinct. First, *numerical* identity is the relationship an individual has to themself in being one and the same individual over time. Second, *narrative* identity involves a person's self-conception or self-told story about herself and her life. We explore four approaches to numerical identity from the philosophical literature: person-based accounts, biological accounts, mind-based accounts, and a social account. The chief findings of the theoretical investigation are that (1) person-based accounts and the social account are implausible accounts of numerical identity, and (2) the biological accounts and mind-based accounts are *both* plausible, motivating a pluralistic approach to personal identity. Our account is pluralistic in the sense that we hold that policies and practices should be consistent with the assumption that the biological and mind-based accounts are both reasonable and worthy of accommodation.

Equipped with these theoretical resources, the discussion turns to three areas of practical application. First, we neutralize some common concerns about human enhancement through biomedical means. Second, we investigate and ultimately vindicate the authority of advance directives in cases of severe dementia. Third, we enter the controversy over the definition of death and associated questions about unilateral discontinuation of life support and vital organ procurement. We find that proper resolution of these issues turns primarily on practical considerations other than the nature of death. The overarching lesson of these practical investigations *deflates* the role of personal identity theory in bioethics. Contrary to the claims of most bioethics scholars who have invoked personal identity, after we have narrowed down the theoretical options to genuinely plausible accounts, the latter do not have far-reaching implications in bioethics.

The final chapter of the book, Chapter 10, addresses the ethics of procreative decision-making. It begins by defending a negative right to procreative autonomy on the basis of more general rights of autonomous agents to control their own bodies. These rights, like other autonomy rights, are limited in scope by potential harm to others. Nevertheless, the negative right to procreative autonomy supports allowing the use of a wide range of procreative technologies. We also contend that while people's interests in procreating may ground claims to assistance on the basis of justice, they have no special weight compared with other interests and so do not qualify as positive rights.

From procreative autonomy the discussion turns to the ethics of making decisions that affect which humans come into existence (or to term). These divide into fixed-identity decisions and identity-determining decisions. The former occur when one chooses whether or not to bring a specific individual into the world – for example, a decision to terminate a pregnancy because the fetus has spina bifida. The pivotal question in fixed-identity cases is whether and in what circumstances abortion is ethically permissible. We contend that presentient fetuses are not harmed by death and that killing them is permissible. Once sentience emerges – probably no earlier than twenty-eight weeks' gestational age – it becomes plausible that death ordinarily harms the fetus. Yet we argue (on the basis of a "gradualist" view of the harm of death) that, due to the weak psychological connections between the fetus and its possible future, the harm of death to the sentient fetus is relatively small. It follows on our view that terminating pregnancy even in the late stages of pregnancy can be justified when there is a weighty reason to do so.

Identity-determining decisions determine *which* of several possible individuals will come into being. A couple might attempt to get pregnant now or – concerned about an outbreak of an infectious disease that might affect a fetus – postpone their attempt for several months. The sperm and egg that would be part of conception now will not be the same gametes that would be involved in a conception a few months later, so the decision about whether or not to delay determines which of two possible individuals will come into being. Identity-determining cases are ethically complex when the individuals who could come to exist differ substantially in their expected quality of life. Many philosophers believe it would be wrong to bring into existence someone whose life would go worse than that of another individual who could, with little cost, be brought into existence instead. But it is hard to understand this judgment once we note that there is no actual individual whose life is made worse by such a decision. We contend that, in at least a subset of these "nonidentity" cases, it is permissible to cause the existence of someone whose life will go worse than that of another possible individual.

The chapter's final two sections apply our theoretical conclusions about fixed-identity and identity-determining decisions to two practical issues: the use of medical technologies for sex selection and public health measures in the context of a Zika virus outbreak.

CHAPTER 2

Methodology

2.1 Introduction

This book is a work of normative theory – specifically, an attempt to provide a general framework that can illuminate and address ethical issues that arise in biomedical contexts. Such normative theorizing requires an appropriate methodology. The methods of the natural sciences – involving the collection of data, the testing of hypotheses through experimentation, and so forth – are insufficient for drawing conclusions about what ethically ought to be done. In this chapter, we describe and defend the methodology that we use in the rest of the book.[1]

Our reasons for explicitly laying out our methodology are threefold. First, doing so facilitates critical engagement. For someone who disagrees with us, it can be very helpful to identify whether the disagreement is a matter of starting from a different set of values, reasoning in different ways from similar starting points, or failing to meet some shared standards for ethical reasoning. Second, doing so displays the standards to which we think we should be held. The arguments we make over the course of the book should be explicable and defensible in terms of the methodology we describe here. Third, presenting our method may be helpful to readers who do not work in philosophical ethics. It is common for nonphilosophers to question how normative theorizing is done: "Do you collect data on what people think is ethical? If not, aren't you just stating your opinions?" Explaining the methodology and demonstrating how to use it may provide both a justification for how we proceed and some helpful examples for readers who are new to bioethics or ethical theory.

---

[1] Each of us has described his methodology in ethics elsewhere. See David DeGrazia, *Taking Animals Seriously* (Cambridge: Cambridge University Press, 1996), chap. 2; and Joseph Millum, *The Moral Foundations of Parenthood* (New York: Oxford University Press, 2017), 4–14. Our discussion here is consistent with those accounts while going beyond them in various respects.

Although normative theorizing and empirical research use different methods, empirical data are highly relevant to normative work in bioethics.[2] It is generally impossible to make action-guiding ethical recommendations in a particular case without taking into account the empirical facts that characterize that case. For example, in thinking about whether to follow a family's request to discontinue treatment for a terminally ill patient, we need to ascertain such matters as the following: what the prognosis would be with and without different treatments, whether the patient is suffering, what the options are for palliation, whether the patient's wishes are known, and what resources are available to the hospital. Answering these questions requires empirical information about the case (such as what wishes the patient expressed) and inferences drawn from empirical studies (such as the likelihoods of different possible outcomes of a treatment).

We begin this chapter with a description of our methodology, which we take to be a version of the method of *reflective equilibrium* that is widely used in philosophy and bioethics. We then describe some methodologies for normative theorizing in bioethics that are often advanced as alternatives to this methodology. Some, such as casuistry, we think are better understood as versions of the method of reflective equilibrium, at least as they are typically practiced. Others, such as particularism and foundationalism, we reject. Next, we defend the method of reflective equilibrium against some prominent criticisms, including skeptical reactions about the use of intuitions that recent work in experimental philosophy has engendered in some commentators. Finally, we turn to metaethics and clarify what we are, and are not, assuming about the nature and foundation of ethics.

2.2 The Method of Reflective Equilibrium

The basic idea behind the method of reflective equilibrium is relatively simple. We start with our existing ethical beliefs about cases and principles, weed out those that are thought to be unreliable, and then adjust the remaining set in order to make it as coherent as possible.[3] The final goal – which may never be

---

[2] There is a substantial amount of rigorous and valuable empirical bioethics research, and multiple academic disciplines contribute to bioethics scholarship. For an overview of the disciplines and their methodologies, see Jeremy Sugarman and Daniel Sulmasy, *Methods in Medical Ethics* (Washington, DC: Georgetown University Press, 2010).

[3] We use the language of "beliefs" because we find it natural to speak of ethical beliefs. We do not intend this usage to beg any questions regarding whether ethical judgments can be true or aim to express truths (see Section 2.5).

reached but stands as a regulative ideal – is a set of principles that fit together as a single theory and which, along with the relevant empirical facts, entail the moral judgments about cases that we think are correct. In the following paragraphs we fill out this idea and make it more precise.

Terminology and Scope

A couple of points regarding terminology and scope merit mention at the outset. First, some writers use "principles" to pick out only the most general of ethical judgments. For example, Beauchamp and Childress distinguish "principles" from "rules" such that principles are more "general and comprehensive" and rules are "more specific in content and more restricted in scope."[4] We make no such distinction. We use "principle" to refer to a universal normative statement, no matter how general or specific. Occasionally, we follow common usage in speaking of "rules" or "rules of thumb," but do not mean these as technical terms.

Second, our initial set of ethical beliefs are not just those judgments that we have already explicitly made. Implicit ethical beliefs can be elicited. The use of cases to prompt intuitions is a common way to demonstrate to someone that they have beliefs of which they were not aware. For example, someone might be persuaded that they already believe in an ethical difference between killing and letting die when they discover that their reaction to a case in which a physician can administer a lethal injection to a patient in terrible pain is different from their reaction to a case in which a physician can withdraw life-support measures from a similar patient. Notice, too, that these ethical beliefs come in different forms. We have intuitive reactions to particular actions or cases – "It would be wrong for Dr. Gomez to kill her patient." We also have intuitive reactions about the plausibility of ethical principles – "It is wrong to provide more benefits to one person than another solely on the basis of gender."

Third, though the ultimate goal of reflective equilibrium is a set of principles, a key part of the process involves articulating what those principles *mean*. Often there are terms used in candidate ethical principles whose meaning is unclear or disputed. Such terms include "well-being," "harm," "autonomy," "equality," "voluntariness," and so on. Settling on the correct principles must then include settling on the correct under-standing of these terms. For example, the principle of nonmaleficence is a

---

[4] Tom Beauchamp and James Childress, *Principles of Biomedical Ethics*, 7th ed. (New York: Oxford University Press, 2013), 14.

prohibition on causing harm. Assuming that we start with the considered judgment that some version of this principle is correct, the process of reflective equilibrium will involve working out the conditions under which it applies (e.g., is it wrong to harm someone who gives consent, or to harm one person to prevent harm to another?). But we cannot apply the principle without also knowing what harm consists in. As we discuss in Chapter 4, there are different accounts of harm. These different accounts can themselves be assessed and amended on the basis of their fit with our considered judgments about principles and cases.

Finally, for clarity of exposition, we mostly restrict our explanation of the method of reflective equilibrium to ethical judgments about principles and cases. However, this does not exhaust the relevant considerations that may be used in moral argument. In the process of attaining what Norman Daniels described as "wide reflective equilibrium" we may bring up all sorts of beliefs about values, reasons, and metaphysics. Daniels writes:

> Though we may be committed to some views quite firmly, no beliefs are beyond revision.... I include here our beliefs about particular cases; about rules and principles and virtues and how to apply or act on them; about the right-making properties of actions, policies, and institutions; about the conflict between consequentialist and deontological views; about partiality and impartiality and the moral point of view; about motivation, moral development, strains of moral commitment, and the limits of ethics; about the nature of persons; about the role or function of ethics in our lives; about the implications of game theory, decision theory, and accounts of rationality for morality; about the ways we should reply to moral skepticism and moral disagreement; and about moral justification itself.[5]

In the arguments of later chapters concerning personal identity, procreation, and moral status, this breadth of relevant considerations should become clear.

From Initial Beliefs to Considered Judgments

From the set of initial beliefs about cases and moral principles we select just those that we think have sufficient credibility. These are the *considered judgments* that form the data for our ethical theory. Our initial ethical judgments may be eliminated as candidates for considered judgments for various reasons. One is that we lack confidence in those judgments; that is,

---

[5] Norman Daniels, "Wide Reflective Equilibrium in Practice," in Daniels, *Justice and Justification* (New York: Cambridge University Press, 1996), 333–352, at 338–339.

we are uncertain about whether they are correct.[6] Cases in which we are uncertain about whether our initial judgment is correct (even where we have certainty regarding relevant empirical facts) are precisely those for which an ethical theory is valuable.[7] After all, unless we are willing to let our theory guide our judgments in at least some cases, working out an ethical theory is just an academic exercise. Another reason to exclude an initial belief from the set of considered judgments is that we have reason to think that the belief results from some distortion in our thinking. For example, someone who is having an affair may have a vested interest in concluding that adultery is not wrongful and this might bias their judgments.[8] Other potential distorting factors include that the judgment is made in a hurry, that it is made while angry, that the person making the judgment has a close relationship with one of the parties to a conflict, and so forth. These are all reasons to exclude individual initial beliefs that reflect our intuitive judgments. In Section 2.4, we consider more wholesale objections to the use of intuitions in moral theorizing.

After weeding out the initial beliefs whose credibility we have reason to doubt, we are left with a set of considered judgments that consists of judgments about individual cases and about principles of varying levels of generality. This set is the data with which we try to construct a theory about the topic that interests us, whether it is a theory of the ethics of paternalism or a complete moral theory. Typically, the set of considered judgments will not be sufficient to specify our theory completely. This is for two reasons. First, there will usually be some inconsistency among the members of the set and so some adjustment is needed. One basic criterion for coherence among a set of beliefs, and one of the most basic virtues of a theory, is that it be internally consistent – that is, free of logical contradictions. Second, our choice of ethical theory will still be *underdetermined*

---

[6] Since we will have different degrees of confidence in our initial beliefs, strictly speaking, we will require more evidence to reject some than others. The dichotomy that we describe here between considered judgments and initial judgments that we reject is a simplification that is useful for explanatory purposes.

[7] As John Rawls explains: "There are questions which we feel sure must be answered in a certain way. For example, we are confident that religious intolerance and racial discrimination are unjust. We think that we have examined these things with care and have reached what we believe is an impartial judgment not likely to be distorted by an excessive attention to our own interests. These convictions are provisional fixed points which we presume any conception of justice must fit. But we have much less assurance as to what is the correct distribution of wealth and authority. Here we may be looking for a way to remove our doubts" (*A Theory of Justice*, revised ed. [Cambridge, MA: Belknap, 1971/1999], 17–18).

[8] Konrad Bocian and Bogdan Wojciszke, "Self-Interest Bias in Moral Judgments of Others' Actions," *Personality and Social Psychology Bulletin* 40 (2014): 898–909.

by our set of considered judgments even when they are consistent – meaning that multiple theories will be consistent with the same set.

A great deal of debate in bioethics involves looking for and exposing apparent inconsistencies. For example, suppose we are interested in the conditions under which consent is valid and have agreed that voluntariness is one such condition. We are now developing a theory of what makes an act (such as giving consent) voluntary or involuntary. A prima facie plausible principle might be "Someone acts involuntarily if they are caused to act by someone or something external to them." Now someone suggests this counterexample: if someone offers me a reasonable hourly rate to tutor them and I agree to do so, then I have been caused to act by something external to me (the prospect of money and satisfying work), but this is surely a voluntary act. After all, if it were not voluntary, then my consent to receive the money would be invalid, and that seems highly implausible. The structure of this simplified dialectic is as follows. We have a principle that was initially part of our set of considered judgments. A case was proposed and a moral verdict rendered about that case (that the action was morally unproblematic and thus voluntary). The case judgment appeared inconsistent with the principle. In such a case, resolving the inconsistency requires rejecting the principle, rejecting our intuitive verdict about the case, or some argument to show that we were mistaken about their inconsistency.

In the process of reflective equilibrium, decisions about how to resolve inconsistencies are very important. In the case just described, we expect that most people would be inclined to reject the principle: our intuitive verdict on the counterexample is one in which we have confidence; similar counterexamples seem likely to arise for many familiar cases in which someone is caused to act; and it seems likely that the principle was over-simplified. The natural course to take is to try to articulate another principle that is intuitively plausible without being subject to such coun-terexamples. But it will not always be obvious which of our considered judgments should be rejected. For principles in which they have more confidence, people may be inclined to preserve the principle and reject the judgment that called that principle into question. This kind of "biting the bullet" is common among philosophers and bioethicists who are seeking to challenge received wisdom and make what they consider to be moral progress. For example, in Chapter 7, our examination of moral status leads us to reject common intuitions about ways in which it is permissible to treat nonhuman animals and preserve the principle that the well-being of all sentient creatures has substantial moral importance.

The underdetermination of theory by data is a long-standing challenge for the development of scientific theories that also applies to theory choice in ethics.[9] Here is a simple version of the problem. Suppose you are collecting empirical data in order to develop a scientific theory. For any finite data set – and all actual data sets are finite – there are infinite functions that would yield those data. This means that there are infinitely many universal generalizations that are consistent with the data. Which we should pick as our scientific theory for the phenomenon being studied is simply not determined by the data alone. Identical points apply to the construction of an ethical theory through the back and forth of the method of reflective equilibrium: the set of considered judgments will not determine which moral theory we should adopt.

Other Theoretical Virtues

The issue of how to resolve inconsistency and the underdetermination of theory by data both imply that the decision about what ethical theory we should adopt must be made on the basis of more than simply asking which theory is consistent with our considered judgments. Logical consistency is only one theoretical virtue. When we compare competing theories, we have to consider others.

One such virtue is the prima facie plausibility of the theory itself. Are the principles that make up a theory themselves ones in which we have a great deal of confidence or are they dubious? For example, many utilitarians find the theory compelling because its basic principle – that individuals should act so as to bring about the greatest overall improvement in well-being – seems so clearly correct to them. By contrast, for many people a moral theory based on the principles articulated by the biblical ten commandments would be implausible in part because it includes principles (e.g., "Thou shalt not steal") whose exceptionless character they find dubious.

A second important virtue is the explanatory power of a theory. An ethical theory has greater explanatory power when it renders verdicts in more types of case than a competitor. We can assess this in two ways. First, one theory may be better able to give a verdict because it is more precise than another. So, for example, a theory that relies on intuitively weighing

[9] Kyle Stanford, "Underdetermination of Scientific Theory," in Edward Zalta (ed.), *Stanford Encyclopedia of Philosophy* (Winter 2017 edition; https://plato.stanford.edu/entries/scientific-underdetermination/).

competing principles will have less explanatory power than one that explicitly says how competing considerations should be balanced. Second, one theory may have broader scope than another, in the sense that it applies to more areas of our moral lives. For example, a theory of consent that is applicable in the domains of clinical research, sexual relations, and contract law has greater explanatory power than one that is tailored solely to clinical research.

Theories with greater explanatory power are more informative since they are able to provide moral verdicts for a wider range of cases. This also means that they are more open to counterexamples. If one theory is more precise than another, then it will be easier to see what it implies. It will be a "clear target," making it easier to identify an implication that is inconsistent with some considered judgment. Likewise, if one theory has broader scope than another, then the first theory is more liable to being inconsistent with considered judgments in the form of principles or case judgments regarding one of the varied domains to which it applies. When we are comparing two theories we therefore need to be careful that we are not rejecting one that is more precise or has broader scope simply because it is easier to identify potential counterexamples to such a theory.

An important test for a theory occurs when it is extended to unfamiliar cases. It is evidence in favor of a theory if it renders verdicts about those cases that are also intuitively plausible – that is, entails moral verdicts about unfamiliar cases that are independently excellent candidates for considered judgments. It is a problem for a theory when its implications for novel cases conflict with considered judgments. In the face of such inconsistency one can adjust one's theory to take account of the apparent counterexample. Such adjustments can then make the theory more or less informative. It will be more informative if we can now apply it to a further range of cases to test how it fits them. It will be less informative if the adjustment simply deals with the problematic cases, but no more. Adjustments like the latter are ad hoc. For example, return to our principle concerning voluntariness. We might adjust it to say: "Someone acts involuntarily if they are caused to act by someone or something external to them that they do not endorse." Or we might adjust it to say: "Someone acts involuntarily if they are caused to act by someone or something external to them unless they want a tutoring job." The latter is ad hoc – it generates almost no new predictions to test against. The former is much more informative – we can now examine various cases of endorsement to see how well the principle answers questions about voluntariness.

A final, related theoretical virtue is simplicity. It is generally thought that if two theories have the same explanatory power but one is derived from fewer or more concisely stated principles, then the simpler one is better. Both utilitarianism and Kantian ethics, for example, might be regarded as simple in this sense, since they (purportedly) derive all their moral verdicts from just one principle applied to the empirical facts of a case. It is widely accepted that simpler *scientific* theories are preferable. For example, in addition to its greater explanatory power, one advantage that Newton's laws of motion and gravitational attraction had over prior physical theories was that their explanation of the movements of celestial bodies was simpler. What justifies this preference for simplicity and whether it applies equally in ethics has received little theoretical attention.[10]

The goal of the method of reflective equilibrium is to develop a moral theory that preserves as many of our considered judgments as possible, while remaining logically consistent, independently plausible, explanatorily powerful, and simple.[11] Naturally, there are trade-offs to be made. For example, we may find ourselves caught between a complex theory with many different principles that captures most of our considered judgments about cases and a theory that is much simpler but which requires us to amend more considered judgments. How to trade off the different theoretical virtues is itself a matter of debate, in ethics as in science.[12]

Reflective Equilibrium and Practical Ethics

The discussion so far may seem rather abstract and distant from ordinary ethical problem-solving. After all, when we are trying to decide what to do – in the clinic or outside it – it does not seem as if we are gathering a set of considered judgments and then constructing a theory from it. However, we think that the method of reflective equilibrium is implicitly used in everyday ethical debates and problem-solving. Consequently, understanding the method will help us adjudicate these debates and problems.

[10] For a discussion of the challenges involved in justifying and applying simplicity criteria in the context of scientific theory choice, see Alan Baker, "Simplicity," in Zalta, *Stanford Encyclopedia of Philosophy* (Winter 2016 edition; https://plato.stanford.edu/entries/simplicity/).

[11] An ethical theory should, of course, also be consistent with what we have most reason to believe about relevant factual matters, including the best natural and social scientific theories. For example, an ethical theory whose scope was limited to human beings because it assumed that no nonhuman animals were conscious or sentient would be deficient due to its implausible factual assumption about animals. And a political theory that assumes that its preferred form of government is most conducive to human happiness is no stronger than this pivotal empirical assumption.

[12] Thomas Kuhn, "Objectivity, Value Judgment, and Theory Choice," in Alexander Bird and James Ladyman (eds.), *Arguing about Science* (New York: Routledge, 2013), 74–86. See also Ben Sachs, *Explaining Right and Wrong* (New York: Routledge, 2018).

First, even when only a narrow topic area is at issue we can often understand a debate in terms of reflective equilibrium. For example, consider what might get brought up in a discussion about the ethics of medical assistance-in-dying (MAiD). The discussants will want to show that their ultimate views are consistent with more general moral principles that they hold. Someone might invoke the importance of the right of competent adults to decide what happens to their bodies, or a physician might note the apparent incongruity between causing death and the role of healer. The resulting back and forth might involve amending their views on MAiD; it might also involve changing how they interpret those more general principles.[13] Someone's views may also be challenged by showing that they appear to be inconsistent with a considered judgment about a case. For example, someone who thinks that it is permissible for clinicians to let someone die but not actively to kill might be confronted with a case in which that distinction does not seem to affect her moral verdict. This is the intended effect of James Rachels's fictional description of two evil uncles: both intend to murder their nephews by drowning them in the bath, but only one carries out his scheme, since the other has the "good fortune" to witness his nephew slip and fall and so only has to watch while he drowns.[14] When one of the people discussing MAiD reflects on these apparent inconsistencies and decides how to respond, she will then have to make use of the considerations we described above. For example, she may be pushed to distinguish those judgments in which she is truly confident (such as that it would be unethical to kill a competent adult against his wishes) from those in which she is uncertain (such as whether it could be permissible for a physician to give a lethal dose to a patient who requests it). For these latter cases she may be seeking guidance from a theory.

Second, when we are debating about ethics – or when we are simply trying to give someone advice – we have to use something like the method of reflective equilibrium if we are to proceed in an effective, mutually respectful way. I can only persuade you of my view about some topic if I start from what you already believe in and show that given your beliefs it is reasonable to draw the same conclusions that I have. For example, suppose that one person is trying to persuade another that he should not eat pork. She might try to show him that eating pork is inconsistent with being a good Muslim. But if he is not religious, this will not be persuasive

---

[13] See Chapter 4.
[14] James Rachels, "Active and Passive Euthanasia," *New England Journal of Medicine* 292 (1975): 78–80.

because he lacks the requisite beliefs. Alternatively, she might ask him whether it is bad to cause humans to suffer. Perhaps he agrees. She might go on to quiz him about whether he can think of a reason why the suffering of humans matters but the suffering of other intelligent mammals does not. Perhaps he cannot. Finally, she may ask whether it is justifiable to cause another to suffer in order to gain a small amount of pleasure and he may agree that it is not. Then, if she presents him with data on how the pigs from which his pork comes are treated, he may be compelled to agree that he should not eat pork. Of course, this dialectic is simplified, but we hope it is recognizable. In starting from where the other person is already, it is possible to persuade them of an ethical view that they did not originally hold. The process of doing so essentially involves showing them that making their set of ethical beliefs optimally coherent requires accepting that ethical view. It is the method of reflective equilibrium.[15]

2.3   Alternative Methodologies

Philosophers and bioethicists have articulated a variety of methods for normative theorizing in bioethics. These methods, such as principlism and casuistry, were articulated within academic bioethics as rivals to one another.[16] For principlists, such as Beauchamp and Childress, the application of mid-level principles to cases is intended to supply guidance as to what to do in those cases. Casuists, on the other hand, contend that the attempt to answer bioethical questions by applying agreed-upon principles to cases fails to take account of the rich contextual details that matter for actual decisions. Instead, bioethicists should proceed by careful description of the case under discussion and analogical reasoning from paradigm cases about which we have confident ethical judgments.[17]

   With a couple of exceptions we think that these are all variants of the method of reflective equilibrium that differ in terms of the relative emphasis that they put on different types of considered judgments. For example, it is not true that casuists refuse to theorize at all. They have to make some

[15] The same process occurs in written work on applied ethics. The writer attempts to show the reader that she should accept the conclusions for which he is arguing *on the assumption* that the considered judgments he cites are shared by her.
[16] John Arras, "Theory and Bioethics," in Zalta, *Stanford Encyclopedia of Philosophy* (Winter 2016 edition; https://plato.stanford.edu/entries/theory-bioethics/).
[17] For a history and defense of casuistry, see Albert Jonsen and Stephen Toulmin, *The Abuse of Casuistry* (Berkeley: University of California Press, 1988).

generalizations in order to draw analogies between similar cases and to decide which features of those cases are in fact relevantly similar.[18] Rather than being simply opposed to universal principles, modern casuists may be understood as putting greater emphasis on the evidentiary weight of case judgments and accepting complexity in their universal principles as the price of ethical accuracy. Scholars who are more sympathetic to principlism, on the other hand, may be characterized as putting more weight on the importance of bringing cases together under universal moral principles. Again, such scholars do not typically deny that their theory should be sensitive to contextual details or to strongly held judgments about cases. Thus, these different methods simply vary in the importance that they attach to the different theoretical virtues described in the previous section.[19]

Bioethicists at either extreme of the methodological spectrum could deny that they are engaged in the method of reflective equilibrium. At one extreme, some particularists deny that moral principles are a source of justification. At the other, some foundational moral theories deny that considered judgments about cases and mid-level principles have any justificatory weight. We now argue against these possibilities in turn.

Some proponents of particularism claim to reject the use of theory altogether. For example, Jonathan Dancy denies that moral principles have any justificatory weight at all: "Moral Particularism ... is the claim that there are no defensible moral principles, that moral thought does not consist in the application of moral principles to cases, and that the morally perfect person should not be conceived as the person of principle."[20] Dancy argues that the moral relevance of any feature varies across cases such that, depending on the situation, the same feature may be morally good, bad, or simply neutral. Pain, for example, is bad in some situations – such as for a patient seeking treatment for his arthritis – but can be good in

---

[18] Albert Jonsen, "Casuistry: An Alternative or Complement to Principles?," *Kennedy Institute of Ethics Journal* 5 (1995): 237–251.

[19] For more extended arguments for the claim that proponents of these different methods are all engaged in versions of reflective equilibrium see, e.g., John Arras, "The Way We Reason Now: Reflective Equilibrium in Bioethics," in Bonnie Steinbock (ed.), *Oxford Handbook of Bioethics* (New York: Oxford University Press, 2007); Mark Kuczewski, "Casuistry and Principlism: The Convergence of Method in Biomedical Ethics," *Theoretical Medicine and Bioethics* 19 (1998): 509–524; and Daniels, "Wide Reflective Equilibrium in Practice."

[20] Jonathan Dancy, "Moral Particularism," in Zalta, *Stanford Encyclopedia of Philosophy* (Fall 2017 Edition; https://plato.stanford.edu/entries/moral-particularism/). For an extended defense, see Jonathan Dancy, *Ethics without Principles* (Oxford: Oxford University Press, 2006).

others – such as when felt by athletes striving to push themselves as hard as they can. Likewise, pleasure is usually good, but can be bad – as when a sadist takes pleasure in another's pain. Principles, such as "Pain is bad" or "Pleasure is good," seem inevitably to be vulnerable to counterexample. Particularists like Dancy think that we can abandon them and simply explain our moral judgments by reference to the reasons that are relevant in each particular case, without the expectation that those reasons will operate in the same way in other cases.

Dancy's view has been subject to extensive philosophical critique else-where.[21] Instead of recapitulating that debate here, we note two key points. First, for extreme particularists like Dancy, we should demand a high burden of proof. If his view were correct, it not only would under-mine the methodological points we made above about selecting a theory but also would require us to revise our everyday practices of discussing and teaching morality, since they often seem to involve searching for, demand-ing, and articulating moral principles.[22] Second, insofar as moral particu-larism is supported by the apparent counterexamples that can be raised to proposed universal principles, so can the contrary view be defended by arguing in favor of specific universal principles. If a purported principle explains our considered judgments and gives us plausible verdicts for cases about which we are uncertain, that is a reason to preserve the principle. The arguments about principles that constitute the majority of this book stand as an attempt to demonstrate this point. We leave it to the reader to decide whether our theorizing is fruitful.

At the other extreme from the particularist position are views that seek to derive their answers to questions of applied ethics from foundational ethical theories, where the evidence for the truth of those theories is independent of how well they fit with more granular considered judgments about principles or cases. For example, Immanuel Kant sought to derive all of morality from the Categorical Imperative, which itself is a principle of rationality for beings like us (that is, embodied and able to act according to reasons).[23] Likewise, some utilitarians reject intuitive judgments as a

[21] See discussions in Mark Lance, Matjaž Potrč, and Vojko Strahovnik (eds.), *Challenging Moral Particularism* (Oxford: Routledge, 2008).
[22] Cf. Margaret Little, who writes: "If we reflect on our shared moral life, it certainly looks as though an important part of how we justify, convince, teach, and clarify is by pointing to explanatory generalizations whose truth we seem to endorse" ("On Knowing the 'Why': Particularism and Moral Theory," *Hastings Center Report* 31 [4] [2001]: 32–40, at 36).
[23] *Grounding for the Metaphysics of Morals*, 3rd ed., trans. James Ellington (Indianapolis, IN: Hackett, 1993; first published 1785).

source of evidence about morality.[24] For such foundationalists, it might seem as though reflective equilibrium is irrelevant: the foundational moral theory justifies verdicts about cases, but verdicts about cases do not provide evidence for or against the foundational moral theory.

Like many others, we have yet to be convinced by a theory that attempts to derive all of morality from a single, allegedly self-evident principle. More importantly, for our point about methodology, one of the main reasons we find them unconvincing is that they fail to give plausible verdicts about cases. For example, one criticism of utilitarianism is that it implies that only the amount of benefits and harms matters, not their distribution. On its face, it therefore suggests that it could be permissible to punish an innocent person to calm an angry mob, or to ignore the needs of people who are severely disabled because it would be so expensive to benefit them. These implications are highly counterintuitive. This counts against any version of utilitarianism that has such implications.

2.4   Reflective Equilibrium: Clarifications and Criticisms

Why Start from Here?

One objection to the use of the method of reflective equilibrium is to ask why we should give any credence at all to our initial set of moral beliefs. What makes us think that starting with the moral judgments we are already disposed to make will lead us to end up with an accurate moral theory?[25] Given that the method of reflective equilibrium seeks to find a theory that preserves our considered beliefs, it seems plausible that one's starting point will bias where one ends up. For example, if you and I start with very different initial moral beliefs, then we are also likely to end up with different moral theories; that is, our reflective equilibria will be different. But why should I think that my starting point is preferable to yours? If I have no reason to think one starting point preferable, then I have no reason to think that one reflective equilibrium is preferable to another either. Skepticism seems to loom.

One possible response would be to claim that the method of reflective equilibrium, properly applied, will in fact lead to convergence between

---

[24] See, e.g., R. M. Hare, "Rawls' Theory of Justice" (in two parts), *Philosophical Quarterly* 23 (1973): 144–155, 241–252; Peter Singer, "Sidgwick and Reflective Equilibrium," *Monist* 58 (1974): 490–517; and R. B. Brandt, *A Theory of the Good and the Right* (Oxford: Clarendon, 1979), chap. 1.

[25] For blunt criticism along these lines, see Hare, "Rawls' Theory of Justice" (Part 1).

people who start with different moral views. Although we think this will be true in some cases – after all, a central point of moral deliberation is resolving disagreement – it seems unduly optimistic to think that this will always be the case. Further, for our skeptic, such convergence on its own might not be reassuring. The problem is not the possibility that we fail to reach agreement; rather, the problem is that our end point seems determined by our starting point and we have no reason to think that the starting point is correct. The possibility of two people coming to different equilibria because they have different starting points simply illustrates this worry. Thus, for the skeptic, convergence would be reassuring only if there were a plausible explanation of the convergence, for example, that the method of reflective equilibrium tracks reasons for belief and so brings us closer to moral knowledge.

At this point it is helpful to distinguish different objectives that we might seek with our methodology. If we want a method that will get us to the moral truth, then we need first to answer the deep questions in metaethics regarding whether moral claims can be true or false, what moral properties are, and how we come to know them. Depending on our answers to these questions, the method of reflective equilibrium may or may not prove to be the best way to access the moral truth. As we explain in Section 2.5, though we think there are strong grounds to reject moral skepticism, we do not have answers to these difficult and highly contested metaethical questions. We therefore regard the function of our methodology as more modest. The method of reflective equilibrium might not tell us how to get to the moral truth. Instead, it guides us to what we should say about novel or difficult moral questions, *given what we already believe*. Thus, it should not be seen as a response to moral skepticism, since it starts from the assumption that in a wide range of situations we already know what we should do. Similarly, with regard to interpersonal reflective equilibrium, we should be modest about what can be shown. It might be that people who start from very different views will not converge in their views on some subjects, even if they are the most patient and well-meaning of interlocutors. We can only attempt to convince those people who already share certain beliefs with us, that, *given those shared beliefs*, they have good reason to draw the same conclusions as we have for some novel or difficult question.

Even if our critic allows that there is no way of engaging in moral theorizing that is entirely independent of one's existing moral beliefs, it might be objected that the method of reflective equilibrium is still liable to give conservative results. After all, it involves trying to find the theory that preserves as many of our considered judgments as possible. Since we start with the ethical beliefs that we (and, we hope, our readers) already have, we therefore stack the deck in favor of a moral theory that is similar to what we already believe.

But even brief reflection on the dominant moral views in Western societies over the last couple of centuries suggests that there have been dramatic changes in what many people believe rather than a conservative preservation of moral outlook. Moreover, it is hard, from our modern perspective, to avoid thinking that many of these changes constitute progress. For example, the prevailing views about people of different races or about women have not only changed, but surely changed for the better. A little humility suggests that there are likely to be equally dramatic changes in the future (perhaps concerning our treatment of nonhuman animals, for example).[26]

Further, we would argue that the moral progress that has been made has occurred because of – not in spite of – the moral beliefs that people already hold. It is by realizing that certain of our beliefs are in tension with each other, that some are propped up by false empirical claims, or that some are clearly self-serving that the societal consensus has been pushed toward radical change. For example, a view that denies that women have the same moral status as men is one that is flatly inconsistent with most people's views about what underlies moral consideration (whether it be rationality, the ability to suffer, or species membership). The push for consistency between moral principles and moral judgments has made that view untenable.[27] Thus, although it is true that we start from where we already are, that fact does not prevent progress.

Empirical Concerns about the Reliability of Moral Intuitions

Recent empirical findings about how people's moral intuitions are elicited have also led some to skepticism about the role of intuitions in justifying moral principles. For example, Eric Schwitzgebel and Fiery Cushman describe a series of experiments in which they present participants with pairs of moral scenarios relating to the doctrine of double effect, the action-

---

[26] Cf. Peter Singer, *The Expanding Circle* (Princeton, NJ: Princeton University Press, 2011).

[27] For classic treatments, see John Stuart Mill, *The Subjection of Women*, vol. 1 (London: Longmans, Green, Reader & Dyer, 1869); and Simone de Beauvoir, *The Second Sex*, trans. Constance Borde and Sheila Malovany-Chevallier (New York: Random House, 2009; first published 1949).

omission distinction, and moral luck.[28] They show that the order in which
the scenarios are presented has significant effects on moral judgments
about the scenarios. Since order is presumably irrelevant to the right
answer in these scenarios, the experiments cast doubt on whether intuitive
judgments are a source of evidence about right and wrong. Joshua Greene
and colleagues have conducted multiple experiments looking at variants of
trolley problems.[29] They argue that people's intuitive responses are highly
sensitive to the use of personal force. Since we do not think that the mere
fact of using personal force rather than something else (e.g., pushing
someone off a bridge rather than using a remote switch to drop him
through a trapdoor) is morally relevant, they argue that we should not
trust these intuitions.

For some philosophers, such findings throw the whole method of
reflective equilibrium into doubt. For example, Peter Singer argues:

> At the more general level of method in ethics, this same understanding of
> how we make moral judgments casts serious doubt on the method of
> reflective equilibrium. There is little point in constructing a moral theory
> designed to match considered moral judgments that themselves stem from
> our evolved responses to the situations in which we and our ancestors lived
> during the period of our evolution as social mammals, primates, and finally,
> human beings.[30]

We agree that empirical findings about the origins of our moral beliefs and
the causes of our moral judgments should be taken seriously. However, we
think that the method of reflective equilibrium, as we have described it, is
able to incorporate their use. For example, if our moral intuitions about
some family of cases are highly sensitive to morally irrelevant features of
those cases, we agree that this gives us reason to question the evidentiary
value of those intuitions (so they should not enter the set of considered
judgments). Thus, scientific evidence can play a helpful debunking role.

---

[28] Eric Schwitzgebel and Fiery Cushman, "Expertise in Moral Reasoning? Order Effects on Moral
Judgment in Professional Philosophers and Non-philosophers," *Mind & Language* 27 (2012):
135–153.

[29] See, especially, Joshua Greene, "Beyond Point-and-Shoot Morality: Why Cognitive (Neuro)
Science Matters for Ethics," *Ethics* 124 (2014): 695–726. A "trolley problem" typically involves a
runaway trolley and a choice between five people dying and one person dying. Variations in the
nature of the choice include throwing a switch to move the trolley from one track to another,
pushing someone off a bridge to block the trolley, and so forth.

[30] Peter Singer, "Ethics and Intuitions," *Journal of Ethics* 9 (2005): 331–352, at 348. But see, e.g.,
p. 347 on the possibility of a wide reflective equilibrium that could "countenance the rejection of all
our ordinary moral beliefs." For a more extended response to Singer with which we are sympathetic,
see Joakim Sandberg and Niklas Juth, "Ethics and Intuitions: A Reply to Singer," *Journal of Ethics*
15 (2011): 209–226.

However, it can only play this role along with considered normative judgments. The judgment that some feature of a case (e.g., the order in which cases are presented) is morally irrelevant is also a considered judgment that we employ in the debunking argument. Even the most hard-core skeptics about the evidentiary value of intuitions acknowledge this general point.[31]

Furthermore, we believe that the available evidence does not impugn the majority of careful work in applied ethics that makes use of judgments about cases. A great deal of this work does not rely on brute intuitions – like a gut response that I should not push someone off a bridge – but uses cases to draw out the structure of moral principles that we already have. For example, analyses of coercion, consent, or the nature of prudential value appeal to complex concepts with which many people are already facile. Take an example from theoretical work on consent. A. John Simmons describes a case in which the chair of a board asks attendees at a meeting if they have any objections to the policy he proposes.[32] Their silence, Simmons points out, constitutes consent to the policy provided that it meets the same standards for voluntariness and the like that affirmative consent would require. But the reader who is persuaded by Simmons that "tacit consent" is morally transformative in the same way as express consent does not have a gut response to the case and conclude that Simmons has given an explanation. Rather, Simmons uses the case to illustrate a view the reader already endorses.

In summary, we welcome the empirical evidence, consider it relevant, and believe it should be used during the process of seeking reflective equilibrium along with the other relevant considerations we have described.

2.5   Metaethics

Work in metaethics involves the attempt to understand the ultimate foundations of ethics. Are there matters of fact regarding ethical

---

[31] Some of these writers think that there are different types of intuition in play here. See Singer, "Ethics and Intuitions," 350–351; and Greene, "Beyond Point-and-Shoot Morality," 724, citing Sidgwick on "philosophical" intuitions. We believe they underestimate the number of such intuitions, which should include intuitions not just about consequences but about the nature of those consequences (e.g., suffering, death), about their distribution, and, as noted, about moral relevance.

[32] A. John Simmons, "Tacit Consent and Political Obligation," *Philosophy & Public Affairs* 5 (1976): 274–291, at 278–279.

judgments? Can such judgments be true or false, objectively correct or incorrect? If ethics admits of truth or objectivity, in what is it grounded: religious truths, some other type of metaphysical truths, facts about the natural world? How can we know the relevant facts? And so on.

These are enormously complicated matters that have been debated at least since antiquity.[33] They are not matters about which this book has much to say. Nevertheless, some of our readers might wonder how we can have a theory of bioethics without addressing them. In the following paragraphs we sketch answers to some of the questions such readers might have.

What are you assuming about the nature and foundation of ethics in using the method of reflective equilibrium? Our assumptions are relatively modest. We are not committed to any specific view of the foundation of ethics. In fact, we do not seek a rationally indubitable foundation for ethics and doubt that such a foundation exists. Further, we assume nothing about the truth or falsity of particular religions or religion in general. We consider it inappropriate to appeal to the supposed authority of some individual, a particular group, or a religious text as the basis of ethical thinking. We do assume that people's beliefs about ethical matters, especially upon reflection and when informed about relevant facts, provide the appropriate starting point for ethical inquiry. In the absence of an indubitable foundation or infallible source of authority for ethics, we think, there is no more credible starting point than what people believe about ethics.

Are you assuming that ethical beliefs can be true or false, that there are facts of the matter regarding ethical issues? The answer may depend on how broadly, or narrowly, one defines "truth" and "facts" – and we do not wish to enter this semantic territory. What we can say is that we assume that ethics is objective in at least the sense that there are better and worse answers to ethical questions, that some ethical judgments are more defensible and worthy of acceptance than others. Without such an assumption there would be little or no point in investigating and debating ethical issues. Why do so if no result is better than any other? We therefore reject *ethical skepticism*, which holds that no ethical judgments are justified and therefore better than any others, period. We also reject *ethical relativism*, which (as we understand it) holds that ethical judgments can be justified only relative to the ethical beliefs of a particular culture or group.

---

[33] For a useful collection of historical and contemporary readings, see Steven Cahn and Andrew Forcehimes (eds.), *Foundations of Moral Philosophy* (New York: Oxford University Press, 2016).

Why do you reject ethical skepticism? Our confidence has several grounds, which we can present only briefly here. First, we find certain ethical judgments – and the belief that they are binding on all human moral agents – more plausible than any arguments we have encountered in support of ethical skepticism. For example, we find the judgment "Raping children is wrong," where this judgment is understood to apply to all human beings, far more plausible than the argument that, because there is no God, everything is morally permissible. Likewise for every other argument we have encountered in support of ethical skepticism. If we accepted the conclusion of the argument, then we would have to accept that all our ethical beliefs are mistaken, and this seems more counterintuitive than that the argument is unsound. Similar points apply to examples of apparent moral progress. Increasing respect for gay persons in Western countries in recent decades seems to represent an ethical advance over the comparative disrespect that preceded it. Unless ethics were objective in the sense that there are better and worse answers to ethical questions, there would be no standard against which we could measure the trend of increasing respect as an improvement rather than simply a change.

Second, it is very difficult to maintain skepticism about ethics without also becoming a skeptic about all reasons for action. Consider a very basic ethical claim: that an individual agent should take the interests of others into account when deciding what to do. The skeptic says that this claim is false. The fact that some act will help or hinder another person is in itself irrelevant to what the individual should do. How should an individual agent decide what to do? Perhaps, our skeptic might suggest, she should think only of her own interests and how to promote them. In that case, her interests provide her with reasons for action. But now we may ask why even her own interests provide her with reasons to act. Certainly, we humans are less prone to doubt that we have good reason to promote our own interests than other people's, but that does not justify the claim that we should care about them. If we should be ethical skeptics, then perhaps we should be prudential skeptics too.

There are three possible ways to respond to this argument. The first is to embrace wholesale skepticism about reasons and say that no one has any reason to do anything. This is logically consistent but seems impossible for any actual agent to adopt. Whenever one faces a novel situation and stops to think about what to do, the decision process involves thinking about the reasons to do one thing rather than another. The second response is to show that there is a difference between prudential and ethical reasons such that we should accept the former but not the latter. This would require some convincing explanation of why our own interests give us reasons, but the interests of others do not. The third, which we prefer, is to accept that there are both prudential and ethical reasons. Your interests matter to you, mine to me, and ours to each other. The challenge for ethical theory is to work out how they matter.[34]

Why do you reject ethical relativism? One reason we do so is the same as for rejecting ethical skepticism: our confidence in some of our ethical judgments. We are confident that committing genocide and raping children is wrong. We have yet to hear the argument for relativism that is convincing enough to shake our conviction that these actions would still be wrong even if a particular culture or group believed otherwise.

A second reason is that ethical relativism does not have a satisfactory way to justify ethical claims to those who disagree with them. Suppose that someone grows up within a culture but comes to disagree with a commonly held view within that culture about gender roles. She finds the views of a different culture with more liberal gender norms more plausible. According to the ethical relativist, the fact that her culture has a specific ethical view is justification for that view: she is wrong to defy these gender norms. But, she may ask, how is it that these norms correctly apply to me but not to women in another culture, just because I grew up in one and not the other? The relativist must say that ethical judgments are ultimately justified just because the majority of people in a culture believe them. This justification seems unsatisfactory: the dissenter is asking for reasons why she should conform to cultural norms, not just the assertion that they are cultural norms – that is, judgments held by the majority.

Finally, some of the most commonly presented grounds in favor of ethical relativism actually support an objective understanding of ethics. For example, one often hears that we should be ethical relativists because it would be disrespectful to condemn the ethical systems of other societies when they differ from our own society's ethical views. This reasoning implies that respect for other cultures is ethically valuable. Yet surely such respect is not valuable only because our own culture says it is. Disrespect seems morally problematic, no matter who the disrespectful agent or culture is. Moreover, those who advance this argument in favor of relativism usually acknowledge limits to appropriate deference to other cultures' views. It is not as if respecting the views of another culture means we

---

[34] For longer and more sophisticated arguments in a similar vein, see Thomas Nagel, *The Possibility of Altruism* (Oxford: Clarendon, 1970). See also Derek Parfit, *On What Matters*, vol. 1 (Oxford: Oxford University Press, 2011), Part 1.

should tolerate, for example, genocide or slavery in another society. The good point the ethical relativist has in mind is that we should not assume that our culture is correct on all ethical matters on which there are differences among cultures. But this point is consistent with believing that there are objectively better and worse answers to ethical questions. As later chapters will make clear, we do not defer to or accept all of our culture's views on ethical matters. For example, we argue that the dominant Anglo-American culture is wrong in not viewing animals as having substantial moral status and in often favoring property rights over the most important needs of the global poor.[35]

Consistent with the method of reflective equilibrium, we should take existing ethical beliefs (of anyone from any culture) to have some initial authority but not as infallible. This approach is appropriately respectful of members of other cultures without falling into the implausibility and impracticality that characterize ethical relativism and ethical skepticism.

This concludes our discussion of methodology in ethics. The task of the next chapter is to sketch our ethical theory.

---

[35] For an approachable overview of reasons why one might be tempted by ethical relativism and why that temptation should be resisted, see Michael Garnett, "Is Morality Relative?" (unpublished manuscript available at https://philpapers.org/archive/GARIMR.pdf).

CHAPTER 3

Outline of the Dual Value Theory

3.1 Introduction

As elaborated in Chapter 2, our methodology in ethics is *reflective equilibrium* – also called *the coherence model of moral reasoning*. Motivating this methodology is the assumption that no single level of ethical analysis – such as a foundational principle, mid-level principles, rules, or judgments about specific cases – deserves priority in our moral reasoning. It is true that considered judgments play a special role. Considered judgments are moral judgments that we have especially good reason to consider reliable; for this reason, an ethical theory may be constructed at least partly on the basis of considered judgments. But the considered judgments that form the starting points of ethical theorizing may be highly abstract and general, very specific and context-dependent, or of any level of intermediate generality.

What counts as an "ethical theory"? We think of an ethical theory as *a structure of general moral norms that helps to render specific ethical verdicts*. For example, utilitarianism at its core is a single ethical principle, the principle of utility – where the principle requires specification in terms of a particular account of utility, its scope, and the like. Once adequately specified, the principle of utility serves as the ultimate normative basis for all of the judgments that comprise utilitarian moral thinking. Another example is Gert's rules-based approach, which comprises a system of ten rules and a decision-making procedure for dealing with conflicts among rules as the basis for sound ethical reasoning.[1] Here, the structure of rules plus the decision-making procedure constitutes the theory.

Our ethical theory cannot be stated so succinctly. This is because the method of reflective equilibrium reveals the best-justified theory to be more intricate than these examples suggest. Nevertheless, our ethical

---

[1] Bernard Gert, *Common Morality* (New York: Oxford University Press, 2004).

theory does have a discernible structure, so it is not just a collection of considered judgments. Understanding that structure will prove valuable for understanding how we specify our theory in the chapters that follow and how the theory would be naturally extended to topics that we lack the space to cover in this book. In this chapter, we sketch our ethical theory at two levels of generality: (1) fundamental values, principles, and scope; and (2) specification in terms of mid-level principles. Our arguments in favor of the theory, as well as more detailed specifications of its parts, comprise the rest of this book. In the final part of the chapter, we discuss how our theory relates to other familiar theories and concepts in moral philosophy, including consequentialism, deontology, virtue ethics, and the ethical theories of other bioethicists.

The theory we describe here is the one that we think applies to ethical reasoning in any area of life, not just bioethics. Bioethics is not special in the sense of needing its own ethical principles or methods. It is special in that it throws up a number of particularly difficult and important ethical questions, which a general ethical theory can help us answer. It may prove helpful to keep this in mind throughout the book. We emphasize those aspects of theory that are especially important for bioethics; illustrate them with examples from medicine, public health, health policy, and the like; and apply the theory to problems in bioethics. But, at its core, the theory is independent of the subject matter to which we apply it.

3.2   Fundamental Values, a Formal Principle, and Scope

At the highest level of generality, our theory consists of two broad substantive values, a formal distributive principle, and a scope determining the set of beings with moral status. The two broad values are *well-being* and *respect for rights-holders*. The distributive principle is *equal consideration* for all beings with moral status. And the scope is the set of *sentient beings*. Although our approach confers equal moral consideration on all sentient beings, it does not regard all sentient beings as rights-holders.

The value of well-being grounds duties to benefit others and prohibitions against harming them. Given the scope of the theory, moral agents have these duties with respect to all sentient beings. For those sentient beings who have moral status but not rights, equal consideration takes a consequentialist form, which means that the well-being of one individual can be traded off against the well-being of another. Moral agents have additional duties to those sentient beings who are also rights-holders. First, duties against harming rights-holders are much more stringent – it is not sufficient to show that causing them harm would result in greater benefit for others. Second, rights-holders who are capable of acting autonomously have a set of autonomy rights whose exercise should be respected. Finally, rights-holders have positive rights held against individuals and institutions on the basis of distributive justice. Difficult bioethical questions frequently involve a tension between the two values of well-being and respect for rights-holders. Since our ethical theory regards both as important, how they should be balanced depends on working through the process of reflective equilibrium for particular cases.

Fundamental Values: Well-Being and Respect for Rights-Holders

The two substantive moral values of well-being and respect for rights-holders may also be understood as ethical principles: "Promote well-being" and "Treat rights-holders with respect." A great deal must be done to explicate these principles before they can help guide action.

First, we must say what well-being and rights are. The account of well-being we defend is a subjective theory, in that what is in an individual's interests is necessarily related to facts about that individual's psychology. According to this account, both enjoyment and the satisfaction of "narrative-relevant" desires – that is, desires that are relevant to one's life story – are prudentially good for an individual. Meanwhile, both suffering and the frustration of narrative-relevant desires are prudentially bad for an individual. In our view, reality has an amplifying effect. Enjoyment contributes more to one's well-being when it responds to a state of affairs that (unlike, say, a delusion) actually obtains. In parallel, the fulfillment of desires contributes more to well-being when those desires are relevantly informed. What unifies enjoyment and desire-satisfaction in our account is the fact that both reflect the lived, self-caring perspective of a conscious subject.

A moral right is a justified moral claim that (1) imposes an obligation on one or more individuals and (2) ordinarily resists appeals to the common good as grounds for overriding the claim. For example, persons have rights against bodily trespass, which protect their interests in controlling their own lives, not being subject to harm, and the like. The right against bodily trespass imposes obligations on moral agents not to interfere with the bodies of other persons. Such obligations can be suspended (for example, if a competent person gives consent to be touched and so *waives* her right) or overridden by overwhelmingly strong reasons based on well-being (for example, in the case of mandatory reporting of certain infectious diseases where someone's privacy right may be infringed in a limited way in order to track the spread of disease and protect other members of society). It is worth noting that writers use the term "right" in different ways. In particular, it is common to say that if one individual owes a duty (or obligation) to another, then the latter has a right against the former.[2] This comprises only half of what we mean by a *right*, since it does not include the restriction on overriding the right for the common good. As we use the term, it is possible to owe duties to non-rights-holders.

The right against bodily trespass is an example of what is called a *negative right* – it imposes obligations on others to refrain from some action or actions. Other important negative rights in contemporary bioethics include rights to medical confidentiality and to nondiscrimination in the provision of services. Autonomous persons have additional *autonomy rights*, which include the power to waive others' obligations. This is what underlies consent, whereby a competent patient is entitled to make a free decision, following adequate disclosure, to either authorize or reject an offer of a particular medical intervention. If a patient gives valid consent to treatment, they thereby waive their right against bodily trespass in this particular circumstance.

Our theory also asserts some *positive rights*, which impose obligations on others to perform some action or actions. For example, patients have the right to be provided with adequate health care as a matter of distributive justice. Such positive rights are typically limited, since resources are limited. The right to adequate health care does not entail that patients have rights to anything they please – for example, to care that is not medically indicated or to care that is so expensive relative to its efficacy that providing it would financially threaten the medical system. While it is important to recognize rights wherever there are solid moral grounds for asserting them and the obligations they entail can realistically be met, it is also important to acknowledge that what individuals have a claim to receive may depend on the resources available and the claims of others.

Well-being and respect are both important in our theory. Neither is supreme. Often, promoting well-being and respecting rights-holders will coincide. Sometimes, however, they will conflict. Where they conflict, there is no simple procedure for settling the conflict. Fortunately, the method of reflective equilibrium frees us from any notion that ethically right action must be *derived* from the most general ethical principles or values. Moral reflection at various levels of generality – and considerations

---

[2] See, e.g., Tom Beauchamp and James Childress, *Principles of Biomedical Ethics*, 7th ed. (New York: Oxford University Press, 2013), 371–372.

of coherence throughout – help to work out what is ethically defensible even when well-being and respect apparently conflict. For example, when a quarantine is morally justified, an individual's right to freedom of movement in public places is overridden by appeal to social utility, settling the conflict between well-being and respect (temporarily) in favor of the former. This resolution of the conflict rests on the conviction that the overall set of norms that incorporates this judgment – that it is permissible to override the right temporarily – is more plausible and coherent than the overall set of norms that includes the contrary judgment upholding the right and prohibiting a quarantine. Consider another example. No matter how much valuable information could be generated by a medical experiment that placed young children at high risk of death with no compensating medical benefits, we judge that such research would be unjustified. Children's right to adequate protection from harm would trump appeals to societal well-being. This way of settling the conflict between well-being and respecting rights – in favor of the latter – rests on the conviction that the overall set of norms that includes this verdict is more plausible and coherent than the overall set of norms that permits overriding pediatric subjects' rights to adequate protection. Because our ethical theory treats well-being and respect as its most fundamental values or principles but not as foundations from which ethical verdicts can be derived, their coequal status does not paralyze ethical analysis.

As the most general values in our ethical theory, well-being and respect for rights-holders call for careful analysis. We elaborate on respect for rights-holders in Chapter 7, "Moral Status." We devote Chapter 8 to the nature of individual well-being. In addition, questions of benefiting and harming, and analyses of individual rights, are integral to the development of our moral theory throughout the book.

A Formal Principle: Equal Consideration

In addition to featuring the general substantive values of well-being and respect, our ethical theory features a very general principle that indicates, for each individual who counts morally or possesses moral status, *how much* they count in relation to others. In our ethical theory the principle of *equal consideration of interests* – or *equal consideration* for short – plays this role. This principle asserts that everyone's interests are to receive impartial consideration. For example, other things being equal, causing x amount of suffering to A is as morally problematic as causing x amount of suffering to B, irrespective of the species, traits, or capacities of A and B. It would be inconsistent with equal consideration to judge that it is worse to cause moderate suffering to A than to B just because A is a competent adult whereas B is a toddler or just because A is a human being and B is a pig. Note that equal consideration is about regarding *individuals* as equally deserving of moral concern (from an impartial standpoint), not treating each individual *the same*. For example, we take a moderate prioritarian view about distributive justice, according to which it is more important to benefit those rights-holders who are worse off than those who are better off. All else being equal, the interests of the worse off are therefore valued more highly. Nevertheless, we think that they receive equal consideration, since if their situations were reversed, priority would again be given to the ones who are worse off.

In asserting that everyone's similar interests are equally morally important, the principle of equal consideration needs a criterion for comparability of interests. The criterion is *prudential*: two interests are of similar magnitude when what is at stake for the individuals is roughly the same in terms of their well-being. So a human's interest in not suffering moderately may be assumed to be comparable to a turtle's interest in not suffering moderately because, we might say, moderate suffering is *moderately awful* whenever it occurs.[3] In contrast, in ordinary cases a person with life plans has a much greater stake in remaining alive than a turtle who has very little sense of the future, so that equal consideration does *not* require attributing equal moral importance to the person's continued life and the turtle's continued life. It is far worse that the person dies than that the turtle dies. What equal consideration requires is that agents give equal moral weight to *prudentially similar interests* irrespective of what sorts of beings the interest-bearers are.

Equal consideration is an extremely general and abstract principle that is assumed – at least for application to persons or human beings – by a wide variety of moral theories. Utilitarianism incorporates equal consideration because the principle of utility gives equal or impartial consideration to all beings who have a welfare. Equal consideration is also assumed in Kantian ethics, libertarianism, and most other prominent deontological theories, although they usually limit the scope of this principle to humanity. Meanwhile, views that attribute rights to animals also assume a type of equal consideration for humans and animals.

---

[3] Here we bracket the complication that suffering may be not only intrinsically bad for a subject but also instrumentally bad in thwarting some of their projects or valued activities, which may vary in value from individual to individual.

Equal consideration is compatible with various theories because it is a formal principle – where what is under consideration is rather abstract, namely, moral importance or how much one's interests matter morally. Indeed, equal consideration is compatible with a nihilism according to which *nothing* matters morally. A nihilist could say, "I give everyone's comparable interests equal moral weight – to wit, none." Thus, the significance of the formal principle of equal consideration depends on substantive values. As we have seen, the two most general substantive values in our ethical theory are well-being and respect (for rights-holders). So, in effect, at a very general level we answer the question "*What* is substantively at issue in ethics?" with the substantive answer "well-being and respect." Again at a very general level, we answer the question, "*How* are individuals to be regarded with respect to these fundamental substantive values?" with the answer "equally, in the sense of giving equal moral weight to individuals' comparable interests." A third question concerns scope: "Who is subject to such equal consideration?"

Scope: Sentient Beings

Some ethical theories limit equal consideration to persons or human beings. If such theories address the moral status of animals or nonpersons, they assert that these individuals have either less moral status or no moral status at all. By contrast, as we discuss in Chapter 7, our theory maintains that all beings who have interests – namely, sentient beings – have moral status and that all beings with moral status fall within the scope of equal consideration.

The value of well-being applies to all beings who have a welfare: sentient beings. Thus all sentient beings, in our view, at least deserve equal *consequentialist* consideration. But the value of respect, in our view, is best understood as *respect for rights-holders*. Again, we use the term "rights" somewhat strictly so that rights-holders have moral claims that generally may not be overridden by appeals to utility. Our theory attributes rights of full strength to persons and not to sentient nonpersons. Persons are defined as beings who have "narrative self-awareness" or "narrative capacity" (the ability to understand the parts of their lives as forming a sort of story). Derivatively, we also attribute rights to human beings who are not persons in this sense but are expected to develop into such persons. Moreover, because the normative importance of self-awareness over time is not limited to its appearance in full-blown narrative self-awareness, we attribute *rights of partial strength* to animals who have nontrivial temporal self-awareness that falls short of narrative self-awareness.

The view that all sentient beings are entitled to equal consideration represents a radical departure from other leading works in bioethical theory. One implication, lying outside the purview of bioethics but exceptionally important to everyday choices and agricultural policy, is that modern industrial animal husbandry – "factory farming" – is ethically indefensible. A second broad implication is that the traditional presumption in favor of conducting animal studies before proceeding to clinical trials involving human subjects is morally backward:[4] there should be a significant presumption *against* involving (sentient) animal subjects in research, in view of their moral status and the fact that nearly all biomedical research involving animals seriously harms them without compensating benefits.

3.3 Mid-level Principles

In Chapters 4–6 we use the method of reflective equilibrium to specify the two values – in light of the formal principle of equality and our views regarding scope – in the form of substantive "mid-level" ethical principles. Here, we describe some key mid-level principles as they relate to nonmaleficence, beneficence, distributive justice, and autonomy rights.[5] Since what we say about them is at a level of specificity that allows moral verdicts to be drawn for particular cases, our specification of the fundamental values into these mid-level principles is a vital part of our overall theory. Thus, we think of the principles not as ones whose content we have *derived* from the two values but as integral components of the theory itself.

Nonmaleficence

The principle of nonmaleficence states that it is pro tanto wrong to harm others – meaning that it is wrong to harm others unnecessarily or without sufficient justification. We believe that nonmaleficence is so deeply plausible as to require no justification. Indeed, one would be justified in rejecting any ethical theory that denied that harming others tended to be wrong, on the basis of this denial alone. Although the principle of nonmaleficence is virtually self-evident, its scope is not. Our argument that all and only sentient beings have moral status implies that the scope of nonmaleficence is much broader than humanity or the set of persons,

---

[4] This assumption is stated in "The Nuremberg Code," reprinted in *Trials of War Criminals before the Nuremberg Military Tribunals* (Washington, DC: US Government Printing Office, 1948), article 3.
[5] We discuss them at length in Chapters 4–6.

extending to sentient beings more generally. In view of this scope, the principle of nonmaleficence as we understand it establishes a moral presumption against harming sentient beings: They should not be harmed unless there is a special justification for harming them. Our further argument, that many sentient beings have rights, guides judgments about the sorts of justifications for harm that are acceptable. For rights-holders, showing that an action would provide greater benefits to others is not sufficient justification for inflicting harm. The magnitude of the benefits must exceed a higher threshold to count as justification.

In stating that it is pro tanto wrong to harm others, nonmaleficence appeals to the concept of harm. What is harm? As discussed in Chapter 4, the concept is somewhat elusive. After critically evaluating several leading conceptions, we suggest the following definition for use in ethical analysis: *A, an agent or event, harms B if and only if A makes B worse off than B would have been in the absence of the event or A's intervention.* This analysis fits our intuitions about whether or not harm has occurred in a broad range of cases. For example, if A punches B, then B is harmed because he is now worse off than he would have been if B had left him alone. Likewise, suppose B has a chronic condition and was about to receive drugs but A steals them. B may be no worse off than he was before – he is still not getting treatment – but he is worse off than he would have been if A had left him alone, so A has harmed him.

The principle of nonmaleficence underlies various rules of thumb pertaining to distinct types of harm. The following moral rules have their basis in nonmaleficence:[6]

1.   Do not cause pain, suffering, or other experiential harm.
2.   Do not kill.
3.   Do not cause illness, injury, or disability.
4.   Do not deprive of goods or opportunities to which the individuals deprived have legitimate claims.
5.   Do not impose excessive risk of harm.

Beneficence

Because we believe distributive justice and beneficence are more closely connected than common morality and most prominent theories of

---

[6] For ease of formulation, we are leaving out such standard qualifications as "unless there is adequate justification for doing so," whose purpose is to allow for exceptions to the unqualified rules.

bioethics suggest,[7] we explore both principles together in Chapter 6. Nevertheless, the *concepts* of beneficence and distributive justice are very different. And there are types of justice other than distributive justice that are important to bioethics. Moreover, beneficence applies in principle to all beings with moral status, whereas distributive justice applies only to rights-holders. So the ethical principles that relate to beneficence and distributive justice merit separate discussion before any connection between them is forged.

Beneficence requires agents to take positive steps to promote the well-being of others. One may promote others' well-being by conferring a benefit upon them (e.g., giving them cash) or by preventing them from being harmed (e.g., by giving them access to effective vaccines or rescuing them from a fire). Sometimes these categories of beneficent measures are difficult to distinguish – for example, when conferring a benefit (e.g., giving food) removes or prevents a harmful condition (e.g., starvation). But just as instances of harming involve making someone worse off than they otherwise would have been, instances of beneficence involve *making someone better off* than they would have been otherwise.

Once we begin to investigate its content more concretely, it becomes apparent that beneficence really splinters into several distinct mid-level principles. We find it helpful to distinguish (1) general beneficence, which is a nonspecific moral obligation to help others in need; (2) a duty to rescue; and (3) special obligations of beneficence that attach to positions within special relationships (e.g., as parents have toward their children and caretakers have toward their pets) or to professional roles (e.g., physician, lawyer, teacher).

General beneficence is the moral obligation to contribute significantly, relative to one's ability and over the course of a lifetime, to assist individuals in need. Potential beneficiaries might include people who are homeless or malnourished, political refugees, victims of human trafficking, and so on. They also include nonhuman animals – such as homeless companion animals and animal victims of organized fighting. General beneficence is what ethicists call an *imperfect* obligation. This means that a moral agent has discretion over to whom and how the obligation is discharged: to what particular causes or individuals, at what particular times, and in what particular forms (e.g., money, volunteer services, blood donations). It is

---

[7] See, e.g., Beauchamp and Childress, *Principles of Biomedical Ethics*; H. Tristram Engelhardt, Jr., *The Foundations of Bioethics* (New York: Oxford University Press, 1986); and Bernard Gert, Charles Culver, and K. Danner Clouser, *Bioethics*, 2nd ed. (New York: Oxford University Press, 2006).

appropriate that this obligation leaves such discretion both because there is far more need in the world than any one agent can hope to address and because there are limits to how much one must sacrifice in order to meet this obligation.

In contrast to classical libertarians, we claim that general beneficence is genuinely *obligatory*, not an ideal that is beyond the call of duty. In contrast to common morality, we claim that this obligation is *fairly strong*. At the same time, in contrast to act-utilitarians and other maximizing forms of consequentialism, we claim that the demands of general beneficence are *limited*. That is, we deny that general beneficence requires agents to do everything they can to promote the best results or make the world a better place.

In addition to the imperfect obligation of general beneficence, our ethical theory recognizes *the duty to rescue*, which is a *perfect* obligation. This means that it is morally binding on specific occasions. The duty of rescue requires an agent to provide a benefit to another when the benefit is very large and the agent can do so at a sufficiently low cost to himself. A paradigm scenario featuring the duty to rescue is one in which a lone passerby spots a nearby child, apparently drowning, in a lake into which the passerby can safely wade to rescue the child. Assuming that the costs to the passerby are just inconvenience and soiled clothing, it seems obvious that she has a duty to attempt to rescue the child.

There are further obligations to benefit that are grounded in special relationships or particular professional roles. Parents have special obligations to house, feed, protect, and nurture their children. One generally has stronger obligations to help friends in distress than to help individuals with whom one has no special relationship. You have perfect obligations to feed and protect your pet, get him veterinary attention as needed, and so on. In professional settings, one's role often generates special obligations to benefit. Physicians, for example, have obligations to provide health benefits for their patients and plausibly to strangers too, as when someone needs urgent medical attention on a plane or boat. Teachers have special obligations to provide their students certain educational benefits and to be available to advise them on educational matters. Firefighters have obligations, while on duty, to fight fires within some geographical area.

Let us consider physicians' beneficence-based obligations in greater detail. Doctors clearly have obligations to benefit patients with whom they have a physician–patient relationship. Moreover, if a physician happens upon a stranger who has just collapsed, she, like any other person who could help, has a duty to attempt to do so (if there is no extraordinary reason why she cannot). Indeed, as a physician, she has a duty to provide medical attention, whereas a layperson may just have a duty to call for assistance. These obligations of beneficence are relatively straightforward.

Matters are less clear when a possible duty of beneficence is very burdensome to discharge, many people need to be rescued, or the reason rescue cases are so costly or so common is that other people are not doing their duty. A physician from a wealthy country may struggle over whether to volunteer to combat a dangerous epidemic in a nation with weak medical and public health infrastructure. In the United States, a physician may have to decide whether to treat indigent, uninsured patients with no expectation of receiving payment. A third physician may live in a part of the world where many people living in slums have serious diseases but could be helped with relatively low-cost medical care.

In the face of such ambiguity about a physician's obligations of beneficence in cases such as these, we emphasize two distinctions: (1) between individual and institutional obligations and (2) between ideal and nonideal background circumstances. Consider again the American physician who must decide whether to treat uninsured patients for free. He faces this dilemma only because of a nonideal background in which the United States, a wealthy nation that can afford to provide universal health care, has failed to meet its obligation to do so. Were the institutional obligations met, US citizens and residents would collectively meet the need of the otherwise-uninsured *indirectly*, by paying taxes that are used by the federal government to ensure universal access to health care.

Given that the United States does not meet this institutional obligation to ensure universal access, does a physician have a beneficence-based obligation to treat uninsured patients who cannot pay? We argue that in such nonideal circumstances those who are in a position to help have much greater obligations than they would in a just world (where the costs of helping would be spread more widely). Not only does a US physician have the duty to attempt to rescue someone who collapses right in her presence; her perfect duties of beneficence require providing a substantial amount of care without charge or at a minimal cost. For example, a physician might charge patients on a sliding scale according to their ability to pay or set aside a certain number of appointments per week in which she provides free care to indigent or uninsured patients.

Distributive Justice

Understood in a highly abstract or formal way, justice may be considered a single moral principle: the principle that requires moral agents to give others *their due*. But, considered so formally, justice provides no actual direction because one needs to have a substantive idea of what different individuals are due. As soon as we turn our attention to substantive mid-level principles of justice, it becomes apparent that there is considerable disagreement about these principles – and, therefore, about what justice actually requires.

Given our commitment to equal consideration, as discussed earlier, our substantive approach to justice must be compatible with equal consideration – that is, with giving equal moral weight to individuals' prudentially comparable interests. This is a very significant commitment when it comes to our dealings with animals, since they are so often treated in ways that give much less than equal consideration to their interests. It is also sufficient to ground a requirement of nondiscrimination among persons – for example, on the basis of race, class, religion, or sexual orientation. Although widely accepted today – at least in liberal democracies – as a requirement of justice, this broad acceptance is a result of hard-won battles in civil rights movements. Moreover, the acceptance in principle does not always correlate with actual practice (e.g., in police's differential treatment of persons of different races), and there continue to be some disputes about what is required in principle (e.g., to instantiate nondiscrimination for transgendered persons). Even so, equal consideration, due to its lack of specificity, is compatible with a broad array of substantive principles of justice as they pertain to persons or human beings.

Let us here distinguish four kinds of justice and clarify the focus of our investigation. *Retributive justice* gives responsible agents what they are due in light of their wrongful acts. As such, this type of justice concerns punishment, a topic that falls outside the purview of this book. *Restorative justice* gives appropriate compensation to individuals who have been wronged so as to "restore" them, in some sense, to their state of well-being prior to being wronged. *Distributive justice*, on which we primarily focus, gives individuals what they are due in the form of benefits (e.g., income, health care access) and burdens (e.g., tax obligations, jury duty) independently of anyone's prior wrongdoing. In morally ideal circumstances, then, neither retributive justice (which responds to agents' having done wrong) nor restorative justice (which responds to individuals' having been wronged) would be relevant. But distributive justice would be relevant so long as there were benefits and burdens to distribute. Finally, *procedural justice* is a matter of the fairness of the process by which decisions are made.

In our view, only rights-holders have claims on the basis of distributive justice. Though we acknowledge a wider set of rights-holders than human persons, for reasons of space we further restrict our discussion of justice in this book to human persons. We address questions of distributive justice within a single state and also internationally. Domestically, we defend a liberal egalitarian view of distributive justice according to which it is presumptively unjust if one person is worse-off than another person as a result of factors beyond their control. When scarce societal resources are allocated among individuals, we balance two goals: giving higher priority to people who are worse off and maximizing the total benefits that are distributed. Thus our distributive principle is a form of *moderate prioritarianism*.

The differences in life prospects between individuals in different countries are vast. For example, life expectancy for a child born in Sierra Leone in 2018 was fifty-four years. For a child born in Japan it was eighty-four years.[8] We regard these unchosen differences as problematic in just the same way as differences within a country. We therefore defend a *cosmopolitan* view of global distributive justice: the principles of justice apply in the same way across states as they do within states.

Here we note two important implications of our approach to justice. First, we argue that people have a right to access affordable health care. As a matter of distributive justice, this right is limited in certain ways. In particular, it is limited by the availability of resources, so that individuals do not have a right to every intervention that would be beneficial – moderate prioritarianism applies to the distribution of health care resources too. Our views about global justice also imply that richer countries (and richer individuals) have substantial duties to provide poorer countries with the means to provide their people with adequate health care. Second, we argue that the current international intellectual property system that grants twenty-year patents on novel pharmaceuticals is unjust. The international community has an obligation to permit poorer countries to purchase cheaper, generic versions of patented medicines and to adopt different methods for incentivizing innovation in medicine.

---

[8] The data come from the World Bank, *World Bank Open Data* (available at https://data.worldbank .org/indicator/SP.DYN.LE00.IN; accessed September 22, 2020).

Autonomy Rights

Autonomy means self-rule. More specifically, autonomous or *competent* individuals are capable of deliberating about their options in light of their own values and priorities, reaching a decision on the basis of such deliberation, and acting accordingly.

Autonomy is of special importance because of its close connection with both well-being and respect for rights-holders. When a competent person exercises their capacity for autonomous action, doing so tends to promote their well-being. Autonomy has *instrumental* value insofar as competent persons tend to know their interests better than other people do, with the consequence that competent persons' self-governance tends to promote their well-being more effectively than paternalistic interventions into their affairs. Autonomous action can also itself be a source of well-being, since many people desire to and enjoy being able to act free of others' control. The value of autonomy in terms of its contribution to well-being can also ground obligations to assist persons to actualize their capacity for autonomous decision-making and action. For example, a mental health professional may have an obligation to foster their patient's confidence, clarity of thinking, and other capacities that enable autonomous choice. Likewise, good parents recognize an obligation to nurture their children's development into autonomous adults.

The capacity for autonomous action is also the ground of autonomy rights, such as the rights to bodily control that allow competent persons to give or refuse consent to medical interventions. Strictly speaking, "respect for autonomy" means respecting the exercise of these rights. Other things being equal, it is wrong to interfere with competent persons' decision-making or control their action through deception, motivational manipulation, or coercion. As we discuss in Chapter 5, awareness of these threats to autonomous decision-making helps to illuminate the conditions of valid consent and of appropriate surrogate decision-making.

Competent individuals may or may not act autonomously in any given case. We analyze autonomous action in this way: *An agent A performs action X autonomously if and only if (1) A performs X (i) intentionally, (ii) with sufficient understanding, (iii) sufficiently freely of controlling influences; and (2) A decided, or could have decided, whether to X in light of A's values.* Condition (2) implies that only beings who have values can act autonomously. Many beings who can act intentionally on the basis of their desires lack the capacity to stand back and evaluate their desires in light of values. A bird, for example, might fly intentionally to her nest on the basis of her desires and perceptions, but she does not thereby fly autonomously.

To head off a possible confusion: it is not necessary, for an action to be autonomous, that the agent actually reflect on and endorse the action in terms of the agent's own values; many or most autonomous actions in everyday life are not preceded by such reflection. What *is* necessary for someone's action to be autonomous is that the agent be capable of such evaluation. For example, Dan may choose to eat a bowl of sugary cereal with milk and do so autonomously but without any reflection. If someone were to point out an inconsistency between his choice of breakfast and his values (relevantly here: good nutrition and abstaining from factory farm products), Dan could change his behavior to bring his choice in line with his values. If Jeri is addicted to nicotine and wishes she did not have a desire to smoke, considering the habit contrary to her value of healthful living, she may smoke intentionally on the basis of her desire, but her smoking may be compulsive rather than autonomous.

Many human beings lack the capacity for autonomous action due to immaturity or substantial cognitive incapacity, yet are capable of performing intentional actions in accordance with their desires and beliefs. The same is true of many animals. We use the term *nonautonomous agents* to refer to all beings – whether human or nonhuman – who can act intentionally but not autonomously. Although the choices of nonautonomous agents do not have to be respected as a matter of rights, these individuals can still have an interest in liberty and freedom from controlling influences. Other things being equal, an eight-year-child has an interest in freedom of movement, as does a dog – it is good for children, dogs, and other nonautonomous agents to enjoy themselves as they see fit and do things they want to do. Yet, frequently, other things are not equal. Considerations of well-being require restricting children's and dogs' liberty in order to keep them safe from potential kidnappers or cars on the highway. For nonautonomous individuals, this sort of paternalistic interference is justified when the benefits outweigh the harms.

Contrast with Principles of Biomedical Ethics

Because the mid-level principles we have described fall under similar categories to the four principles featured in Tom Beauchamp and James Childress's prominent textbook, *Principles of Biomedical Ethics*, it may be helpful to identify some of the main respects in which our treatment of these principles differs from the approach of Beauchamp and Childress.

Our chapter on nonmaleficence, unlike the corresponding chapter in *Principles*, includes an extensive exploration of the concept of harm, canvassing several theoretical options and issues before arriving at our own analysis.[9] In addition, differences between Beauchamp and Childress's (partly sketched) model of moral status and our own model of moral status entail differences in how nonmaleficence is to be interpreted in relation to sentient animals. One clear difference is that, whereas Beauchamp and Childress assert degrees of moral status such that some beings with moral status deserve less than equal consequentialist consideration,[10] our commitment to equal consideration denies this assertion. Consequently, there is a stronger presumption against harming sentient animals on our view than on theirs.

There are several important differences between our approach to beneficence and justice and that of Beauchamp and Childress.[11] Unlike these authors, we find beneficence and distributive justice to bear significant overlap in their substantive moral demands. This is related to the fact that we acknowledge moderately strong obligations of general beneficence (as explained above), whereas Beauchamp and Childress remain neutral on the strength of such obligations.[12] Relatedly, Beauchamp and Childress treat classical libertarianism, which expressly denies that people have general obligations of beneficence, as one among several respectable theories of justice; by contrast, we reject and attempt to refute libertarianism. The principle of distributive justice at which we arrive is a form of moderate prioritarianism, whereas Beauchamp and Childress embrace several distributive principles without clarifying whether they can be integrated.

Finally, our treatment of autonomy differs from Beauchamp and Childress's approach in several ways. Although our analysis of autonomous action significantly converges with theirs,[13] only ours requires that agents have the ability to evaluate their prospective actions in terms of their own values. This feature of our analysis substantially limits the class of agents who are capable of acting autonomously – as opposed to merely intentionally – and coheres with our ascription of rights only to beings with substantial self-awareness. In addition, we analyze the conditions for valid consent – arguably the most central autonomy-related concept in bioethics – differently from Beauchamp and Childress. For example, whereas they, like many other commentators, require significant comprehension as

---

[9] Their analysis of the concept of harm is limited to four paragraphs and discusses neither recent nonstandard analyses nor challenges to standard analyses such as theirs (*Principles of Biomedical Ethics*, 153–154).
[10] Ibid., 82–85.   [11] Ibid., chap. 7.   [12] Ibid., 203–206.   [13] Ibid., 104.

a condition of valid consent,[14] we do not, instead placing great emphasis on adequate disclosure and the avoidance of deception.

3.4 Other Ethical Theories and Concepts

It is common today to divide ethical theories into three broad categories: consequentialism, deontology, and virtue ethics. Our approach may be understood in terms of consequentialism and deontology, both of which rely on principles that prescribe certain actions. However, in addition to specifying action-guiding norms, we can also identify moral virtues that correspond to some of these norms. As we understand moral virtues, their primary role is to support moral conduct by complementing agents' ability *to know what actions are right* (such knowledge being facilitated by such action-guides as principles and rules) with the strength of character that makes them more likely *to act accordingly*. Here we describe the key features of these three categories of ethical theory and note how our theory relates to them.

Consequentialism

Consequentialism is the class of ethical theories that converge on the general idea that *right action is that which is expected to produce the best (or good enough) results*. Utilitarianism is the most prominent type of consequentialist theory. It features a single supreme principle: the principle of utility. The principle of utility directs agents to act in ways that can be reasonably expected – either directly or via utility-promoting rules – to maximize well-being or utility. Important utilitarian thinkers in bioethics include Joseph Fletcher, a theologian and pioneer of the newly recognized discipline of bioethics, and the renowned philosopher Peter Singer.[15] We agree with utilitarians that the well-being of individuals is a central value to be promoted, but disagree that it is the only general value at the heart of ethics. For this reason, we cannot commit to the principle of utility, which directs agents to *maximize* – rather than merely promote – well-being or utility.

Consequentialist theories differ along two dimensions. First, they differ regarding how consequences matter morally. For example, in contrast to

---

[14] Ibid., 124.
[15] See, e.g., Joseph Fletcher, *Situation Ethics* (Louisville, KY: Westminster John Knox Press, 1966); and Peter Singer, *Rethinking Life and Death* (New York: St. Martin's, 1994).

utilitarian theories, other types of consequentialist theories either interpret
the value at stake in the "best results" in different terms (for example,
taking into account both well-being and priority to the worst-off), moderate the demand for the *best* results so that an agent is required to do
enough to promote well-being rather than having to maximize it, or both.

Second, consequentialist theories differ in terms of how they think the
norms that guide our behavior should take into account the consequences
that ultimately matter. *Direct* consequentialism asserts that agents ought to
act in such a way that can be expected, on each occasion, to produce the
best (or, in some versions, good enough) results. Direct utilitarianism –
which is often called *act*-utilitarianism – instructs the agent to act in ways
that can be expected to maximize well-being. This directive, however,
would seem to justify some actions that conflict with our considered
judgments. For example, it would apparently justify the discreet murder
of a hospital patient in order to salvage his organs to save several other
individuals. Further, direct utilitarianism would justify the most barbaric
torture of an animal if the enjoyment of a large number of sadistic
spectators outweighed the harm to the animal and no other activity could
be expected to offer a greater gain in overall well-being. These apparent
implications of direct utilitarianism contradict our considered judgments
that killing an innocent person as a means to save others wrongfully
violates the victim's rights and that torturing an animal for fun cannot
be justified. By contrast, *indirect* consequentialists believe that in the long
term the good is best promoted by complying with certain rules and
constraints.[16] These might include a prohibition on killing the innocent
without their consent and a rule against tormenting animals for entertainment. Even if the immediate consequences of murdering an innocent
appear to be positive, on balance, given human nature it would ultimately
lead to worse consequences if we endorsed making these judgments on a
case-by-case basis.[17]

Given its emphasis on individual rights, our ethical theory is inconsistent with direct forms of consequentialism. It might, however, be consistent with a form of indirect consequentialism. Consequentialism offers a
principled basis for identifying the rare justified exceptions to well-
fashioned rules and their corresponding rights that we accept. To return
to an earlier example, it tends to promote well-being and the best results
for society if we grant people a right to freedom of movement in public

[16] For a recent example, see Brad Hooker, *Ideal Code, Real World* (Oxford: Clarendon, 2000).
[17] See R. M. Hare, *Moral Thinking* (Oxford: Clarendon, 1981).

spaces, but this right is appropriately overridden whenever imposing a quarantine on infectious individuals is justifiable – and it is plausible that the basis for overriding the right is utility or the public welfare. A further reason to think our approach is consistent with indirect consequentialism is that the consequentialist commitment to promote well-being can straightforwardly justify the moderately strong imperfect obligation to help those in need that our theory embraces. Our hesitation in asserting that our ethical theory is consistent with indirect consequentialism is the fact that this assertion depends on the speculative empirical claim that general acceptance of and compliance with the norms we defend would, in fact, be conducive to the best results in the long term.

Deontology

Deontology is the broad class of ethical theories that agree with conse-quentialism (against virtue ethics) that right action is the most central concept in ethics but disagree with the consequentialist thesis that criteria for right action concern only its results. Deontologists hold that moral duties constrain what we are permitted to do, even when our actions would produce the best results. For example, our duty not to kill innocent people without their consent means that we may not murder one person even if we expect thereby to save several people's lives. Deontologists also generally hold that morality includes "options" that permit agents to pursue their own projects and interests, rather than do everything they can to bring about the best results.[18] Thus, deontology is *stricter* than consequentialism in that it sets constraints on the pursuit of the best results or any other ends. Deontology is *more permissive* than utilitarianism – and other types of consequentialism that require acting so as to bring about the *best* results – in not requiring agents to do all they can to make the world a better place. Frances Kamm is an important contributor to bioethics whose thinking is distinctively deontological.[19]

The most influential deontological theory derives from the work of Immanuel Kant.[20] Kantian ethics features a single supreme principle, the Categorical Imperative. One way to understand the substance of the Categorical Imperative's content is in terms of respect: one must always

---

[18] See, e.g., Samuel Scheffler, *The Rejection of Consequentialism* (Oxford: Oxford University Press, 1982).

[19] See, e.g., Frances Kamm, *Bioethical Prescriptions* (New York: Oxford University Press, 2013).

[20] *Grounding for the Metaphysics of Morals*, 3rd ed., trans. James Ellington (Indianapolis, IN: Hackett, 1993; first published 1785).

act in ways that are consistent with respecting persons and never in ways that treat them as mere means to an end. Moreover, the fact that the Categorical Imperative does not require one to do everything one can to promote well-being – since one can live in compliance with this principle while devoting much time and energy to one's own personal projects – might also be understood in terms of respect. At issue here is respect for a moral agent, who has sovereignty over their own life and may pursue their own ends, consistent with the Categorical Imperative, rather than facing a never-ending obligation to make the world a better place. An important neo-Kantian contributor to bioethics is Onora O'Neill.[21]

We agree with Kantians that respect is a central value at the heart of ethics. We disagree with Kantians by denying that respect constitutes a supreme principle that always overrides the promotion of well-being in cases of conflict. Moreover, we recast respect for persons as respect for *rights-holders*, a conception that leaves open whether rights-holders are limited to persons, include all sentient beings, or comprise a range of beings wider than the set of persons but narrower than the set of sentient beings. We defend a version of the latter, intermediate view of rights-holders.

Deontology, as noted, sets constraints on the pursuit of ends but allows moral agents considerable freedom to decide what to do within those constraints. A modern example of a *pure* deontology might feature absolute rights, which correspond to absolute rules binding all moral agents. For example, libertarians, such as bioethicist Tristram Engelhardt,[22] assert rights to life, liberty, and property that cannot be overridden by appeals to utility. Unlike libertarians, neo-Kantians accept that individuals have an imperfect obligation to help those in need, but they generally assert some absolute constraints such as against killing innocent persons without their consent. Our theory, in contrast, holds that nearly all such constraints have thresholds such that they may be overridden if the gain in overall well-being from doing so is sufficiently great. In brief, constraints, yes, but not absolute ones.[23] Hence our view is a form of *moderate* deontology. Further, because our approach embraces stronger obligations to promote the good than many deontologists acknowledge, our deontology is

---

[21] See Onora O'Neill, *Autonomy and Trust in Bioethics* (Cambridge: Cambridge University Press, 2002).

[22] See Engelhardt, *Foundations of Bioethics*.

[23] As we note in Chapter 4, in practice we regard certain rights – including rights against torture, rape, and enslavement – as absolute. There are, we maintain, no actual situations in which these acts are justified by the expectation of uniquely valuable consequences.

moderate in terms of how much freedom it gives persons to pursue their own projects rather than assist others in need.

Virtue Ethics

Virtue ethicists take moral character, rather than the results of actions or their consistency with moral rules, to be fundamental to ethics. Virtues are character traits such as courage, honesty, and generosity. A virtuous agent is someone who possesses these character traits such that they recognize which situations call for, say, courage – as opposed to being timid or overly rash – and are motivated to act accordingly. Edmund Pellegrino was an important contributor to bioethics who represented the tradition of virtue ethics.[24]

Though our view does not take virtues as foundational, we acknowledge that they are vital parts of an ethical life. An ethical theory like ours that captures a defensible normative structure in the form of principles, rules, obligations, and rights can help moral agents identify the right action to perform or the right policy to support. But knowing what is right is one thing, doing it quite another. It is possible to know what is right and fail to do it due to insufficient motivation, weakness of will, being overwhelmed by peer or institutional pressure to do something else, or major character defects – that is, moral vices. *Moral virtues*, as we understand them, are character traits that facilitate right conduct. Also important are *intellectual virtues*, traits of mind that facilitate good thinking, including good ethical thinking. One might think that mastery of a good theory would make intellectual virtues unnecessary in ethics, since the theory would tell you the right action or policy. This reasoning would miss the important point that any theory needs to be *applied*, which requires intellectual work (e.g., "Would saying X be deceptive?"), and sometimes needs to be *interpreted* (e.g., "What does equal consideration for animals imply about the permissibility of killing them?"). Both moral virtues and intellectual virtues are crucial to living ethically.

Which traits of character and mind are virtues? Beginning with traits of character – moral virtues – we can distinguish two types. *First-order virtues* have a moral content that guides action. They include respectfulness, benevolence, compassion, honesty, discretion, fairness, and passion for justice. *Second-order virtues* do not directly guide action. They function

---

[24] See, e.g., Edmund Pellegrino, "Toward a Virtue-Based Normative Ethics for the Health Professions," *Kennedy Institute of Ethics Journal* 5 (1995): 253–277.

1. Fundamental values

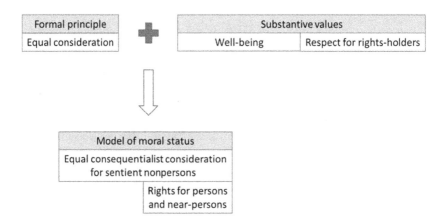

2. Specification

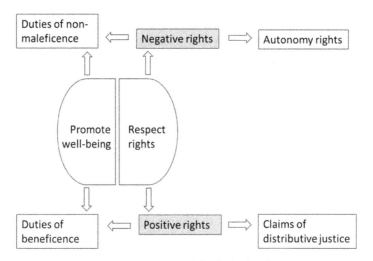

Figure 3.1   The dual value theory.

to make it more likely that one will do the right thing when it is difficult to do so. These virtues include conscientiousness or integrity, moral courage, mindfulness (which counteracts impulsivity), and strength of will. Meanwhile, intellectual virtues or traits of mind that are important to ethical living include intellectual honesty, open-mindedness, clarity of thinking, perceptiveness, the capacity to master and remember salient information, and sound judgment or practical wisdom. We believe that the importance of both second-order moral virtues and intellectual virtues in ethical living tends to be underappreciated.

This completes a sketch of our ethical theory. A fuller picture will emerge with the details of later chapters. Figure 3.1 gives a pictorial representation of the theory.

CHAPTER 4

Nonmaleficence and Negative Constraints

4.1 Introduction

The principle of nonmaleficence states a prohibition on causing harm to others in the absence of justifying circumstances. Among general ethical principles, *nonmaleficence* has the strongest claim to being self-evident.[1] If an ethical theory claimed that harming others had no tendency to be wrong, we would be justified in rejecting the theory on this basis alone. But to accept the obvious claim that harming others tends to be wrong leaves open several important issues. It leaves open exactly what constitutes a harm, when harming others is permissible, and the range of beings that fall within the scope of the prohibition on harm.

At a general level, the concept of harm is very familiar. We know that such actions as tormenting, assaulting, and killing others generally involve harming them. We know that harm is bad for an individual and that its opposite, benefit, is good for an individual. Relatedly, we generally think that harming someone for no good reason is unethical, and the fact that someone is attempting to harm another person can provide grounds for restricting the former person's liberty. In most instances, we are confident in our attributions of harm and our grasp of its practical significance.

However, the precise nature of harm is surprisingly difficult to capture. This is important because, depending on which account of harm is correct, an action may, or may not, cause harm, with apparent implications for whether the action is wrong. Consider these questions. Does it harm a patient to end his life if he is terminally ill, wants to die, and reasonably believes that he will never again enjoy an acceptable quality of life? What if the patient has entered an irreversibly vegetative state and had no settled preferences regarding continued life in this state? While it is obvious that

[1] For an excellent discussion of self-evidence in ethics, see Robert Audi, *The Good in the Right* (Princeton, NJ: Princeton University Press, 2004), 48–54.

58

sentient animals can be harmed, most obviously by being caused to suffer, what about nonsentient animals and plants? They are living organisms, and can be damaged or killed, but can they be harmed? In the case of beings who can be harmed, does harming them require *changing their condition*, making them worse off in some way? An affirmative answer might seem obvious, but any sense of obviousness dissipates in the context of "creation cases": situations in which we bring someone into being. For example, one might hold that it harms a human being to bring her into an existence that involves unrelenting misery. Yet, since the individual did not exist before coming into existence, bringing her into existence did not change her condition.

Special circumstances in which harming others is sometimes regarded as permissible include self-defense, punishment, consent by the person harmed, or causing someone a minor harm in order to prevent a worse harm to the same individual. The latter two circumstances arise frequently in clinical care and research. More challenging are cases in which one person is harmed to save others from greater harms. These require some analysis of how nonmaleficence relates to individual rights.

Accepting the principle of nonmaleficence also leaves open the range of beings that fall within its scope. A small number of ethical theorists maintain that our obligations to refrain from harming ultimately concern only persons or human beings.[2] Because we have obligations of nonmaleficence to a set of beings that includes persons, and because sentient animals can be harmed – they can feel pain and, more generally, have an experiential welfare – a reasonable *presumption* is that obligations of nonmaleficence extend beyond persons and humanity to include sentient animals. This leaves open whether obligations of nonmaleficence are *equally strong* as applied to persons and to sentient nonpersons. Chapter 7, on moral status, defends the thesis that sentient beings have moral status, implying that the scope of nonmaleficence extends this far. It also addresses the question of the strength of the prohibition on harming by distinguishing sentient beings with rights of differing strengths and sentient beings without rights.

We begin this chapter by surveying some prominent accounts of the nature of harm. We defend a counterfactual account: you harm someone if and only if you make them worse off than they would have been in the absence of your intervention. Though this account does not capture all the

---

[2] For a classic representative, see Immanuel Kant, *Lectures on Ethics*, trans. Peter Heath, ed. Peter Heath and J. B. Schneewind (Cambridge: Cambridge University Press, 1997).

ways in which the term "harm" is used, it does capture what matters about harm for the purposes of ethical analysis. Using this account we then specify nonmaleficence into several general moral rules corresponding to ways in which individuals can be harmed. These foundational reflections are followed by discussions of three areas of ethical concern in which rules concerning harm are prominent: (1) the ethics of torture, including health professionals' involvement in torture; (2) the limits of permissible risk in pediatric research; and (3) the ethics of medical assistance-in-dying.

4.2   What Is Harm?

Three Accounts

Accounts of the nature of harm can be divided into comparative and noncomparative accounts. *Comparative accounts* hold that one is harmed when one is made *worse off* in some way. If you kick a dog hard, causing substantial pain, you make the dog worse off – in at least two senses. Because of your action, the dog is worse off than she was before your assault, and she is worse off than she would have been had you left her alone. These two senses in which one can be made worse off correspond to two more specific comparative accounts of harm. According to the *historical* account, you harm someone if and only if you make them worse off *than they were before your intervention*. According to the *counterfactual* account, you harm someone if and only if you make them worse off *than they would have been in the absence of your intervention*.[3]

As the dog example illustrates, these two accounts typically coincide – someone is made both worse off than they were beforehand and worse off than they would have been otherwise. But the accounts can diverge. Suppose a sick child needs a full dose of some medication, which her attending physician prescribes, but an inattentive pharmacist provides only a partial dose, which the child receives. The child's condition improves, but less than it would have with a full dose. In this case, the pharmacist's error seems to harm the child – even though she is not made worse off than she was before receiving the medication – because it makes her worse off than she would have been in the absence of the error.

---

[3] Kicking the dog for no good reason also makes her worse off than she *should have been*, indicating the possibility of a *normative* account of the relevant comparison. The possibility of defining harm partly in normative terms will resurface later when we consider harm by omission.

Cases like that of the inattentive pharmacist lead us to reject historical accounts of harm as inadequate for use in ethical analysis. First, they fail to capture the fact that harms can take place even though there is no historical worsening. These are often harms that matter for evaluating the ethics of a course of action. Second, without knowing what would have happened without the event that caused the harm (a counterfactual matter), it is impossible to assess the magnitude of the harm. How bad was it for the child that she only received a partial dose? That depends on the difference between the course of her illness following the partial dose and what its course would have been with the full dose. Assessing the magnitude of harm is often an essential part of an ethical analysis.

Proponents of *noncomparative accounts of harm* claim that making someone worse off is not a necessary condition for harming them. Instead, harming someone involves putting them in an intrinsically bad, or harmful, state. According to one formulation of this alternative account, "An action harms a person if the action causes pain, early death, bodily damage, or deformity to her...."[4] Kicking harms the dog because it puts her into a state of pain. One reason for adopting a noncomparative account of harm is that it explains a common intuitive reaction to some creation cases that comparative accounts appear unable to explain. Consider a child who is brought into existence with a significant, genetically determined disability that causes her substantial pain. According to the noncomparative account the child is harmed by the act of procreation because she is thereby put into harmful states like pain. Comparative accounts seem unable to draw this plausible conclusion, because being brought into existence does not make the child worse off. She is not made worse off than she was beforehand because she *wasn't* beforehand. She is not made worse off than she would have been otherwise because she *wouldn't have been* otherwise.

We do not think that it is necessary to adopt a noncomparative account of harm to deal with these cases. In Chapter 10, when we discuss the "nonidentity problem," we deny that the child in this sort of case is harmed. The child could not have existed in a better state because the disability was caused by genetic factors and any child who came into existence with a different genome would have been a different individual.

---

[4] Elizabeth Harman, "Can We Harm and Benefit in Creating?," *Philosophical Perspectives* 18 (2004): 93. Seanna Shiffrin presents a different noncomparative account of harm in "Wrongful Life, Procreative Responsibility, and the Significance of Harm," *Legal Theory* 5 (1999): 117–148.

The parents did not harm their child even if they anticipated that the child would come into existence with a significant disability.

For us, the central problem with noncomparative accounts of harm is that they seem unable to make sense of the harm of death.[5] Nearly everyone agrees that death (ordinarily) harms the individual who dies, and we concur. Since an afterlife might be an improvement over earthly existence, the common assumption that death is a harm tacitly assumes that there is no afterlife and that death involves our going out of existence. The problem for noncomparative accounts is that nonexistence cannot be an intrinsically bad state of an individual because it is not a state of the individual at all. Rather, someone's having died entails that the individual does not exist. By contrast, a counterfactual account of harm can explain why death is bad for the individual by looking at how the individual would have fared were they not to have died. If they would have continued to live a life worth living, then death harmed them. (The historical account of harm also has difficulty explaining the harm of death because, in order to do so, it would have to compare the condition of an individual right before death with the condition of the individual upon becoming dead – but, once death occurs, there is no individual in any condition.)

Having rejected historical and noncomparative accounts of harm, we endorse a counterfactual account of harm as the one best suited for ethical analysis. We think that defining harm using such an account can explain why we care about harm in the first place – because making someone worse off than they would otherwise have been is typically a bad thing to do to them. As noted above, the counterfactual account also has the advantages that it can plausibly include failures to benefit as harms in certain cases, explain why death can be a harm, and allow us to calculate the magnitude of the harm that someone incurred. Moreover, the historical account of harm may be understood as *implicitly presupposing* the counterfactual account. Why, in determining whether Joe was harmed, should we ask how Joe *was faring* just before the putatively harmful event? Because how he was faring suggests (in ordinary cases) how he *would be faring* in the absence of that event. Despite these strengths of the counterfactual account, it faces several important challenges. Addressing them will show how the account is useful in ethical analysis, make the view's implications more precise, and allow us to acknowledge that we are biting some intuitive bullets by accepting it.

---

[5] See Ben Bradley, "Doing Away with Harm," *Philosophy and Phenomenological Research* 85 (2012): 390–412, at 400–401.

Challenges to the Counterfactual Account

Preemption Cases

Suppose that Dan dies of a brain aneurism precisely at noon. One second later his body is riddled with bullets shot by a firing squad. Had the aneurism not occurred, Dan would have died a second afterward. So the aneurism does not make Dan worse off than he would have been in its absence, which on the counterfactual account entails that the aneurism does not harm Dan. Many writers consider this implication counterintuitive.[6]

One theoretical option for those who want to preserve their intuition that the aneurism harms Dan would be to adopt a hybrid comparative account of harm. On such a view, an event would constitute a harm if it made someone worse off than they would otherwise be *or* if it made them worse off than they were before. Though we are sympathetic to this hybrid account as a way to capture those events we intuitively judge to be harmful, we think that it is unnecessary and unhelpful for the purpose of ethical analysis.

The historical account is unnecessary because the counterfactual account can identify harms in the cases in which they matter ethically. In Dan's case, for example, there would seem to be no reason to expend resources to prevent the aneurism, if we cannot save him from the firing squad. Why? Because he is not, on balance, made worse off because of the aneurism.[7] On the other hand, if we could prevent both, that would provide a reason to do so: the aneurism *plus* the bullets make Dan worse off than he would otherwise be by depriving him of life.

Consider another case, in which unconscious Suraj will lose a leg unless his infected toe is amputated. Removing the toe harms him on the historical account, since he is – let us assume – worse off than he was just before the amputation, but benefits him on the counterfactual account, since he would otherwise go on to lose his leg from the infection's spreading. Now, one might interpret the historical account such that it reaches the same verdict about amputating Suraj's toe: doing so confers an overall benefit insofar as it removes a dangerous infection that could spread. But this interpretation depends on counterfactual reasoning.

---

[6] See, e.g., Michael Rabenberg, "Harm," *Journal of Ethics & Social Philosophy* 8 (3) (2015): at 8–10.
[7] Could there be something wrong with killing someone who was about to die anyway? Absolutely, but it is not helpful to think in terms of harming them. Killing someone who is about to die might violate their rights, although it does not, on balance, make them worse off.

Why might it be plausible to think that Suraj would be better off *after the amputation than he was beforehand* (a historical comparison)? Because, *if the toe had not been removed, the infection would have led to Suraj's losing his leg* (a counterfactual comparison). Even where it delivers plausible verdicts, the historical account of harm is unnecessary, and often, as in this case, it depends on the counterfactual account. Returning to practical ethical concerns, what should we do for Suraj? Barring very unusual circumstances, we should operate and remove the toe, since he will be much worse off if we do not. Labeling the amputation as a harm does nothing to help the ethical analysis, which should be concerned only with what would otherwise happen to Suraj.[8]

By rejecting the historical account and a hybrid comparative account we end up denying that some intuitively "harmful" events (like the aneurism) are actually harmful. We accept this consequence. Our definition of harm has a particular function. The definition is not intended to capture all common language uses of the term "harm." Instead, it is intended to capture the part of our usage that is important for ethics.

Omission Cases

A second challenge to the counterfactual analysis of harm denies that making someone worse off than they would otherwise have been is a *sufficient* condition for harming that individual. One argument motivating this challenge appeals to our judgments about "omission cases." Suppose you buy a drum that you intend to give to Manuel, which would please him greatly. But Kevin sees you leaving the store and persuades you that you would enjoy it if you kept it for yourself. So you do, and never mention the earlier intention or the omission to Manuel.[9] The counterfactual account suggests that you harm Manuel by not giving him the drum, because you make him worse off than he would have been had you given it to him. Yet it seems implausible that your decision not to give Manuel the drum harms him.

This objection identifies a challenge for accounts of harm generally, not only counterfactual accounts. In fact, we can construct parallel cases for historical and noncomparative accounts. For example, suppose that your neighbor Manuel is out in the sun without a hat or sunscreen. You could

---

[8] There may be cases in which someone is benefited on one dimension but harmed on another (for example, an operation saves their sight but leaves an ugly scar). Still, we can capture what matters on the counterfactual account by comparing what would have happened with and without the operation. The historical account does not help.

[9] This case is similar to one presented in Bradley, "Doing Away with Harm," 397.

cross the road and offer him a hat, but you don't – he is capable of getting his own. Manuel gets sunburned. As a result of your omission, Manuel is worse off than he was before and so the historical account suggests that you harmed him. Moreover, as a result of your omission, Manuel is in a harmed state, so the noncomparative account also suggests that you harmed him. But, as with the drum example, it is implausible to say that you harmed him.

The challenge here is thus not about which account of harm we adopt, but how we should attribute harms in omission cases. We do not want to hold you responsible for Manuel's being harmed by the sun, because you do not cause the harm. However, we do, plausibly, want to hold the negligent pharmacist responsible for failing to prescribe a high enough dose of medication to her patient. How to distinguish causing an event from failing to prevent it is a difficult philosophical question. We do not attempt to solve it in this book. For the purposes of ethical analysis we rely on intuitive judgments about which behaviors are acts and which are omissions. *In terms of responsibility for harms, we hold someone responsible only if they cause the harm or if they have an ethical duty to prevent it from occurring.*

Fair Competition Cases

Another potential counterexample to comparative accounts of harm represents what we might call "fair competition cases." Suppose Al is excelling in a calculus class. Eager to get into a top doctoral program, he realistically believes that a letter from his professor stating that Al was the top student in the class will significantly improve his prospects. Unfortunately for Al, Jill (but only Jill) outperforms him, and their honest professor is unwilling to write that Al was the top student. Through her excellent work, Jill has made Al worse off than he would otherwise have been. But we might hesitate to attribute harm here. Not only does it sound a little odd to say that Jill's excellent performance *harmed* Al; surely, in doing work superior to Al's, Jill did nothing pro tanto (presumptively) wrong. Yet it is widely believed that it is pro tanto wrong to harm other persons. If we retain this belief and the intuition that Jill does nothing wrong, then we must judge that Jill's excellent performance does not harm Al, in which case making someone worse off is not sufficient for harming him.

In response, we accept that Jill may do nothing wrong but nevertheless harms Al. Disadvantaging someone, with no ill intent, in a fair competition is a plausible example of a harm where the perpetrator does not act even pro tanto wrongfully. Our account is intended to capture when something is a harm and what the magnitude of the harm is in ways that are relevant to ethical analysis of cases involving harm. It does not entail that all harms are even pro tanto wrongful. Our account is descriptive, not normative, so it is a separate matter to decide how to evaluate a specific harm. Note that the claim that Jill's action is not at all wrongful is consistent with the thesis that *intentionally* harming is always pro tanto wrong; had Jill intended to set back Al's dreams, it is plausible to think that her behavior would have been morally problematic. It is also consistent with the thesis that basing admission to doctoral programs on relative rankings of students within a program is unfair, in which case Al would be wronged, but not by Jill.

4.3 Types of Harm and Preliminary Specifications of Nonmaleficence

The principle of nonmaleficence states, at a first approximation, that it is pro tanto wrong to harm others. This approximation will be qualified in several ways in our discussion, including for fair competitions, where consent has been given, and to take account of cases where a *risk* of harm is imposed. To say that harming others is pro tanto wrong means that the fact that an act will harm another individual is a reason not to do it, but a reason that can be outweighed by sufficiently important opposing reasons. Nonmaleficence may be specified into the following relatively general rules, each concerned with a way in which individuals can be harmed:

1. Do not cause pain, suffering, or other experiential harm.
2. Do not cause illness, injury, or disability.
3. Do not deprive of goods or opportunities to which the individuals deprived have legitimate claims.
4. Do not kill.[10]

These are good rules of thumb for everyday life. As our later discussions show, they work less well to guide action in difficult cases. In such cases it can be important to understand the underlying harms that the rule prohibits. Here we comment briefly on each rule.

[10] One might include an additional rule, "Do not deprive of liberty," insofar as interfering with individuals' liberty tends to harm them. But we understand such harm in terms of the content of rules 1 and 3. Note that a moral presumption against interfering with people's autonomous choices is relevant only to those who can act autonomously and raises moral concerns that are independent of nonmaleficence, as discussed in Chapter 5.

The first rule concerns *experiential harms*, which take the form of unpleasant, disagreeable, or aversive states of consciousness. The second rule concerns the harm of *dysfunction*, or loss of functioning, which can occur in the absence of either experiential harm or death. A person could lose a great deal of mental functioning through being pleasantly drugged and experience no unpleasant consequences of their new condition. According to most accounts of well-being, one would be harmed by this loss of functioning (see Chapter 8). The third rule concerns losses of valuable experiences (e.g., enjoyments), resources (e.g., property), and opportunities (e.g., job prospects). These losses may or may not occur in conjunction with experiential harm or dysfunction. Stealing, for example, can harm someone even if that individual never learns of the theft and is not harmed in any of the other three major ways noted here. As argued in the previous section, it is implausible that all instances in which someone causes someone else to lack goods or opportunities are cases of harming (consider omission cases), and there are even some types of harm that are not even pro tanto wrong (as in fair competition cases). Thus, in order to fashion a useful rule, we limit it to cases where the object of deprivation is something *to which one has a legitimate claim*. So, for example, even though Manuel has no claim on you to give him a drum, you would harm him if you stole a musical instrument from him.

The fourth rule focuses on the harm of *death*, that is, loss of life – a conceptually complex matter that merits more sustained reflection than the harms associated with the first three rules. The harm of death is distinct from experiential harm because (we assume) dead bodies have no experiences. The dying process can involve considerable experiential harm, yet most people regard death as bad for the person who dies over and above the harms involved in dying. We go to great lengths to avoid death and most people are willing to undergo considerable experiential harm and illness to prolong their lives. For example, chemotherapy for cancer is often debilitating and extremely unpleasant for the patient, yet where it offers a reasonable prospect of cure almost all patients accept it.

To some, the idea that death is a harm to the decedent seems odd. The individual who dies will not be around to experience any effects of death, and so in what sense is there a subject of the harm?[11] We find it plausible to understand the harm of death in terms of instrumental disvalue: death

---

[11] As Epicurus wrote: "So death . . . is nothing to us, since so long as we exist, death is not with us; but when death comes, then we do not exist" ("Letter to Menoeceus," in *The Stoic and Epicurean Philosophers*, ed. W. J. Oates, trans. C. Bailey [New York: Modern Library, 1940], 30–34).

deprives the one who dies of whatever goods their life would have contained had they lived.[12] The counterfactual account of harm then allows us to say how bad it is for someone that they die. The disvalue of someone's death is a function of what goods their life would have contained had they not died. A young man killed in a car crash might be greatly harmed because he would otherwise have lived a flourishing, healthy life for the next fifty years. An elderly man who dies of a stroke at age eighty-five would likely be harmed much less by death because he misses out on less by dying.

Another complication relating to the harm of death is worth exploring here. It seems plausible that the death of a young adult is, all else equal, worse for them than the death of an older adult. According to one possible extension of this reasoning, the death of a baby is even worse for her than the death of the young adult. After all, the baby likely misses out on even more valuable life than the young adult. This reasoning can be extended back to the earliest point at which we are individuated, so that the very worst death would be that of a sentient fetus, presentient fetus, embryo, or zygote (depending on which account of personal identity is correct, as discussed in Chapter 9). To many, this seems implausible. Jeff McMahan writes:

> If we thought that the death of a fetus or infant [were] as serious a misfortune as the death of an older child or adult, we would have to think of the vast number of spontaneous abortions that occur as a continuing tragedy of major proportions. We would surely mobilize ourselves, as a society, to lower the prenatal death rate. Yet the level of social spending on the prevention of spontaneous abortion remains exceedingly low – lower by far than the social investment in the search for a cure for diseases, such as AIDS, that result in far fewer deaths. The explanation for this is that we simply do not regard the death of an embryo [or] fetus as a serious misfortune. . . .[13]

The solution that McMahan proposes, and which we endorse, is to distinguish two factors that are relevant to the harm of death. The first, mentioned already, is the total good (the amount of valuable life and its quality) of which the decedent is deprived. The second is the connection between the individual who dies and the valuable life of which they are deprived. Most adult humans have strong psychological connections to themselves in the future and the past. They are aware of themselves as

[12] Thomas Nagel, "Death," *Noûs* (1970): 73–80.
[13] Jeff McMahan, *The Ethics of Killing* (Oxford: Oxford University Press, 2002), 165–166.

temporal beings: I am the person I was yesterday and will be tomorrow and so forth. They make plans for the future, have fears about it, and have desires regarding it. In other words, it matters to them what will happen in their future. Less cognitively developed individuals have much weaker connections to their futures. A creature who is sentient, but not self-conscious, cannot conceive of itself as someone who persists through time. It might have desires and fears, but not plans. Some sentient beings might even be so cognitively simple that they are not really connected to their futures at all. How bad it is for someone to miss out on future goods, then, is a matter of their connection to those future goods, and this varies with their cognitive capacities. In general, it is worse for a mature human to die than for a mature tortoise to die, even if death deprives each of comparable quantity and quality of life, because the human, we believe, is more closely psychologically connected to the life of which they are deprived.

When we combine these two factors that are relevant to the harm of death, we get a *gradualist* account of how bad death is for typical humans. Early in development, before they are sentient, embryos and younger fetuses miss out on a great deal if they die, but since they are not yet sentient, there is no psychological connection to their future lives and so it is not actually bad for them if they die. Once sentience is reached, death starts to be bad for the decedent, but older fetuses and young infants are much less psychologically connected to their future selves than typically developing older children and adults are. Thus, how bad it is for a human to die typically increases during early childhood, peaks close to the point where all the psychological capacities relevant to the harm of death are present, and then declines as the human ages because they miss out on decreasing amounts of valuable life.[14]

Turn now to a different complication that frequently arises in assessing how bad a potential harm is and that motivates an additional rule. While some types of actions are inherently or nearly always harmful, other types of actions sometimes are and sometimes are not harmful. If someone at a crowded beach throws a rock without aiming at anything in particular, whether this action causes harm depends on whether the rock strikes someone. Both the agent's choice and luck play a role in determining whether harm occurs. Because such a choice is subject to moral evaluation – most likely, in this case, that throwing the rock was irresponsibly

---

[14] For discussion of how we might put numerical values on the harm of death, see Joseph Millum, "Putting a Number on the Harm of Death," in Espen Gamlund and Carl Tollef Solberg (eds.), *Saving People from the Harm of Death* (Oxford: Oxford University Press, 2019), 61–75.

reckless – the scope of nonmaleficence includes not only actions that are expected to harm others but also actions that *risk harm to others*. It is generally wrong to cause such harms as death, suffering, injury, and loss of goods or opportunities to which one has a legitimate claim. But it is also wrong to cause *excessive risk* of these and related harms to others. This is true even where the risky act does not eventuate in harm. Throwing a rock at a crowded beach may be excessively risky even if the rock does not hit and harm anyone.

One might think we should add this rule to the four general rules identified earlier: *Do not impose risk of harm.* But this rule would be implausibly strict. Nearly everything we do imposes some risk of harm on someone. Every time one opens a storm door while exiting a house, for example, one takes an extremely slight risk of injuring some toddler who wandered up and happens to have his head next to the door. The other rules operate well as rules of thumb, so that in everyday life we can mostly follow these rules and only occasionally have to consider whether acts falling under them really involve harms or whether the harms are justified. But for risks of harm this rule would not even be helpful as an approximation. The imposition of risk is so ubiquitous in life – including in medicine – that we find it more helpful to formulate our fifth general, nonmaleficence-based rule this way:

5.   Do not impose excessive risk of harm.

A judgment as to whether an imposed risk is excessive should take into account both (1) the degree of risk and (2) whether or not, in the circumstances, taking that degree of risk is justified. The degree of risk associated with a possible harm is, in turn, a function of two factors: (a) the likelihood (probability) that the harm will occur and (b) the magnitude of the harm, if it occurs. For example, injection with a local anesthetic has a high probability of transient pain at the injection site and soreness once the anesthetic has worn off. There is a very low probability that it will cause a life-threatening allergic reaction. Taking into account the factors of both likelihood and magnitude, these two risks of local anesthesia – even in combination – are generally considered to be very low. Whether imposing some degree of risk is justified will depend on various factors, including what other expected harms and benefits will result from the action. A good illustration of this point is available in the context of pediatric research, as discussed later.

From a theoretical standpoint, it is helpful to specify a principle such as nonmaleficence into some general rules, as above. It is, if anything, even more helpful to engage a moral principle and one or more of the rules that specify it with an important problem in practical ethics. This sort of engagement is often called an "application" of a principle or theory. Such applications can both illuminate the concrete problem area and extract some of the content and moral significance of the general principle. With this in mind, the remainder of the chapter discusses three areas of practical ethical concern in which nonmaleficence plays a prominent role: the right not to be tortured, nontherapeutic pediatric research, and medical assistance-in-dying. The discussion of torture brings out several important issues, including the question of when preventing harm to others can justify inflicting harm and the distinction between what is justified in principle versus what is justified in practice. Torture is, in a sense, the easy case, since we argue that it is never actually justified. Pediatric research is more philosophically challenging, since sometimes risking harm to children will be justified on the basis of preventing harms to others. Both the right not to be tortured and nontherapeutic pediatric research are topics where our conclusions are not dependent on any particular account of harm – much of the time, in bioethics, the competing accounts of harm coincide in their verdicts. The case of medical assistance-in-dying is one where it matters how we conceptualize harm, since it requires judgments about the magnitude of harm caused by someone's death, and the counterfactual account is uniquely capable of explaining the harm of death and assessing its magnitude.

4.4 The Right Not to Be Tortured

The United Nations characterizes torture as follows:

> [a]ny act by which severe pain or suffering, whether physical or mental, is intentionally inflicted on a person for such purposes as obtaining from him or a third person information or a confession, punishing him ..., or intimidating or coercing him or a third person ... when such pain or suffering is inflicted by or at the instigation of ... a public official or other person acting in an official capacity.[15]

Torture violates the nonmaleficence-based rule against causing pain, suffering, and other experiential harm. Torture also frequently causes injuries, such as broken limbs, and sometimes lasting physical or psychological

---

[15] United Nations General Assembly, "Convention against Torture and Other Cruel, Inhuman or Degrading Treatment or Punishment" (adopted December 10, 1984; available at www.un.org/documents/ga/res/39/a39r046.htm), Article 1.

disability, such as mangled fingers or posttraumatic stress disorder. In these instances, torture violates the rule prohibiting the infliction of injury, illness, and disability. Another feature of torture – coercion – violates the victim's autonomy rights, as discussed in Chapter 5, but here we focus on torture in relation to nonmaleficence.

In view of the enormous, inherent harmfulness of torture, nonmaleficence supports a moral obligation on the part of governments and individuals not to torture. Major international bodies have interpreted the moral obligation not to torture as absolute – as having no exceptions. They have also generally regarded the injunction against torture as a *legal* obligation within the body of international law that rests on a *human right* – a fundamental moral right common to all human beings. In 1948, the United Nations prohibited torture in the Universal Declaration of Human Rights.[16] In 1984, the UN adopted the Convention against Torture and Other Cruel, Inhuman or Degrading Treatment or Punishment (the source of the above definition of "torture").

Despite these prohibitions, torture remains widespread. Over a five-year period, Amnesty International reported on torture in three-quarters of the countries in the world.[17] The use of torture by state officials ranged from (presumed) isolated instances to routine practice. For example, it is now widely accepted that the US government, following the September 11, 2001, terrorist attacks, practiced torture in the name of national security. Suspected terrorists held in Guantanamo Bay, Cuba were subjected to such forms of torture as waterboarding (simulated drowning); mock executions; sexual humiliations of various kinds, including rectal forced-feeding; being forced to stand, handcuffed, for up to forty continuous hours; menacing with dogs; sleep deprivation for as long as a week; hypothermia (in one case to the point of death); and threats to kill or rape prisoners' family members, including children.[18] Justice Department legal counsel wrote memos in 2002 and 2005 in an attempt to provide legal cover for these practices, which the administration called "enhanced interrogation techniques" rather than "torture." In 2014, a scathing report by the Senate Intelligence Committee asserted that the post-9/11 torture

[16] United Nations General Assembly, "Universal Declaration of Human Rights" (1948; available at www.un.org/en/documents/udhr/index.shtml).
[17] Amnesty International, "Torture in 2014: 30 Years of Broken Promises" (available at www.amnestyusa.org/files/act400042014en.pdf).
[18] US Senate, Senate Select Committee on Intelligence, *Committee Study of the Central Intelligence Agency's Detention and Interrogation Program* (declassified December 9, 2014; available at www.intelligence.senate.gov/study2014/sscistudy1.pdf).

techniques were more brutal than the CIA acknowledged to the Bush administration – so brutal, in fact, that some CIA personnel tried to have them halted, only to be rebuffed by senior officials who demanded their continuation. The report also went to great lengths to refute the agency's leading arguments justifying the harsh forms of interrogation: that the torture was both necessary for and effective in thwarting terrorist plots and capturing senior Al Qaeda figures, including Osama bin Laden.[19]

Involvement in torture by physicians and other medical professionals is also widespread.[20] Physicians may be asked to devise methods of torture, to assess whether a prisoner can be tortured without fatal consequences, to treat a prisoner so that torture can continue, and to falsify records and otherwise act so as to conceal torture. In the case of Guantanamo Bay, there is ongoing controversy over the role of psychologists and physicians in the design of interrogation methods, the treatment of tortured detainees, and the neglect or concealment of evidence of torture.[21] The UN's resolution on *Principles of Medical Ethics* states:

> It is a gross contravention of medical ethics, as well as an offence under applicable international instruments, for health personnel, particularly physicians, to engage, actively or passively, in acts which constitute participation in, complicity in, incitement to or attempts to commit torture or other cruel, inhuman or degrading treatment or punishment.[22]

In Chapter 3, we analyzed moral rights as valid moral claims that protect important interests and ordinarily trump appeals to the general welfare. The moral right not to be tortured is a valid moral claim, grounded in nonmaleficence, that protects an individual's important interests in avoiding terrible pain and distress, injury, disability, and so on. Thus, to say that someone has a right not to be tortured implies that appeals to the general welfare are not – at least ordinarily – sufficient to justify overriding their

---

[19] Ibid. See also Mark Mazzetti, "Senate Panel Faults C.I.A. over Brutality and Deceit in Terrorism Interrogations," *New York Times* (December 10, 2004), A1.

[20] Jesper Sonntag, "Doctors' Involvement in Torture," *Torture* 18 (2008): 161–175.

[21] Vincent Iacopino and Stephen Xenakis, "Neglect of Medical Evidence of Torture in Guantanamo Bay: A Case Series," *PLoS Medicine* 8 (2011): e1001027; Task Force on Preserving Medical Professionalism in National Security Detention Centers, *Ethics Abandoned* (New York: Institute on Medicine as a Profession and the Open Society Foundation, 2013); David Hoffman et al., *Independent Review Relating to APA Ethics Guidelines, National Security Interrogations, and Torture* (Chicago: Sidley Austin LLP, 2015).

[22] United Nations, Principles of Medical Ethics (1982): Resolution 37/194 (Geneva: United Nations, 1982). Whether and under what conditions medical professionals may treat tortured prisoners in the face of possible complicity with the torturing regime is a complex question that we cannot address here (see Chiara Lepora and Joseph Millum, "The Tortured Patient: A Medical Dilemma," *Hastings Center Report* 41 [3] [2011]: 38–47).

moral claim not to be tortured. Imagine that police in a particular district calculated that they could produce more public benefit than harm, overall, by torturing gang members and using elicited information to make key arrests of gang leaders, thereby greatly reducing gang violence and drug trafficking in the district. Even if their calculations were accurate, this appeal to the public welfare would not justify torturing the gang members. As we noted in Chapter 3, *sometimes* rights give way when the difference in the net gain in public welfare becomes sufficiently large. This motivates the question: *Is it ever permissible to override someone's right not to be tortured?* We argue, "Yes, but only in principle; never in practice."

The classic case that is invoked to support the permissibility of torture is the ticking bomb case.[23] Imagine that government agents know the following:

1. There is a terrorist plot to explode a massive bomb, very soon, in a crowded urban center in their nation.
2. The plot has a high chance of succeeding if it is not prevented by their agents.
3. A convicted terrorist in their custody is known to possess information that would permit their agents to prevent detonation of the bomb.
4. Torturing this particular man has a high chance of eliciting the required information in time to prevent the tragedy.
5. There is no feasible alternative means to averting the tragedy.

If government agents really knew statements (1)–(5) to be true, then, we think, the government would be justified in applying torture because the harm involved in torturing this one man would be very small in comparison with the harm to be averted by preventing the explosion of a massive bomb in a crowded urban setting, no better option exists, and the right not to be tortured is not absolute. Even when we factor in additional, secondary harms that are fairly likely to occur – such as possible psychological harms to the agents of torture, societal distress that the government was willing to apply torture, and resentment on the part of persons sympathetic to the terrorist – the opportunity to prevent the disaster would appear

---

[23] See, e.g., Alan Dershowitz, *Why Terrorism Works* (New Haven, CT: Yale University Press), chap. 4, although Dershowitz argues for the permissibility of torture in real-life circumstances, not just in principle. In response to Dershowitz, Oren Gross defends an absolute legal ban on torture yet defends the very occasional resort to (real-life) torture – in an act of official disobedience – as a necessary means to averting a catastrophe ("Are Torture Warrants Warranted? Pragmatic Absolutism and Official Disobedience," *Minnesota Law Review* 88 [2004]: 1481–1555).

sufficiently valuable to dwarf the harms that might accrue if the individual is tortured.

We accept that torture would be justified in these circumstances. If any reader is inclined to disagree, we could raise the stakes higher and more fantastically by stipulating that it is not just a large population in an urban setting whose lives are at stake, but an entire nation or even all of humanity. We could even stipulate that the prospective torture victim himself will die if the bomb goes off, and that he himself is likely to suffer in dying from nuclear radiation far more than he would suffer if tortured. When the stakes are this high, it seems to us that it would be irrational and fanatical to deny the permissibility of torturing someone to prevent such cataclysmic results.

So we accept that torture can, in principle, be justified in some conceivable circumstances. But this is very different from claiming that torture is ever, in fact, justified in real life. We deny that it is actually justified in real life, which involves the world as we know it and human beings as we know them. Crucial differences between the scenario described above, in which torture would be permissible, and the actual world concern *the limits of human knowledge*[24] *and the frailties of human character.*[25]

Consider first the limits of knowledge. It is highly improbable that actual human beings would ever be in the position of knowing the truth of statements (1)–(5) enumerated above. To be sure, that a particular terrorist plot exists can sometimes be known, where intelligence is reliable and the evidence robust. (Of course, intelligence is often unreliable, as when the United States relied on faulty intelligence about supposed weapons of mass destruction in justifying an invasion of Iraq.) Perhaps, in favorable circumstances, we can also know that a particular plot has a high chance of succeeding if it is not thwarted. Much more doubtful is that agents will really know that a particular person – say, a suspected terrorist – has the crucial information. It is very difficult for individuals to know that someone else, who is not in a cooperative relationship with them, has information that they do not themselves possess. But suppose the captive does have the crucial information. Perhaps the most dubious of the five assumptions is that torture will yield the correct information and do so in time to prevent the tragedy. After all, the torture victim can stop the

---

[24] See Vittorio Bufacchi and Jean Maria Arrigo, "Torture, Terrorism and the State: A Refutation of the Ticking-Bomb Argument," *Journal of Applied Philosophy* 23 (2006): 355–373, sect. V.

[25] Henry Shue discusses both types of limits in opposing the use of torture ("Torture in Dreamland: Disposing of the Ticking Bomb," *Case Western Reserve Journal of International Law* 37 [2006]: 231–239).

torture, at least for the time being, by *appearing* to cooperate and *appearing* to supply the desired information. The final assumption enumerated above – that there is no other way of obtaining the desired information – also seems to us well worth questioning in practice.

In sum, officials cannot know in any given case that torturing a particular individual will enable averting a disaster and will be the only way of doing so. A rebuttal is available, however, to a consequentialist who focuses on probabilities and the magnitude of the disaster to be averted: "It is true that we cannot be absolutely certain that torturing a person of interest will work and be the only way to avert a catastrophe. But we're talking about a *catastrophe*, or the possibility of one, not the prospect of saving a couple of people. Even if there were only a very small chance, say 5 percent, of being correct in a given case, there must be some magnitude of harm to be averted that would justify taking that chance. So your argument, while successfully showing that we will always lack 100 percent certainty about the relevant facts, does not succeed in showing that torture is always wrong in the real world."

In response to this argument, we appeal to further consequentialist considerations. Suppose a government sanctioned torture, in the name of averting great harms, despite the impossibility of knowing in any given case both that doing so will be effective and that no less morally problematic alternative would work. What would happen? First, even if the agents of torture and their superiors had morally perfect intentions, there would be "false positives": cases in which individuals are tortured uselessly (because the torture was ineffective) or needlessly (because torture was not necessary to avert the catastrophe). And because the chances of getting everything right in a given case are unlikely to be very high, false positives will almost certainly outnumber true positives or successes. If there is a 5 percent chance of being correct, then 95 percent of the time there will be unnecessary torture. Second, in the real world we cannot expect agents of torture and their superiors to have morally perfect intentions. If a government gives officials the prerogative to torture, they will surely use this prerogative more often than would be justified. As Henry Shue notes, "history does not present us with a government that used torture selectively and judiciously."[26] And recent experience in the United States should remind us that human beings simply cannot be trusted with the

---

[26] Ibid., 234.

power to torture.[27] Third, if a powerful nation such as the United States or United Kingdom permits torture, it sends a signal that even powerful nations cannot adequately defend their citizens without resorting to torture, suggesting a fortiori that less powerful nations cannot be expected to do so. In effect, the result is implicit permission to engage in torture. We believe that this message is more likely to lead to catastrophe than a strict policy of refraining from torture. For these reasons, we submit that even the most resourceful consequentialist defense of torture cannot succeed.

4.5   Permissible Risks in Pediatric Research

Children, like adults, need validated medicines and medical procedures to be available for treatment or prevention of disease. Such validation requires rigorous biomedical research. Because children's bodies differ from adults' bodies in complex ways, this research typically requires pediatric subjects; research results based on adult subjects cannot simply be extrapolated to children. Most children cannot give valid consent to the intrusive and potentially risky interventions that biomedical research involves. But then when is it permissible to place some children at risk for the sake of benefiting the health of other children in the future? The answer, presumably, will depend on the amount of risks and the extent of the potential benefits. Children have a moral right to adequate protection from harm, but this must be considered together with the value of conducting the research.

What constitutes *adequate* protection in pediatric research? How much risk to pediatric subjects is ethically permissible? The answer depends partly on the circumstances. The most important distinction in this context is that between (1) *therapeutic* pediatric research, which offers the prospect of direct medical benefit to the pediatric subjects themselves, and (2) *nontherapeutic* pediatric research, which does not offer the prospect of such benefit to the subjects.

Consider, first, a ten-year-old boy who suffers from a form of leukemia for which no successful treatment is known. He is likely to die within months if he does not receive effective treatment, the only possibility of receiving which is in a single clinical trial. The risks of the trial drug are not insubstantial, but initial tests have suggested some promise of effectiveness. In this situation, the child's right to adequate protection from harm would

---

[27] See, e.g., Karen Greenberg and Joshua Dratel (eds.), *The Torture Papers* (New York: Cambridge University Press, 2005).

permit his entering a trial that poses considerable risks to his health so long as the expected benefit – from possibly saving his life – along with the risks is preferable to the risks and benefits of the only alternative: receiving no treatment. In general, if the risk/benefit ratio of entering a trial offering the prospect of direct medical benefit is better than the risk/benefit ratio of any alternative (and the risks of entering the trial are minimized with optimal research design and sound medical practices), then the pediatric subject's right to adequate protection has been respected. In therapeutic contexts where there are few options, adequate protection can be compatible with high risks.

Our conclusion here does not imply that it is permissible to accept high risks whenever some direct medical benefit is in prospect for pediatric subjects. It would be wrong to enroll a child in a trial in which the expected therapeutic benefit was relatively modest while the risks were extremely high. For example, if a promising medication offered a child relief from a case of atopic dermatitis (eczema) that standard treatments failed to ameliorate, but it posed a significant risk of a fatal allergic reaction, the prospect of direct medical benefit would likely not justify the risks. The prospect of benefit, taking into account both the magnitude and likelihood of benefit, must at least roughly offset the risks, taking into account the magnitude of possible harms and their likelihood of occurring.[28]

Consider another case. The parents of a healthy ten-year-old girl are thinking of enrolling her in a trial of a vaccine that is hoped to protect children against a chemical agent that might be used in a terrorist attack. The vaccine has already been found safe and effective in adults. The girl does not have a medical condition that might be treated by enrolling in the trial, and there is no particular reason to expect an attack anytime soon, so this trial would clearly count as nontherapeutic research. Because she does not stand to benefit medically from participating (setting aside the extremely remote possibility that a terrorist attack would occur, she would be exposed to the noxious agent, *and* the vaccine she had taken in the trial would protect her), the trial is unlikely to be in her interests. An adult may accept significant risks to benefit society through participation in research, but children lack the capacity to consent and therefore need special

---

[28] We say "roughly offset" in response to a suggestion by Dave Wendler (personal communication): that just as minimal (but nonzero) risk is permissible in *nontherapeutic* pediatric research, it would make sense to allow *a bit more* risk than is compensated for by the prospect of direct medical benefit in *therapeutic* pediatric research.

protection. What protection would be adequate for nontherapeutic pediatric research?

An approximate answer is suggested by our intuitive judgments regarding the risks parents can responsibly allow their children to undergo.[29] Because nontherapeutic research does not offer the prospect of direct medical benefit to pediatric subjects, we may think analogously about risks undertaken by children in nonmedical activities whose primary purpose is to benefit others. How much risk could parents responsibly allow their children to take in helping others? The following activities seem within the range of reasonable risk: delivering groceries by bicycle to an elderly neighbor; helping to rebuild a damaged building; and running an eight-kilometer race for charity in the rain.[30] These examples suggest that parents may responsibly allow their children to undergo *some nonnegligible risks* in activities that are primarily altruistic, yet the risks would still have to be *relatively minor*.

This way of thinking about permissible risk in pediatric research can be stated more precisely in terms of the *reasonable subject standard*, which we defend in Chapter 5 as the appropriate standard for medical decision-making when the informed-consent and advance-directive standards are inapplicable.[31] According to the reasonable subject standard, a surrogate decision-maker should decide on behalf of someone lacking decision-making capacity as that individual would decide if she were a rational agent choosing prudently within the constraints of morality. Prudent decision-making in the present context would require not accepting high risks in nontherapeutic trials. Meanwhile, beneficence requires that an agent make some significant contributions to the public good over the course of a lifetime (as discussed in Chapter 6). One way of partly discharging this obligation is to enroll in important nontherapeutic trials. So parents should have the discretion to enroll their children in nontherapeutic pediatric studies to the extent that doing so would be consistent with how a prudent person would discharge their duties to benefit society.

Current US regulations state four risk categories for research involving children.[32] They permit nontherapeutic research that poses "minimal

---

[29] This approach is further developed in David DeGrazia, Michelle Groman, and Lisa Lee, "Defining the Boundaries of a Right to Adequate Protection: A New Lens on Pediatric Research Ethics," *Journal of Medicine and Philosophy* 42 (2017): 132–153.

[30] Cf. David Wendler, "A New Justification for Pediatric Research without the Potential for Clinical Benefit," *American Journal of Bioethics* 12 (2012): 23–31.

[31] See also Joseph Millum, *The Moral Foundations of Parenthood* (New York: Oxford University Press, 2018), chap. 6.

[32] The regulations are found in 45 Code of Federal Regulations (CFR), Sections 46.404–46.407 (for the Department of Health and Human Services) and in 21 CFR, Sections 50.51–50.54 (for the Food and Drug Administration). Hereafter we will cite only 45 CFR 46.

risk" – where "minimal" is said to be no greater than the degree of risk that
children face in everyday activities and in routine medical examinations.[33]
(Follow-up discussions have led to general agreement that here we should
imagine healthy children living in safe neighborhoods.) They also permit
research that involves greater than minimal risk where the risks associated
with participation are compensated "by the anticipated benefit to the
subjects."[34] This corresponds to what we called therapeutic research. In
cases in which the research offers no prospect of direct medical benefit to
pediatric subjects, but is deemed "likely to yield generalizable knowledge
about the subject's disorder or condition," the permitted risk level is
"a minor increase over minimal risk."[35] However, we do not think the
likelihood of illuminating the subject's condition is a cogent justification
for a higher risk level.[36] The justification we gave for exposing children to
risk in nontherapeutic research rests on considerations of beneficence,
which apply whether or not the individuals in need share a condition with
their potential benefactor. We regard the minor-increase-over-minimal-
risk category as justifiable independent of the disease status of
the participants.

This third category is not universally acknowledged in regulations for
pediatric research. Both Canada and the United Kingdom are more
restrictive in terms of the risks that they allow children to undergo in
research. Canada limits the involvement of children to research with
minimal risks or where the benefits to participants outweigh the risks –
that is, to the first two categories we just described.[37] The terminology in
the United Kingdom is different than that used in North America. The
Medical Research Council's guidelines allow nontherapeutic research only
where the risks are "minimal" or "low," where "low risk" appears to
include similar procedures to those regarded as "minimal risk" in Canada
and the United States (e.g., blood draws).[38] Again, higher risks are permissible in the case where the prospect of direct benefits to participants
outweighs the risks.

Even if the US category of "a minor increase over minimal risk" is
something of an outlier internationally, we believe that – as commonly

[33] 45 CFR 46.404.   [34] 45 CFR 46.405.   [35] 45 CFR 46.406.
[36] Cf. David Wendler, Seema Shah, Amy Whittle, and Benjamin Wilfond, "Non-Beneficial Research
    with Individuals Who Cannot Consent: Is It Ethically Better to Enroll Healthy or Affected
    Individuals?," *IRB* 25 (2003): 1–4.
[37] TCPS 2 (2018): 53.
[38] Medical Research Council, *Medical Research Involving Children* (2004) (available at https://mrc.ukri
    .org/documents/pdf/medical-research-involving-children/).

interpreted in practice – it is justified. This standard is commonly understood as permitting not only such procedures as blood draws (considered minimal risk) but also skin biopsies and chest X-rays, but not procedures much riskier than these.[39] We believe this level of risk is consistent with adequately protecting pediatric subjects from harm.

Nearly all pediatric studies that are approvable under current US regulations will fall under one of the three categories described: (1) therapeutic studies, (2) studies posing minimal risk, and (3) studies posing a minor increase over minimal risk but likely to yield generalizable knowledge about the subjects' medical condition. The regulations also mention a fourth, "wild-card" category of approvable pediatric studies: those posing more than minimal risk with no prospect of direct medical benefit to individual subjects and without the prospect of illuminating a medical condition that affects the individual subjects. Such a study is approvable if it presents a significant prospect of furthering the understanding, prevention, or treatment of a serious problem affecting the health or welfare of children, though approval would require national expert review rather than the usual review by a local institutional review board.[40] Earlier we considered a candidate study for approval under this provision: a pediatric study of a vaccine against a particular chemical agent that could be used in a terrorist attack. Assuming the risks would be more than minimal, and considering the fact that the potential participants do not have a medical condition that the trial is designed to illuminate, the risks they would face in this trial would be considered excessive and therefore unjustified – unless the study is approvable under the wild-card category.

We think that this fourth category identifies a class of permissible research studies, and offer several suggestions with regard to it. First, the regulations would be improved by specifying a limit to the risk levels to which children may be subjected in this category of studies, just as there are limits specified for the other approvable categories. Second, the risk ceiling should still be limited to those that parents could responsibly permit for their children in altruistic activities, consistent with the burdens that someone could reasonably be asked to assume on the basis of beneficence. Third, we anticipate that this limit may be higher than a minor increase over minimal risk, but not much higher. Fourth, as with

---

[39] For examples from one high-volume pediatric research institutional review board, see Children's Hospital of Philadelphia Research Institute, "Risk of Common Procedures" (2020) (available at https://irb.research.chop.edu/risk-common-procedures).

[40] 45 CFR 46.407.

other research studies, pediatric studies that deserve to be approved under the wild-card category are ones in which risks are minimized.

This last category raises an interesting question. It is easy to understand how adequate protection of children in therapeutic research allows greater risks than adequate protection permits in nontherapeutic research: a sufficient prospect of direct medical benefit compensates for higher risks. What may be difficult to understand is why the higher risk standard pertaining to the last category, which we have argued is compatible with children's right to adequate protection, is not the appropriate standard for *all nontherapeutic research*.

Our answer is that this higher risk standard would be the appropriate standard for all nontherapeutic pediatric research in certain ideal circumstances. These would be circumstances in which research institutions and investigators were not biased in favor of conducting research; the government and its officials reliably treated individual children with as much care and protection as good parents treat their children; and prospective subjects and their proxies never felt pressured by biomedical personnel into joining particular studies. Given that these ideal circumstances do not obtain, it is appropriate that in most instances children receive more protection than they would need in ideal circumstances. In this light, the more restrictive standard of a minor increase over minimal risk is the one we endorse as a default level of permissible risk. Occasionally, however, this additional downward (protective) pressure on permitted risk may be appropriately relaxed due to extraordinary circumstances. In these instances, the limits of permissible risk may – if necessary – be raised. But in these instances, as the regulations stipulate, national expert review is required. Thus, while the *substantive* protection is slightly relaxed with an increased level of permissible risk, the *procedural* protection increases.

Might there be rare cases in which it would be ethically permissible to conduct even riskier research on children where the expected social benefits are very high? Here our response is the same as it was to the question of whether there were exceptions to the right not to be tortured: in principle, yes, but not in practice. We can imagine circumstances in which (1) enrolling children in nontherapeutic research with net risks substantially higher than a minor increase over minimal risk would offer the prospect of the best overall consequences *by far*, while (2) decision-makers would have all the information needed to make this judgment reliably, and (3) they would possess the intellectual and moral character needed to resist institutional pressures biased in favor of research. But, in the world as we know it with people as we know them, we believe it would be better to maintain a strict ceiling on the net risks to which children may be exposed.

Let us take stock. In this chapter, so far, we have articulated the ethical principle of nonmaleficence, investigated the concept of harm at the heart of this principle, and identified several general moral rules that capture different aspects of nonmaleficence. In addition, we have noted that nonmaleficence supports a variety of moral rights in the form of negative constraints, including a right not to be tortured. We have also found that nonmaleficence supports negative constraints and moral rights, regarding the imposition of risk, exploring in some detail the appropriate risk-related constraints in pediatric research. In our final application of the principle of nonmaleficence, we explore its implications for medical assistance-in-dying. We find, perhaps surprisingly, that whether death constitutes a harm depends not only on one's circumstances but also on one's values.

4.6 Medical Assistance-in-Dying

Conceptual and Legal Background

Consider two types of harm. *Experiential harm* includes pain, distress, suffering, and other unpleasant experiences. Accordingly, one of the general moral rules that we derived from the principle of nonmaleficence was "Do not cause pain, suffering, or other experiential harm." And one of the commonly acknowledged goals of medicine is to alleviate pain and suffering. A second type of harm is *death*. In ordinary cases, death harms a human being by depriving them of the goods that their life would have contained had they lived. So one of the general rules we mentioned earlier was "Do not kill." And one of the goals of medicine, of course, is to preserve life.

In some cases, the objectives of avoiding or ameliorating experiential harm and of preventing death conflict because the continuation of life entails suffering due to painful or debilitating medical conditions. In many cases, the conflict is tolerable because the suffering is not so great as to call into question the assumption that continuing to live is in someone's best interests. This might be the case, for example, where imperfect recovery from a surgery has caused a low level of recurring pain that is not fully relievable with medications. But there are also cases in which the prospect of unrelenting, severe suffering causes the patient or their proxies to doubt that their remaining alive is worthwhile.

Such a patient might have an end-stage metastatic cancer that has defeated the best treatments and is causing pain and discomfort that pain medications cannot satisfactorily alleviate. Or they might be a patient with locked-in syndrome whose paralysis permits them to move only their eyelids, and who has determined after trying to adjust to their disability that they would prefer dying sooner than later. Cases could be multiplied indefinitely. What such patients have in common is that their situation, in their opinion, reverses the usual presumption that death constitutes a harm. In their view, on balance, the continuation of life constitutes a harm for them. Such cases have motivated the movement away from the traditional medical imperative of preserving human life in all cases toward assertions in law and medical ethics of "a right to die." Here, we explore the ethics of pursuing various ways to bring about a patient's death, with special attention to the concept of harm. We assume, unless otherwise specified, that the patient in question is a competent adult.

In a medical setting, there are various ways of bringing it about that a patient dies sooner rather than later. We may distinguish five modalities:

1. Forgoing of life support
2. Unintentional killing through escalating use of pain medications with the intention of relieving pain
3. Terminal sedation
4. Physician-assisted suicide
5. Euthanasia.

Each merits a brief explanation.

Medical life-support measures such as respirators, feeding tubes, and antibiotics for a potentially lethal infection can be forgone either through stopping their use or withholding them (not starting). Because it is well-established in law and ethics that a competent adult patient has a right to refuse medical treatment, it is widely accepted that such patients have the right to forgo life support.[41]

A distinct modality, widely accepted in practice yet less often discussed in the literature, involves unintentional killing or shortening of life. In these cases, a physician does not intend to end a patient's life but is willing to increase the dosage of an opioid to reduce or eliminate pain *even if there is a significant chance that the medicine will induce respiratory failure, causing*

---

[41] See Ruth Faden and Tom Beauchamp, *A History and Theory of Informed Consent* (New York: Oxford University Press, 1986), Part II; and Gregory Pence, *Medical Ethics*, 6th ed. (New York: McGraw-Hill, 2011), Part I.

the patient to die. So long as the physician does not use more medication than she judges necessary to reduce suffering and does not intend to cause the patient's death, then if the patient dies as a result of opioid-induced respiratory failure, the killing is deemed unintentional and consistent with appropriate medical practice. In the legal jurisdictions of which we are aware, killing in these circumstances is not considered homicide under the law. Properly used, however, this method cannot guarantee a patient's death because pain relief might prove successful while the patient is alive.

In *terminal sedation*, a patient agrees to be sedated to the point of entering a coma, remaining in the coma due to continuing sedation, and to withholding of life-support measures. By this method, a patient can be assured of dying painlessly from an underlying illness or from dehydration.[42] Although the legal status of terminal sedation tends to be somewhat ambiguous, at least in certain cases it would appear to be legal by virtue of the legality of two separate acts: providing sedatives to a suffering patient and forgoing life support, including nutrition and hydration.[43]

A fourth modality is *physician-assisted suicide (PAS)*, in which a physician provides crucial support for a patient who commits suicide.[44] In order for an act to be an instance of suicide and not euthanasia, it must be the patient who performs the act that causes death. One way a physician may provide assistance is by writing a prescription for a lethal dose of medicine and providing instructions for how to take the medicine. A doctor might also supervise the process or even give a bedridden patient the pills and water to swallow. At the time of this writing PAS is legal in Belgium, Canada, Luxembourg, the Netherlands, Switzerland, Columbia, the Australian province of Victoria, and eight US states and the District of Columbia. PAS remains illegal in, for example, New Zealand, the United Kingdom, and most US states.

The most controversial mode of medically bringing about a patient's death is *euthanasia*, in which a physician intentionally causes a patient's

---

[42] Any patients who prefer to remain conscious during their remaining days can refuse hydration and be sure of dying from dehydration within two weeks. Palliative measures can reduce pain and discomfort without inducing coma.

[43] In 1997 the US Supreme Court provided at least some support for terminal sedation: "A patient who is suffering from a terminal illness and who is experiencing great pain has no legal barriers to obtaining medication from qualified physicians, even to the point of causing unconsciousness and hastening death" (Justice Sandra Day O'Connor, Concurring Opinion in *Glucksberg v. Washington* [521 U.S. 702, 737 (1997)]). In 2016 France legalized terminal sedation in cases of refractory pain and imminent death within two weeks (Ruth Horn, "The 'French Exception': The Right to Continuous Deep Sedation at the End of Life," *Journal of Medical Ethics* 44 [2018]: 204–205).

[44] Our use of the term "physician" in "physician-assisted suicide" refers – as it does throughout the book – to any medical doctor.

death. The standard method of euthanasia involves injection of a lethal agent, such as potassium chloride.[45] Of the five modalities under consideration, it is the only one (at least on standard interpretations) in which a physician intentionally kills a patient.[46] Because of the moral rule against intentionally killing human beings and corresponding laws against homicide, acceptance of euthanasia is considered somewhat radical. The practice is currently illegal in the United Kingdom and the United States, for example, but legal in Belgium, Canada, Columbia, Luxembourg, and the Netherlands. In the 1990s euthanasia was also briefly legal in the Northern Territory of Australia.

Conventional Thinking about This Issue and Its Limitations

All five modalities are ways in which a patient's death can be made to occur earlier than it would with full application of life-support measures. But conventional thinking about the ethics of end-of-life decision-making does not regard all of the modalities as morally equivalent. It is widely believed – among scholars in medical ethics and among the general public – that forgoing life support, unintentional killing through appropriate use of opioids, and terminal sedation can be morally permissible, assuming certain conditions are met. It is also widely – though by no means universally – thought that euthanasia is morally impermissible under any circumstances and should be illegal. Attitudes about physician-assisted suicide are more ambivalent. PAS is legal in some, but not all US states, legal in Canada, and illegal in the United Kingdom."

Reflections on nonmaleficence and the nature of harm put the coherence of this conventional thinking in doubt. Consider this view's prohibition of euthanasia. At first glance, the prohibition seems reasonable insofar as nonmaleficence supports a rule forbidding the killing of human beings. Reflection on unintentional killing in pursuit of the legitimate goal of pain relief motivates specifying the rule so that it forbids only *intentional* killing. Reflection on killing as a last resort in self-defense against an aggressor

---

[45] This practice is sometimes called "active euthanasia" and contrasted with "passive euthanasia," the forgoing of life support. Probably due to widespread acceptance of the latter practice and (for some people) negative connotations of "euthanasia," the term "passive euthanasia" is rarely used today. So we reserve the term "euthanasia" for intentional medical killing of a patient by a physician.

[46] Some commentators argue that terminating life support, in some circumstances, intentionally causes the patient's death and therefore constitutes intentional killing. It has also been argued that a patient's decision to forgo life support can, depending on details, constitute a decision to commit suicide, in which case a physician's complying with the request constitutes assisted suicide. We set aside these conceptual complexities.

motivates a further specification, so that the rule forbids the intentional killing of *innocent* human beings. Even with these refinements, prohibiting euthanasia seems quite reasonable, because euthanasia standardly involves the *intentional* killing of *innocent* human beings. And that, according to common morality, is wrong.[47]

But we must ask *why* common morality considers such killing wrong. The most cogent answer is that intentionally killing innocent people is wrong because (1) death is a terrible harm, (2) killing violates a victim's rights, (3) the victim's innocence removes special justifications of killing (e.g., self-defense), and (4) the intentional nature of the act removes excuses that may apply to accidental killing (e.g., in pursuit of pain relief). Focus now on reasons (1) and (2), which underlie the general pro tanto wrongness of killing human beings. We are considering situations in which patients give *valid consent* to administration of a lethal injection. So the second reason does not apply. Meanwhile, we have been considering cases in which a patient does not regard staying alive, given her condition and prognosis, as worthwhile in view of the suffering involved. Given our subjective view of well-being, which we defend in Chapter 8, the counterfactual account of harm has a momentous implication. Provided that the patient correctly judges that her life will involve more suffering than enjoyment and her desire to die is suitably informed and responsive to her values, *death is not a harm*. Indeed, in these cases, it is the continuation of life that is harmful. A "good death" – the literal meaning of "euthanasia" – would put an end to the harm.

The recognition that death is not a harm in the relevant set of cases, while euthanasia would be respectful of patients' autonomy, suggests that the basic reasons for opposing the intentional killing of innocent human beings simply do not apply. Why, then, do so many people and so many jurisdictions favor the prohibition of euthanasia? Is there any cogent basis for doing so?

One possibility is that euthanasia is to be condemned on the basis of a moral principle of *avoiding killing* that is independent of nonmaleficence. The idea would be that intentionally killing a human being is at least pro

---

[47] In this discussion, we bracket the morality of suicide. Some thinkers consider it wrongful to end one's own life, and this would, of course, have implications for the ethics of others' helping one to end one's life. Interested readers might turn to Margaret Battin, *Ethical Issues in Suicide* (Englewood Cliffs, NJ: Prentice Hall, 1995); Tom Beauchamp and Robert Veatch (eds.), *Ethical Issues in Death and Dying*, 2nd ed. (Upper Saddle River, NJ: Prentice Hall, 1996), Part 3; and Margaret Battin (ed.), *The Ethics of Suicide* (New York: Oxford University Press, 2015).

tanto wrong, independently of whether it would harm or violate the rights of the individual in question.[48]

We find this an unpromising strategy for defending a prohibition on euthanasia. It seems that, when killing is wrong, it should be possible to say why it is wrong. Consider that killing human beings is usually wrong, killing nonhuman animals is often wrong, and killing some living things (e.g., bacteria, ivy) doesn't seem at all morally problematic. These points are easily understood on the basis of differences in the harms or rights violations typically involved in each case. Human death is ordinarily a very substantial harm, and killing an innocent human person against their will violates their rights. The death of sentient nonhuman animals is ordinarily somewhat harmful to them. The strength of our reasons not to kill nonhuman animals plausibly depends on both the magnitude of this harm and our views about whether they have rights. The death of insentient creatures is not plausibly regarded as harmful to them, and their lack of sentience means there is no subject who could have rights. The harm of death and the violation of rights involved in killing some creatures seem sufficient to explain what is wrong about killing. But this explanation would not support a prohibition of euthanasia – in which death is not a harm and the patient's rights against bodily trespass have been waived.

Defense of a More Progressive View

The foregoing arguments suggest that euthanasia is morally justified, in principle, in some circumstances. We mean two things in saying that euthanasia is sometimes justified *in principle*: (1) negatively, that nothing about the act of euthanasia justifies an automatic prohibition, and (2), positively, that strong reasons – concerning avoiding the harm of continuing life and promotion of patient autonomy – count in favor of allowing euthanasia in some circumstances. But a type of action might be justified in principle without being justified in practice, after accounting for factors such as the possibility of well-intentioned error and some people's willingness to act wrongly. We argued that this is true of torture.

So let us consider practical concerns that might justify prohibiting euthanasia. Some of these practical concerns are especially acute in the United States, which has a highly inequitable distribution of income,

---

[48] For a defense of this view, see Robert Veatch, *A Theory of Medical Ethics* (New York: Basic Books, 1981), chap. 10. Cf. William Frankena, *Ethics*, 2nd ed. (Englewood Cliffs, NJ: Prentice-Hall, 1973), 55–56.

wealth, and access to health care (see Chapter 6). The major concerns about the legalization and practice of euthanasia, among those who acknowledge that this act may sometimes be justified in principle, are concerns about five possibilities: (1) error, (2) coercion or undue pressure, (3) abuse of the discretion afforded to physicians, (4) a slippery slope toward unacceptable practices or policies, or (5) inconsistency with the role morality of clinicians. We address these possibilities in turn.

The most important type of error in this context is incorrectly thinking that a particular person is an appropriate candidate for euthanasia. Suppose, for example, that a patient is suffering terribly, and professionals involved in the patient's care believe there is no realistic hope of relief – although in fact there is a method of pain alleviation available that caretakers have not attempted or considered. With the best palliative care, let us suppose, this person would not want to die. It would be tragic for them to die unnecessarily as a result of this error. Of course, such an error would be equally tragic if it led to a patient's death via terminal sedation or simply the withdrawal of life support.

The second concern is that, once euthanasia is an option, individuals may be coerced or otherwise pressured into agreeing to undergo it. Suppose a nursing home patient lacks insurance that covers nursing home care and has multiple medical problems requiring costly services to address. The patient's care providers now face the choice of either not providing needed services or providing them without compensation. Such a patient might feel pressure to consent to euthanasia, for example, as a result of cues from staff members that the patient's care is very costly. This concern will be particularly pressing in countries like the United States where many people are uninsured or underinsured. But they will also arise in countries with universal health care, like Canada and the United Kingdom, where public provision of some services is limited. Even in a country with a strong health care system, individuals may feel pressure to consent to euthanasia on the basis of feeling that they pose a disagreeable burden on family members and hospital staff. Pressure to agree to euthanasia might undermine the voluntariness of the decision, if it involves a threat (see Chapter 5). But even pressure that does not have this effect – simply being reminded of the sacrifices others have to make and the option of euthanasia to relieve them – could lead someone to make a decision that they would rather not make.[49] Death would then be contrary to the

---

[49] J. David Velleman develops an argument against giving patients the right to request euthanasia on the grounds that providing that option may make people worse off, even though it may be rational

patient's wishes and potentially seriously harmful insofar as his death, given his values and priorities, would deprive him of a life worth continuing. Once again, this concern also applies to terminal sedation and withdrawal of life support, both widely accepted ways to hasten death.

In addition to concerns about patients being pressured into accepting euthanasia, there are concerns about possible abuse. Some health professionals, knowing that euthanasia is an accepted practice, may commit involuntary euthanasia – killing a patient *against* the patient's wishes – and claim that the patient had validly consented. This is a truly disturbing possibility. Like the other concerns, though, it applies to even the most widely accepted modalities for hastening death. For example, a health professional might also discontinue life support without the patient's permission and then claim that the patient had consented to the decision.

A fourth concern is the possibility of a slippery slope. The idea here is that institutionalization of morally acceptable forms of euthanasia might lead to the widespread practice and perhaps institutionalization of forms of euthanasia that are morally wrong. An early critic of euthanasia, Yale Kamisar, referred to "the danger that legal machinery initially designed to kill those who are a nuisance to themselves may someday engulf those who are a nuisance to others."[50]

In order to be persuasive, a slippery slope argument against euthanasia must combine a reasonable projection about where acceptable euthanasia practices are likely to lead and a considered moral judgment that the end point is morally unacceptable. In other words, a strong slippery slope argument against euthanasia must be both empirically and morally plausible. Let us consider three specific "slopes" on which acceptable euthanasia practices might be thought to slide toward unacceptable ones.

First, in terms of *medical condition*, a policy that requires terminal illness as a condition for euthanasia might slide to a practice or policy in which terminal illness is not required, greatly expanding the pool of candidates for euthanasia. Second, regarding the *basis for decision-making*, a euthanasia policy that requires consent might slide, over time, to permitting cases in which consent is impossible but an advance directive had earlier been completed and now applies; then later, to permitting cases in which consent is impossible and no advance directive had been left, but there

for them to exercise the option once it is available ("Against the Right to Die," *Journal of Medicine and Philosophy* 17 [1992]: 665–681).

[50] "Some Non-Religious Views against Proposed 'Mercy-Killing' Legislation," *Minnesota Law Review* 42 (1958): 969–1042. Cited in L. W. Sumner, *Assisted Death* (Oxford: Clarendon, 2011), 175.

are thought to be adequate grounds for euthanasia based on the patient's previously expressed preferences; and, finally, to permitting cases in which no such judgment can be substantiated, but death is judged to be in the patient's interests. Third, regarding the *patient's age*, a policy that initially includes only adults as eligible for euthanasia might slide, over time, to include adolescents and then younger children and finally infants.

The three slippery slope arguments just presented are empirically fairly plausible. Indeed, in at least Belgium and the Netherlands, all three slides have already occurred: terminal illness is not required; decision-making standards less demanding than informed consent have been accepted in certain cases; and there is euthanasia involving minors.[51] Even in more "conservative" jurisdictions in which there were greater emphasis on safeguards it would seem reasonable to judge that each slide down a slippery slope is *quite possible and not at all far-fetched*. But there remains the question of whether these arguments are morally plausible – that is, whether the bottom of each projected slide is clearly morally wrong. We answer negatively for all three.

In terms of the patient's medical condition, we favor not requiring terminal illness. Many patients who are appropriate candidates for euthanasia, such as individuals with cancer or a progressive neurological disorder, will be terminally ill. But, in our view, some patients who are appropriate candidates for euthanasia lack a terminal illness but are suffering terribly, with no reasonable prospect of relief, as a result of a medical condition they cannot bear. This might be the situation of certain patients who have medical conditions such as locked-in syndrome or other severe forms of paralysis and have grown weary of struggling with their physical limitations. So we do not regard the slide in question as morally unacceptable. With sufficient safeguards, it is appropriate not to require terminal illness.[52]

The other possible slides may give greater pause. Yet we believe it would be ethically permissible to permit euthanasia in some cases in which consent cannot be obtained. Euthanasia would be morally permissible,

[51] See, e.g., Andrew Siegel, Dominic Sisti, and Arthur Caplan, "Pediatric Euthanasia in Belgium: Disturbing Developments," *JAMA* 311 (2014): 1963–1964; Barron Lerner and Arthur Caplan, "Euthanasia in Belgium and the Netherlands: On a Slippery Slope?," *JAMA Internal Medicine* 175 (2015): 1640–1641; and Scott Kim, Raymond De Vries, and John Peteet, "Euthanasia and Assisted Suicide of Patients with Psychiatric Disorders in the Netherlands 2011 to 2014," *JAMA Psychiatry* 73 (2016): 362–368.

[52] For arguments in support of requiring terminal illness as a condition for any form of physician-assisted death, see Lynn Jansen, Steven Wall, and Franklin Miller, "Drawing the Line of Physician-Assisted Death," *Journal of Medical Ethics* 45 (2019): 190–197.

in our view, where a *valid* advance directive was completed, was never put in doubt by an apparent change of mind, and now *clearly applies* to the patient's situation and calls for euthanasia. For example, a patient's directive might call for euthanasia in the event that her inoperable brain tumor has deprived her of medical decision-making capacity, apparently irreversibly, and she appears to be suffering greatly with no realistic prospect of relief. In these cases, euthanasia is justified on the basis of an autonomous decision that the patient made at an earlier time – rather than on the basis of a judgment about what she would have wanted or what is best for her. So we are confident about the permissibility of euthanasia in some cases in which a patient currently lacks decision-making capacity.

We are less confident about permitting euthanasia in cases that lack any autonomous authorization (via consent or an advance directive) by the patient. We believe that euthanasia *might* occasionally be permissible, given the right sorts of safeguards, on the basis of the reasonable subject standard. In any such cases, prudential considerations on behalf of an incapacitated adult or a minor would favor a quick, minimally painful exit from life, which could be achieved with either euthanasia or terminal sedation. Chapter 8 discusses a small number of cases involving severely impaired newborns in which euthanasia might be appropriate from the standpoint of our theory.

At this point, even those who agree with us that euthanasia is not inherently wrong may challenge our position on the following grounds: *With each step away from the decision-making authority that accompanies an individual informed consent process, the possibilities of error or abuse increase.* The power of decision-making moves farther away from the patient's current will and toward other people's interpretations of what he wanted or, where there was no advance directive, what a reasonable choice for him would be.

Yet these possibilities of error and abuse already attend widely accepted modalities for hastening death, including withdrawal of life support. In addition, more restrictive policies also have a terrible downside: preventing the death of individuals for whom continuing life is worse than ending it. The best approach is not to prohibit euthanasia but to institutionalize safeguards that deal sensibly with these areas of concern. Suppose, for example, that a child suffering from an intractable type of leukemia with no hope of relief (while alive) satisfied all reasonable criteria for euthanasia in principle. If euthanasia were precluded for minors, then what options would he have? He might commit suicide with the help of a physician (if this were permitted). But that expectation might be cruel for a child.

He could be subject to pain relief that may or may not be effective and may or may not end his life, which seems less than optimal. He could undergo terminal sedation, in which case it is unclear how this has any advantage over euthanasia. Or life support could be withdrawn without sedating him to unconsciousness, in which case he would suffer more than necessary. Once we understand that euthanasia is not wrong in principle and that a practice of euthanasia is generally no more vulnerable to error, undue pressure, or abuse than clearly acceptable modalities of hastening death, we must accept that euthanasia is acceptable in practice. The key is to implement safeguards that best reconcile the importance of protecting vulnerable patients while permitting a quick exit from a life whose continuation is harmful to the patient.

A somewhat different concern remains: that euthanasia might be inconsistent with the role morality of clinicians – that is, with the professional ethics of the doctors, nurses, and others who would be involved in its administration. Some opponents of euthanasia claim that the role morality of physicians, for example, includes not only certain traditional goals, as discussed at the outset of this section, but also a negative constraint: "the inviolable rule that physicians heal and palliate suffering but *never intentionally inflict death.*"[53] Another group of authors argues, "The essence of medicine is healing, managing pain, and alleviating suffering. Doctors [participating in PAS or euthanasia] jeopardize the moral integrity of the medical profession."[54] However, these claims beg the question of the goals of medicine in assuming that euthanasia is inconsistent with those goals. An international group of scholars convened by the Hastings Center, a respected bioethics think tank, listed among the goals of medicine the relief of suffering caused by medical maladies, the care of patients who cannot be cured of their maladies, and the pursuit of a peaceful death.[55] Euthanasia can serve all three of these goals. In our estimation, appeals to the role morality of clinicians do not undermine our arguments in favor of euthanasia in some circumstances.

Policy Suggestions

Although we cannot offer a full characterization of an adequate policy here, we offer several suggestions for a policy that permits euthanasia.

---

[53] C. L. Sprung et al., "Physician-Assisted Suicide and Euthanasia: Emerging Issues from a Global Perspective," *Journal of Palliative Care* 33 (2018): 197–203, at 197 (emphasis added).

[54] Ibid., 200.

[55] See Daniel Callahan, "The Goals of Medicine: Setting New Priorities," *Hastings Center Report* 25 (6) (1996): S1–S26, at S10–S13.

- *Physician-assisted suicide would be legal (under constraints similar to those for euthanasia) and, in most cases involving adults, encouraged as an alternative to euthanasia. Euthanasia would be permitted when PAS was either infeasible due to the patient's condition, inappropriate due to the patient's young age (if euthanasia is permitted for minors), or unpalatable to the patient for some other reason.* The rationale for a presumption favoring PAS for competent adults is that it affords the patient slightly more control over the final act that causes death. An example of a condition making PAS infeasible is one in which the patient cannot swallow. The reason PAS may be inappropriate for children is that the prospect of committing suicide may be emotionally overwhelming to them. An example of a reason that PAS may be unpalatable to a given patient is that she finds the prospect of swallowing an enormous number of pills (if that is required in her jurisdiction) excessively arduous.

- *Euthanasia would generally be permitted only if the patient is suffering badly enough that her life is reasonably judged not worth living, the suffering is due to one or more medical conditions, and there is no reasonable prospect of recovery or of relief from the suffering while alive.* What makes it the case that continued life constitutes a harm rather than a benefit for the patient is the presence of great suffering without the prospect of relief, not the length of life remaining. So we do not endorse a requirement of terminal illness. Nor would we restrict the causes of suffering to "physical illness." It is possible that psychiatric conditions could cause sufficient suffering with no realistic prospect of relief (see below). The reason to require that the suffering be due to medical conditions is that other reasons for preferring a quick death are not the business of practicing physicians. If medical centers became places in which individuals could receive a quick exit from life for reasons unrelated to medicine, this development might badly damage public trust in the medical profession.[56]

- *In rare instances, euthanasia may be permissible in a patient who is not currently suffering badly enough but is expected – on the basis of highly compelling evidence – to experience sufficiently bad suffering in the future.* There is necessarily some risk of error in permitting euthanasia on the basis of a *prediction* of the degree to which someone will otherwise suffer. But we believe that, in some rare cases, the risk of someone's

---

[56] See Franklin Miller, "Should a Legal Option of Physician-Assisted Death Include Those Who Are 'Tired of Life'?," *Perspectives in Biology and Medicine* 59 (2016): 351–363.

suffering terribly and unnecessarily is even graver. This may be true of some impaired infants whose conditions worsen relentlessly over time. As we discuss in Chapter 8, death as a self-aware child may be far more traumatic than death as an unaware infant.

- *The patient must either (1) provide valid consent for euthanasia in a nonpressured environment with a thorough discussion of alternatives, including all available palliative care and terminal sedation, and reaffirm consent after a waiting period (perhaps a week); (2) have completed a valid advance directive that now unambiguously applies; or (3) be determined by a legally authorized proxy to be in a state in which the reasonable subject standard recommends euthanasia.* The third condition is one for which particularly stringent safeguards would be needed, including independent third parties who could confirm that the proxy decision-maker was deciding according to the appropriate standard and taking into account all the relevant facts.

- *An independent physician must confirm the patient's condition and prognosis and, if the patient retains decision-making capacity or presents a reasonable hope of regaining capacity, must rule out reversible depression.* Confirmation by an independent physician helps to reduce the possibilities of error or abuse. The relevance of reversible depression is that a patient, while depressed, may see less value in remaining alive than a patient who recovers from depression and is closer to his psychological and cognitive baseline. It is worth noting here that euthanasia in response to suffering due to psychiatric conditions – not only depression but also, for example, schizophrenia, personality disorders, and posttraumatic stress disorder – is a highly complex and hotly contested issue.[57] Some authors argue that euthanasia (and perhaps also physician-assisted suicide) should not be available on the basis of suffering due to psychiatric disorders.[58] We have reached the opposite judgment – where the other conditions detailed above are met. Our position rests significantly on the thesis that the value basis for determining whether a competent adult's life is worth continuing is that individual's well-informed judgment. It also depends on a fair measure

---

[57] Marie Nicolini et al., "Should Euthanasia and Assisted Suicide for Psychiatric Disorders Be Permitted? A Systematic Review of Reasons," *Psychological Medicine* 50 (2020): 1241–1256.

[58] See, e.g., Scott Kim and Trudo Lemmens, "Should Assisted Dying for Psychiatric Disorders Be Legalized in Canada?," *Canadian Medical Association Journal* 188 (October 4, 2016): E337–E339; and, for empirical data that can motivate this view, Kim, De Vries, and Peteet, "Euthanasia and Assisted Suicide of Patients with Psychiatric Disorders in the Netherlands 2011 to 2014."

of confidence in the possibility of adequate safeguards to protect adequately against errors and abuse.

This is a very rough sketch of the policy we recommend. At this point, a reader might wonder why we have defended a policy permitting euthanasia when terminal sedation, which offers equally fast relief from suffering, is already available in some jurisdictions. Our answer has three parts. First, although terminal sedation has the practical advantage of already being legal, *it has no ethical advantage over euthanasia*. The cases in which either modality would be appropriate are cases in which it is continued life, rather than death, that would be harmful to the patient. And terminal sedation does not afford more control to the patient than euthanasia does. By contrast, PAS does afford the patient a bit more control at the time of causing death and so is appropriately encouraged as an alternative to euthanasia. The second reason for permitting euthanasia despite the availability of terminal sedation is that many patients, and their families, may prefer that the patient undergo a "clean" death rather than dying more slowly from dehydration or an underlying medical condition. Even though the dying process would be unconscious, sparing the patient from suffering and awareness of his deterioration, the patient and his family may find the prospect of dying this way repugnant. We believe this sensibility ought to be accommodated. Third, it is wasteful to devote costly medical resources to keeping someone alive as she gradually dehydrates to the point of death if that individual meets appropriate criteria for euthanasia.

CHAPTER 5

Autonomy

5.1   Introduction

The concept of autonomy has played a pivotal role in modern bioethics, as it has in the liberalism that has dominated political discourse over the last half-century. The focus on the importance of patient autonomy – with its emphasis on informed consent, patient rights, and the value of people making their own decisions about medical care – has transformed medical practice and clinical research. In this chapter, we analyze autonomy and relate it to the other components of our ethical theory.

We begin by describing what we take autonomy to consist in and distinguish two ways in which autonomy is morally important for bioethical questions. We then discuss respect for autonomy and its relationship to rights before delineating a taxonomy of ways in which someone's autonomy can be interfered with. We briefly evaluate two justifications for interfering with someone's actions: paternalistic justifications and the prevention of harm to others. One key normative role that respect for autonomy plays is in grounding the requirement to obtain consent from competent patients and research participants. We provide a detailed analysis of the conditions for valid consent. When someone is not competent to make their own decisions, someone else must decide on their behalf. The last part of our ethical analysis discusses this surrogate decision-making. Finally, we turn to two more specific applications of the theory that we have developed: the right to refuse treatment and the ethics of direct-to-consumer advertising of pharmaceuticals.

A preliminary point about terminology. Sometimes a distinction is drawn between the terms *capacity* and *competence* in the context of talking about someone's ability to make their own decisions autonomously. According to this way of distinguishing them, *capacity* describes someone's ability, whereas *competence* describes a legal power – someone is competent to make their own decisions if they have the legal right to do so. We do not distinguish the terms in this way; when speaking in the legal sense we explicitly qualify the terms we use. Second, the term "autonomy" is used in multiple overlapping ways in everyday discussion, as well as in discussions of medical ethics. We attempt neither to provide an account of all these uses nor to capture everyday use of the term. Instead, we identify specific normative functions that autonomy talk serves and restrict our use of it to those functions. Similar points apply to the use of terms such as *coercion*, *manipulation*, and *persuasion*.

5.2   The Nature and Value of Autonomy

Autonomy means self-rule. In the words of the Belmont Report, "An autonomous person is an individual capable of deliberation about personal goals and of acting under the direction of such deliberation."[1] In a moment, we will go into more detail concerning the criteria for determining whether someone is autonomous. Before that it will be helpful to distinguish two roles that autonomy plays in our ethical thinking: as a component of a flourishing life and as a ground for rights claims.[2] First, it is widely thought that having the capacity for autonomous action and the opportunity to exercise that capacity is good for human beings. Good parents bring up their children to be autonomous because they judge that it is good for a child to become someone who can think and act for herself. Autonomy might be intrinsically valuable for human beings, in the sense of being a component of well-being. In any case, autonomy is certainly instrumentally valuable: valuable because autonomous people tend to be good at identifying and pursuing what is in their own interests, and because the exercise of autonomy is (often) itself enjoyable or satisfying.[3] However, autonomy is only one component of – or contributor to – well-being. Someone might be more autonomous than their friend but also more depressive: ceteris paribus, they are then better off on one dimension of well-being and worse off on another. Indeed, it is possible that someone's autonomy could actively interfere with other valuable aspects of their life. For example, someone who is excessively focused on remaining independent from the influence of others might be inhibited from enjoying personal relationships that require some reliance on other people.

---

[1] National Commission for the Protection of Human Subjects of Biomedical and Behavioral Research, *The Belmont Report* (Washington, DC: US Government Printing Office, 1978).
[2] See Stephen Darwall, "The Value of Autonomy and Autonomy of the Will," *Ethics* 116 (2006): 263–284.
[3] See the discussion of subjective and objective theories of well-being in Chapter 8.

In addition to being a component of a flourishing human life, autonomy plays a distinct normative role insofar as autonomous individuals have certain *rights* that are grounded in their autonomy. Crucially for bioethics, an autonomous person has the right to decide whether other people may do things to his body. He can exercise this right by refusing a medical treatment that his doctor thinks would benefit him. On the other hand, he can also exercise it by giving consent to a research procedure that will do him no good at all, but will provide data that may help other people in the future. Respecting this *autonomy as personal sovereignty* is therefore quite different from promoting someone's well-being. Although it may be good for someone to be autonomous, she may exercise her autonomy in ways that are actually detrimental to her well-being, and her autonomy grounds her right to do so. As Joel Feinberg puts it: "There must be a right to err, to be mistaken, to decide foolishly, to take big risks, if there is to be any meaningful self-rule; without it, the whole idea of *de jure* autonomy begins to unravel."[4]

Autonomy thus matters morally in two quite different ways. Both arise frequently in discussions of bioethical questions. For example, the benefit of being autonomous arises in discussions of patient empowerment and helping patients to make better, more informed decisions. The rights that are grounded in autonomy arise in discussions of informed consent. Thus, the contexts in which we care about these two types of autonomy overlap considerably. Nonetheless, for the purposes of making progress with problems in bioethics it is important to keep them conceptually distinct.[5]

Turn now from the normative role that autonomy judgments play to the nature of autonomy. We have already roughly indicated what it means to be autonomous: to be able to deliberate about one's actions in the light of one's values, make a decision on the basis of that deliberation, and act accordingly. It is also helpful to distinguish autonomous *agents* from autonomous *actions*. Most adults are autonomous agents in the sense that they have the capacity for autonomous action and the decision-making rights grounded in that capacity. It does not follow that every one of their actions is autonomous. We might doubt, for example, that an adult acts autonomously when they are heavily drugged or furiously angry. Roughly speaking, *an agent A performs action X autonomously if and only if (1)*

---

[4] Joel Feinberg, "Autonomy, Sovereignty, and Privacy: Moral Ideals in the Constitution," *Notre Dame Law Review* 58 (1982): 445–492, at 461.

[5] These two normative roles are frequently mixed together in bioethical discussion under the umbrella of "respect for autonomy." See, e.g., Tom Beauchamp and James Childress, *Principles of Biomedical Ethics*, 7th ed. (New York: Oxford University Press, 2013), 106–107.

*A performs X (i) intentionally, (ii) with sufficient understanding, (iii) suffi-
ciently free of controlling influences; and (2) A decided, or could have decided,
whether to X in light of A's values.*[6]

The conditions presented in this analysis merit some explication. First,
to perform an action intentionally involves doing what one *has in mind* in
acting. Suppose the action under consideration is lending someone money.
To lend someone money intentionally involves acting with the idea of
lending the money, rather than, say, handing it over as a gift. To lend it
with sufficient understanding involves not only knowing what one is
doing, but also grasping its major implications (e.g., that the other party
is now indebted to you). To perform this action sufficiently free of
controlling influences is to perform it more or less voluntarily, as would
not be the case if one were coerced by another into advancing a loan or
driven to do so by an irresistible compulsion to lend money. As a final
condition of our analysis, one performs an action autonomously only if
one is able to make the decision to act in light of one's own values
(whether or not those values are actually considered during decision-
making). In the case of the loan, for example, this means that if the
individual had concluded that she *should not* make the loan, all things
considered, then she could have refrained from doing so. This condition
implies that only individuals who have values can act autonomously.

For bioethicists, one critical question concerning what it means to be
autonomous centers on how to ascertain the threshold at which someone is
competent, such that he has autonomy rights. In the remainder of the
section, we address this question.

At the critical threshold of competence, someone is sufficiently autonomous to govern her own life. Among other things, this means that it can be
appropriate to hold her responsible for her voluntary actions and that she is
capable of being swayed by reasons. These implications correspond to
aspects of the conditions for autonomous action. Only someone who is
capable of acting intentionally and understanding what she is doing can be
held responsible for her actions. Only someone who can be swayed by
reasons is able to decide on the basis of her values. Being sufficiently
autonomous does not mean that all of an agent's actions are rational or that
they are based on full understanding of the possible consequences – no

---

[6] This analysis is nearly identical to that presented in Jennifer Desante, David DeGrazia, and Marion
Danis, "Parents of Adults with Diminished Self-Governance," *Cambridge Quarterly of Healthcare
Ethics* 25 (2016): 93–107, at 95. It is also similar to the one presented in Beauchamp and Childress,
Principles of Biomedical Ethics (104–105) except that the latter analysis has nothing approximating
our second condition.

human being is completely autonomous. Nevertheless, all who meet a critical threshold are equally in possession of autonomy rights.

The capacity for autonomous action is frequently regarded as a global capacity: someone is either competent or not. A typical middle-aged adult has autonomy rights; a typical young child does not. This global view has come under sustained criticism from bioethicists who regard the capacity for autonomous action as task- or domain-specific.[7] On the domain-specific view someone can be autonomous with respect to some decisions but nonautonomous with respect to others, such that she has the moral right to make decisions with regard to some aspects of her life but not all.

This domain-specific view is suggested by laws that assign different legal powers at different ages. For example, the age at which someone can give consent to sexual intercourse in the United Kingdom is sixteen, but the age at which someone has the right to vote is eighteen.[8] It is also not uncommon to take a domain-specific attitude to the assessment of someone's capacity in certain medical contexts. For example, assessments of a prospective participant's ability to consent to research in the Clinical Center of the US National Institutes of Health are tailored to the specific research protocol in which he would be enrolled. These assessments evaluate, for example, the prospective participant's understanding of the risks, benefits, and purpose of that protocol, and his reasoning regarding the participation decision.[9]

The domain-specific view can be justified in the following way. There is a threshold level of ability to make decisions for oneself that grounds one's right to do so. If someone does not meet this threshold, then she lacks the right to make her own decisions. But different decisions can be easier or more difficult for an individual to make. For example, decisions about

---

[7] For discussions of decision-making competence that defend the domain-specific view, see Allen Buchanan and Dan Brock, *Deciding for Others* (New York: Cambridge University Press, 1989), 17–86; Bernard Gert, Charles Culver, and K. Danner Clouser, *Bioethics* (New York: Oxford University Press, 1997), 131–148; and Beauchamp and Childress, *Principles of Biomedical Ethics*, 115–120.

[8] Of course, nothing magical happens during development such that at age sixteen or eighteen someone transitions from being unable to make their own decisions to being able to do so. The process of normal development is gradual and, in any case, varies among individuals. However, for purposes of public policy it is helpful to have clear lines to determine when people acquire the relevant legal powers for the majority of the population. Since age is correlated with cognitive development, it is sensible to use it for a first approximation to competence.

[9] Some of the commonly used instruments for assessing capacity to consent to clinical care and research assume a global view. Others are designed to be adapted to the specific decisions that patients and prospective participants are asked to make. See L. B. Dunn, M. A. Nowrangi, B. W. Palmer, D. V. Jeste, and E. R. Saks, "Assessing Decisional Capacity for Clinical Research or Treatment: A Review of Instruments," *American Journal of Psychiatry* 163 (2006): 1323–1334.

participation in clinical research may be more cognitively demanding than decisions about clinical care; decisions about what to wear today may not require the ability to plan that is necessary to make decisions about college or retirement, whose effects will not be felt for many years. A person may therefore be capable of making some decisions sufficiently well that she has a right to do so, but not others.

5.3 Respect (and Disrespect) for Autonomy

Respect for Autonomy and Rights

To respect someone's autonomy, as we understand it, requires respecting her autonomy rights. Common to these rights is the right to make certain decisions for oneself. For example, a competent individual's right to control her own body gives her a claim against other people that they not touch her without permission. Interference with someone's exercise of autonomy involves a prima facie (that is, apparent) rights violation. It will not be a rights violation, however, if it uses a permissible method of interfering (e.g., persuading someone of a course of action by providing compelling reasons) or if the person interfering has the right to do so (e.g., despite having a right to freedom of movement you have walked onto my property, so your right does not extend this far).[10] Moreover, as argued in Chapter 2, we consider rights to be morally very important, but not absolute. A rights violation is therefore pro tanto wrongful: the wrongfulness of violating someone's rights can sometimes be outweighed, on balance, by other morally important considerations. What is needed to outweigh a rights claim will depend on the nature of that claim, including the importance of the interest the right protects. For example, one's interest in controlling personal information is very substantial but not as great as one's interest in avoiding torture. Consistent with this judgment, we think there are multiple situations in which it is justifiable to require people to disclose personal information, overriding their right to privacy, but no actual cases in which it is permissible to override someone's right not to be tortured (Chapter 4).

In bioethics, cases involving disrespect for autonomy commonly arise as a result of attempts to control someone's decision. For example, if a

---

[10] We use the term "interference" in a deliberately broad manner here, so as to include those ways of intervening in someone's decision-making that prove to be morally innocuous, even though they might vex the actor in question.

hospital's staff insist on providing treatment to a competent patient who has refused it, they attempt (illegitimately) to control her decision about what care she will receive. It will therefore prove helpful to lay out a taxonomy of ways in which one party may control or attempt to control another's decision.[11]

Coercion, Offers, Undue Inducements, and Exploitation

Coercion is the bluntest method of control. *Occurrent coercion* involves the direct use of physical force: a patient who is being held down on a bed or locked into a room is coerced in this way. *Dispositional coercion*, by contrast, occurs when one party issues a credible threat to another in order to secure compliance with her demands.[12] For example, a public-sector pharmacist who refused to dispense needed medicines without a kickback would be engaged in dispositional coercion.

Someone who engages in coercion attempts to control another individual by altering the options that are open to him (or, at least, purporting to do so). For example, the robber who says "Your money or your life!" purports to alter her victim's options by removing from him the option of keeping both his money and his life. This is not the only way in which it is possible to influence someone's behavior by altering his options. Offers can also have this effect. In contrast to a threat, an *offer* is a proposal to make someone better off if he complies with the request of the person making the offer. For example, someone who enrolls in a research study because she will be paid $100 has been motivated by an offer.[13]

Before proceeding to the ethical analysis of these methods of control, it is worth noting the relationship, or the lack of it, between the method used

---

[11] This taxonomy draws on the taxonomy in Amulya Mandava and Joseph Millum, "Manipulation in the Enrollment of Research Participants," *Hastings Center Report* 43 (2013): 38–47.

[12] The distinction is from Thomas Mappes, "Sexual Morality and the Concept of Using Another Person," in Thomas Mappes and Jane Zembaty (eds.), *Social Ethics*, 3rd ed. (New York: McGraw-Hill, 1987): 248–262. The account of dispositional coercion according to which coercion essentially involves a threat to violate another's rights unless they comply with the coercer's demands can be found in Alan Wertheimer, *Coercion* (Hoboken, NJ: John Wiley & Sons, 1987).

[13] Note that someone might not be better off *overall* if they accept an offer. For example, if you offer me $5 to wash your truck, I might be worse off overall if I accept since my time would be better spent doing something else. Nonetheless, you make me an offer, since you attempt to motivate me by making me better off relative to my current financial situation if I do as you request. Likewise, complying with a threat could make someone better off overall, even though the threat is a proposal to make the person worse off if they do not comply. For example, if Fabian threatens to punch the drunk Arturo unless he hands over his car keys, it may make Arturo better off by preventing him from getting into an accident.

and its effectiveness. One might find it natural to assume that coercion is more forceful and effective than making an offer. Yet physical force may be weak – a slight shove may not move me anywhere, for example. A threat may be easy to resist – your saying that you'll spill water on my shoes is a threat, but likely one I'll laugh off. On the other hand, an offer may be impossible for a reasonable person to resist – if you promise to pay for my child's otherwise unaffordable chemotherapy, then I will likely agree to whatever you propose. All these methods, then, vary in their ability to control someone's actions, and none is intrinsically more controlling than the others. Instead, one person's ability to control the actions of another will depend on that person's psychology and the context in which the interaction takes place.

Turn now to the ethical analysis. Threats and offers are generally distinguished on the basis of whether they involve a proposal to make someone worse off or better off. This naturally prompts the question: Worse off or better off than what? One possibility is to use a *descriptive baseline*. For example, by threatening to kill her victim, the robber proposes to make her victim worse off than she would otherwise have been. But descriptive baselines struggle with cases of omission. For example, the pharmacist who refuses to provide medicine to a patient without a bribe seems to coerce him (we would not say that the pharmacist now had a legitimate claim to the bribe money). Yet the patient is not worse off than he otherwise would have been. We therefore favor using a *normative or moralized baseline*. Whether a proposal is a threat depends on whether carrying out the threat would make the person threatened worse off than she *should* be.[14]

On our view, coercion, whether occurrent or dispositional, typically involves the violation of the coercee's rights.[15] The robber's threat, for example, violates her victim's right to dispose of his property as he sees fit by presenting a risk of harm that the robber has no right to impose. There is therefore a high bar that must be passed in order to justify coercion. Offers, on the other hand, typically do not involve violating someone's rights.

---

[14] Note that an analysis of threats based on normative baselines has difficulty making sense of the idea of legitimate coercion. For example, legal sanctions – such as the threat to fine or imprison citizens who do not pay their taxes – are generally regarded as paradigmatic instances of coercion. Yet, if the government has the right to force its citizens to comply with the tax laws, then it does not propose to violate their rights by punishing those who do not comply. For discussion, see Scott Anderson, "Coercion," in Edward Zalta (ed.), *Stanford Encyclopedia of Philosophy* (Winter 2017 edition; available at https://plato.stanford.edu/archives/win2017/entries/coercion/).

[15] Here we follow Wertheimer, *Coercion*.

To see the contrast, consider a parallel case to the case of the robber. Suppose that a surgeon honestly advises her patient that he needs an operation if he is to survive. In effect, she says, "This operation or your life!" As with the robber's victim, the patient faces death if he does not comply. Yet we would not say that the surgeon acts wrongly here. This is because she is not responsible for the risk of death that her patient faces. Relative to the appropriate baseline – which is the patient facing death if he goes without surgery – she is proposing to make him better off.

Though offers do not typically violate anyone's rights, that does not mean that their effect on decision-making is wholly unproblematic. In the context of research, one common objection to paying substantial amounts of money to research participants is that such payments constitute "undue inducements" to enroll in the research study. For example, the Council for International Organizations of Medical Sciences (CIOMS) states in their guidelines: "Compensation must not be so large as to induce potential participants to consent to participate in the research against their better judgment ('undue inducement')."[16]

Clearly, inducing someone to act by offering them an incentive is not in itself ethically problematic. It is not wrong to pay someone to work when they would not work for free. The concern that animates CIOMS seems to be about how the incentive might affect the quality of someone's decision-making. If an offer led someone to make a poor decision, by their own lights, then one might be concerned that their autonomy had been compromised. For example, if the immediate prospect of payment made a prospective research participant irrationally downplay the risks of a research study, this might be problematic.[17] It is important to be precise about when this is a problem. We are not saying that an offer impedes someone's autonomous decision-making whenever it induces her to act in a way that she would not act in the absence of the offer. A rational decision about whether to take up an offer must be one that includes weighing the value of what is offered. Rather, an offer would be problematic if it induced her to act in a way that she would not act if she were thinking clearly.

It is common to raise concerns about "undue inducement." Whether offers of payment often present real risks to the autonomy of people's

[16] Council for International Organizations of Medical Sciences, *International Ethical Guidelines for Health-Related Research Involving Humans*, 4th ed. (Geneva: CIOMS, 2016), Guideline 13.
[17] Ezekiel Emanuel, "Undue Inducement: Nonsense on Stilts?," *American Journal of Bioethics* 5 (2005): 9–13.

decision-making is an empirical matter. We do not know of data that support the claim that payment worsens decision-making. The limited data that exist on the relationship between perceptions of risks and payment for research enrollment suggest that payment does not impair decision-making.[18]

The issue of "undue inducement" is usually raised when an offer is thought to be too high. But offers are more often unethical because they are too low. Suppose that a clinical research group is conducting a study that involves infecting healthy volunteers with malaria parasites in order to test the effectiveness of a new antimalarial drug. The study involves a battery of invasive tests, a week-long inpatient stay, the risks of malaria infection, and treatment with an experimental drug. Studies like this usually pay participants several thousand pounds. In this case, the research is recruiting in an area with pervasive high unemployment. The research group's recruiter therefore thinks that they could get sufficient volunteers to enroll if they cut the remuneration to £500. If this would be wrongful, it is because it is exploitative.

Exploitation occurs when one party takes advantage of another's vulnerability in order to obtain an unfair distribution of benefits and burdens from their interaction.[19] In the malaria study, the research group would be able to offer an unfairly low payment because the people in the area are so desperate for paid employment. They take unfair advantage of the poverty of prospective research participants. Questions of exploitation frequently arise in bioethics – for example, one might perceive exploitation in charging patients high prices for drugs or in conducting research in a population that does not stand to benefit from the results of the research.

A final way in which offers can be ethically problematic may arise when a conditional offer is made to someone who lacks any reasonable alternative to accepting. Suppose someone is suffering from chronic kidney disease and can no longer afford the medical bills for dialysis. Faced with a choice between kidney failure and, at best, a transplant that he also would not be able to afford, they would do whatever it takes to get treatment, whether that be borrowing money at very high rates of interest

---

[18] See J. P. Bentley and P. G. Thacker, "The Influence of Risk and Monetary Payment on the Research Participation Decision Making Process," *Journal of Medical Ethics* 30 (2004): 293–298; Scott Halpern et al., "Empirical Assessment of Whether Moderate Payments Are Undue or Unjust Inducements for Participation in Clinical Trials," *Archives of Internal Medicine* 164 (2004): 801–803; and Leanne Stunkel et al., "Comprehension and Informed Consent: Assessing the Effect of a Short Consent Form," *IRB* 32 (2010): 1–9C.

[19] Alan Wertheimer, *Exploitation* (Princeton, NJ: Princeton University Press, 1999).

or enrolling in research studies where care is subsidized.[20] The alternative – not having life-preserving medical care – is so bad that almost any condition could be attached to an offer that would provide the care. Assuming that the party to whom he turns has no obligation to help, this is not a situation that involves coercion in the sense just discussed. However, if the lender can put whatever terms he likes on the loan or the researcher can dictate the terms on which people enroll in her study, then, in that regard, the patient is subject to someone else's will.[21] Since independence from the will of others is usually one contributor to well-being, subjection to another's will typically makes someone's life go worse. Many of the cases in which people are prone to describing offers as "coercive" are cases in which the alternative to accepting the offer is unbearable. We think that this analysis in terms of subjection to the will of another better captures the underlying ethical concern that motivates them.

Three points are worth making about this idea that a conditional offer can be bad for someone when the alternative to accepting the offer is unbearable. First, if the offer is effective, then it is likely to make the recipient of the offer better off overall. The person who chooses to enroll in a research study in order to get free care may be worse off in one respect because he is subject to the researcher's will, but much better off in another respect because he gets treatment for his disease. On balance, then, he is likely to be better off. It is therefore an open question whether such offers should be prohibited. It is also an open question whether the party making the offer ought to avoid making it (thereby keeping her hands clean, but not benefiting someone she could benefit) or should just sweeten it (further compensating for the setback to autonomy interests by promoting other interests). Second, many cases of so-called coercive offers will also be exploitative. Someone whose situation is so desperate that a conditional offer leaves him subject to the will of the person making the offer will also be someone who is likely to agree to an unfair distribution of benefits and burdens. Likewise, in both cases there is an identical solution: providing

---

[20] In the United States, nondirected kidneys for transplantation are considered a public resource. However, the costs of the medical procedures associated with transplantation, including pre- and postoperative care, fall upon the individual and their medical insurance. Assessment of transplant candidates therefore includes assessment of their ability to meet financial costs. See, e.g., UC Davis Transplant Center, "The Evaluation Process" (2016) (available at https://health.ucdavis.edu/transplant/heart/the-evaluation-process.html; accessed September 28, 2020).

[21] For a complete articulation and defense of this claim, see Joseph Millum and Michael Garnett, "How Payment for Research Participation Can Be Coercive," *American Journal of Bioethics* 19 (9) (2019): 21–31.

greater benefits both makes an offer less bad for the recipient overall and makes the transaction less exploitative. Finally, it is important to emphasize that these cases arise only when someone has no good alternative to complying with the wishes of the person making the offer. As noted above, the fact that someone is motivated by an offer is not sufficient to show that it is ethically problematic.

Deception, Manipulation, and Persuasion

Thus far, we have described forms of control that involve altering the options available to someone. An alternative way to affect someone's decision is instead to alter their perception – broadly speaking – of the choice situation. One way to do this is through deception. *Deception* involves one person deliberately inducing another to believe something that the first party believes to be untrue.[22] This might involve telling a lie – "This won't hurt a bit!" But deception might also be achieved through *conversational implicature*, as when a crucial fact is omitted from a description that the listener is expected to interpret as complete. Telling a patient that side effects of a surgery "include possible infection, bleeding, and postoperative pain" but not mentioning the risk of stroke or seizure would be deceptive, since he can reasonably expect, and the surgeon can anticipate that he reasonably expects, that she would mention those risks if they were known. Though it is common for people to try to avoid lying directly and instead to deceive in other ways, we do not regard the differences between these methods of deception as ethically important in themselves.[23]

Someone's perception of his choice can also be affected through *motivational manipulation* – which occurs when one party intentionally causes another to act on desires that, on reflection, he would not consider sufficient reason to engage in the action.[24] Consider, for example, a patient who wants to change his primary care doctor and so asks his current doctor

---

[22] See, e.g., Sissela Bok, *Lying* (New York: Vintage, 1978), 14; and James Edwin Mahon, "The Definition of Lying and Deception," in Edward Zalta (ed.), *Stanford Encyclopedia of Philosophy* (Winter 2016 edition; available at https://plato.stanford.edu/archives/win2016/entries/lying-definition/).

[23] For an attempt to argue that lying, as opposed to other forms of deception, is particularly bad, see Jennifer Jackson, "Telling the Truth," *Journal of Medical Ethics* 17 (1991): 5–9. For a response, see David Bakhurst, "On Lying and Deceiving," *Journal of Medical Ethics* 18 (1992): 63–66. For further analysis of the wrongfulness of deceit, see Colin O'Neil, "Lying, Trust, and Gratitude," *Philosophy & Public Affairs* 40 (2012): 301–333.

[24] Mandava and Millum, "Manipulation in the Enrollment of Research Participants," 40.

to transfer his medical records. She sighs, looks him in the eye, and tells him she feels really bad that he's severing their relationship. If he now feels guilty and backtracks, then she will have successfully manipulated him. Note that this need involve no threats and no deception: simply by stimulating a desire in him not to make her feel bad, the guilt-tripping physician gets her way.

Consider a different doctor–patient encounter. Suppose that a patient is contemplating surgery for his lower back pain. His doctor lays out the evidence regarding the effectiveness of surgery as opposed to continuing with physical therapy, as well as the possible side effects of the operation. She reminds him that his pain tends to wax and wane and that his current pain is likely to diminish of its own accord over the next couple of weeks. Suppose that over the course of their discussion, this information is sufficient to make him decide against surgery, just as the doctor thinks he should. Nevertheless, it would be a stretch to say that she has manipulated him, where that has a negative connotation. When someone attempts a balanced presentation of facts that she considers relevant to someone's decision, or when she shows him the logical links between his reasons and an action, she is engaged in *persuasion*, not manipulation.[25]

These three ways to alter someone's perception of his options warrant quite different ethical judgments on the basis of the different ways that they affect an individual's ability to act autonomously. Deception directly interferes with someone's ability to make decisions according to her own preferences and values. This makes deception pro tanto wrongful.[26] Deception may also have additional normative effects. For example, the fact that someone was deceived into performing some action might constitute an excuse for what they did. Likewise, consent from someone who is deceived about a fact that would be material to his decision will be invalid because it will violate the disclosure requirement (as discussed below).[27] On the other hand, we consider persuasion, defined as an attempt to affect someone's decision through the honest use of reasons, to be ethically unproblematic. Persuasion does not undermine someone's

---

[25] For a similar definition of persuasion, see Ruth Faden and Tom Beauchamp, *A History and Theory of Informed Consent* (New York: Oxford University Press, 1986), 261.

[26] For further discussion on what exactly makes it wrongful, see O'Neil, "Lying, Trust, and Gratitude"; Alan Strudler, "The Distinctive Wrong in Lying," *Ethical Theory and Moral Practice* 13 (2010): 171–179; and Bernard Williams, *Truth and Truthfulness* (Princeton, NJ: Princeton University Press, 2002), chap. 5.

[27] This observation does not preclude the possibility of someone giving valid consent to being deceived (David Wendler and Franklin Miller, "Deception in the Pursuit of Science," *Archives of Internal Medicine* 164 [2004]: 597–600).

capacity to make her own decision in the light of her values and preferences; if anything, it augments it.

The ethical analysis of motivational manipulation is more complex. First, when one party successfully manipulates another, he causes her to act on the basis of her immediate desires, not the values and preferences that she would, on reflection, choose to involve in her decision-making (or, more subtly, not putting the same weight on those values and preferences that she would without his influence). She makes his decision-making process worse, relative to his values, without his agreement to do so. Thus, we think that motivational manipulation is pro tanto wrongful.[28] However, although motivational manipulation is morally problematic because of how it interferes with autonomous decision-making, it does not follow that it is on a par with coercion or deception. Someone subject to motivational manipulation can still have other good options available and can still have all the information that she needs to make her own decision. That is, she retains the ability and access to the information necessary to make a decision that reflects her own values and preferences. We do not, therefore, think that being manipulated is sufficient to excuse someone from wrongdoing or to invalidate his consent.

Consider the following example. A patient with a treatable form of cancer has nonetheless refused the recommended chemotherapy because hair loss and severe nausea are among the side effects. His oncology team, having provided all the information about the pros and cons of the treatment and recommended that he proceed, now consider alternative strategies. In discussion, his family reveals that he has a soft spot for one of the younger doctors, who reminds him of the daughter he never had. The team sends this doctor into the patient's room, where she listens to his stories, laughs at his jokes, mildly reprimands him, and asks why he's delaying getting treatment. Feeling buoyant and wanting to please, the patient agrees to start chemo.

If the patient agreed to the treatment because the doctor threatened him, or because the doctor lied about whether there were any side effects, then his consent to the procedure would clearly be invalid. Those would be cases of coercion or deception. In this case, however, the fact that he was manipulated into agreeing does not render his consent invalid. Moreover, the fact that receiving the treatment was very much in his interests makes it plausible that the manipulation was in fact morally justified. It would be justified, we think, if the expected net benefits of the treatment were large

---

[28] Mandava and Millum, "Manipulation in the Enrollment of Research Participants," 40.

enough to outweigh the pro tanto wrong of manipulation, and if there were no other ways to get his agreement that were less ethically problematic.

Recent discussions of "nudging" in the context of health care have also generated concerns about manipulation. According to Richard Thaler and Cass Sunstein's characterization: "A nudge . . . is any aspect of the choice architecture [i.e., the context in which individuals make decisions] that alters people's behavior in a predictable way without forbidding any options or significantly changing their economic incentives."[29] Examples include setting as a default that people are organ donors and requiring them to opt out if they do not want to donate; attaching photographs of patients to X-rays to encourage radiologists to read them more carefully; and describing cancer treatments in terms of probability of survival versus probability of mortality, thereby making it more likely that patients will opt for treatment.[30]

Thaler and Sunstein, and others since, have documented a wide variety of nudging techniques, and there is not space here to evaluate them all. As they understand the term, a "nudge" will not involve coercion or deception, since it is designed to leave people free to decide for themselves. Some nevertheless will involve manipulation. Take the framing effect of describing the probabilities of treatment outcomes in terms of survival or mortality. Multiple studies presenting participants with hypothetical choices have found that they are more likely to select surgery and more invasive or toxic medical treatments when they are presented with information framed in terms of survival than in terms of mortality.[31] For example, patients in the waiting room of a multispecialty outpatient clinic were asked to watch one of two videos and then presented with a hypothetical choice about whether to undergo angioplasty on the advice of their doctor.[32] Both videos described the potential risks of angioplasty, but one ended by saying, "ninety-nine percent of patients undergoing the procedure do not have any of these complications." The other ended saying, "These complications are seen in one out of a hundred people who undergo the

---

[29] Richard Thaler and Cass Sunstein, *Nudge* (New Haven, CT: Yale University Press, 2008), 6.
[30] These examples and others are listed in Jennifer Blumenthal-Barby and Hadley Burroughs, "Seeking Better Health Outcomes: The Ethics of Using the 'Nudge,'" *American Journal of Bioethics*, 12 (2012): 1–10.
[31] Annette Moxey et al., "Describing Treatment Effects to Patients," *Journal of General Internal Medicine* 18 (2003): 948–959.
[32] Hitinder Singh Gurm and David Litaker, "Framing Procedural Risks to Patients: Is 99% Safe the Same as a Risk of 1 in 100?," *Academic Medicine* 75 (2000): 840–842.

procedure." When the reason for angioplasty was simply to relieve chest pain, significantly more respondents who watched the former (positively framed) video said they would agree to the treatment than those who watched the latter (negatively framed) video. Since the information that is provided is the same, one interpretation of what is going on in cases like this is that describing it in terms of survival makes the positive outcome more salient and describing it in terms of mortality makes the negative outcome more salient.[33] Insofar as this leads the decision-maker to give too much or too little weight to the risks of the procedure, it is manipulative.[34]

We noted above that in some cases manipulation seems clearly permissible, given the benefits to the individual manipulated. Does this mean clinicians should regularly set up discussions to manipulate their patients into making the decision that the clinician thinks best? No. First, motivational manipulation is still pro tanto wrong because it is disrespectful of autonomy, even though the wrong can be outweighed. Second, competent adults are frequently better judges of what is in their own interests than are others. Third, clinicians may have their own biases to guard against; for example, they may tend to favor more aggressive interventions than someone's situation warrants. Fourth, clinicians and medical researchers have a duty of beneficence to help patients and prospective research participants make good decisions, where this means making good decisions *by their own lights*. Thus, they have a (limited) duty to enhance patient and participant autonomy. Fifth, it is plausible that warranted trust in medical professionals and medical institutions will be better for patients over the long run. Frequent manipulation for short-term benefit is likely to undermine that trust. Finally, even if manipulation were in a patient's interests, it could be justified only if the clinician lacked ways to benefit him that would be less morally problematic, such as taking the time for persuasion. Permissible manipulation, then, is the exception, not the rule. We discuss this issue again later in the chapter when we examine the ethics of direct-to-consumer pharmaceutical advertising.

5.4 Justifying Interference

The autonomy rights of competent persons restrict what others may do to them without permission. People typically also have interests in acting

---

[33] R. Noggle, "Manipulation, Salience, and Nudges," *Bioethics* 32 (2017): 164–170.

[34] Note that framing effects may be correctable with relatively simple debiasing interventions (Sammy Almashat et al., "Framing Effect Debiasing in Medical Decision Making," *Patient Education and Counseling* 71 [2008]: 102–107). It may therefore be possible to present data on survival and mortality rates without manipulating the decision-maker toward one outcome or another.

autonomously, and some justification must be given for interfering with those interests. In this section, we address two broad classes of interference with autonomy: interference for someone's own good and interference for the good of others.

Paternalism

When we interfere with someone's choices or decision-making for their sake but without their consent, we engage in *paternalism*. If I hide your cigarettes so that you won't smoke because I'm concerned that you will get cancer, I act paternalistically. If a physician deceives a patient so that they will consent to a procedure the physician thinks is in the patient's best interests, the deception is paternalistic. Likewise, according to common understandings of the term, when we stop a curious child from rifling through the knife drawer, we act paternalistically. Institutions, too, may be paternalistic. For example, the US Food and Drug Administration (FDA) regulates the sale of food, drugs, and medical devices. Without sufficient evidence of the safety and efficacy of a new drug, the FDA will not allow its sale.[35] Making these drugs available only with a prescription from a physician may also be regarded as paternalistic: the most plausible justification for not allowing individuals to decide for themselves which drugs to buy is that this prohibition protects them.

It is helpful to distinguish hard and soft paternalism.[36] *Hard paternalism* is typically understood to involve one party interfering with the voluntary, relevantly informed actions or decision-making of an autonomous agent for the sake of that agent. *Soft paternalism* involves one party interfering with the actions or decision-making of someone who is not competent for that individual's sake. Both types of paternalism involve one party's substitution of their own judgment for that of the individual who is treated paternalistically. Human beings typically have interests in governing their own lives, even when they lack the capacity for autonomous action and so lack autonomy rights. Thus, even soft paternalism bears some burden of justification, though the bar for justifying it is much lower. It must be justified by showing that it is in the interests of the person whose acts are interfered with, where we understand interests sufficiently broadly to encompass their interest in choosing for themselves.

---

[35] Similar functions are performed by the European Medicines Agency and Health Canada.
[36] Joel Feinberg, *Harm to Self* (New York: Oxford University Press, 1986), 12–16.

Though most cases of paternalism involve interfering with someone's actions for the sake of their well-being, Seana Shiffrin gives an amended analysis that both expands the scope of what counts as paternalistic and explains what is ethically problematic about hard paternalism. She notes that, first, paternalism does not always entail that the person acting paternalistically thinks that the agent's judgment *about* his interests is inferior to hers.[37] She may act paternalistically because she judges him unable to act in the way that would best *secure* his interests (according to his own judgment) – as when she interrupts a friend who is speaking to articulate one of his points better than she thinks he would. Second, paternalism does not have to relate to the well-being of the agent at all. If I hide a friend's cigarettes because I am concerned that his wife will be grief-stricken if he dies, then I act paternalistically toward him.[38] What unites these phenomena as hard paternalism is that the person acting paternalistically substitutes her own judgment or action for the other party's in a sphere over which the other party has legitimate control. Shiffrin writes: "The essential motive behind a paternalist act evinces a failure to respect either the capacity of the agent to judge, the capacity of the agent to act, or the propriety of the agent's exerting control over a sphere that is legitimately her domain."[39] Someone who acts paternalistically toward an autonomous agent therefore disrespects him by disregarding his authority to govern his own life and by implicitly asserting that her own judgment or action is superior or more effective.

Hard paternalism involves one party substituting her judgment or action for that of an autonomous person who is acting voluntarily and knows, basically, what she is doing. Since, by definition, this is an interference with someone's decision about a matter over which she has legitimate control, hard paternalism is pro tanto wrong. Like other rights violations, such interference faces a high bar for justification. By contrast, soft paternalism can generally be justified by showing that it is in the individual's interests. Challenges arise in cases of uncertainty and marginal autonomy.

Suppose a middle-aged patient is going to have his wisdom teeth removed and asks the dentist not to anesthetize him. The clinician may be uncertain whether the request is autonomous: Is the patient ignorant of

[37] Seana Shiffrin, "Paternalism, Unconscionability Doctrine, and Accommodation," *Philosophy & Public Affairs* 29 (2000): 205–250, at 215.

[38] Ibid., p. 217.

[39] Ibid., p. 220. Shiffrin does not distinguish hard and soft paternalism, but we consider her insights about what she calls "paternalism" helpful for understanding what we classify as hard paternalism.

some key fact, such as what it means to have a tooth extracted? Is there a problem with his capacity to understand what is going on and make decisions for himself? Or is he perfectly capable of making decisions and places a very strong value on having genuine experiences? Here, the dentist may need to assess her patient's understanding of the operation and his decisional capacity before she proceeds.

Note that delaying the operation in order to reeducate a patient or check that he is really capable of making a decision in the light of his own values need not be paternalistic in a problematic way, even if the clinician is doing it because she judges that the patient's original decision is probably a bad one.[40] According to Shiffrin's analysis, the wrong of hard paternalism involves a failure to respect someone's capacity to judge or act. We can only fail in this way once we have good reason to think that someone is acting autonomously. Thus, there is nothing problematic about delaying an operation until the dentist is confident that her patient's decision is autonomously made. Moreover, this suggests that in cases where someone might be choosing nonautonomously, and where acting on that nonautonomous choice might have serious consequences, there are good reasons to take the time and effort to ascertain the true status of the choice. If it seems as though someone would not make the choice they have selected were they acting autonomously, this is reason to check. Likewise, if the consequences of their choice would be a severe harm.

Some people's capacity for autonomous action is marginal. For example, someone with mild to moderate Alzheimer's disease may be able to reason well and have settled values and preferences, but be unable to retain in short-term memory enough information about her condition and the care options presented to her to make good decisions on her own. Similar considerations apply to marginal cases as to cases of uncertainty. Again, where there is doubt about someone's decision-making, it is not paternalistic to check it. And where the decision is particularly consequential, this gives stronger reasons to be sure that the person making it is capable of doing so autonomously. Finally, it is important to remember that making decisions for oneself is conducive to well-being, not just a matter of rights.

---

[40] Note that ignorance about some pertinent facts is not sufficient to justify interference by others. If you happen to have a much better understanding of stereo equipment than I do, that does not license you interfering with me buying a new set of speakers, even if you correctly judge that my preferences would be better satisfied by your selection. I still understand what I'm doing – exchanging money for speakers. On the other hand, if I were confused enough that you realized I was buying cupboards under the misapprehension that they were speakers, that would justify interference. I would no longer be autonomously *buying speakers*.

People with marginal autonomy who are judged to lack capacity with regard to a particular decision should still be involved in decision-making as far as that is possible because it is (typically) good for them. For example, it would generally be good for a ten-year-old to play as active a role as possible in deciding whether to enroll in a pediatric clinical trial.

Interference for the Sake of Others

It is one thing to interfere with someone's decisions for that person's own sake. It is quite another to do so for the sake of other people. Virtually everyone, including those who would object to hard paternalism, accept that there are substantial limits on what autonomous individuals are ethically permitted to do. Earlier in the chapter, we characterized the basis of autonomy rights in terms of a person's sovereignty over their own life. A key question for determining the limits of autonomy rights is therefore what the boundaries of someone's own life are. One commonly accepted boundary is at the point where one person's actions would pose excessive risk of harming another or would otherwise violate their rights. Consider a patient who is admitted to a hospital with active tuberculosis and a cough. Such a patient is highly contagious. The standard of care for infectious tuberculosis patients includes isolation from other patients. We would think it perfectly legitimate for the hospital to require this patient to accept isolation within the health care facility as a condition of admission, because otherwise they would impose a substantial risk of harm to others.[41]

The prevention of harm to others is one clear justification for restricting the liberty of autonomous individuals. Are there other justifications? According to John Stuart Mill's "harm principle," there are not. In *On Liberty* Mill writes:

> The object of this Essay is to assert one very simple principle … that the sole end for which mankind are warranted, individually or collectively, in interfering with the liberty of action of any of their number, is self protection. That the only purpose for which power can be rightfully exercised over any member of a civilized community, against his will, is to prevent harm to others. His own good, either physical or moral, is not a sufficient warrant.[42]

[41] See World Health Organization, *Ethics Guidance for the Implementation of the End TB Strategy* (2017) (available at http://who.int/tb/publications/2017/ethics-guidance/en/).

[42] John Stuart Mill, *On Liberty*, in John Gray and Gordon Smith (eds.), *JS Mill's on Liberty in Focus* (London: Routledge, 2012), 30.

Mill here clearly rejects paternalism as a justification for interfering with autonomous action. The harm principle would also rule out interfering with someone's actions on the grounds that what they are doing offends others or is contrary to their moral beliefs (*legal moralism*). For example, the fact that many people are disgusted by the idea of human cloning, or gender reassignment, is not sufficient reason to prohibit either, if we adopt the harm principle. Likewise, that some people regard suicide as immoral does not provide grounds for preventing other people from taking their own lives. In these cases, some harm to other parties, or some violation of the rights of other parties, would have to be demonstrated in order to justify restricting someone from doing as they wish.

The harm principle has been extremely influential in liberal thinking and has served as a bulwark against both legal moralism and hard paternalism. However, we think that preventing harm to others is neither necessary nor sufficient to justify interfering with the liberty of autonomous individuals. It is unnecessary because there are other wrongs that justify intervention. For example, we think that the government may legitimately prohibit exploitative wage offers and impose a minimum wage, even if no one is harmed by the unfair level of compensation.[43] Likewise, harm to others is insufficient because rights have thresholds such that the obligation to respect someone's rights is only pro tanto. If the benefits to others of overriding someone's rights – including autonomy rights – are sufficiently great, then this can justify doing so.[44] In the context of liberty, we can see this principle at work in many areas of everyday life where a low risk of harm to innocent nonconsenting others is nevertheless thought to be justifiable. For example, it is commonly thought that parents are permitted to take their children on car trips, thereby putting them at a very small risk of serious harm, even when there is no benefit to the children themselves. Presumably, insofar as this practice is ethically

---

[43] In Chapter 4, we argued that depriving someone of something to which they have a legitimate claim constitutes a harm. One might think that individuals have claims to fair wages, in which case paying less than a fair wage would indeed be harmful. Whether this is correct depends on the appropriate counterfactual for assessing what would otherwise have happened to the worker. It would be ethically permissible for the employer to pay them a fair wage or not employ them at all. Thus the unfairly low wage is either a *harm* because less than they would have received if their claims were respected or a *benefit* because more than they would have received if their claims were respected. We are not certain which comparison is most apt. However, it seems to us that the wrong of exploitation does not depend on a judgment that it is harmful and neither does the justification for prohibiting exploitative transactions.

[44] At least in principle. See Chapter 4's discussion of torture for an example of a right that we think should never be overridden in practice.

acceptable, it is because the costs to the parents of restricting their liberty in order to avoid this risk of harm to their children would be too great.

5.5   Consent

One way in which autonomy rights are commonly exercised is through consent. By giving valid consent to an act, an individual can transform it from an act that would be morally forbidden into a permissible act. They do this by *waiving* their right with respect to the other party. For example, if a surgeon attempted to operate on a competent patient without his permission, she would be assaulting him. With his valid consent, the surgeon's acts of cutting her patient's body open are transformed from assault into appropriate surgery. He has waived his right against her cutting him in specific ways. Given how frequently decisions regarding health care and research involve someone giving consent, it is important that we analyze the conditions under which consent is valid. We do so here under the assumption that consent in the context of medicine is the same normative phenomenon as consent in other areas of life, such as sexual relations, even though the contexts may be very different. In each of these contexts, valid consent involves one person exercising an autonomy right to transform an act that would be a rights-violation into one that is permissible (provided no other ethical constraints apply). Differences in the information that is required for consent or the institutional safeguards needed to protect voluntariness, for example, should emerge from how the same conditions for valid consent can be met when the context is different. Further, we do not draw a distinction between "consent" and "informed consent." Whether someone has successfully exercised their rights depends on whether *valid* consent has been obtained and all forms of valid consent include informational components.

In analyzing consent it is vital to separate the question of whether someone's choice constitutes valid consent from whether it was a good choice. Here it is helpful to recall the two roles that autonomy plays in our ethical thinking (Section 5.2). One is that the capacity for autonomous action is a ground for autonomy rights. The other is that being and acting autonomously is a contributor to or component of one's well-being. As we saw in our earlier discussion of autonomy, someone may exercise her autonomy rights in foolish ways. In other words, she may make a poor choice but have the right to do so. Someone might, for example, give valid consent to having her lip pierced, but this might end up being a decision she regrets.

The process of obtaining consent in clinical care and research can and ideally should serve the goals of both helping someone make a good decision and obtaining his valid consent. However, these two goals can come apart. Someone might give valid consent but choose something that predictably does not best serve his values and preferences. Conversely, someone's consent to an act can be invalid – say, because he has been deceived about what is proposed – even if the act in question would be best for him. In this regard, it is important to note that the obligations to help people make good decisions are much weaker than the obligation to obtain valid consent. It is beneficial for someone to make a better decision, but the obligations of clinicians and researchers to benefit other people are limited (Chapter 6). On the other hand, not obtaining valid consent to an act that requires it would constitute a violation of the person's rights.

Consent can be analyzed in terms of five elements: (1) capacity, (2) disclosure, (3) understanding, (4) voluntariness, and (5) authorization.[45] The satisfaction of each of these elements is required in order for consent to be valid. In the paragraphs that follow, we explain what is required for each and note the ways in which consent can be invalidated, drawing on our analysis in Section 5.2. We then turn to the question of how decisions should be made for people who cannot decide for themselves.

Capacity

An individual has the capacity to give consent when she is autonomous in the sense described at the beginning of this chapter: she is capable of deliberating about her actions in the light of her values and making a decision on the basis of that deliberation. An individual has the capacity to make a specific consent decision when she is capable of deliberating and deciding about that specific choice in the light of her values. Centrally, this involves being able to understand the aspects of the decision that relate to the rights she is being asked to waive through consent and being able to reason about whether to waive those rights. Note that it does not require that she be able to understand *everything* that might be germane to her decision. Nor does it require that her ultimate choice is a rational one. As just discussed, respect for autonomy includes respect for decisions that are

---

[45] See, e.g., Ruth Faden and Tom Beauchamp, *A History and Theory of Informed Consent* (New York: Oxford University Press, 1986), 274, although the authors use the term "consent" instead of "authorization."

poorly made, provided that it is the agent herself who is responsible for the quality of the decision-making.

We do not have more specific criteria for identifying the threshold of ability to reason, understand, and make decisions on the basis of one's values that underlies the capacity to consent for oneself.[46] For certain individuals – such as adolescents and addicts – this uncertainty is reflected in uncertainty about whether such individuals should be allowed to make important decisions. Suppose Alfred, an adult patient, leaves a psychiatric unit, knowing he needs the care offered there, only because he is addicted to alprazolam (a sedative) and believes he can find relief by getting some alprazolam outside the unit. Does Alfred have decision-making capacity? This is a difficult case and might remain difficult even with further details. Arguably, Alfred understands both his need for treatment and his addiction, but is incapable of deciding (rationally, in accordance with his own values) to remain in the psychiatric unit; his addiction undermines his capacity. On the other hand, perhaps he understands the advantages of remaining in the hospital but places a higher value on the immediate relief that alprazolam can deliver and on freedom from institutional rules; in this case, his choice to leave might reflect genuine capacity. A third possibility is that the only rational choice (given his own values and priorities) was to remain in the hospital, and he had the capacity to do so, but he simply did not because he did not try hard enough to resist the temptation to leave. This would be an instance of weak will rather than incapacity.

Disclosure

Ethically and legally, many acts of consent require the prior disclosure of certain information. For example, contracts are expected to include information about what is being agreed to by both parties, what process will be followed if one party does not act as agreed, and so forth. Likewise, clinicians and researchers are expected to disclose pertinent information about what they are proposing to do. One common view is that this disclosure requirement is derived from the understanding requirement: the information that must be disclosed for consent to be valid is the information that must be understood, and it must be disclosed because it must be understood.[47] In the words of Alexander Capron: "Plainly,

---

[46] For discussion see citations in notes 7 and 9.
[47] Consistent with such a view, it might be that more information should be disclosed than must be understood, but that the additional information is not information that is required for *valid consent*.

comprehension is essential for truly informed consent, for the act of disclosure would otherwise be pointless."[48] This view would make sense if the function of the disclosure requirement were to enable understanding. However, we believe that the function of the disclosure requirement *as it relates to the validity of consent* is not to enable understanding but to respect the right of autonomous individuals to make their own decisions. That means not illegitimately controlling someone's decision regarding consent by intentionally withholding relevant information or providing false information. It does not mean ensuring that the person giving consent understands all the information that would help them make a good decision.[49]

An example can show why we hold this view. Suppose Diego mentions to his friend that he has a really sore neck. The friend innocently suggests that he help Diego "crack" it. Diego agrees and his friend holds his head and twists vigorously in both directions, producing a satisfying pop. In fact, Diego's friend has yanked his neck beyond its safe range of motion and the next day it is so stiff he cannot turn his head. Here, we take it, though both people might be acting foolishly, there is nothing awry with Diego's consent. Contrast this case with one in which Diego mentions the same thing to an osteopathic doctor. Suppose that doctor tells Diego that she can help by twisting his neck in exactly the same way. However, she knows that this would be past the safe range of motion (perhaps she hopes to drum up more business for her practice by injuring him). In such a case, most people would judge that Diego's consent to the twisting would be invalid. But his understanding of what will happen is identical. The difference lies in what he has been told (or not told). In the latter case, but not the former, information is withheld that Diego would reasonably expect to be told. Withholding the information about the risks of twisting his neck allows the osteopath to control Diego's decision. His ignorant friend does not control his decision because his friend knows no more than Diego about the risks.[50]

For example, we would not be concerned if a research participant did not recall the name and number to call if they had questions about the research. However, it is plausible that this information should be included on the consent form.

[48] Alexander Capron, "Legal and Regulatory Standards of Informed Consent in Research," in Ezekiel Emanuel et al. (eds.), *Oxford Textbook of Clinical Research Ethics* (New York: Oxford University Press, 2008), 625. For statements of this view, see, e.g., Declaration of Helsinki, Paragraph 26; and Beauchamp and Childress, *Principles of Biomedical Ethics*, 124, 131–137.

[49] The discussion that follows is derived from Danielle Bromwich and Joseph Millum, "Disclosure and Consent to Medical Research Participation," *Journal of Moral Philosophy* 12 (2015): 195–219.

[50] Note that this sort of control can arise through negligence, as well as deliberate action. For example, if the osteopath did not care either way whether Diego agreed, but knew that she was omitting relevant information, this would also constitute illegitimate control.

Analyzing the disclosure requirement in terms of illegitimate control reveals the information that must be disclosed in order to fulfill the requirement. The person requesting consent must disclose all the information about the act she is proposing that she knows, has reason to think is relevant to the individual's consent decision, and that she thinks the person giving consent would reasonably expect to receive. She must disclose the information in a manner that gives him a fair opportunity to understand it. If she does all this, then she does not make use of her informational advantage in order to control what he does. To play this out with another simple example, consider what must be disclosed in order to give consent to participate in a clinical research study. The information that we might reasonably predict would be relevant to someone's decision includes what the study is about, what procedures will be conducted and what they involve, what the risks and potential benefits are, and how participation in the study augments or replaces alternative treatment options. Moreover, in the context of clinical research, it is plausible that potential participants would expect to receive this information, so that withholding it would be deceptive. In order that potential participants have a fair opportunity to understand this information, it should be disclosed in lay language, in simple writing or orally for people who are illiterate or do not read well, and so on. The clinician seeking consent should encourage follow-up questions and answer any questions patiently.

Understanding

We have established what information must be disclosed in order to obtain valid consent and how that information must be disclosed. We have argued that it is a separate question what must be understood.[51] Provided that the disclosure requirement has been met and the person giving consent is competent, the understanding requirement is minimal. Three conditions are necessary and sufficient to meet it.[52] The person giving consent must understand (1) that he is giving consent and not doing something else; (2) what signifies consent in this context, that is, how to

---

[51] Understanding has been studied most thoroughly in the context of consent to clinical research. Surveys of research participants around the world suggest that understanding of facts about risks, procedures, and study purpose is highly variable and often very poor. See Amulya Mandava et al., "The Quality of Informed Consent: Mapping the Landscape: A Review of Empirical Data from Developing and Developed Countries," *Journal of Medical Ethics* 38 (2012): 356–365.

[52] Joseph Millum and Danielle Bromwich, "Understanding, Communication, and Consent," *Ergo* 5 (2018): 45–68.

indicate consent; and (3) what he is agreeing to, that is, what the person obtaining consent will be permitted to do that she was not permitted to do before. The first two conditions are necessary for a token of consent to constitute the act of intentionally giving consent. The last condition derives from the point of consent, which is to redraw the normative boundaries in the way that the two parties agree upon.

An example may make these conditions clearer. Suppose that a nurse asks his patient for consent to draw her blood and she agrees. If she mishears and thinks that he asked whether she's feeling comfortable, her agreement will not constitute consent. Likewise, if he asks her to sign a consent form and she does not realize that her signature signifies consent – instead, she thinks she's signing a petition – then she will not have consented in any morally relevant sense at all.[53] These possible errors concern the first two conditions. Third, prior to consent, the nurse was not ethically permitted to penetrate his patient's arm with a needle nor to remove her blood. The third condition is met when she understands that the nurse will now be permitted to do those things – that is what redrawing the normative boundaries consists in.

The minimal nature of the understanding requirement is consistent with the underlying function of autonomy rights, which is to protect the sovereign authority of a competent individual to decide what happens in their own life. This includes the right to decide foolishly, for example, by declining information that is made available. The minimal understanding requirement also allows individuals to pursue their interests by agreeing to actions and transactions that they fail to fully grasp. For example, Franklin Miller and Steve Joffe describe the misunderstandings that are rife among participants in phase 1 oncology trials.[54] Such participants frequently conflate clinical care and research, underestimate the risks and overstate the benefits, and exaggerate their personal prospects of benefit. Nevertheless, Miller and Joffe contend, the decision to enroll in phase 1 trials is frequently consistent with participants' values and preferences. Provided that the participants are given a fair opportunity to understand the information relevant to their decision, we think that they are able to give valid consent despite these misunderstandings.

---

[53] It does not follow that the nurse would be at fault if he innocently believed her to have understood what signing the consent form signified. It is one thing to ask whether someone has given valid consent and another to ask whether someone proceeding on a token of consent has acted in a blameworthy manner.

[54] "Phase 1 Oncology Trials and Informed Consent," *Journal of Medical Ethics* 39 (2013): 761–764.

Here, it is worth noting again the dual functions that the consent process may play. Assuming the disclosure was adequate, *valid* consent is consistent with very minimal understanding. A *good* decision may require much more understanding. In circumstances in which the person proffering consent does not have a right to an intervention, it may therefore be legitimate to refuse to provide it until they demonstrate substantial understanding of what it entails. For example, consider a first-in-humans trial of a new drug in healthy volunteers, that is, in research participants who do not have a health condition that the drug is designed to treat. Plausibly, the volunteers do not have any right to be offered participation in the trial. In that case, it is no violation of their rights to exclude participants who fail a quiz that assesses their understanding of the procedures and associated risks that the trial involves. By contrast, patients in ordinary clinical settings often have a right to the intervention that is indicated for their condition. Requiring such patients to demonstrate a higher level of understanding than that required for valid consent would illegitimately deprive them of something to which they have a right.

Voluntariness

Saying that consent is voluntary means that the token of consent is proffered intentionally and free of the illegitimate control of another party. Failure to meet the disclosure requirement involves illegitimate control and so invalidates consent through rendering it involuntary. This applies to cases of outright deception, as well as cases where information is withheld or is disclosed in a way that the person can be expected to misunderstand. Voluntariness may also be undermined by coercion, which is another form of illegitimate control. For example, someone who consents to a medical procedure because her husband wants her to undergo it and she is afraid of what he will otherwise do has not given voluntary consent.

Consent is either valid or it is not. But, as noted earlier, control is a matter of degree. Thus, whether a form of illegitimate control renders consent invalid will depend on how controlling it is. A weak threat – say, a physician's threat to reveal some rather trivial piece of private medical information to her patient's child – may be noncontrolling, while deception about some fact that would make a difference between consenting and declining would be enough to render consent invalid. The exact threshold at which this occurs will be a matter of judgment.[55]

---

[55] See the taxonomy of control in Section 5.3.

Authorization

Depending on the context, various tokens can signify authorization or consent. In many situations, saying "Yes," to a request for consent is sufficient. In others, a simple gesture may be enough (such as in response to "May I sit here?"). It is even possible for consent to be tacit – implied without being explicitly expressed. When the chair of a meeting proposes a motion and asks, "Any objections?" then the silence of the other members of the committee may be sufficient to signify consent.[56]

Medical research typically involves written authorization. Medical care may involve written authorization for some procedures, such as those that are risky or involve the transfer of private information. In terms of the validity of consent, there is nothing special about having the token in writing. Provided that its significance is understood by all parties involved, a nod can confer valid consent just as well as a signature on a form. What matters is that all five conditions are met. Nonetheless, there can be reasons for preferring one token to another that are not related to the validity of consent. For example, *used correctly*, a written informed consent form can help to ensure that all the relevant information is conveyed to potential participants in a study, give them time to go over the information they have been provided, and provide a record of the consent token. In other situations a written consent form would be problematic. For example, when research is conducted with a stigmatized population a written consent form could put research participants at risk. For example, an HIV study enrolling gay men might not require participants to sign consent forms if study sponsors are concerned about a potential breach of privacy.[57]

Exceptions to the Consent Requirement

Consent to medical care or research is not always required. In some cases, this is because the acts performed by the relevant professionals are not acts against which people have rights. For example, consider a research study that involves recording how people behave in public places. Generally speaking, people have neither a right against being observed when they

[56] A. J. Simmons, "Tacit Consent and Political Obligation," *Philosophy and Public Affairs* 5 (1976): 274–291, at 278–281.
[57] See David Wendler and Jonathan Rackoff, "Informed Consent and Respecting Autonomy: What's a Signature Got to Do with It?," *IRB* 23 (3) (2001): 1–4, for some cases in which different social and cultural contexts affect the appropriate form that consent tokens should take.

are in public nor a right against someone making written notes of what is observed. Thus, research that involves these acts does not require consent from the subjects of research – there is no right for them to waive through consent.

In other cases, there is a right involved, but there are good reasons to override it. For example, suppose that a researcher obtained blood samples and medical histories from a large number of patients with type II diabetes. She got consent from these patients to carry out diabetes research. Ten years later, with many new tools for genetic analysis at their disposal, she and her colleagues want to use the samples to see if people who become obese are more likely to have genes that predispose them to heart disease and mood disorders. Is she permitted to do so?

The first question to answer is whether the scope of the original consent covered the new research studies. If the consent form, interpreted as we could reasonably expect the participants to interpret it, would include heart disease and mood disorder research, then they would likely already have given valid consent for this research. Assume that the consent form signed by the participants clearly restricts the scope of the research, so they did not give consent to these new research uses. The second question is then how difficult it would be to obtain consent for the new proposed research. If it would be straightforward – names and contact information are on file and the research will not be unduly affected by excluding participants who cannot be recontacted – then further consent (or "reconsent") should be obtained. If it would be very burdensome or impossible to obtain consent for the new research study, then we must assess, third, whether carrying out the research without consent can be justified. Since, we are assuming, consent would ordinarily be needed for what is proposed, it is pro tanto wrongful to proceed without consent. The value of the research must therefore be sufficiently great to outweigh this pro tanto wrong. How great that value must be will depend, in turn, on how serious the rights violation is.[58] Fourth, just as when conducting risk/benefit assessments we look to minimize the risks consistent with the scientific goals, when the consent of research participants is not going to

[58] More precisely, the calculation involves weighing the incremental net value of conducting the research without obtaining consent against the bad of overriding participant rights in the specific ways the research involves. The incremental net value is found by subtracting the predicted net value of the research that could be done consistent with obtaining consent from the predicted net value if consent is not obtained. The net value includes both the valuable outputs of the research and the costs of conducting it (with and without reconsent).

be obtained, the extent to which the researchers interfere with their rights should be minimized.[59]

Finally, there are cases in which consent does not need to be obtained from a patient or research participant because they lack the capacity to give their own consent – for example, because they are unconscious, are cognitively impaired, or have not yet developed sufficient capacity to reason about their actions. We now turn to such cases.

5.6 Decision-Making for Others

Consider a patient with moderate dementia as a result of Alzheimer's disease. Though she can still recognize family members and still expresses preferences, she is confused about her condition and cannot recall details of what her doctor tells her thirty seconds later. There is no doubt that she lacks the capacity to make her own decisions about health care. She has been diagnosed with breast cancer and there are multiple options regarding treatment. Someone must decide what to do. Who should make that decision and how should they make it?

Regarding who should decide, there are two possibilities: either the patient, while competent, appointed someone to make decisions on her behalf or she did not. If she did – for example, by completing a written advance directive – then that person should be her surrogate decision-maker, provided that he is himself capable, available, aims to make ethically appropriate choices, and so forth. If she did not herself assign a surrogate decision-maker, then someone must be appointed to take that role. This will be the case for many people who are incapable of making their own decisions. Only a minority of adults in Canada, the United Kingdom, and the United States have completed advance directives, and there are many people – including children and people who are congenitally severely cognitively disabled – who are never competent to decide for themselves.[60] Some incompetent individuals have court-appointed

---

[59] Related issues arise in the context of research that involves deceiving participants. This is common practice in a great deal of psychological research, for example, where participants are often not told the true purpose of the study in which they are enrolled until after their participation. For an overview, see David Wendler and Franklin Miller, "Deception in Clinical Research," in Emanuel et al., *The Oxford Textbook of Clinical Research Ethics*, 315–324.

[60] See D. Aw, B. Hayhoe, and L. K. Bowker, "Advance Care Planning and the Older Patient," *QJM: An International Journal of Medicine* 105 (2011): 225–230; Pew Research Center, *Views on End-of-Life Medical Treatments* (November 2013); available at: www.pewforum.org/2013/11/21/views-on-end-of-life-medical-treatments/; Jaya Rao et al., "Completion of Advance Directives among US Consumers," *American Journal of Preventive Medicine* 46 (2014): 65–70; and Ana Teixeira et al.,

guardians who are legally granted decision-making power for health care and research participation (among other things). Children also typically already have parents or guardians with the legal power to make decisions on their behalf. For other incompetent patients, the individual legally authorized to make decisions varies considerably by jurisdiction. In many US states and Canadian provinces, legislation provides a next-of-kin hierarchy for clinicians to identify an appropriate surrogate.[61] For example, in Maryland, they would select the highest person on the following list who is available: spouse, adult child, parent, sibling, other relative. Other jurisdictions have further detailed categories of relatives further down the hierarchy (e.g., grandparent, aunt or uncle, grandchild), explicitly allow for unmarried partners or close friends, and may specify how disagreements are to be resolved and what range of decisions can be made by the surrogate. By contrast, in the United Kingdom, unless a surrogate decision-maker has been designated by the patient or a court, health care professionals have the authority to make decisions about treatment.[62]

Whether appointed by the patient or not, a surrogate decision-maker does not have carte blanche to decide as they wish, ethically speaking. First, if the incompetent person has completed an advance directive that expresses specific preferences for care or research, then those preferences should usually be followed, subject to the same constraints on the use of resources that apply to everyone.[63] For example, someone might write in his advance directive that he does not want to be kept on life support if he is not expected to recover consciousness. That constitutes an exercise of his autonomy right to refuse treatment and so should be honored. However, second, in many cases there will not be specific instructions from the

"What Do Canadians Think of Advanced Care Planning? Findings from an Online Opinion Poll," *BMJ Supportive & Palliative Care* 5 (2015): 40–47.

[61] For the United States, see Erin DeMartino et al., "Who Decides When a Patient Can't? Statutes on Alternate Decision Makers," *NEJM* 376 (2017): 1478. For Canada, see statutes listed at Canadian Nurses Protective Society, "Consent for the Incapable Adult" (available at https://cnps.ca/consent-adult; accessed September 28, 2020).

[62] British Medical Association, "Advance Decisions and Proxy Decision-making in Medical Treatment and Research: Guidance from the BMA's Medical Ethics Department" (London: BMA, 2007).

[63] Where someone's stated preferences seem to deviate substantially from what would be in their interests, there is room for caution about following the advance directive to the letter. First, this may be an indication that the advance directive, as stated and interpreted, does not actually express what the individual meant to express. Second, the individual's present interests could yet be important enough to override their prior exercise of autonomy. For detailed discussion of these points in the context of advance directives and dementia patients, see Ronald Dworkin, *Life's Dominion* (New York: Vintage, 2011); and Rebecca Dresser, "Dworkin on Dementia: Elegant Theory, Questionable Policy," *Hastings Center Report* 25 (1995): 32–38.

incompetent person or the instructions that have been given require interpretation. In that case, some standard must be used to guide surrogate decision-making.

Two standards are widely cited: *substituted judgment* and *best interests*. According to the substituted judgment standard, the surrogate should decide as she judges the patient would decide, were he competent. According to the best-interests standard, the surrogate should choose the option that she judges to be in the best interests of the patient or would bring about the greatest net benefit to him. Sometimes these standards are ordered hierarchically: the surrogate should use the substituted judgment standard if the patient's preferences are known or can be reasonably inferred and otherwise should use the best-interests standard.[64] As will become clear, we partly dissent from this mainstream understanding of standards for surrogate decision-making.

In this context, it is crucial to distinguish between the speech act of making a decision about one's health care and simply expressing one's preferences about treatment. When someone completes an advance directive, they exercise an autonomy right. Likewise, when someone gives consent to a medical intervention they exercise an autonomy right. Simply saying what one thinks about treatment – "I would never want to be kept on a machine like that" – is expressing a preference but not exercising a right.[65] Likewise, a substituted judgment, even one that is highly accurate, does not constitute the exercise of a right.

What then is the moral relevance of a substituted judgment? We think that substituted judgments can sometimes play an important role as a result of the close relationship between a person's preferences and what is in her interests. As we discuss in Chapter 8, any plausible theory of well-being should show considerable deference to each individual's authority regarding what is good for her. To a large extent what someone would decide to do, on reflection and taking relevant facts into account, is likely to be a good guide to what would be good for her. Thus, substituted judgment is relevant *insofar* as it predicts what would be in an incompetent individual's interests. There will be important exceptions to the generalization that substituted judgment is a guide to someone's interests. For example, someone might have an exaggerated fear of radiation, such that he would have refused a clinically indicated X-ray if he were conscious. Absent explicit instructions to the contrary, if he is unconscious and a

---

[64] For a nuanced treatment, see Buchanan and Brock, *Deciding for Others*, 93–151.
[65] Cf. ibid., 115–117.

surrogate must decide on his behalf, she should probably disregard this fear and do what she judges to be in his interests. Here, a substituted judgment would give the wrong result.

We also think that it is a mistake to adopt a best-interests standard in those cases in which there is no advance directive. In fact, it is widely accepted that the best-interests standard, literally understood, cannot be the right standard for making decisions on another person's behalf.[66] This is because people's interests frequently conflict and so trade-offs must be made. Consider, for example, the triage decisions made at admissions for the emergency room of a hospital. Even though each individual would benefit from being seen sooner rather than later, not everyone can see a physician immediately. The triage nurse must therefore make decisions that weigh factors such as the urgency of someone's condition, how long she has been waiting, the capacity of the hospital, and so forth. He cannot – and therefore is not obliged to – act in each person's best interests. This is true whether the people in line for care are able to make their own decisions or not.

A more plausible conception of the best-interests standard would accept that there are limits to what can be done to promote someone's interests, but say that surrogate decision-makers should still choose on someone's behalf whatever would maximize her well-being within the constraints of distributive justice.[67] However, we think that even this is too weak. A competent individual should sometimes not put her interests above those of others, even if she has the right to do so. Likewise, if she is deciding on behalf of someone else, she should not always put his interests above those of others, even if justice does not forbid it.

In fact, we think very similar moral constraints apply to incompetent as to competent individuals. The standard we prefer for making decisions on someone else's behalf is a *reasonable subject* standard.[68] According to this standard, the surrogate should decide on the incompetent individual's behalf as he would decide if he were a rational agent acting prudently within the constraints of what morality requires. That is, the surrogate should do what is in the incompetent individual's interests when they are

---

[66] For discussion in the context of making decisions for children, see David Archard, "Children's Rights," in Edward Zalta (ed.), *Stanford Encyclopedia of Philosophy* (Winter 2014 edition; available at http://plato.stanford.edu/archives/win2014/entries/rights-children/). The points Archard makes generalize to other noncompetent patients.

[67] See Buchanan and Brock, *Deciding for Others*, 192.

[68] For a full elucidation and defense of this standard, see Joseph Millum, *The Moral Foundations of Parenthood* (New York: Oxford University Press, 2018), chap. 6.

the only interests that are relevant. But when other people's interests or claims are also implicated by a decision, then those interests and claims should be taken into account just as they should be by a competent individual. This standard will frequently coincide with choosing the option that best promotes the patient's well-being, but it allows us to justify certain exceptions. For example, it explains why it can be permissible to enroll an incompetent individual into research that poses net risks to him – for example, in some pediatric studies featuring no prospect of direct medical benefit to child participants (Chapter 4).

To summarize, if someone has completed an advance directive while competent, when he loses decision-making capacity his surrogate decision-maker should first endeavor to follow the guidance in the advance directive. Where this is indeterminate, she should follow the reasonable subject standard by making decisions on his behalf that promote his interests within the constraints of morality. Where someone has not completed an advance directive while competent, when he loses decision-making capacity his surrogate decision-maker should go straight to following the reasonable subject standard. For those individuals, such as young children, who have never had the capacity to make their own decisions, the reasonable subject standard likewise applies.

This chapter's first five sections have elaborated relatively theoretical aspects of autonomy. In the final two sections we illustrate with a pair of specific bioethical applications of our theoretical account: the right to refuse treatment and the ethics of direct-to-consumer marketing of pharmaceuticals.

5.7 The Right to Refuse Treatment

Respect for autonomy grounds stringent rights against interference with one's body. As a result, with very limited exceptions, other people may not do things to the body of a competent adult without their permission. In particular, as the discussion of paternalism showed, attempting to promote someone's interests is not a sufficient ground to justify bodily interference. This right has been widely – and we think correctly – interpreted as grounding a right to refuse treatment. For example, if my doctor recommends prescription painkillers for my lower back pain, it is up to me whether I take them or not. The right to refuse treatment is the mirror of the requirement that professionals obtain consent to treatment. Both are grounded in respect for autonomy rights.

The right to refuse treatment includes the right to refuse life-saving treatment. Someone with advanced cancer may still have treatment options that offer a good prospect of extending her life for a few months. Nevertheless, she may decide that the life extension is not worth the horrible side effects of going through more chemotherapy. She would rather be made as comfortable as possible and allowed to die from her disease. If she is competent, well-informed about her treatment options, and decides voluntarily, then we see no reason not to respect her wishes.[69] (If she is not competent, then the considerations of the earlier discussion of decision-making for others apply.) The right to refuse life-saving treatment includes both forgoing and withdrawing life-sustaining treatment. For example, a competent individual might exercise this right to demand that mechanical ventilation or intravenous nutrition be stopped.

Matters become more controversial when the decisions being made seem less reasonable to other parties. Consider the case of Dax Cowart.[70] In 1973, a propane gas explosion left Cowart blind, unable to use his hands, and severely burned over two-thirds of his body. He repeatedly refused treatment and asked to be allowed to die. A psychiatrist who was brought in to evaluate Cowart judged him competent to make his own decisions. Nevertheless, his requests were overruled and he underwent a series of incredibly painful treatments. Many years later, Cowart no longer wanted to die, but maintained that he should have been allowed at the time to die rather than experience the pain.

Many people regarded Cowart's decision as unreasonable. But the fact that he made different decisions than they would make on his behalf does not entail that he was incapable of making his own decisions. Being autonomous means being able to make decisions in the light of one's values and preferences, not having some specific set of values and preferences. Nor should we assume that severe pain renders someone incapable of making decisions about treatment. Provided that he was capable of understanding information about his situation and reasoning about what to do, Cowart was competent to make his own decisions. As we discussed in Section 5.3, if a decision seems unreasonable and is likely to have serious consequences, this gives clinicians a reason to take the time to ensure that it is indeed the voluntary decision of an informed, competent adult. Once they are confident of this, overruling the person's refusal of care would constitute objectionable paternalism.

---

[69] See also the discussion of physician assistance-in-dying in Chapter 4.
[70] For discussion, see Dax Cowart and Robert Burt, "Confronting Death: Who Chooses, Who Controls?," *Hastings Center Report* 28 (1998): 14–24.

While we acknowledge that cases like Dax Cowart's are challenging for all involved, we think that the ultimate moral verdict is clear: the patient's autonomous decision should be respected. Other cases are harder to resolve. Jodi Halpern describes the case of Ms. G, a fifty-six-year-old woman with diabetes mellitus and kidney failure who had just had a second above-the-knee amputation.[71] Ms. G's husband had informed her that he no longer loved her and was leaving her for another woman. Believing that she would never be loved again, Ms. G refused life-saving dialysis. Here, there was reason to think that Ms. G was mistaken in her certainty about the hopelessness of her postamputation future: she had been equally depressed following her first surgery and yet had recovered to lead a fulfilling life. Should her doctors respect her repeated refusal of treatment?

The first question to ask in cases like these is whether the patient's beliefs are actually unreasonable, in the sense of clearly not being warranted by the evidence. If the patient and her clinicians disagree about her prognosis or overall life prospects, then this does not mean that she is being irrational. Suppose, though, that it is clear that what she is saying is not warranted. The second question to ask is whether she is really expressing beliefs about how the world is or is expressing something else. To say, "No one will ever love me again" might be an expression of one's belief that the future will be as lonely as the present; but it might instead be an expression of just how lonely one feels right now. Such feelings are not in themselves reason to doubt someone's capacity either. Suppose, though, that the patient's statements are unwarranted and are also really expressing beliefs. The third question to ask is whether those beliefs can be swayed by evidence or by having different people talk to her, or whether they will change with time. To attempt to persuade someone in this situation that she is mistaken, and to have multiple people attempt to do so, seems caring rather than objectionably paternalistic. It is as though a man about to cross a shaky bridge is refusing to believe that the bridge will collapse, despite strong evidence to the contrary, and passersby are doing everything they can to persuade him not to continue.

Finally, if a patient is refusing treatment on the basis of unwarranted beliefs that are resistant to change, we must decide whether her decisions should be respected or overridden. Is she competent to make this decision or does her recalcitrant belief render her incompetent and justify soft paternalistic intervention? Here, we think that a responsible clinician faces

---

[71] Jodi Halpern, *From Detached Concern to Empathy* (New York: Oxford University Press, 2001), 1–4.

a dilemma for which we do not have a ready resolution. On the one hand, it is hard to square acceding to such decisions with the underlying motivation for respecting autonomy – that it allows people to live their own lives in accordance with their own values and preferences. After all, someone cannot actually live her life in accordance with her values and preferences if she is fundamentally mistaken about the facts relevant to making decisions about her life. On the other hand, if someone is incompetent whenever they make decisions on the basis of mistaken beliefs, then this standard risks expanding the scope of incompetence too far. For example, given the complexity of the stock market, it is possible that everyone whose retirement fund includes investments in stocks is making some of their financial decisions on the basis of false beliefs. But surely we do not want to treat all adults of only moderate numeracy as unable to make their own financial decisions.

5.8   Direct-to-Consumer Marketing of Pharmaceuticals

In the majority of jurisdictions around the world, direct advertising of prescription pharmaceuticals to patients, or "direct-to-consumer advertising" (DTCA), is prohibited. The United States and New Zealand permit it, provided certain safeguards are in place. In the United States, in 2014, drug makers spent \$4.5 billion on DTCA, including print media, television, and online advertising.[72] The majority of these advertisements are product-specific: they name a drug, state its therapeutic uses, and make claims about its effectiveness and safety. Following FDA requirements, they must also include information about the most significant risks.[73] Most, however, omit other information that might be pertinent to a patient's decision about treatment, such as success rates for the drug, risk factors for the condition, costs, and alternative treatments (including nonpharmaceutical lifestyle changes patients could make).[74] Moreover, like marketing for other products, pharmaceutical advertisements do not rely simply on propositional content but deliver that content in ways that

---

[72] Jason Millman, "It's True: Drug Companies Are Bombarding Your TV with More Ads than Ever," *Washington Post* (March 23, 2015) (www.washingtonpost.com/news/wonk/wp/2015/03/23/yes-drug-companies-are-bombarding-your-tv-with-more-ads-than-ever/).

[73] Food and Drug Administration, "Basics of Drug Ads" (www.fda.gov/Drugs/ResourcesForYou/Consumers/PrescriptionDrugAdvertising/ucm072077.htm; accessed September 28, 2020).

[74] Michael Wilkes, Robert Bell, and Richard Kravitz, "Direct-to-Consumer Prescription Drug Advertising: Trends, Impact, and Implications," *Health Affairs* 19 (2000): 110–128.

are intended to sway their audience, such as by associating their products with attractive people leading desirable lifestyles.

DTCA has been widely criticized on the grounds that it increases demand for more expensive medications, misleads patients about the risks and benefits of different therapies, leads to inappropriate prescriptions, distorts the doctor–patient relationship, and contributes significantly to the overmedicalization of the US population.[75] In 2015 the American Medical Association adopted a policy that supported a ban on DTCA.[76]

The effectiveness of pharmaceutical advertising in increasing prescriptions for brand-name drugs is not in doubt. Its overall effect on patient well-being is less clear, since that depends on whether a patient population is currently undertreated or overtreated with pharmaceutical products. DTCA seems both to encourage people with serious health conditions to seek treatment and to lead patients to request interventions that are not medically appropriate. For example, a randomized controlled trial sent standardized patients to their primary care physicians with requests for brand-name medications, general requests for medication, or no request at all.[77] The standardized patients reported either symptoms of major depression (for which medication would be indicated) or adjustment disorder (for which medication would not generally be recommended). Requests for medication of any type substantially increased the proportion who were offered "minimally acceptable initial care" for major depression, but also substantially increased the proportion of those presenting with adjustment disorder who were prescribed antidepressants.

In analyzing the ethics of DTCA it is important to separate the question of what individual pharmaceutical companies and advertising agencies should do from the question of how the behavior of these actors should be regulated. We start with the former. Consider a simple case first. In 2008, the FDA wrote a warning letter to Bayer Healthcare Pharmaceuticals regarding two of its television advertisements for Yaz, an oral contraceptive also approved for treatment of premenstrual dysphoric disorder (PMDD) and moderate acne in women choosing to use an oral

---

[75] For an overview of arguments on both sides, see C. Lee Ventola, "Direct-to-Consumer Pharmaceutical Advertising: Therapeutic or Toxic?," *Pharmacy and Therapeutics* 36 (2011): 669.

[76] American Medical Association, "AMA Calls for Ban on DTC Ads of Prescription Drugs and Medical Devices" (November 17, 2015 press release; www.ama-assn.org/press-center/press-releases/ama-calls-ban-dtc-ads-prescription-drugs-and-medical-devices).

[77] Richard Kravitz et al., "Influence of Patients' Requests for Direct-to-Consumer Advertised Antidepressants: A Randomized Controlled Trial," *JAMA* 293 (2005): 1995–2002. Note that "standardized patients" here is a euphemism, in that these individuals were pretending to have the symptoms in question.

contraceptive. The letter criticizes the advertisements for suggesting that Yaz would be appropriate for treating the more common and milder premenstrual syndrome (PMS), an indication for which it was not approved.[78] Advertisements that are misleading in this way are straightforward to evaluate. Deception disrespects the autonomy of the people viewing the advertisement, and false beliefs about the safety or efficacy of pharmaceutical products are likely to be detrimental to patient well-being.

Note that, as discussed earlier in this chapter, deception does not have to involve outright lying. If an advertisement does not make literally false statements but implies propositions that are untrue, it is deceptive. For example, if a medication were known to increase the risk of stroke and this information were not revealed in an advertisement, it would be deceptive. It would be deceptive because it is reasonable for a consumer to believe that the major risks of a medication will be stated in a pharmaceutical advertisement, and so the omission of stroke implies that stroke is not one of the risks.

But most of the advertising that is criticized is not outright deceptive in this way. For example, footage of handsome middle-aged people playing sports and picnicking together in the sunshine might engender positive feelings, but it is not (usually) conveying propositional content. Likewise for stirring music, calm colors, and reassuring voices. Following the taxonomy given in Section 5.2, if this advertising is ethically problematic, it is because it involves motivational manipulation.[79] It may dispose people to be positively inclined toward a drug even though they have been given no reason to be so inclined and even though – on reflection – they would likely reject the nonpropositional content of the advertisements as a reason to take the drug.

---

[78] Food and Drug Administration, Warning Letter (October 3, 2008; available at http://wayback.archive-it .org/7993/20170111082225/http://www.fda.gov/Drugs/GuidanceComplianceRegulatoryInformation/ EnforcementActivitiesbyFDA/WarningLettersandNoticeofViolationLetterstoPharmaceuticalCompanie s/ucm049750.htm).

[79] Paul Biegler and Patrick Vargas argue that these features of pharmaceutical advertisements are ethically problematic because this nonpropositional content involves evaluative conditioning, whereby a stimulus with positive valence (e.g., the attractive couple picnicking) is paired with something that has neutral valence (e.g., the drug being marketed), thereby transferring its positive valence. Consequently, the authors claim, this leads viewers to develop unjustified beliefs about the efficacy and safety of advertised pharmaceutical products ("Ban the Sunset? Nonpropositional Content and Regulation of Pharmaceutical Advertising," *American Journal of Bioethics* 13 [2013]: 3–13). This undermines the autonomy of the viewers' choices about treatments. We think that the ethical wrong that Biegler and Vargas identify is better captured by the sort of insult to autonomy that motivational manipulation involves – it is pro tanto wrongful because it involves illegitimately bypassing the viewer's rational belief-forming mechanism.

Motivational manipulation illegitimately interferes with autonomous decision-making and so is pro tanto wrongful. It is also liable to reduce the quality of someone's decisions and so reduce the autonomy of those decisions, which is detrimental to their well-being. These consequences are added to whatever the net effects of pharmaceutical advertising are on other aspects of patient well-being – an empirical question and one for which there is probably not a single answer for all products and indications. How are we to evaluate the ethics of this sort of advertising? Since the manipulation is pro tanto wrongful, if there is a way to obtain the beneficial effects without manipulative advertising, that alternative should be taken. The propositional content of the advertisements clearly could be conveyed without the rest – an advertisement could provide the information about the product in a way that is designed to be as neutral as possible. Thus, the burden of proof for an individual company defending its DTCA is to show that the net benefit to patients of the manipulative advertisements is so much larger than the net benefit to them of non-manipulative advertisements that it justifies the affront to autonomy. Though this is an empirical matter, we suspect that it is a high hurdle to surmount.

For individual companies, then, we think it likely that much of their advertising should be more neutral in tone.[80] This does not yet tell us what would be the optimal policy, that is, whether regulations and oversight should be highly restrictive or could be relatively lax (as they currently are in the United States). Set aside the substantial legal difficulties that would stand in the way of restricting nondeceptive advertisements in the United States, where commercial speech is protected by the Constitution. Still legislators would have to address additional empirical questions. To what extent would restrictions on DTCA affect the overall volume of pharmaceutical sales? What difference would this make to longer-term research and development priorities? Would lower levels of prescriptions be overall beneficial to society or detrimental? We do not have the data and economic models to provide an answer to these questions here.

---

[80] Note that this judgment applies well beyond pharmaceutical advertising. Any company whose marketing predictably makes consumers' decision-making worse will be acting in a way that requires ethical justification. Some people will find it implausible that so much marketing could be unethical. We challenge them to explain why it should be ethically permissible to undermine someone's decision-making without their permission and without counterbalancing benefits to them. As with pharmaceutical advertising, of course, how such marketing should be regulated is a distinct question.

CHAPTER 6

Distributive Justice and Beneficence

6.1   Introduction

Justice is a matter of giving individuals what they are due. Four broad concepts of justice can be distinguished. *Retributive justice* gives people what they are due – for example, punishment – in virtue of their wrongful acts. *Restorative justice* gives people what they are due – for example, compensation – in virtue of past wrongs they experienced. *Distributive justice* gives people what they are due independent of past wrongful actions. It includes the distribution of valuable resources (such as medical care and job opportunities), the distribution of burdens (such as taxation and jury duty), and the assignment and enforcement of certain legal rights (such as regarding marriage and inheritance). Finally, in contrast to these concepts of substantive justice, there is also *procedural justice*, which concerns the fairness of the processes by which decisions regarding matters of substantive justice are made. Our main interest here is in distributive justice, though, as will become clear, restorative justice may also be relevant to some of the applications of our views on distributive justice.

Beneficence concerns our duties to benefit other individuals. Being benefited is the converse of being harmed: someone is benefited when they are made better off than they would have been otherwise (Chapter 4). We can distinguish three types of duties of beneficence. The *imperfect duty of beneficence* is a duty to contribute substantially, relative to one's ability, to assist individuals in need over the course of one's life. Individual agents have discretion over exactly how and when this duty is discharged. The *perfect duty of beneficence* or *duty of rescue* is a duty that all agents have to provide large benefits to others when they can do so at a sufficiently low cost to themselves. Finally, there are *special duties of beneficence* that attach to agents in virtue of their relationships and the roles they occupy, such as the special duties of parents to their children or of clinicians to their patients.

At first blush, it might seem peculiar that we treat distributive justice and beneficence together. Although each addresses the provision of benefits and burdens, in the bioethics literature they are usually treated as distinct.[1] For the purpose of answering certain, limited questions relating to clinical care and research we agree that it can be helpful to separate them. However, as the following discussion reveals, we think that the content of one depends on the content of the other.

This chapter divides the theoretical landscape in two ways: (1) between the ideal and the nonideal and (2) between how institutions should be arranged and how individuals should behave. The distinction between ideal and nonideal theory comes from political philosophy.[2] *Ideal theory* concerns how just social and international institutions should be organized and how individuals ought to act against a background of just institutions and on the assumption that other people will act as they should. *Nonideal theory* concerns what ought to be done when the institutional background is unjust and other people cannot be relied upon to act well. More specifically, we take nonideal theory to address what particular individual actors – including states and persons – should do in the world as it is now.

Regarding institutions, domestically, we defend a relatively generic *liberal egalitarian* view about distributive justice according to which unchosen differences in individual advantage within a society are prima facie unjust.[3] Plausible justifications for differences in individual advantage include that the benefits to other parties of inequality are sufficiently large, that the inequality is necessary to secure a fundamental right, or that the inequality results from voluntary, informed decisions by the disadvantaged parties. Globally, the reasons that lead us to endorse liberal egalitarianism also lead us to endorse a form of *cosmopolitanism*. According to this view, similar principles of justice apply internationally as apply domestically. For individuals, we argue for extensive duties of beneficence, albeit consistent with considerable leeway for people to prioritize their own projects.

In our nonideal world these conclusions have far-reaching consequences for the setup of institutions and the actions of individuals. We show how they imply that national governments should ensure that all their residents have access to affordable health care and how they give us

[1] See, e.g., Tom Beauchamp and James Childress. *Principles of Biomedical Ethics*, 7th ed. (New York: Oxford University Press, 2013).
[2] See, e.g., John Rawls, *A Theory of Justice* (Cambridge, MA: Harvard University Press, 1971), 351.
[3] We borrow this notion from Douglas MacKay, who articulates a form of "generic liberalism" ("Standard of Care, Institutional Obligations, and Distributive Justice," *Bioethics* 29 [2015]: 262–273, at 264).

reasons to amend the global intellectual property regime that governs pharmaceutical patents.

6.2   Just Institutions

A Defense of Liberal Egalitarianism

Social institutions – understood broadly to include legal regimes, as well as government bodies and their characteristic activities – are a source of tremendous benefits. The particular ways in which they distribute benefits require justification. For example, property laws convey benefits by facilitating economic transactions that are beneficial to the parties transacting. Specific property laws stand in need of justification since what counts as property and how it is obtained affect who benefits and how much from these transactions. Likewise, health care funded through general taxation provides benefits to patients in the form of better health and financial risk protection. Government-funded health care stands in need of justification since it involves distributing resources that would otherwise belong to the general population to patients and health care providers. We take it that the way in which social institutions distribute resources, rights, opportunities, and so on is just if it could be justified to each person affected by those institutions. We submit that social institutions that are consistent with liberal egalitarianism can be justified in this way.

Egalitarians like us regard it as presumptively unjust if one person is worse off than another person as a result of factors beyond their control.[4] All else being equal, such a difference should be prevented if possible. This rules out treating people differently on the basis of morally irrelevant features, such as race or sexual orientation.[5] However, it does not mean that people should always be treated the same. Most obviously, people have different needs. If we want to give them equal opportunities to

---

[4] We therefore approach distributive justice through the lens of "luck egalitarianism." This view may be contrasted with "social egalitarianism," which bases concerns of justice in the value of individuals being able to participate as free and equal citizens in their society (see Alex Voorhoeve, "Why Health-Related Inequalities Matter and Which Ones Do," in Ole Norheim, Ezekiel Emanuel, and Joseph Millum [eds.], *Global Health Priority-Setting* [New York: Oxford University Press, 2019], 145–161). For an early representative of an implicitly luck egalitarianism approach in bioethics, see Robert Veatch, *A Theory of Medical Ethics* (New York: Basic Books, 1981).

[5] We regard these as good examples of morally irrelevant features in the ideal case (that is, the case where institutions are just and individuals act justly). It does not follow that they are morally irrelevant in the nonideal (actual) case. For example, it might be justified to give preferential treatment in hiring to members of a racial group that has historically been discriminated against.

flourish, then they may need to be given unequal amounts of resources.[6] For example, someone who is near-sighted and someone with 20/20 vision differ in their need for corrective lenses. It is consistent with egalitarianism to supply only the former with glasses.

There may be reasons for treating people in ways that lead to unchosen inequalities in well-being. One prominent reason is that allowing some inequalities may substantially increase the total resources that are available for distribution and so increase the total well-being of a society. For example, allowing variation in wages plausibly incentivizes individuals to work more, to invest in economically productive skills, and to pursue careers for which there is high demand. Under the right conditions, this increases net economic productivity.

Egalitarians disagree about when these unchosen inequalities in outcomes are consistent with treating everyone as an equal.[7] Rawls, for example, defends the *difference principle*, according to which inequalities are permissible only when they most benefit the least well-off:

> No one deserves his greater natural capacity nor merits a more favorable starting place in society. But, of course, this is no reason to ignore, much less to eliminate these distinctions. Instead, the basic structure can be arranged so that these contingencies work for the good of the least fortunate.[8]

Rawls restricted the scope of his theory of justice to representative persons holding different social positions and set aside any special problems raised by those in need of health care.[9] But consideration of cases other than healthy workers in the paid economy is necessary for thinking about problems in bioethics and affects which allocative principles seem plausible.[10] In practice, particularly when it comes to the allocation of resources for medical care, we think that the difference principle would be

---

[6] We do not engage here with the debate about exactly what egalitarians should seek to equalize – that is, what the ultimate currency of distributive justice is – but assume that it is something like opportunities to flourish, where flourishing is synonymous with positive well-being. For a helpful discussion of some key philosophical positions, see Gerald Cohen, "On the Currency of Egalitarian Justice," *Ethics* 99 (1989): 906–944.

[7] For an introduction to political theory that interprets leading theories as attempts to articulate the principle that everyone should be treated as an equal, see Will Kymlicka, *Contemporary Political Philosophy*, 2nd ed. (Oxford: Oxford University Press, 2002).

[8] Rawls, *Theory of Justice*, 87.

[9] Ibid., 83–84. Norman Daniels has attempted to apply a Rawlsian view to health care (*Just Health* [New York: Cambridge University Press, 2007]).

[10] Feminist scholars have criticized theories of justice like Rawls's that bracket issues of justice outside those that relate to individual workers. See, e.g., Susan Moller Okin, *Justice, Gender, and the Family* (New York: Basic Books, 1989).

too strict.[11] The people who are worst off within high-income countries (HICs) are probably individuals who are born with painful, debilitating congenital conditions that dramatically curtail their life expectancy.[12] The difference principle would imply that society should invest vast amounts of money into research and incremental improvements in the quality of life for these individuals, even when far greater benefits could be provided to other patients whose quality of life is not quite as bad but who have greater prospects for improvement. We noted above that a just institution is one that could be justified to each person affected by it. In this case, we would justify to the very worst off not focusing all our resources on them by pointing out how much more could be done with some of those resources if directed to more treatable conditions. Such cases suggest that in justifying unchosen differences in resources there is a balance to be struck between giving higher priority to people who are worse off and maximizing the total benefits that are distributed.[13] We should care both about the distribution of benefits and about the amount of benefits.[14] Both factors are relevant to a just distribution, consistent with our egalitarian approach.

We are not only egalitarians, but liberal egalitarians. Our liberalism shows up in two important ways. First, we argued in Chapter 5 that there is a strong moral presumption against interfering with the voluntary actions of autonomous individuals, except where it is necessary to protect other parties. This presumption also applies to the state. The state – via the various social institutions that it enables or creates – should give high priority to respecting, protecting, and fulfilling the autonomy rights of individuals. Contrary to libertarian views, however, this liberal defense of autonomy does not imply that redistributing resources is presumptively wrongful. Insofar as a different distribution of resources is required *as a matter of justice*, the current holders of those resources do not have rights to

---

[11] Cf. Derek Parfit, "Equality and Priority," in Andrew Mason (ed.), *Ideals of Equality* (Oxford: Blackwell, 1998), 1–20; Dennis McKerlie, "Equality," *Ethics* 106 (1996): 274–296; and Richard Arneson, "Egalitarian Justice versus the Right to Privacy," *Social Philosophy and Policy* 17 (2000): 91–119.

[12] Examples include Tay-Sachs disease, Lesch-Nyhan syndrome, and juvenile Batten disease, which we discuss in Chapter 8.

[13] Compare Norman Daniels, "Justice, Health, and Healthcare," *American Journal of Bioethics* 1 (2) (2001): 2–16, at 9–10.

[14] We do not attempt to give a formula for how this trade-off should be made. For some data on public preferences regarding how much priority should be given to those who are worse off, see Koonal Shah, "Severity of Illness and Priority Setting in Healthcare: A Review of the Literature," *Health Policy* 93 (2009): 77–84.

them and so do not have autonomy rights with respect to them that the state has a duty to respect.

Second, the state should adopt a default of neutrality among different views people may have about what constitutes a good life. This is partly for reasons of autonomy. It is typically valuable for individuals to lead an autonomous life in which they are able to set and follow their own goals. Some people may aim to live lives that sacrifice their well-being, to some extent, for valued projects. It would be paternalistic to insist that they do otherwise. State neutrality is also justified by reasons of epistemic humility in light of our subjective account of well-being, according to which what is ultimately good for someone depends on what they desire and what they enjoy (Chapter 8). Unsurprisingly, then, people are often the best judges of their own well-being.[15] Such state neutrality is compatible with recognizing that certain resources are likely to be *instrumentally* helpful to virtually everyone, regardless of their specific aims and priorities. This idea justifies the state's role in promoting, for example, universal basic education and public health measures.

Finally, we should mention our views on the *site* of social justice. By the site we mean the sort of entity or agent that is a candidate for being distributively just or unjust. Some writers think that only social institutions – or some subset of social institutions – can be judged according to whether they conform to principles of justice. Others think that we can also criticize individuals on the grounds that their actions lead to unjust outcomes. We accept the latter view. This is because the reasons why we care about how social institutions are set up – such as the substantial effects they have on people's life prospects – also seem to apply to the actions of individuals.[16]

In many cases, differing views on the site of social justice will not affect specific conclusions about justice in bioethics. But occasionally it will matter. To illustrate, consider the challenge many health systems face of ensuring sufficient coverage for rural communities. Those who think that only social institutions are amenable to criticism on the basis of justice may argue that governments or community health providers are responsible for

---

[15] Cf. John Stuart Mill, *On Liberty* (London: Parker & Son, 1859), 91–92. Note that this need not entail state neutrality about how (nonautonomous) children should be raised, since neither consideration – the value of autonomously directing one's own life and epistemic humility – applies in the same way.

[16] For an accessible overview of this debate and an argument in favor of judging individual actions as well as social structures, see G. A. Cohen, *If You're an Egalitarian, How Come You're So Rich?* (Cambridge, MA: Harvard University Press 2000).

incentivizing doctors to work in remote areas. Those who take the contrary view will say that doctors who refuse to work in rural communities unless they are given much higher pay are also open to criticism.

To summarize, according to the liberal egalitarianism we endorse:

1. Unchosen differences between individuals in terms of their opportunities to flourish are presumptively unjust.
2. In justifying unchosen differences a balance must be struck between giving higher priority to people who are worse off and maximizing overall benefits.
3. Infringements on individual liberty require substantial justification.
4. The state should be neutral among competing conceptions of the good life for an individual.
5. We may evaluate individuals, as well as institutions, in terms of justice.

It is worth noting four questions within liberal egalitarianism on which we have not taken a position.

First, though we maintain that the distribution of resources is critical to justice, we have not spelled out precisely how to conceptualize distributive concerns. Regarding the egalitarian criterion of distribution, we have left open whether it is ultimately about equality per se (a comparative notion) or about helping those who are worse off (a prioritarian notion). Normally, helping the worse off will promote equality, and vice versa, but in principle the two aims can diverge.[17] We have also not committed to any precise way of weighing the egalitarian criterion (whether conceptualized ultimately as equality or priority) against other considerations, such as maximizing the amount of benefit that can be distributed. We regard this as a task that will involve intuitive weighing and might not be susceptible to more structured analysis.

Second, we endorsed the "luck egalitarian" thesis that *chosen* inequalities are not unjust. This implies that, in principle, people can be held responsible for their decisions and the consequences of those decisions. But we have not said under what conditions a choice is voluntary and informed enough that someone should be held responsible for its consequences. In bioethics, this issue arises when someone's behavior can influence their

---

[17] For an argument that this distinction will rarely make a difference in practice, see Marc Fleurbaey, "Equality versus Priority: How Relevant Is the Distinction?," *Economics & Philosophy* 31 (2015): 203–217.

health. For example, diet and exercise affect the likelihood that someone will develop type II diabetes. For some, this connection implies that it would be acceptable for public health providers and private insurers to incentivize healthful behaviors and penalize risky behaviors.[18] Others consider such policies unwarranted because they deny that the bad outcomes are chosen sufficiently voluntarily and knowingly for people to be legitimately held responsible for them.[19] Furthermore, many individuals whose health behaviors are associated with negative health outcomes are unjustly disadvantaged in other ways. For example, in HICs, smoking is negatively correlated with socioeconomic status.[20] Even if such individuals are responsible for some part of their ill health, they are already deserving of much better treatment by state institutions than they currently receive.[21]

Third, it is one thing to identify a social injustice and another to say what policy responses are appropriate ways to address it. For example, unjust inequalities in wages might be appropriately redressed through legal systems that empower collective bargaining, set minimum standards for compensation, and institute a progressive taxation system to fund government programs. By contrast, unjust inequalities that resulted from employers discriminating on the basis of race or gender would not be appropriately addressed by simply paying more to those who were discriminated against. For some important bioethical questions, the acceptable policy responses are hotly debated. For example, someone with a disability may be unjustly disadvantaged in getting and keeping jobs as a result of their disability. One response would be to try to "correct" disabilities as much as possible through medical intervention. Another is to reduce the disadvantages through providing a more accommodating environment, such as wheelchair-accessible workplaces and flexible working hours. A third is to provide additional benefits, such as monetary support, to individuals with disabilities that impede their ability to work.

---

[18] A. M. Buyx, "Personal Responsibility for Health as a Rationing Criterion: Why We Don't Like It and Why Maybe We Should," *Journal of Medical Ethics* 34 (2008): 871–874.

[19] Rebecca Brown, "Moral Responsibility for (Un)Healthy Behaviour," *Journal of Medical Ethics* 39 (2013): 695–698.

[20] Rosemary Hiscock et al., "Socioeconomic Status and Smoking: A Review," *Annals of the New York Academy of Sciences* 1248 (2012): 107–123.

[21] Eric Cavallero, "Health, Luck, and Moral Fallacies of the Second Best," *Journal of Ethics* 15 (2011): 387–403. A policy that holds people responsible for some negative health outcomes also needs a fair method for determining which health outcomes people are responsible for. Given the multitude of influences on health outcomes – behavioral, environmental, and genetic – and the multiple possible influences on behavior, it is typically very hard to determine which individual health outcomes are the result of voluntary decisions.

Depending on the context, there may be very good reasons to prefer one of these ways of responding to unjust differences in opportunities to flourish to others.[22]

A fourth, and related, question concerns the extent to which egalitarians should consider issues other than the distribution of resources. Critics of luck egalitarianism have argued, among other things, that it has focused too much on redistribution and neglected the importance of the relationships in which individuals in a society stand to one another.[23] For example, the successful businessman who is discriminated against because he is black or gay suffers injustice, but the injustice results not from maldistribution of resources but from failure to treat him as an equal. As Nancy Fraser put it, egalitarians should care about "recognition," not only about "redistribution."[24] We do not seek to take a position on this debate here. However, we acknowledge that our primary focus is indeed on the distribution of benefits. This is not because we think these other concerns do not matter. Rather, given limited space, it is more important for the development of our theory to show its links with individual obligations of beneficence, which also concern distributing benefits.

Though these four questions are important and sometimes relevant to policy, liberal egalitarians who disagree about them still share extensive common ground. In many cases, as we hope this chapter demonstrates, this common ground is sufficient to give guidance regarding questions of bioethics.

Rejecting Libertarianism

In high-income Anglophone countries, the most prominent alternatives to liberal egalitarian views of distributive justice are libertarian views.[25] Though defended by relatively few academics who work on justice, they have been very influential in the wider political culture. Libertarians

---

[22] J. Wolff, "Disability among Equals," in Kimberly Brownlee and Adam Cureton (eds.), *Disability and Disadvantage* (New York: Oxford University Press, 2009), 113–137.

[23] Elizabeth Anderson, "What Is the Point of Equality?," *Ethics* 109 (1999): 287–337. For some responses, see Kok-Chor Tan, "A Defense of Luck Egalitarianism," *Journal of Philosophy* 105 (2008): 665–690; and Kasper Lippert-Rasmussen, *Luck Egalitarianism* (London: Bloomsbury, 2016).

[24] Nancy Fraser, "Social Justice in the Age of Identity Politics: Redistribution, Recognition, and Participation," in Nancy Fraser and Axel Honneth, *Redistribution or Recognition?* (New York: Verso, 2003), 7–109.

[25] Utilitarianism also provides an alternative account of the requirements of distributive justice. We present our reasons against adopting utilitarianism as a moral theory in Chapter 3.

prioritize individual autonomy rights, including negative rights against interference with persons and their property.[26] They deny that it is permissible for the state to use people's property except in order to secure the resources necessary to enforce autonomy rights. Consequently, libertarians typically reject the sort of wholesale and ongoing redistribution of resources – as provided, for example, by public health care programs and unemployment benefits – that egalitarians support.[27]

Libertarian views would have very different implications for many issues in bioethics than the liberal egalitarianism we just defended. For example, Tristram Engelhardt argues:

> Rights to health care constitute claims against others for either their services or their goods. Unlike rights to forbearance, which require others to refrain from interfering, rights to beneficence require others to participate actively in a particular understanding of the good life. Rights to health care, unless they are derived from special contractual agreements, depend on the principle of beneficence rather than that of autonomy, and therefore may conflict with the decisions of individuals who may not wish to participate in realizing a particular system of health care.[28]

The upshot, for Engelhardt, is that there is no moral right to health care. We reach the opposite verdict in this chapter's penultimate section. Given the substantial disagreement between our conception of justice and the libertarian approach, we think it important to explain why we think libertarianism is mistaken.[29]

For the libertarian, the way that resources are ultimately distributed in a society is not what matters for justice. What matters for justice is the *process* through which the distribution of resources comes about. Provided that someone legitimately acquires a resource, it is up to her how to dispose

---

[26] For prominent statements of this position, see F. A. Hayek, *The Constitution of Liberty* (Chicago: University of Chicago Press, 1960); Robert Nozick, *Anarchy, State, and Utopia* (New York: Basic Books, 1974); and Jan Narveson, *The Libertarian Idea* (Philadelphia: Temple University Press, 1988).

[27] For the purposes of discussion, we set aside so-called *left libertarians*, who share libertarian views about the importance of individual self-ownership, but have much more egalitarian views about the distribution of natural resources. See, e.g., Michael Otsuka, *Libertarianism without Inequality* (Oxford: Clarendon, 2003); and Peter Vallentyne and Hillel Steiner, *Left Libertarianism and Its Critics* (New York: Palgrave, 2000).

[28] Tristram Engelhardt, *The Foundations of Bioethics* (New York: Oxford University Press, 1986), 336.

[29] By contrast, other competing political theories either would tend to have similar implications for many questions in bioethics (such as moderate communitarian views) or are no longer prominent in political debates or in the bioethics literature (such as Marxism).

of it. If others interfere with how she disposes of her resources, they violate her rights.[30] This includes interfering in order to redistribute the resources to those who need them more. By contrast, liberal egalitarians can endorse the allocation and reallocation of resources according to individuals' present needs.

In order to defend their view, libertarians need to explain how individuals obtain rights over resources in the first place. One way to obtain property rights over an object is for someone to make the object out of resources they already own. For example, if I build a house on land I own with materials that I buy, then I will own the house. This prompts the question of how individuals came to own the resources that they use to make other things. For most resources, this comes about through a transfer of property rights: one person gives a resource to a second person. But, of course, this will be a legitimate way to obtain rights to a resource only if the first person already had a legitimate claim to the resource. In turn, that person will have had a legitimate claim to the resource only if she received it from someone who had a legitimate claim, and so on. Somehow, the initial acquisition of individual property rights over resources must be justified. This poses what we believe are insuperable challenges for the libertarian approach to justice.

The first challenge is that the actual processes by which private property in land and other resources were originally acquired were clearly not legitimate in most cases. For example, land in the Americas was mostly acquired through the conquest and displacement of native peoples by colonizing Europeans. Land title in European countries traces back to similarly inglorious events.[31] The libertarian must either accept that acquiring property by force is a legitimate way to obtain it (in which case it may be taken from its present owners) or, more plausibly, say that it is not (in which case the current ownership of a great deal of property is illegitimate on their view).[32]

The second challenge is that it is difficult to find a principled justification for the initial acquisition of private property, even for a hypothetical case. Many libertarians look to John Locke's labor-mixing theory of

---

[30] Nozick, *Anarchy, State, and Utopia*, chap. 7.

[31] For example, much land in the United Kingdom is privately owned as a result of its removal from common use during the "enclosures." Enclosure was the source of considerable resistance from the rural poor who were thereby deprived of access to fruits of the land. See Pauline Gregg, *Modern Britain* (New York: Pegasus, 1965).

[32] Kymlicka, *Contemporary Political Philosophy*, 111.

property rights for a justification of the initial acquisition of property.[33] Since I own my body, I own my body's labor. If I mix my labor with unowned materials, I thereby gain ownership of the product of that mixing, as well. This acquisition is subject to the proviso that there is "enough, and as good, left in common for others."[34]

The proviso, taken literally, cannot be met in the modern world, since most of the earth's resources are now privately owned – there is definitely not enough and as good left for people who are born now. Acknowledging this, libertarians such as Robert Nozick argue that the proviso should be interpreted as saying that the acquisition of private property is legitimate only when it does not make anyone worse off. Yet, interpreted this way, the proviso seems unjustified because a transaction might treat someone unfairly even if it does not make them worse off. Suppose that some area of outlying land is jointly held by a town's residents. Each resident, we suppose, might be better off if the land were the private property of a small number of people: this would be more efficient than common ownership, the landowners could employ the landless, and so on. Thus the proviso is met and a small group of individuals claim the land. However, it might be that this group is much better off as a result of becoming landowners, while the others, now waged laborers, are only slightly better off than before. How is it that the small group can claim so much of the gains of the new system just by virtue of working on this land first? And, given how important autonomy rights are for the libertarian, how is it that they do not need the others' consent for the acquisition? Again, the problem is particularly stark when we think about generations born after most land is already divided up. They had no opportunity to labor on the land first, and so had no chance to be the ones who benefited most – and, of course, they had no opportunity to consent to the acquisition.[35]

It might seem that a one-time redistribution of resources could meet both challenges. The redistribution would establish a starting point at which everyone had a fair share of resources. After that, the libertarian might argue, it should be up to each person to decide what they do with their property. No further redistribution should be allowed.

[33] John Locke, *Second Treatise of Government*, ed. C. B. Macpherson (Indianapolis: Hackett, 1980/ 1690), chap. V. See also, e.g., Nozick, *Anarchy, State, and Utopia*, chap. 7.

[34] Locke, *Second Treatise of Government*, chap. V, para. 27.

[35] Compare G. A. Cohen, *Self-Ownership, Freedom, and Equality* (Cambridge: Cambridge University Press, 1995), 79–87. See also Kymlicka, *Contemporary Political Philosophy*, 107–127.

However, this proposal fails on at least two counts. First, it does not help with the problem of new people entering the population. How is their share of natural resources to be worked out? Second, it does not address the fundamental counterintuitive aspect of the libertarian's view. No matter what choices people make, they will end up with very unequal amounts of resources and opportunities to flourish. This is because in every generation some people will be given more resources than others (for example, through inheritance or education), some people will have greater opportunities than others (for example, because they have abilities that are more highly valued), and some people will be unlucky (for example, children whose parents die or do not provide for them). For the egalitarian, such cases drive the perception that unchosen differences in opportunities for flourishing are unfair and should be corrected. The libertarian has to bite this counterintuitive bullet.

Note that although we reject libertarianism as a theory of distributive justice, this does not mean that we always oppose the use of markets for distributing goods. Under certain conditions markets are very efficient ways to incentivize the production of needed goods. The liberal egalitarian can happily support the existence of markets in goods and services for these instrumental reasons. But they are instrumental reasons: she is also willing to constrain those markets in cases in which doing so would produce more just outcomes. Market transactions can also be one way in which individuals exercise autonomy rights over their persons or property. There is therefore a strong presumption against interfering with them, except when they lead to unjust outcomes or otherwise involve wrongdoing.

Global Justice: A Defense of Cosmopolitanism

We have argued that unchosen differences in opportunities to flourish within a society are prima facie unjust. Within certain constraints social institutions should be set up in order to mitigate those differences. But, in our nonideal world, there are not only substantial differences in outcomes between compatriots; there are huge differences between people across national borders. Take life expectancy, which is a good summary indicator of expected well-being. Life expectancy for a child born in Sierra Leone in 2018 was fifty-four years.[36] For a child born in Japan it was eighty-four

---

[36] The data come from the World Bank, *World Bank Open Data* (available at https://data.worldbank.org; accessed August 18, 2020).

years.[37] The thirty-year difference cannot be plausibly ascribed to differences in voluntary decisions made by individuals in the two countries. Rather, it results from massive differences in material wealth, nutrition, access to health care, and so forth.[38] Gross domestic product (GDP) per capita is $43,240 in Japan and only $1,790 in Sierra Leone.[39] Globally, 734 million people live in extreme poverty,[40] 2 billion lack access to improved sanitation facilities (with nearly 700 million defecating in the open),[41] and 785 million do not have access to a basic water service.[42] An estimated 5.3 million children under the age of five die each year.[43] The average under-five mortality rate in low-income countries is fourteen times greater than the average rate in HICs. Literacy rates vary from 43 percent in Afghanistan to almost 100 percent in HICs.[44] Like many other important outcomes, literacy is also gendered: of the 750 million illiterate adults in the world, nearly two-thirds are women.[45]

What is the ethical significance of these transnational differences in individual prospects? The intuitive judgments that motivated liberal egalitarianism in the case of the state might seem to support treating these differences in the same way. The nation into which someone is born is unchosen and appears morally arbitrary – that is, there seems to be no sense in which one person deserves a worse life than another in virtue of having been born in a different country. Consequently, the vast differences

---

[37] Ibid.
[38] In any case, the large difference in *life expectancy* – an average measure – is substantially a product of much greater child mortality in Sierra Leone, for which the question of individual responsibility cannot arise.
[39] World Bank, *World Bank Open Data* (available at https://data.worldbank.org; accessed August 18, 2020). Gross domestic product represents the monetary value of all finished goods and services produced within a country's borders. These figures are in 2017 international dollars adjusted for purchasing power parity. An international dollar has the same purchasing power in a specific country as a US dollar has in the United States. It thereby takes account of the differences in the cost of goods and services in different countries.
[40] These are data for 2015 (available at www.worldbank.org/en/topic/poverty/overview; accessed August 18, 2020). Extreme poverty is defined by the World Bank as less than $1.90 international dollars per day (so, for US readers, this is the equivalent of $694 annually for all expenses, including housing, food, transport, medical care, and schooling).
[41] UNICEF, "Sanitation" (June 2019; available at https://data.unicef.org/topic/water-and-sanitation/sanitation/; accessed August 18, 2020).
[42] UNICEF, "Drinking Water" (June 2019; available at https://data.unicef.org/topic/water-and-sanitation/drinking-water/; accessed August 18, 2020).
[43] These 2018 data are from World Health Organization, Global Health Observatory (available at www.who.int/gho/child_health/mortality/mortality_under_five_text/en/; accessed August 18, 2020).
[44] The World Bank, *World Bank Open Data* (available at https://data.worldbank.org; accessed August 18, 2020).
[45] US Central Intelligence Agency, *World Factbook* (available at www.cia.gov/library/publications/resources/the-world-factbook/fields/370.html; accessed August 18, 2020).

in life prospects between individuals born in different countries seem as unjust as they would if they arose between compatriots. Considerations like these support a *cosmopolitan* view of global justice: principles of justice apply in the same way across states as they do within states.[46]

For some theorists, this extrapolation from the national to the international context is unwarranted. While unchosen and arbitrary differences indicate injustice within a society, the existence of such differences is not sufficient for principles of justice to apply. Instead, these *statists* argue, the fact that conationals are part of the same society is necessary for differences between them to matter.[47] Rawls writes:

> For us the primary subject of justice is the basic structure of society, or more exactly, the way in which the major social institutions distribute fundamental rights and duties and determine the division of advantages from social cooperation.[48]

If the existence of the "basic structure" is a precondition for concern about distributive justice, and if there is no such basic structure internationally, then it is a mistake to apply our liberal egalitarian views to the global distribution of resources.[49]

For this statist response to be compelling, it must be true both that there is no global basic structure and that the existence of a shared basic structure is indeed necessary for questions of distributive justice to arise. Both claims are dubious.[50]

First, as various theorists have argued, the extent of international interdependence and shared global institutions is great enough that we should

---

[46] Cosmopolitanism is defined in various ways. See Charles Beitz, "Rawls's Law of Peoples," *Ethics* 110 (2000): 669–696, at 677; Thomas Pogge, "Cosmopolitanism and Sovereignty," *Ethics* 103 (1992): 48–75, at 48–49; and Gillian Brock, *Global Justice* (Oxford: Oxford University Press, 2009), 11–14. Our particular choice of terminology should not beg any substantive questions.

[47] Statists need not deny that we have some obligations to people living outside our national borders. They can agree, for example, that we have duties not to harm foreigners and even duties of beneficence to benefit foreigners who are especially needy. The key point is that these duties do not result from relative differences in people's prospects. We return to this point shortly.

[48] Rawls, *Theory of Justice*, 6.

[49] Whether Rawls believed that there is no global basic structure is a matter of interpretation (see Arash Abizadeh, "Cooperation, Pervasive Impact, and Coercion: On the Scope [not Site] of Distributive Justice," *Philosophy & Public Affairs* 35 [2007]: 318–358, at 319 note 3). In any case, this view is implicit in Rawls's writing and he certainly denies that the same principles apply globally as apply domestically (see John Rawls, *The Law of Peoples* [Cambridge, MA: Harvard University Press, 2001]).

[50] See Abizadeh, "Cooperation, Pervasive Impact, and Coercion," for a comprehensive treatment of the several possible conceptions of the basic structure and an argument to show that each leads to the conclusion that distributive justice is global in scope.

be concerned about the distribution of resources internationally as well as intranationally.[51] All states are heavily dependent on trade for their economic prosperity, so the policies (including internal policies) of other countries also affect them. For example, tax breaks for corporations in one country can negatively affect other countries by incentivizing the movement of capital. Immigration policies that target highly educated individuals may contribute to a "brain drain" from poorer to richer countries. The fact that other countries typically treat the de facto controller of a territory as its legitimate government allows autocratic governments to sell natural resources and borrow money in the name of their people. These international resource and borrowing privileges encourage autocratic governments, coups, civil war, and corruption.[52]

In addition to the substantial effects policies in one country can have on another, there are global institutions that regulate global affairs. Important global institutions include the various organs, subsidiaries, and agencies of the United Nations System – which include the World Bank and the World Health Organization – as well as the World Trade Organization (WTO). The WTO illustrates nicely why some theorists think there is, contrary to the statist's claim, a global basic structure. Currently, 164 states are WTO members and another twenty-two are observers, thereby covering the vast majority of the world. According to WTO figures, 96.4 percent of world trade is accounted for by WTO members, who govern 90.1 percent of the world's population.[53] WTO members have sixty agreements, implemented through domestic legislation, that cover trade in goods and services, intellectual property laws, technical standards, food safety, and many other areas. Membership also involves commitment to a dispute settlement mechanism through which compliance with the other agreements is enforced.[54] Thus, becoming a WTO member involves signing up to a large number of far-reaching rules that affect all aspects of economic life and can be coercively enforced. Nor, given the WTO's global coverage and the trade opportunities it affords, is there much of an option for countries who would prefer a different system. Perhaps state

---

[51] See Charles Beitz, *Political Theory and International Relations* (Princeton, NJ: Princeton University Press, 1979); and Allen Buchanan, "Rawls's Law of Peoples: Rules for a Vanished Westphalian World," *Ethics* 110 (2000): 697–721.

[52] Thomas Pogge, *World Poverty and Human Rights* (Cambridge: Polity, 2002), 112–116.

[53] World Trade Organization, *Handbook on Accession to the WTO*, Chapter 1 (available at www.wto .org/english/thewto_e/acc_e/cbt_course_e/c1s1p1_e.htm; accessed August 18, 2020).

[54] World Trade Organization, "Understanding the WTO: Settling Disputes" (available at www.wto .org/english/thewto_e/whatis_e/tif_e/disp1_e.htm; accessed August 18, 2020).

governments impose more rules, with greater effects on individuals' lives, but even if so, this seems to be a difference of degree rather than kind.[55]

Second, even if a shared basic structure would require more extensive social institutions than the current global order constitutes, we may ask why these more extensive institutions are necessary in order for principles of distributive justice to apply. Rawls suggests an answer in saying that the "basic structure is the primary subject of justice because its effects are so profound and present from the start."[56] But this will hardly separate the domestic from the international case: as the statistics cited above show, whether someone is born into a poor or a rich country makes a huge difference to their life prospects.

We think that the arguments in favor of some sort of cosmopolitanism are compelling. However, we acknowledge that this is an area of considerable disagreement and we have only scratched the surface of an ongoing debate.[57] For this reason, it is important to note that even noncosmopolitans generally acknowledge obligations to foreigners in severe need. Rawls, for example, claimed that there is a duty of assistance to "other peoples living under unfavorable conditions that prevent their having a just or decent political and social regime."[58] This duty has a cutoff – the point at which everyone is living under conditions sufficient to secure their basic needs. But were this duty to be fulfilled, it would dramatically transform the situation of people living in poverty.

6.3   Individuals and the Demands of Beneficence

General Considerations

So far we have examined – through the lens of distributive justice – the ways in which institutions are ethically required to benefit people.

---

[55] Michael Blake argues that the state is distinctive because of its *way* of coercing its residents ("Distributive Justice, State Coercion, and Autonomy," *Philosophy & Public Affairs* 30 [2001]: 257–296). Cf. Thomas Nagel, "The Problem of Global Justice," *Philosophy & Public Affairs* 33 (2005): 113–147. For a response, see Abizadeh, "Cooperation, Pervasive Impact, and Coercion."

[56] Rawls, *Theory of Justice*, 7.

[57] For example, we have not even touched on arguments that seek to justify partiality to conationals on the basis of shared nationality, which may obtain independently of sharing a state (see, e.g., David Miller, *On Nationality* [Oxford: Clarendon, 1995]).

[58] Rawls, *Law of Peoples*, 37. Compare Nagel: "The facts are so grim that justice may be a side issue ... some form of human assistance from the well-off to those in extremis is clearly called for quite apart from any demand of justice, if we are not simply ethical egoists. The urgent current issue is what can be done in the world economy to reduce extreme global poverty" ("The Problem of Global Justice," 118).

Individual agents have related obligations. Some include individuals' obligations to obey the law and play their part in supporting (sufficiently) just institutions.[59] Questions of civil obedience and disobedience – as well as the fundamental question of whether the state can be justified to those who live within it – are fascinating and important.[60] However, we lack the space to address them.

In addition to their duties to support and comply with just institutions, individuals have duties of beneficence that require them to provide benefits to others in need (either directly or indirectly – for example, through institutional means). That we have some such duties is suggested intuitively by examples such as the classic *pond case*.[61] Suppose you are an able-bodied adult walking by a large pond. In the pond you notice a struggling child. Though the child is very likely to drown unless aided, the pond is only a meter deep, so you could safely wade out to save him. If you did so, however, the muddy water would likely ruin your suit. No one else is around. Do you have a duty to save the child? Most people agree that you do; indeed, someone who walked on by would be regarded as a moral monster.

Thought-experiments like the pond case suggest that we are sometimes morally required to assist others at some cost to ourselves. Everyday moral thinking also suggests that there are limits on this requirement to assist. I do not have a duty to benefit another every time I could provide a greater benefit to them than the corresponding cost to myself. Agents appear to have a limited liberty – or "prerogative" – to act in ways that do not maximize the good consequences of their actions.

On the surface, these so-called agent-centered prerogatives might seem mysterious. After all, from a neutral perspective my interests are no more important in virtue of being mine than yours are in virtue of being yours. What makes it acceptable for me to prefer myself rather than doing what is best for everyone?

Note, first, that there is a strong intuitive case for the view that asserts that it is sometimes impermissible to favor one's own interests but also

---

[59] Rawls, *Theory of Justice*, 99–100.

[60] On civil disobedience, see Hugo Adam Bedau (ed.), *Civil Disobedience in Focus* (New York: Routledge, 2002). On possible sources of political obligations, see A. John Simmons, *Moral Principles and Political Obligations* (Princeton, NJ: Princeton University Press, 1981). In bioethics such questions arise, for example, regarding clinicians who have conscientious objections to carrying out abortions or breaking patient confidentiality to assist law enforcement officials.

[61] For the classic description of the case, see Peter Singer, "Famine, Affluence, and Morality," *Philosophy & Public Affairs* 1 (1972): 229–423, at 231.

sometimes permissible not to do what is impartially best.[62] That is, it is intuitively plausible that we have some duties of beneficence, but those duties are limited. Nonetheless, as we stress in multiple places in this book, an initially intuitive view can still be mistaken. We therefore need a principled justification for it as well.

The agent-centered prerogative is a particular type of right, which consists in the liberty not to maximize the good consequences of one's actions. We think that the ground for this right is of the same type as for many other rights: the important interests that it protects. Having agent-centered prerogatives allows autonomous individuals to flourish because it allows them to set their own goals and pursue their own projects according to what they find valuable.[63] This acknowledges that each person's point of view has special weight for her and thereby takes her seriously as someone whose values and goals give her reasons, not merely treating her as a means to making the world a better place. Respecting agent-centered prerogatives, then, is one way in which we show respect for rights-holders (one of the two foundational values in our ethical theory).

We have argued that agents are sometimes morally required to benefit others and are sometimes permitted not to benefit others when they could. It is worth emphasizing that the view does not imply that our starting judgments about *how much* we should care about the interests of others and *how much* we are permitted to benefit ourselves are correct or close to correct. That will depend on the results of using the method of reflective equilibrium, which can lead to dramatic revisions in what we believe we ought to do (Chapter 2).

To get a handle on the extent of our duties to benefit others we must explore the grounds for the duty of beneficence. Duties of beneficence arise in response to the morally important needs of others. The strength of those duties is plausibly greater the more significant the benefits someone could provide. All else being equal, it is morally more important to save someone's life than to save them from losing a limb, and, consequently, their claim to help is greater. Likewise, the strength of the duties is

---

[62] Shelly Kagan describes three positions: *extremist, moderate,* and *minimalist.* The extremist claims that we must always act in a way that is impartially optimal. The minimalist denies that we are ever morally required to benefit others. Kagan argues that moderate views that lie between these two extremes are unsustainable (*The Limits of Morality* [Oxford: Clarendon Press, 1989]).

[63] For discussions of this theme, see Samuel Scheffler, *The Rejection of Consequentialism*, 2nd edition (Oxford: Oxford University Press, 1994); and Bernard Williams, "A Critique of Utilitarianism," in J. J. C. Smart and Bernard Williams, *Utilitarianism* (Cambridge: Cambridge University Press, 1973), 108–117.

plausibly greater the lower the cost to the agent of providing that benefit. If all I have to do is wade into the pond and get my clothes wet in order to save a life, then the victim has a stronger claim than if I had to risk my own life to save his. So, as the benefits we could supply to others grows and the cost to us diminishes, their claim to our help increases.[64]

What does this imply about our duties of beneficence? The claims of some potential victims will be strong enough to override an individual agent's prerogative to pursue her own projects. In such cases, the individual acquires a *perfect duty of beneficence* (the *duty to rescue*). For claims that are weak enough that they do not override the agent-centered prerogative, she may choose to do something other than fulfill those claims. As noted just above, this prerogative is grounded in considerations such as the value of governing one's own life, pursuing the projects one thinks valuable, and so forth. However, satisfying the interests that this prerogative serves to protect is perfectly possible while responding to some of the morally important need that underlies these claims. A typical agent could sometimes provide benefits to needy others without compromising her ability to govern her own life. She therefore ought to do so. Thus, the combination of morally important need and agent-centered options entails what is called the *imperfect duty of beneficence*.[65] This is a duty to provide some benefits to others but where the agent has some discretion about exactly when and how she does so. Having this discretion allows individuals freedom to pursue their interests and allows them to incorporate beneficence into their personal projects.

The Perfect Duty of Beneficence

We have little further to add regarding the content of the imperfect duty of beneficence and do not regard our interpretation of it as controversial.[66] The perfect duty of beneficence – or the duty to rescue – is another matter.

---

[64] Other conditions may apply, too, but we keep the case simple for the moment in order to clarify the underlying normative structure.

[65] The terminology of perfect and imperfect duties comes from Immanuel Kant, *Foundations of the Metaphysic of Morals*, trans. L. W. Beck (New York: Liberal Arts Press, 1959/1785). Compare John Stuart Mill: "[D]uties of perfect obligation are those duties in virtue of which a correlative *right* resides in some person or persons; duties of imperfect obligation are those moral obligations which do not give birth to any right" (*Utilitarianism*, ed. George Sher [Indianapolis, IN: Hackett, 1979/1861], 48).

[66] Relatively little has been written on the imperfect duty of beneficence. One exception is Barbara Herman's work in Kantian ethics. See Herman, "Being Helped and Being Grateful: Imperfect Duties, the Ethics of Possession, and the Unity of Morality," *Journal of Philosophy* 109 (2012): 391–411, and "The Scope of Moral Requirement," *Philosophy & Public Affairs* 30 (2001): 227–256.

As the pond case illustrates, this duty arises for agents when they are in situations such that they can prevent a very serious harm to another at a low cost to themselves.[67] Peter Singer, describing what he takes to be a feature of ordinary moral thought, states it in the following way: "If it is in our power to prevent something very bad from happening, without thereby sacrificing anything morally significant, we ought, morally, to do it."[68]

Potential rescue cases are common. For example, a clinician working in a resource-poor setting may encounter patients who are in desperate need but unable to pay for care. Where she could herself provide potentially life-saving treatment for malaria or take the time to refer someone for cataract surgery to save their eyesight, she has the opportunity to provide a rescue. Clinical researchers may diagnose serious medical conditions in their participants or identify genetic variants that predict increased health risks. Whether they are obliged to inform participants or treat them following these incidental findings may depend on whether the duty to rescue applies.[69] Any clinician may face a potential duty to warn, which – interpreted as an ethical imperative – is best understood as a sort of preventive duty to rescue. This, in effect, was the duty that a majority of justices ascribed to a psychiatrist in the famous *Tarasoff* case of 1976, in which a psychotherapy patient revealed his intention to kill a specific woman, Tatiana Tarasoff: the psychiatrist's duty to warn, the majority reasoned, overrode his duty of confidentiality to his patient.[70] Even at the systems level, policy-makers make rescue decisions. For example, the Cancer Drugs Fund that was introduced in England in 2011 provided funding for National Health Service (NHS) patients to receive expensive cancer drugs that had been assessed as not cost-effective. One charitable interpretation of the motivation behind the fund is that providing access to last-ditch therapies offered a chance of rescue to terminally ill patients.[71]

[67] Compare Beauchamp and Childress on the *duty of rescue* (*Principles of Biomedical Ethics*, 206–207) and Rawls on the *duty of mutual aid* (*Theory of Justice*, 98).
[68] Peter Singer, "Famine, Affluence, and Morality," 231. He originally states a stronger version of the principle: "If it is in our power to prevent something bad from happening, without thereby sacrificing anything of comparable moral importance, we ought, morally, to do it" (ibid.).
[69] For an overview of ethical considerations pertaining to incidental genetic findings, see Gabrielle Christenhusz, Koenraad Devriendt, and Kris Dierickx, "To Tell or Not to Tell? A Systematic Review of Ethical Reflections on Incidental Findings Arising in Genetics Contexts," *European Journal of Human Genetics* 21 (2013): 248–255.
[70] *Tarasoff v. Regents of the University of California*, 17 Cal. 3d 425 (1976); 131 California Reporter 14.
[71] The Cancer Drugs Fund (CDF) was widely criticized as a waste of scarce resources and an inappropriate prioritization of cancer patients over other patients. Following a parliamentary review it was incorporated into the body making other decisions about which of new

Whether the duty to rescue applies to a situation is clearly very important. If it does, then the potential rescuer is under a stringent moral duty to act. We therefore need to assess carefully which considerations are relevant to the duty.

Two considerations that are sometimes thought to be relevant are the proximity and the identifiability of the victim. Faced with a child drowning in front of me, it is clear to all that I ought to attempt to save her. We appear to be much more blasé about more distant and less individually identifiable victims. For example, it is widely regarded as optional whether I give money to help the victims of natural disasters in other countries, even in the face of starvation or outbreaks of easily treatable diseases.

We think that neither of these considerations is in fact morally relevant. First, upon reflection it is implausible that one's proximity to a victim or one's ability to identify in some way who that victim is should be relevant to a duty to help them. Such considerations do not play a role elsewhere in our moral theorizing and seem inconsistent with the idea that persons matter equally.[72] Thus, there is a burden of proof on those who would defend their relevance here.[73]

Second, the considerations that seem most likely to underlie duties of beneficence do not require reference to proximity or identifiability. Most salient, in this regard, are the need of the potential beneficiary and the ability of the agent to meet that need, which presumably play a central role in explaining duties to provide benefits.[74]

Third, in cases where proximity and identifiability affect our moral judgments, there are usually alternative explanations. These take both normative and empirical forms. Consider how we might explain why an individual judges it morally imperative to save the child in the pond at the cost of her expensive suit but does not donate a similar amount of money

---

technologies the NHS should fund: the National Institute for Health and Care Excellence (NICE). A review concluded that the "CDF has not delivered meaningful value to patients or society" (A. Aggarwal et al., "Do Patient Access Schemes for High-Cost Cancer Drugs Deliver Value to Society? Lessons from the NHS Cancer Drugs Fund," *Annals of Oncology* 28 [2017]: 1738–1750).

[72] Cf. Dan Brock's use of the "Principle of the Equal Moral Worth of All Human Lives" in his "Identified versus Statistical Lives: Some Introductory Issues and Arguments," in I. Glenn Cohen, Norman Daniels, and Nir Eyal (eds.), *Identified versus Statistical Lives* (New York: Oxford University Press, 2015), 43–52, at 43.

[73] For one attempt to defend the relevance of proximity, see Frances Kamm, *Intricate Ethics* (New York: Oxford University Press, 2007), 386–388. Her justification in terms of the agent-centered prerogative is too thinly articulated for us to evaluate properly. For arguments for and against the relevance of identifiability, see Cohen, Daniels, and Eyal, *Identified versus Statistical Lives*.

[74] We consider the relevance of roles and special relationships shortly. Here we are concerned only with general duties of beneficence.

to a charity distributing bed nets to prevent malaria transmission. Normatively, we might defend her decision on the grounds that she judges it much less certain that her money will save a child's life than that her wading into the pond will do so. That is, despite the charity's claims, she does not think that the cost per life saved is really the same. Empirically, we might explain her tendency to make judgments like these in terms of the evolution of our moral sensibilities. Humans evolved living in small groups where the plight of those we could help was salient because they were close and identifiable.[75] Our strongest impulses to help arise when we empathize with the situation of another.[76] Thus, it is unsurprising that the urge to rescue is more powerful when we are dealing with a local situation involving a particular person.

Although we think that proximity and identifiability are morally irrelevant in themselves, they may to some extent track considerations that matter. As just noted, more distant rescue scenarios are often ones about which we have much less information and so are likely to be much less certain about the effectiveness of our actions. Whereas the person who jumps into the pond to save a child might have a good idea of whether she can reach him and whether he would drown without her help, this is not always true of the victims of famines or natural disasters. The need may be very real, but whether we can have a beneficial effect may be much more dubious. This skepticism is borne out by data about the effectiveness of many – though not all – attempts to aid distant others. Government-to-government aid, for example, has been notoriously ineffective in improving development outcomes.[77] And donations to causes that are highly salient, such as in the immediate aftermath of natural disasters, often result in minimal incremental benefit to victims, given other available resources.[78]

The fact that we are sometimes right to be skeptical about whether a particular action – like donating to a charity – will have its intended effect should not engender global skepticism about our ability to help. Instead, it illustrates the importance of taking uncertainty into account in assessing the cost-effectiveness of our actions and the importance of collecting data

[75] See, e.g., Joshua Greene, *Moral Tribes* (New York: Penguin, 2013).
[76] See, e.g., Martin Hoffman, *Empathy and Moral Development* (Cambridge: Cambridge University Press, 2000).
[77] See Carol Lancaster, *Aid to Africa* (Chicago: University of Chicago Press, 1999); and Christopher Coyne, *Doing Bad by Doing Good* (Stanford, CA: Stanford University Press, 2013).
[78] Benjamin Hilton, "Heart vs. Mind: A Review of Emergency Aid" (August 1, 2014); available at www.givingwhatwecan.org/post/2014/08/heart-vs-mind-review-emergency-aid/).

to reduce that uncertainty. The latter point is obscured when we think about pond cases, which are one-off events.[79] Other potential rescue cases, like those experienced by clinicians and researchers, predictably arise, and so systematic assessment of the costs and benefits of interventions is possible.

The costs to the agent of attempting a rescue, the probability of success, and the magnitude of the loss averted for the victim, then, are all clearly relevant to whether a duty to rescue applies. Nevertheless, specifying the limits of the duty has proven challenging. Three types of case illustrate the key challenges. *Costly rescues* are cases in which it would be possible to rescue someone in great need, but the cost to the agent is not low. For example, malaria researchers in Mali identified a serious congenital heart defect in one of their pediatric participants.[80] Care was not available for her in Mali, where she consequently faced a high risk of death. She could be airlifted to a European hospital for expensive and possibly life-saving surgery. But were the researchers obliged to do this?[81] *Endless rescues* are cases in which it is possible for someone to execute an easy rescue – as with the pond example – but where there are many such easy rescues she could make and she cannot make them all. Some charitable appeals seem to implicate endless rescues: the present authors would be broke before they could provide every child who needs one with an insecticide-treated mosquito net. Clinicians working in very underserved regions may more directly experience this challenge. There may be no apparent end to the patients waiting outside a clinic with serious and treatable conditions. Finally, there are *noncompliance cases*. Typically, these are cases in which the rescues are costly or endless only because other people are not doing what they should (that is, others are not compliant with the demands of morality).

All of these cases highlight uncertainty about the upper bounds of the perfect duty of beneficence. As we now argue, this turns out to be relatively unproblematic in the ideal case where the burdens of rescue will be fairly distributed. In the nonideal case, it is much trickier.

---

[79] We mean that cases involving individuals happening upon drowning children whom they can easily rescue are exceptional. Drowning, however, is a huge global problem and one of the leading causes of child deaths (World Health Organization, *Drowning* [fact sheet, updated February 2020; available at www.who.int/mediacentre/factsheets/fs347/en/; accessed September 28, 2020]).

[80] Neal Dickert and David Wendler, "Ancillary Care Obligations of Medical Researchers," *JAMA* 302 (2009): 424–428.

[81] Compare the case of *Bob's Bugatti* (Peter Unger, *Living High and Letting Die* [New York: Oxford University Press, 1996], 136).

Individual Duties of Beneficence in a Just World

In the ideal case, institutions are just and individual agents do what they should. Just institutions would dramatically reduce the number of rescue cases, since morally important needs that could be met are generally ones that would be met in a just society. For example, in a just world, no one would lack adequate nutrition or be sleeping without a bed net in a malaria-endemic region. We could imagine that there would still be unpredictable emergencies – like the child in the pond – but they would be very rare. Thus, the problem of endless rescues would not apply. Moreover, since individual agents would be doing what they should, the problem of noncompliance would, by definition, not apply.

There might still be costly rescues. Individual agents might face high financial burdens, as with the child needing expensive surgery. Alternatively, they could find themselves in a position where they had a chance of rescuing someone but the risk to themselves was high. Perhaps they could dash into a burning building to save a child but might themselves be overwhelmed by the smoke.

In the ideal case, however, there are institutional remedies for these problems. Even if a rescue would be ethically required, it might still impose unfair (because unchosen) burdens on the rescuer. If providing such a rescue – such as life-saving surgery – would be extremely expensive, then a just society would presumably reimburse the rescuer for this cost. For example, providing health care funded by taxation is one way in which a country can spread out the costs of providing very expensive interventions to the relatively few people who end up needing them. Institutional remedies like these convert the question of whether an individual should be expected to bear a great cost to benefit another into a question about whether society should collectively bear the cost. It therefore becomes a question of distributive justice.

Other rescue costs are not as easy to distribute across members of society. The risks to the person contemplating running into a burning building cannot be spread out so that everyone gets a single smoky breath. However, there are ways in which even these risks can be managed in an ethical way. For example, rather than relying on untrained passersby, a society can employ professional firefighters. The risks of performing rescues are lower for such professionals: they are trained and equipped to perform specialized tasks. Further, they are usually voluntarily taking on the risks by taking up the profession. Thus, professional duties to rescue

are one institutional solution to the challenge of costly rescues.[82] Joel
Feinberg states this point as follows:

> Each of us has a duty to call the fire department whenever we discover a fire.
> Beyond that we have no positive duty to fight the flames. That is the special
> responsibility of the skilled professionals we support with our funds. The
> reason why we have the duty to report the fire but not the duty to fight it is
> not just that there is minimal effort required in the one case and not in the
> other. It is rather that the very strict social duty of putting out fires is most
> effectively and equitably discharged if it is split up in advance through the
> sharing of burdens and the assigning of special tasks.[83]

This way of conceptualizing the functions of taxation and professionals
who are specialized for particular types of rescue case suggests two further
insights. First, taxation can be used to enforce and coordinate the fulfillment of individual duties of beneficence. Second, there may be professional duties of beneficence that are more demanding and more specific
than the general duties we have been discussing. These special duties
plausibly require that firefighters take on greater risks to save people from
fires than members of the public, that lifeguards take on greater risks to
save drowning swimmers, and so forth. Germane to our focus in this book,
these more demanding duties of beneficence may also apply to medical
practitioners. We say more on this topic shortly.

Individual Duties of Beneficence in an Unjust World

Turn now to the nonideal (actual) case. We do not always have institutions
in place that can spread out the burdens of rescue among many people.
Moreover, many people and institutions do not do what they should.
Some people help only those close and dear to themselves. Others do
nothing or actively make things worse by harming or exploiting others.
This goes for institutions, too. Whether it be through war, supporting
corrupt governments, or imposing unfair terms of trade, governments
often make things worse for individuals around the world, even when they
have an obligation to make things better.

In the actual world, then, individuals frequently face rescues that appear
costly or endless as a result of the noncompliance of others. The researchers

---

[82] Tina Rulli and Joseph Millum, "Rescuing the Duty to Rescue," *Journal of Medical Ethics* 42 (2016):
260–264, at 262–263.

[83] Joel Feinberg, *Harm to Others* (New York: Oxford University Press, 1984), 170–171; see also
157–159.

who faced the question of whether to pay to airlift a child for heart surgery in Europe faced this dilemma because, partly as a result of global injustice, Mali is poor and its health care system is underdeveloped. Similar points apply to clinicians working in environments where there is no limit to the number of patients they could benefit or to those of us living in HICs who would impoverish ourselves before we could make a noticeable dent on the extreme need in the world. Because the majority of people do not do what even a minimal duty to rescue would require, everyone else confronts a world with much greater need. For virtuous agents, the question of where to locate the limits of perfect obligations of beneficence cannot be ignored.

There are differing views on how an agent's responsibilities change when others are not doing what they should. At one extreme is the view that we should treat the noncompliance of others as a fact of nature. For Singer, for instance, each individual has at least a duty to provide benefits to others up to the point where she would be sacrificing something of moral significance. In the face of noncompliance, this would require affluent individuals in HICs to give away much more of their wealth and time than most people think they are obligated to give.

To some theorists, the implications of Singer's view seem unfair. If each of us were to do our duty – that is, if we had full compliance with duties of beneficence – then each of us would have to contribute only a little. Now, the objection goes, many people are not even contributing that little amount (set aside the people who are make things worse). Why should I have to do so much more because they are not doing their part? This apparent unfairness leads Liam Murphy to the view that individual agents are not obliged to do more than they would have to do under conditions of full compliance.[84] He writes: "a principle of beneficence should not increase its demands on agents as expected compliance with the principle by other agents decreases."[85]

Murphy has surely identified something important here. It would be unfair to make those who are willing to do their part shoulder all the burdens of the rescues that should be collectively provided for. However, the agents on whom obligations of beneficence fall are not the only parties who are treated unfairly. As Michael Ridge points out, if we accept Murphy's view, then all the burden of noncompliance falls on the people

---

[84] Liam Murphy, *Moral Demands in Nonideal Theory* (Oxford: Oxford University Press, 2000). Note that Murphy does express some uncertainty about following through with this principle to the case of extreme poverty ("The Demands of Beneficence," *Philosophy & Public Affairs* 22 [1993]: 267–292, at 276–277).

[85] This is what Murphy labels the "compliance condition" (ibid., p. 278).

who are in need of our help.[86] Moreover, these people are the people who are already most unfortunate! That seems even more unfair. Instead, Ridge suggests, in cases where not everyone does what they should, we need to distribute fairly the burdens of noncompliance. In cases where some of the parties involved are much better off than others, fairness will demand that more of the burdens of noncompliance should fall on the better-off party.

To make this idea more concrete, suppose that if everyone did what they should, then each affluent person in the United Kingdom would have a duty to contribute £2,000 on the basis of beneficence as a contribution to alleviating the worst effects of global poverty. Not everyone does this, and so many people in the world suffer from malnutrition and preventable diseases of poverty who otherwise would not. It would be unfair to ask all the people in the United Kingdom who are willing to do their part to contribute substantially more in order to make up the gap. On the other hand, it would be unfair to ask people living in extreme poverty to continue to suffer from easily preventable illness so as to save affluent Brits money. There will be unfairness either way for which we can blame the people who are not contributing anything. But between affluent Brits and the global poor, it is surely the former who should shoulder most of the burden of this noncompliance. On the assumption that there are sufficient opportunities for affluent Brits to continue to give more money to effectively alleviate extreme poverty, those who give should be doing so up to the point where it has a nontrivial impact on their household's well-being. For the typical affluent British household, we would expect this to be thousands of pounds more than they would have to give under full compliance.

Finally, consider the implications of our discussion for clinicians in a wealthy country like the United States where 11.1 percent of the adult population under age sixty-five is uninsured[87] and 23 percent are considered underinsured.[88] These people either cannot access needed care or face

---

[86] "Fairness and Non-Compliance," in Brian Feltham and John Cottingham (eds.), *Partiality and Impartiality* (Oxford: Oxford University Press, 2010): 194–222.

[87] These 2018 data come from Centers for Disease Control and Prevention, "Health Insurance Coverage" (available at www.cdc.gov/nchs/fastats/health-insurance.htm; accessed August 18, 2020).

[88] "Underinsured" is defined by the Commonwealth Fund as someone with health insurance whose out-of-pocket costs, excluding premiums, are 10 percent or more of household income (5 percent if poor), or whose deductible is 5 percent or more of household income (Sara Collins, Petra Rasmussen, Sophie Beutel, and Michelle Doty, "The Problem of Underinsurance and How Rising Deductibles Will Make It Worse. The Commonwealth Fund [2015]"; available at www.commonwealthfund.org/publications/issue-briefs/2015/may/problem-of-underinsurance).

large out-of-pocket expenditures and medical debt when they do. As we argue in the following section, the health care system in the United States is a long way from meeting the demands of distributive justice. What obligations do clinicians, such as physicians, have to provide care to such patients?

We maintain that these obligations are quite substantial. The need is great, physicians have the skills to meet the need, and many could do so without great personal hardship. Thus, it is plausible that they have perfect duties of beneficence to provide a substantial amount of care without charge or at a minimal cost. For example, a physician who has a private practice might charge patients on the basis of a sliding scale of fees proportionate to patients' ability to pay; alternatively, they might charge the same amount for most patients while setting aside a number of appointments per week in which they serve indigent or uninsured patients for free.[89]

Now, it is true that if the health care system were reformed, then individual physicians would not have to volunteer their time to treat poorer patients. It is also true that if all physicians volunteered time, then each would have only a small contribution to make. But neither of these conditions is met in the actual world. Each individual physician therefore has the duty to do considerably more than they ideally would to provide care for patients who would otherwise go without.

Note, finally, that we have been discussing only physicians' general duty to provide care to those in need – that is, a duty grounded in the physicians' ability to provide assistance at relatively low cost to themselves. One might think that physicians have further, *special* duties to provide care to the needy that are grounded in the role morality of physicians. It is undisputed that physicians have some role-based duties to their existing patients.[90] In addition to such duties as truth-telling and confidentiality, which are derivable from respect for patient autonomy, physicians have

---

[89] Strictly speaking, physicians would not have to fulfill their duties of beneficence by providing medical care to those who cannot otherwise access it. They could, instead, practice in a lucrative specialty and donate a substantial proportion of their earnings.

[90] A classic statement of physicians' duties that reflected traditional paternalism toward patients is the Hippocratic Oath (reprinted in David DeGrazia, Thomas Mappes, and Jeffrey Brand-Ballard [eds.], *Biomedical Ethics*, 7th ed. [New York: McGraw-Hill, 2011], 69–70). For more up-to-date statements, see the American Medical Association Council on Ethical and Judicial Affairs, "Fundamental Elements of the Patient–Physician Relationship," in *Code of Medical Ethics: Current Opinions with Annotations* (2008–2009 edition); and Edmund Pellegrino, "The Virtuous Physician and the Ends of Medicine," in Earl Shelp (ed.), *Virtue and Medicine* (Dordrecht: Reidel, 1985), 248–253.

obligations to provide their patients excellent medical care and actively support their capacity to make autonomous medical decisions, which are role-based duties of beneficence. One might think that such duties to one's existing patients do not exhaust the content of the physician's role. A more expansive view of the role morality of physicians – and other health care practitioners – might include wider duties to improve health care provision within their society or abroad.[91]

6.4 Domestic Justice: The Right to Access Health Care

In nearly all HICs, all citizens have access to a wide range of medical services as a matter of government policy. The United States is one important exception where, as just noted, there are still millions of people who lack, or have inadequate, health insurance. The situation in low- and middle-income countries (LMICs) varies tremendously. For example, Thailand has massively expanded its publicly funded health insurance schemes over the last two decades to cover millions more people and to cover more services; while total health expenditure grew from 3.1 percent of GDP in 2000 to 3.7 percent of GDP in 2017, the proportion that is public expenditure nearly doubled – to 2.9 percent of GDP – and private expenditure nearly halved.[92] By contrast, in India, 70 percent of health care expenditure is still private and nearly 90 percent of that is paid out of pocket. Disparities in care in India are vast: around 40 percent of women reported giving birth in a health facility for their most recent birth in 2005–2006, and women in the highest wealth quintile were six times more likely to do so than women in the lowest quintile.[93] Nonetheless, with the encouragement of the WHO, many countries are pushing to provide more health care coverage to more of their population.[94]

Many people regard access to affordable health care as a right.[95] A right to health – and correlatively to health care – is enshrined in the

---

[91] See, e.g., Project of the ABIM Foundation, ACP-ASIM Foundation, and European Federation of Internal Medicine, "Medical Professionalism in the New Millennium," *Annals of Internal Medicine* 136 (2002): 243–246.

[92] The World Bank, *World Bank Open Data* (available at https://data.worldbank.org; accessed August 18, 2020).

[93] Yarlini Balarajan, Selvaraj Selvaraj, and S. V. Subramanian, "Health Care and Equity in India," *The Lancet* 377 (2011): 505–515.

[94] World Health Organization, "Universal Health Coverage" (available at www.who.int/health-topics/universal-health-coverage; accessed August 18, 2020).

[95] According to WHO, in this context "affordable" means that there is "a system for financing health services so people do not suffer financial hardship when using them" (World Health Organization,

constitution of many states.[96] It is recognized in multiple human rights documents, including the International Covenant on Economic, Social and Cultural Rights, the realization of which includes "creation of conditions which would assure to all medical service and medical attention in the event of sickness."[97] And the Sustainable Development Goals (SDGs) that replaced the Millennium Developmental Goals include among the targets for Goal 3: "Achieve universal health coverage, including financial risk protection, access to quality essential health-care services and access to safe, effective, quality and affordable essential medicines and vaccines for all."[98]

Here, we argue that individuals have a right to affordable health care by showing how it follows from the liberal egalitarianism we have defended.[99] We also show that the right will have limits: it does not require that all potentially beneficial services be provided for free, nor that all such services must be covered.

The first step is to note that diminished health can have an enormous negative impact on an individual's well-being. Indeed, on most measures, the severity of a disease is a function of its impact on patients' quality of life and reduction in their lifespan.[100] Daniels takes the negative effects of ill-health on the range of opportunities open to individuals to be so significant that universal access to health care is necessary for equality of opportunity.[101] We do not need to go so far in order to accept that health and so access to health care are frequently very important for a flourishing life. In large part, the impact of disease on well-being is unchosen: individuals do not usually become ill as a result of informed, voluntary decisions. (Possible exceptions are the source of much debate over personal responsibility for health.) Hence, it is presumptively unjust for individuals to bear the costs of averting or treating ill health and premature death.

"Questions and Answers on Universal Health Coverage"; available at www.who.int/healthsystems/topics/financing/uhc_qa/en/; accessed August 18, 2020).

[96] Eleanor Kinney and Brian Clark, "Provisions for Health and Health Care in the Constitutions of the Countries of the World," *Cornell International Law Journal* 37 (2004): 285–355.

[97] United Nations, *International Covenant on Economic, Social, and Cultural Rights*, Article 12.

[98] United Nations, *Sustainable Development Goals* (available at www.un.org/sustainabledevelopment/health/; accessed August 18, 2020).

[99] For more discussion and alternative arguments for a right to health care, see Norman Daniels, in Edward Zalta (ed.), "Justice and Access to Health Care," *Stanford Encyclopedia of Philosophy* (Winter 2017 edition; available at https://plato.stanford.edu/entries/justice-healthcareaccess/).

[100] This is true, for example, of both quality-adjusted life-years (QALYs) and disability-adjusted life-years (DALYs).

[101] Norman Daniels, *Just Health Care* (New York: Cambridge University Press, 1985).

Second, health care has some distinctive features that make it unlike some other goods – such as nutritious food or potable water – that are also essential prerequisites to human flourishing. Unlike food and water, individual needs for health care are often hard to predict and can be extremely expensive. For some high-cost, high-value procedures – for example, ICU treatment for victims of traffic accidents – it would be impossible to ensure that everyone had the money to pay out of pocket for needed care. The uncertainty and variability in need for health care, along with its potentially high cost, means that some sort of risk pooling is necessary. One might then think that it would be sufficient for the state to ensure that everyone had the money to buy insurance against excessive health costs. But here the partial *predictability* of health care needs becomes a problem. Some people, such as those with diagnosed chronic conditions that require ongoing treatment, will definitely have high health care costs. Others – such as young, currently healthy individuals – know that they are much less likely to need care in the short term. A free market in health insurance therefore leads to *adverse selection*, as those who know themselves more likely to need health care are more likely to buy insurance than those who expect to use less health care. Insurers must then increase insurance premiums to cover the increase in expected per capita use of health care. Increased premiums price more of the healthier people out of the market, further driving up per capita costs, and so on. Affordable health insurance therefore requires some way to prevent adverse selection. On a national scale, this requires state intervention to ensure that everyone has access to health care.

Liberal egalitarianism entails a right to access affordable health care. It does not entail that all services must be supplied for free, only that costs involved are ones that people can afford without risk of impoverishment. Nor does it entail that all medically beneficial services must be provided to those who would benefit from them. The right to health care derives from the same foundation as other justice-based claims to resources. Since the total resources available are limited, there will inevitably be trade-offs, as we described above. Those may involve trade-offs between health care and other important goods, as well as trade-offs among health care services that would benefit populations with different health needs.

Last, though liberal egalitarianism entails a right to access affordable health care, it does not tell us what mechanism should be used in order to fulfill this right. Some HICs, such as the United Kingdom, provide most care through a public health care system. Others have substantial private provision, but the government is the main payer, as in Canada. Still others have multiple payers, but mandatory health insurance and premiums that reflect ability to pay, as in Germany. Our view of justice does not favor one of these institutional structures over another. Any of them can implement a right to health care access. The current US approach – with its gaps in insurance coverage and high out-of-pocket costs even for individuals who have insurance – clearly cannot.

6.5   Global Injustice: Intellectual Property Laws and Pharmaceuticals

Of the approximately $240 billion spent each year on medical research,[102] about three-fifths is spent by for-profit companies. The vast majority of research supported by for-profit companies (henceforth "companies") is aimed at developing and testing new drugs and devices that they hope to market. The development of new medical technologies is expensive. In order to receive marketing authorization – from, say, Health Canada, the US Food and Drug Administration, or the European Medicines Agency – a company must demonstrate the safety and efficacy of the new drug or device. This requires multiple scientific studies in humans and nonhuman animals. Most promising drugs and devices fail during the testing process. The revenue from successful products must therefore make up for the costs of all this research. The primary function of patent law is to incentivize companies to develop new drugs and devices, despite the substantial upfront costs of doing so.[103]

A patent on an invention grants its holder exclusive property rights over the invention for an extended period of time. For pharmaceutical products – we focus on drugs here for ease of writing, but the same points apply to devices – the resulting monopoly allows companies to set prices far greater than the marginal cost of manufacture. As a result, brand-name drugs under patent are typically much more expensive than those whose patent has expired and which therefore face competition from the manufacturers of generic copies. In 1994, the WTO adopted the Agreement on Trade-Related Aspects of Intellectual Property Rights (TRIPS agreement). This legally binding agreement requires all WTO members to provide

---

[102] John-Arne Røttingen et al., "Mapping of Available Health Research and Development Data: What's There, What's Missing, and What Role Is There for a Global Observatory?," *Lancet* 382 (2013): 1286–1307.

[103] This is the commonly accepted *instrumental* justification for intellectual property. For discussion of alternative justifications, see Justin Hughes, "The Philosophy of Intellectual Property," *Georgetown Law Journal* 77 (1988): 287–366.

protections for intellectual property rights, including patents on inventions that extend for at least twenty years.[104]

The global intellectual property regime has two especially pernicious effects on poorer patients. First, monopoly pricing means that many pharmaceutical products in LMICs are priced out of the reach of the majority of the patients who could benefit from them. For example, most patients in India are unable to afford highly effective treatments for breast cancer and leukemia.[105] Second, because revenue from inventions is directly tied to sales, the international patent regime encourages companies to focus on developing patentable technologies for conditions that affect richer patient groups. This means that research into diseases that predominantly affect the poor – including many infectious tropical diseases – is woefully underfunded relative to the disease burden.[106]

Is the lack of affordable drugs for non-rich patients in LMICs unjust? Two argumentative strategies have been proposed to show that it is.

The first argumentative strategy, championed by Thomas Pogge, is to contend that the international patent regime is unjust because it harms patients.[107] Since all political views accept that we should not harm innocent others without their consent (or some weighty countervailing consideration), if Pogge is correct, then the international patent regime is illegitimate.[108] Pogge's view relies on several key normative and empirical premises.

---

[104] Developing countries were granted a transition period until 2005. "Least developed countries" have had this transition period for pharmaceutical products extended until at least 2033 (www.wto .org/english/news_e/news15_e/trip_06nov15_e.htm). The Doha Declaration on the TRIPS Agreement and Public Health in 2001 clarified that the TRIPS agreement "should be interpreted and implemented in a manner supportive of WTO Members' right to protect public health and, in particular, to promote access to medicines for all" (www.wto.org/english/thewto_e/ minist_e/min01_e/mindecl_trips_e.htm). Use of the exceptions noted in the Doha Declaration has been limited and fiercely contested by HIC governments and pharmaceutical companies.

[105] Daniel Goldstein et al., "A Global Comparison of the Cost of Patented Cancer Drugs in Relation to Global Differences in Wealth," *Oncotarget* 8 (2017): 71548–71555.

[106] Nick Chapman et al., "Neglected Disease Research and Development: Reaching New Heights," *G-FINDER Report* (2018) (available at www.indiaenvironmentportal.org.in/files/file/G-FINDER_ Full_report.pdf).

[107] Thomas Pogge, "Are We Violating the Human Rights of the World's Poor?," *Yale Human Rights & Development Law Journal* 14 (2011): 1–33. Though there has been some debate about whether the global institutional order as a whole harms the global poor, we find the arguments regarding the harmfulness of the international patent regime, in particular, compelling. For some critical discussion, see Mathias Risse, "How Does the Global Order Harm the Poor?," *Philosophy & Public Affairs* 33 (2005): 349–376.

[108] Might the harms caused by the international patent regime be *the result of a fair competition* and so not wrong the victims (Chapter 4)? The harms to companies whose products do not succeed plausibly do not involve wrong-doing for this reason. The harms we are discussing here, though, are harms to patients who are not part of the competition at all, so we answer our question negatively.

One key premise, that the putative victims of harm did not consent to it, is highly plausible: though the governments of all parties to the TRIPS agreement did agree to it, it is implausible that this agreement constitutes the *consent* of *patients* affected by the agreement. For one, membership of the WTO is not possible without accepting TRIPS, and the costs to a country's economy of not being in the WTO are very high. Thus, the voluntariness of a particular government's decision to implement its TRIPS obligations is questionable. Perhaps more importantly, individuals in WTO countries are very unlikely to have known about TRIPS before its implementation, unlikely to have anticipated that their representatives would be acceding to foreign powers restricting their access to medicines, and (in many cases) unlikely to have had a real say in who those representatives were.

A second premise of Pogge's harm argument is that the international patent regime causes harm. This requires showing that patients are worse off than they otherwise would be.[109] If we hold fixed the state of medical knowledge, this claim seems highly plausible. We argued in the previous section that persons have a right to health care, which will include a right to access important medicines. High prices for medicines can interfere with the realization of that right. (Even though we construed the right to health care as a right of individuals against their own government or society, the high drug prices permitted by the current international regime interfere with a state's ability to meet the obligations entailed by this right.) Moreover, up until recently, many countries had weaker intellectual property laws, which allowed for the production of generic medications much earlier than the current system. For example, until 2005 India allowed patents only on processes, not products, and for much shorter periods than the twenty years TRIPS prescribes.[110] As a result, India developed a huge generic medicines industry that supplied domestic and international markets. The patent regime that the TRIPS agreement brought in therefore appears to be reducing access to needed medicines.

One might respond that this argument ignores the gains in terms of medical innovation that result from stricter patent laws. Certainly, patients now are worse off with respect to *existing medicines* than if we abandoned patents, but doing so would cause future patients to miss out on preventive and treatment interventions for diseases that we cannot currently address. Thus, the argument that the current international intellectual property

---

[109] See Chapter 4 for a discussion of how to conceptualize harm.
[110] The product/process distinction meant that competitors could manufacture identical drugs if they could find an alternative process by which to make them.

regime harms patients must show that there are alternatives to the current system that would be as good or better for future patients. We turn to this point shortly.

The second argumentative strategy for showing that lack of affordable drugs in LMICs is unjust derives from the cosmopolitan view that we defended earlier. Cosmopolitans also have reason to criticize the international patent regime. It benefits some of the best-off people in the world, such as the shareholders of pharmaceutical companies. Moreover, the benefits it provides them – in terms of actual welfare gains – are very small, since they are already materially well-off. Their gains come at the expense of poor patients who would otherwise have access to medical interventions that would provide substantial health benefits and sometimes save their lives. No matter how we treat the trade-off between gains to the disadvantaged and maximizing total benefits, the current system of patent protection looks unjust.

This cosmopolitan argument, like the harm argument, relies on the claim that there are alternatives to the present system. Such alternatives should be ones that would still lead to the development of beneficial medical interventions, but make drugs more affordable, more attuned to global health needs, or both. The literature on drug development suggests multiple alternative models.[111]

Some alternatives to the intellectual property system would involve minimal deviation from the current system. For example, the prices of existing medications could be dramatically reduced if individual countries made much greater use of compulsory licensing. A compulsory license involves a government permitting manufacture of generic versions of a drug that is still under patent provided that the manufacturers pay the patent holder a reasonable fee. Though permitted under the TRIPS agreement, the use of compulsory licenses in the context of pharmaceutical patents is strongly discouraged by richer countries and has been subject to legal challenges where used.[112] One might argue that extensive use of compulsory licenses by LMICs would disincentivize research by reducing the expected profits for patent-holders. This seems unlikely: the vast

---

[111] For a number of examples, see Thomas Pogge, Matthew Rimmer and Kim Rubenstein (eds.), *Incentives for Global Public Health* (Cambridge: Cambridge University Press, 2010).

[112] For example, Thailand has issued a number of compulsory licenses for expensive drugs, including second-line antiretrovirals for HIV/AIDS. This led to objections from the European Union Commissioner for External Trade, the United States Trade Representative putting Thailand on its "Special 301" Priority Watch List, and Abbott Laboratories, one of the patent holders, temporarily refusing to register new drugs in Thailand. See Jonathan Burton-Macleod, "Tipping Point: Thai Compulsory Licences Redefine Essential Medicines Debate," in Pogge, Rimmer, and Rubenstein, *Incentives for Public Global Health*, 406–424.

majority of the patients who can afford expensive patented drugs are living in HICs, and so allowing patients in LMICs to obtain cheaper versions of them would not substantially reduce sales.[113]

Other proposals would involve bigger changes to the current system for drug development. Some writers have suggested that prizes could provide the necessary incentive for private actors to innovate.[114] Thus, for example, the United Kingdom's recent Longitude Prize offers £10 million for the creation of "a cheap, accurate, rapid and easy-to-use point of care test kit for bacterial infections," as a tool to combat antibiotic resistance.[115] Pogge proposed a related scheme – the Health Impact Fund – whereby companies could take out an alternative patent which would mean they were reimbursed proportional to the actual effect of a new drug on the burden of disease.[116] Finally, a great deal of health research is already directly publicly funded, for example, via competitively allocated grants to academic researchers.[117] The development of new interventions for diseases of poverty already relies heavily on such funding sources.[118] One might then imagine expanding public support for developing new health technologies that could be privately manufactured without patent protection or with licenses conditional on affordable pricing.

The current international intellectual property regime is unjust. It substantially reduces access to important medicines for billions of people for benefits that could be better realized in other ways. Governments, especially those of richer countries, have a duty to permit the manufacture of affordable existing medicines and to adopt alternative means to incentivize the development of new ones.

---

[113] Jens Plahte, "Tiered Pricing of Vaccines: A Win-Win-Win Situation, not a Subsidy," *Lancet Infectious Diseases* 5 (2005): 58–63.

[114] William Fisher and Talha Syed, "A Prize System as a Partial Solution to the Health Crisis in the Developing World," in Pogge, Rimmer, and Rubenstein, *Incentives for Public Global Health*, 181–208.

[115] Nesta, "Longitude Prize" (https://longitudeprize.org; accessed September 28, 2020).

[116] Health Impact Fund (http://healthimpactfund.org; accessed September 28, 2020).

[117] Røttingen et al. estimated 30 percent of health research funding is from government entities ("Mapping of Available Health Research and Development Data").

[118] For example, BRV-PV (or Rotasil) is a new oral rotavirus vaccine that is expected to be much cheaper than existing vaccines. Its development was supported by PATH (a nonprofit funded largely by governments and foundations) using BRV strains developed by the US National Institutes of Health, and it is manufactured by the Serum Institute of India (a private company). See Prasad Kulkarni et al., "A Randomized Phase III Clinical Trial to Assess the Efficacy of a Bovine-Human Reassortant Pentavalent Rotavirus Vaccine in Indian Infants," *Vaccine* 35 (2017): 6228–6237.

CHAPTER 7

Moral Status

7.1 Introduction

As earlier chapters have discussed, morality generates obligations pertaining to nonmaleficence, autonomy rights, distributive justice, and beneficence. But to whom are these obligations owed? To address this question is to engage the concept of *moral status*.

Someone who gratuitously harms another person not only does something wrong; she also wrongs the victim. By contrast, someone who gratuitously destroys a beautiful painting or a functioning car does not wrong the painting or the car. If she acts wrongly it is because she wrongs other people who have legitimate claims over the objects in question. This is because persons have moral status whereas paintings and cars do not. Thus far what we have said is uncontroversial. What about nonhuman animals (henceforth "animals")? We have an obligation not to be cruel to dogs, but does such cruelty wrong the dogs themselves, or does it wrong only persons such as the dogs' caretakers? Are any animals persons? What about those human beings who are not persons on some definitions of the term – for example, embryos, fetuses, and individuals in irreversibly unconscious states? Do they have moral status? These are among the issues on which disagreement persists.

This chapter explores these and related questions. The discussion begins with the concept of moral status, unpacking its elements and commenting on its usefulness. It proceeds to a sketch of our account of moral status, which is presented in the form of five theses. The remainder of the theoretical portion of the chapter gradually elaborates and defends these theses, in part by contrasting them with and arguing against alternative positions. With our account in hand, we explore ethical implications for research involving human embryos, rodents, and great apes.

7.2   The Concept of Moral Status

What is moral status? Persons have it, paintings and cars do not, while dogs and fetuses might. To have moral status, an individual must be vulnerable to harm or wrongdoing. More specifically, a being has moral status only if *it is for that being's sake* that the being should not be harmed, disrespected, or treated in some other morally problematic fashion. So, if dogs have moral status, a compelling reason for not kicking dogs is that doing so harms them for no good reason. If, on the other hand, dogs lack moral status, kicking them would be wrong only insofar as it implicated the interests of other individuals, presumably persons.

These points are captured by this formal analysis: *X has moral status if and only if (1) moral agents have obligations regarding their treatment of X and (2) it is for X's sake that moral agents have these obligations.* In developing an account of moral status, we find it helpful to employ the concept of interests. If someone has an interest in something, then that interest can be promoted or set back, which means that matters can go well or badly for that individual with regard to that interest. We find it plausible that only beings with interests have moral status, such that *X has moral status if and only if (1) X has interests, (2) moral agents have obligations regarding their treatment of X, and (3) these obligations are based on X's interests.* We can explain the fact that paintings and cars lack moral status on the grounds that they lack interests. A plausible explanation for some people's belief that not only persons and sentient animals but also insentient animals and plants have moral status is that these people believe that all living things have interests. Meanwhile, much of the controversy over whether embryos and fetuses have moral status can be explained by differing opinions as to whether these prenatal human beings have interests – including an interest in surviving.[1]

One might wonder about the usefulness of the concept of moral status.[2] Our formal analysis suggests that whatever we want to say about moral

---

[1] Some might construe the concept of moral status broadly enough to include sacred objects – such as shrines or idols – even if they do not have interests. On this broad construal, moral status characterizes anything whose properties provide basic or nonderivative reasons to moral agents to treat the thing in question in particular ways (e.g., respectfully). We are skeptical of the idea that sacred objects matter nonderivatively, given that attributions of sacredness vary so much across different cultures, religions, and nations. Instead, we think that someone's regarding an object as sacred may give that person a reason to treat it in a certain way based on the object's significance to them. It may also give others a reason to treat it in a certain way in virtue of the interests of the person who regards it as sacred. None of this implies that the object has some independent moral status.

[2] Benjamin Sachs, "The Status of Moral Status," *Pacific Philosophical Quarterly* 92 (2011): 87–104.

status could be stated instead in terms of interests, obligations, and the basis of obligations. Instead of saying, for example, that dogs have moral status, we could say that moral agents have obligations regarding how they treat dogs that are based on the dogs' interests. If it is possible to reduce the concept of moral status in this way, then perhaps it is redundant. What does the concept of moral status add? First, it adds a measure of convenience. One can make a single claim – say, that dogs have moral status – rather than spelling out the three specific assertions embodied in the claim. In addition, the concept of moral status captures the global idea of *a being's mattering inherently* – mattering in way that is not simply a function of instrumental value to other beings.

One might challenge the usefulness of the concept of moral status in a different way. One might argue that while the concept conveniently captures the idea of a being's mattering inherently, so does the more familiar notion of *moral rights*. If possessing moral status is simply a matter of having moral rights, it might be simpler to speak only of rights. We disagree, because our conception of moral rights does not imply that beings with moral status are necessarily the same as beings with moral rights (see Chapter 3).[3] Indeed, the account we defend in this chapter attributes rights to only a subset of the individuals who have moral status.

7.3   A Sketch of Our Account

Our account of moral status advances five theses.

1.   *All and only sentient beings have moral status.* The reason *only* sentient beings have moral status is that moral status requires having interests, which only sentient beings possess. The reason *all* sentient beings have moral status is that there is no justification for denying the moral importance of the interests of any being who has interests. For example, the principle of nonmaleficence would appear at first glance to apply to all beings who can be harmed, and, on our view, there is no compelling reason to restrict its application to only some beings who can be harmed.

2.   *Sentient beings are subject to equal consequentialist consideration in the sense that (1) their comparable interests count or matter equally, and (2) utilitarian trade-offs among individuals' interests are permissible unless*

---

[3] For an example of a theorist who conflates the two concepts, see Peter Carruthers, *The Animals Issue* (Cambridge: Cambridge University Press, 1992), 1.

prohibited by rights. Where two sentient individuals have roughly the same thing at stake, such as avoiding a moderate amount of pain, their interests count equally, so that, for example, it is as morally problematic to cause moderate pain in one individual as in the other. At the same time, if causing one individual moderate pain is necessary in order to prevent a greater amount of harm to another individual, sacrifice of the first individual's interest in avoiding pain is permissible unless they have rights that block such a trade-off.

3. *Different individuals have different interests and quantities of interests.* For example, a cognitively simple sentient animal may have interests in avoiding unpleasant experiences and having pleasant ones, but little else. A person ordinarily has these same interests and more – such as interests in having meaningful relationships with other people, completing valued projects, and living in accordance with their values. The person has a much broader array of interests than the cognitively simple animal. For this reason, equal consequentialist consideration would ordinarily accord a much higher priority to preserving the person's life.

4. *Some individuals have moral rights that block appeals to the greater good as justifications for sacrificing their interests.* In consequentialist reasoning, comparable interests count equally, but some individuals' interests may be sacrificed for a greater gain to others. Rights protect rights-holders from such trade-offs in a way that makes sense of the idea that *individual rights-holders* (not just their interests) count significantly and equally. We argue that persons have moral rights in virtue of having a narrative identity. Those sentient beings who have some nontrivial awareness of themselves over time but lack a full-fledged narrative identity have rights too, but the threshold for overriding them is lower.

5. *Some individuals who have moral status lack moral rights.* We hold, at a first approximation, that sentient nonpersons who lack self-awareness lack moral rights.

The next several sections elaborate and defend these central theses while considering a variety of alternative views about moral status.

7.4 Sentience as Necessary and Sufficient for Moral Status

The Relevance of Personhood

Every ethical theory that is respected today concurs with common morality that, whoever else may have moral status, persons do. Seeing no reason to challenge this claim, we take it as axiomatic. Personhood, then, is *sufficient* for moral status. Is personhood also *necessary?*

As noted in several places in this book, the concept of a person is contested, and, therefore, who should count as persons is contested. In this book, we adopt a philosophical conception of personhood that traces back to John Locke. Locke wrote that the term *person* refers to "a thinking intelligent being, that has reason and reflection, and can consider itself as itself, the same thinking thing, in different times and places."[4] This and many similar definitions emphasize temporal self-awareness – awareness of oneself as persisting over time – and the capacity to reason. For the purposes of ethics, including the need to develop a model of moral status, we find it most useful to interpret this concept of personhood in terms of "narrative identity." A person is a being who has a narrative identity – a *relatively complex understanding of herself as persisting over time and as having an implicit life story.* Such individuals are agents with the ability to make and pursue plans; they have episodic memory (the ability to remember experiences from their own past). *Human* persons tend to be highly social and to view certain other individuals as figuring significantly in their own life stories. Human persons include at least all cognitively normal human beings beyond the toddler years. We argue in a later section that persons in our sense – individuals with narrative identities – have rights grounded in certain longer-term interests that such beings possess. We also argue, for different reasons, that certain other human beings should also be extended rights.

On our neo-Lockean account, persons include at least all cognitively normal human beings beyond the toddler years. But human newborns are not persons on this view, yet they surely have moral status. So personhood cannot be necessary for moral status.

One might reply as follows: some philosophers and nearly all lawyers and laypeople use the term "person" in such a way that includes newborns.[5] From this standpoint of popular usage, the obvious moral status of human newborns is consistent with the idea that being a person is necessary for moral status.

These are fair points. However, they are consistent with the claim that personhood *as we have defined "person"* cannot be necessary for moral status. In addition, we think that there are compelling grounds for denying

[4] John Locke, *Essay Concerning Human Understanding*, 2nd ed. (1694), Bk. II, chap. 27.
[5] Among philosophers, see, e.g., Marya Schechtman, *Staying Alive* (Oxford: Oxford University Press, 2014).

that personhood is necessary that do not appeal to the moral status of newborns or any other human beings. We need only invoke the moral status of certain animals.

Consider an ordinary bird. Birds are not persons in our sense – or in any other sense that attempts to capture the ordinary descriptive sense of the term.[6] Yet it is wrong to treat a bird cruelly. Imagine someone repeatedly beating a bird until she dies. Assume the bird was not attacking someone or providing some other possible justification for the violence. This is a clear instance of gratuitous and substantial harm – in a word, *cruelty*. We know cruelty is morally wrong. But why is it wrong in the present case? Is it because beating the bird would damage someone's property? Setting aside the question of whether birds can rightfully be considered property, we may stipulate that the bird is not a pet or a farm animal. She has no human caretaker or "owner." Might the wrongness come down to the fact that cruelty to animals offends the sensibilities of those who care about animals? This response is inadequate. First, the bird-thrashing could occur in circumstances in which one can be sure that no other person will learn about it – yet such secrecy would not defeat the judgment that the cruelty is wrong. Second, if birds truly lacked moral status, then it *would* seem permissible to consider birds in one's lawful possession as one's property. In that case, the possibility that cruelty to one's bird would offend others would seem insufficient to overturn the presumption that one may do as one pleases with one's property so long as one does not *harm* others who have moral status.

The only adequate explanation of the wrongness of cruelty to animals attributes moral status to its victims. Birds and many other animals have an experiential well-being that makes them possible victims of cruelty. All such sentient creatures have moral status. Yet not all of these animals are persons. So personhood cannot be necessary for moral status.

The Irrelevance of Species Membership

Personhood is sufficient but not necessary for moral status. What about membership in our species, *Homo sapiens*? Is being human in this biological sense necessary or sufficient for moral status? We have already partly

---

[6] One might use the term "person" in a moralized sense to mean "being with full moral status." In this case someone who believes that all sentient beings have equal moral status would classify birds as persons. See, e.g., Gary Francione, *Animals as Persons* (New York: Columbia University Press, 2009).

answered this question by noting that animals can have moral status. So being human cannot be necessary. Might it be sufficient?

If so, then every member of our species would have moral status. This strikes us as implausible in some instances and as theoretically dubious. The idea that being human is sufficient for moral status implies that not only all postnatal human beings are persons, but so are fetuses and embryos. This will strike some people – but, to be sure, not some others – as counterintuitive. But the thesis in question also implies that human *corpses* (as members of our species) have moral status. Yet we hold that corpses – as distinct from the previously living human beings – do not have interests, so they cannot have moral status. Even if only *living* human beings count, this would still imply that living human beings whose neurological impairment precludes their ever having conscious experience – such as anencephalic infants – have moral status. We therefore find the attribution of moral status to all human beings, or even all living human beings, highly doubtful.[7]

There is also a theoretical difficulty: it is dubious that the biological factor of species membership can carry so much moral importance. To be a *Homo sapiens* is, from a biological standpoint, nothing more than being a member of a certain cluster of animals who share a particular evolutionary lineage. On its own this is not a reasonable basis for moral status. It would have to be something about the species in question – some characteristic of its members – that underlies human beings' moral status. But whatever the relevant characteristic is – whether personhood, moral agency, rationality, or something else – not all members of our species possess it, even potentially. It is certainly *characteristic* of human beings that they are, or develop into, persons, moral agents, rational beings, and so on, but not every human being does. One might claim that every member of our species is *of a kind* whose members characteristically develop in these ways.[8] That is true. But every human being is a member of innumerable kinds, including many biological ones. For example, while every human

---

[7] Ronald Dworkin argues that common attitudes about human beings and human death suggest that all human life is, in some important sense, sacred (*Life's Dominion* [New York: Vintage, 1993], chap. 3) – a thesis that might be understood to imply, in our terminology, that all human life has at least some moral status. Although Dworkin's discussion of common attitudes toward human life is insightful, we believe many of these attitudes represent prejudices or overgeneralizations that will not stand up under critical scrutiny. See also note 1.

[8] See, e.g., Carl Cohen, "The Case for the Use of Animals in Biomedical Research," *New England Journal of Medicine* 315 (1986): 865–870.

being is a member of the kind *Homo sapiens*, each is also a member of the kinds hominid, primate, mammal, vertebrate, animal, organism, and so forth. It is arbitrary to single out species as the one biological kind that bears on moral status.

Sentience and Interests

Sentience is the capacity to experience feelings or, more precisely, to have at least some pleasant or unpleasant experiences. Feelings include conscious *sensations* such as pleasant tactile sensations, pain, discomfort, and nausea; *emotional states* such as excitement, delight, surprise, fear, and anxiety; and *moods* such as cheerfulness and irritability. A creature who is capable of having any of these feelings, even just pain, is sentient. Moreover, as we understand the concept of desire, creatures who can have desires are sentient. That is because having a desire for some state of affairs – say, one's eating food – involves a tendency, or disposition, to feel satisfaction or other pleasant experiences at the satisfaction of the desire and to feel frustration or other unpleasant feelings at the frustration of this desire. Put another way, to have a desire for something involves caring about it, and caring is impossible without the capacity for pleasant or unpleasant experiences.

In Chapter 8, we argue that both enjoyment and the satisfaction of desires that are relevant to one's life story are components of well-being. The argument just given implies that all and only sentient beings have interests that contribute to well-being. At a minimum sentient beings possess an interest in not experiencing pain, distress, or other unpleasant experiences – *suffering*, in a broad sense of the term. Our analysis of the concept of moral status suggested that having interests is necessary for having moral status. Moreover, we see no compelling reason to deny the moral importance of *any* being's interests. The fact that an action would cause suffering seems like a reason not to perform the act. So having interests is also sufficient for grounding obligations in moral agents – at the very least, an obligation not to harm wantonly any being with interests. This means that having interests is sufficient for moral status.

To have interests in the sense we are discussing is to have a welfare or a stake in how things go for one. But for an individual to have a welfare means that matters can go better or worse for them *from the individual's own point of view*. Only beings capable of consciousness can have a point of view in this prudential sense and so have interests. Hence we think all and only sentient beings – whose consciousness features pleasant or unpleasant experiences – have interests and so have moral status.[9]

Which Beings Are Sentient?

In addition to (sufficiently mature) human beings, many animals are sentient. But which ones? Might plants also be sentient? Here a consideration of evidence is indispensable. The major types of evidence for particular types of mental states in nonhuman creatures are (1) behavioral evidence; (2) neuroanatomical evidence, in particular, the presence of a nervous system and brain parts associated with certain kinds of mental states; and (3) evolutionary-functional considerations.

Arguments for the attribution to nonhuman creatures of mental states involving sentience proceed from the premise that mature, typically developing human beings have the mental states in question. In each case, the reasoning takes the form of an argument by analogy – that a particular type of animal is similar enough to human beings in relevant ways to support an inference that members of that species can experience a particular mental state. For example, fish exhibit pain behaviors – that is, behaviors commonly associated with pain – in response to the application of a noxious chemical on their lips but decrease such behaviors after morphine is administered as an analgesic.[10] In this respect, the fish's behavior is much like a human's, consistent with the idea that both can experience pain and that analgesia can ameliorate it. Consider another example. Human anxiety is mediated by benzodiazepines, and human brains have receptors for these compounds. Research has demonstrated that the brains of many other vertebrate species also have benzodiazepine receptors, providing some evidence that members of these species can experience anxious states.[11] This thesis is further supported when animals with these same receptors engage in apparently anxious behaviors in vaguely threatening situations featuring novelty. A third example features a disanalogy between

---

[9] Some will insist that the biological "needs" of plants and insentient animals should qualify as interests, challenging our thesis that only sentient beings have interests and moral status. However, we believe such "needs" of insentient creatures have no more relevance to moral status than the "need" of a car to have gas. These entities need certain things *in order to function in their characteristic ways*, but the absence of any conscious, caring standpoint undermines the claim that they have a welfare and interests in any sense relevant to moral status.

[10] Lynne Sneddon, "The Evidence for Pain in Fish: The Use of Morphine as an Analgesic," *Applied Animal Behaviour Science* 83 (2003): 153–162.

[11] M. Nielsen, C. Braestrup, and R. Squires, "Evidence for a Late Evolutionary Appearance of a Brain-Specific Benzodiazepine Receptor," *Brain Research* 141 (1978): 342–346.

humans and nonhuman animals. Many insects fail to display pain behaviors in situations where we would expect that animals who could feel pain would feel pain. For example, locusts, aphids, and mantids continue to feed while being eaten and insects will put their full weight on injured limbs.[12] Humans in similar situations would feel pain and display self-protective behavior such as trying to escape or inhibitory behavior such as reducing weight on an injured limb. The behavioral disanalogy motivates doubt that the insects in question experience pain.

Although we cannot give comprehensive details here about the scientific evidence for sentience or about the proper interpretation of that evidence, we believe that conclusions drawn from available evidence, judiciously interpreted, can be summarized as follows.[13] There is overwhelming evidence that mammals and birds are sentient creatures. The evidence that reptiles are sentient is also quite strong; the evidence for amphibians, more intermediate. Meanwhile, the evidence that bony fishes and cephalopods (octopi, squid, and cuttlefish) are sentient is fairly strong. As for cartilaginous fishes such as sharks and stingrays, jawless fish such as lampreys and hagfish, and some invertebrates other than cephalopods such as crustaceans and insects, the evidence is mixed. For most other invertebrates (e.g., worms, jellyfish, urchins, sponges), the evidence suggests that they are probably not sentient. As for plants, although there is evidence that they can process information from their immediate environment and use that information to move their parts adaptively,[14] we doubt there is any evidence that they actually *feel* anything. The present picture of sentience among known creatures leaves much uncertainty, but it suggests that many animals – including mammals and birds and probably many others as well – are sentient, have an experiential welfare, and therefore have moral status.

While sufficiently mature human beings are paradigm instances of sentient beings, what about very immature members of our species? Embryos and early fetuses lack sufficient neurological development to be sentient. Indeed, based on what we know about the neuroanatomy of pain,

[12] C. H. Eisemann et al., "Do Insects Feel Pain? A Biological View," *Experientia* 40 (1984): 164–167. Note, however, that some studies report pain behavior – and its usual physiological foundation, nociception – in certain insects (see, e.g., Ewan Smith and Gary Lewin, "Nociceptors: A Phylogenetic View," *Journal of Comparative Physiology* 195 [2009]: 1089–1106).
[13] For a fuller discussion and overview of the evidence, see David DeGrazia, "Sentience and Consciousness as Bases for Attributing Interests and Moral Status: Considering the Evidence and Speculating Slightly Beyond," in Syd Johnson, Andrew Fenton, and Adam Shriver (eds.), *Neuroethics and Nonhuman Animals* (New York: Springer, 2020), 17–31.
[14] See Stanfano Mancuso and Alessandra Viola, *Brilliant Green* (Washington, DC: Island Press, 2015).

fetal sentience apparently does not emerge before the third trimester of pregnancy.[15] Anencephalic fetuses and infants, moreover, are commonly assumed to be irreversibly unconscious and therefore insentient due to the complete absence of cerebral hemispheres in the brain.[16]

Potential

One difference between embryos and pre-sentient fetuses, on the one hand, and members of species that are incapable of developing sentience, on the other, concerns *potential*. Unless afflicted with an extraordinary neurological disability, human embryos and pre-sentient fetuses have the natural potential to develop into sentient human beings. We have argued that sentience is sufficient for moral status. Is (actual) sentience also necessary for moral status or might potential sentience be sufficient?

Part of our answer is that *potential sentience itself* is irrelevant to moral status. The fact that an embryo, for example, has the potential to develop into a sentient human being does no more to confer moral status on the embryo than the fact that a particular seed has the potential to develop into an apple tree means that the seed already has leaves. Being potentially X does not confer on an entity the status or characteristics associated with X.

While potential sentience per se is irrelevant to moral status, in our view *the actual likelihood of becoming sentient in the future* is relevant. This point requires careful explication. Consider a two-month-old fetus, which lacks sentience but could develop into a sentient individual. Our claim is not that what will happen in the future if the fetus becomes sentient will somehow, magically, confer moral status on the two-month-old fetus. Our claim concerns how to think in a helpful ethical way about the fetus. If we expect it to become sentient because the pregnant woman intends to carry it to term, then it makes sense to think of the fetus as already having moral status. If the pregnant woman abuses drugs or alcohol while pregnant, or a

---

[15] See, e.g., Susan Lee et al., "Fetal Pain: A Systematic Multidimensional Review of the Evidence," *JAMA* 294 (2005): 947–954.

[16] Bjorn Merker challenges this common assumption ("Consciousness without a Cerebral Cortex: A Challenge for Neuroscience and Medicine," *Behavioral and Brain Sciences* 30 [2007]: 63–134). Merker argues that while a functioning cortex (the outer layers of the cerebrum) may be necessary for normal consciousness in human beings, it may not be necessary for a more basic consciousness, which he claims is apparent in the behavior of certain children with hydrancephaly. Whatever the merits of Merker's argument, it is noteworthy that children with this condition, unlike anencephalic infants, retain some of their cortex.

partner physically abuses her in a way that injures the fetus, there is a high likelihood that the later sentient human being will suffer harm as a consequence. If instead the fetus is well cared for, there is a high likelihood that the later sentient human being will benefit as a result. For these reasons, we find it helpful to regard a pre-sentient fetus that is expected to become sentient as already having moral status. (In keeping with the thesis that all and only beings with interests have moral status, we might think of the fetus who is likely to become sentient as already having "derivative interests" – deriving from interests she is expected to have later as a sentient being – in conditions conducive to the later fulfillment of her interests.)

If some readers find this way of conceptualizing the moral status of such fetuses unhelpful, they might instead think of only the later sentient human being as having moral status and understand the wrongness of causing prenatal injury as resting on the expectation of *future* harm. It is not very important which way of conceptualizing the situation is adopted. Moral status, as we understand it, is not a real property that individuals possess. Rather, as suggested in our earlier analysis of the concept, talking about moral status is a way of talking about obligations regarding how to treat certain individuals and the basis of these obligations in the individuals' interests.

However one prefers to conceptualize our view about fetuses that are expected to become sentient, our position plausibly implies that (intentionally or negligently) causing prenatal injury is wrong. Meanwhile, it does not imply that aborting a pre-sentient fetus is wrong, because there is no expectation that such a fetus will become sentient (see also Chapter 10).

Now consider human beings who had been sentient but have irreversibly lost the capacity for consciousness and therefore sentience. Do they have interests and moral status? According to our criterion, they do if, prior to losing sentience, they had preferences with implications for their treatment in their current state that are relevant to their life story (see Chapter 8). If, for example, Grampa had a strong preference not to receive life-support measures in a state of irreversible unconsciousness, then he has an interest that this wish be honored in his current state of irreversible coma.[17] Because he retains this and perhaps other interests, despite his irreversible unconsciousness, Grampa has moral status. In

---

[17] Our view does not imply that corpses have interests and moral status because we hold that we are essentially *living* beings, a thesis that entails that death ends our existence. A corpse or pile of ashes is the physical remains of one of us but not, strictly speaking, one of us in a state of death.

Chapter 8 we discuss in detail the interests of patients in irreversibly unconscious states.

7.5 Clarifying the Idea of Differences in Moral Status

We have argued that sentience is the basis for having moral status. More precisely, it is necessary and sufficient for having moral status that an individual is sentient, is expected to become sentient, or was sentient and had (narrative-relevant) preferences regarding their current treatment. Personhood is sufficient for moral status because persons are a type of sentient being. But some people think that there are different degrees, or levels, of moral status. Perhaps, then, sentience entails some minimal moral status, whereas personhood is necessary for *full* moral status. In this section we clarify this idea. The following two sections critically assess the alternative views regarding differences in moral status.

As a first approximation, views granting *equal consideration* to everyone with moral status assert equality of moral status, whereas views that embrace *unequal consideration* assert different degrees, or levels, of moral status. As explained in Chapter 3, equal consideration involves a commitment to ascribe to persons' prudentially comparable interests – interests where roughly the same thing is at stake for each individual – equal moral weight. Such equal consideration can take different forms. Utilitarianism demands equal consideration in the form of impartial utility calculation with the aim of maximizing overall utility. Human rights theories protect important interests more rigorously with rights-claims that (ordinarily) prohibit the sacrificing of some individuals' important interests for the common good. That each person's important interests are given equal protection by rights is a form of equal consideration. The religious idea that all human beings are "equal in the eyes of God" expresses in a different way this idea of moral equality among human beings.

If equal consideration applies not only to all persons but to all sentient beings, then it applies to many animals. This is where it becomes crucial to have a precise understanding of equal consideration as attributing equal moral weight to *prudentially comparable interests*. Members of different species have different interests based on their differing characteristics.

Consider, first, the stake that persons ordinarily have in their own survival. Setting aside cases in which death might be desired or desirable, most persons have a great interest or stake in remaining alive. Death ordinarily deprives an adult human of the many goods she would have had in her life had she continued to live: enjoyments, meaningful activities, the continuation of valued relationships, opportunities to complete various projects, and so on. Now consider a healthy cat who is having a good feline life. Premature death would deprive the cat of whatever good her life would otherwise have contained, so it seems appropriate to judge that she, like the human, has an interest in remaining alive. But are the typical adult human's life-interest and the cat's life-interest comparable? Do they have roughly the same thing of value at stake in remaining alive? We think not: the person may be expected to lose more from dying prematurely and so would be harmed more extensively by death. In addition, the human will likely have a much deeper set of psychological connections to her possible future and for this reason may be judged to be harmed more extensively by death (as discussed elsewhere in this chapter and in Chapter 4).[18]

Now consider liberty – the absence of external constraints. Whether or not liberty has intrinsic value for an individual, it clearly has instrumental value insofar as it allows the individual to do more things he wants to do or values. Compare a significant external constraint – forced restriction within a single house – in the cases of a healthy adult human and a healthy cat, both of whom would like to do things outside the house and could do these things in reasonable safety. Both are harmed by the restriction of liberty. Yet it seems plausible to judge that (ordinarily) the human is harmed more by such confinement. The human, unlike the cat, is likely to have plans, projects, and relationships that require extensive liberty, suggesting that the human is cut off from more that is prudentially important than is the cat. So, while both the human and cat have an interest in liberty, their respective liberty-interests are not prudentially comparable.

Recall that equal consideration requires attributing equal moral weight or importance to comparable interests. Given our reflections about the differences between an adult human's and a cat's life-interests and the two beings' liberty interests, we can see that equal consideration does *not* require ascribing equal moral weight to the human's interests and the cat's. The human's interests would be more extensively set back by death or imprisonment. Even though it is pro tanto wrong to kill cats (when they have lives worth living) and to restrict cats' liberty (beyond what is necessary for their safety), the moral presumptions against killing and against severely constraining the liberty of typical adult humans are

---

[18] This idea is developed in David DeGrazia, "Sentient Nonpersons and the Disvalue of Death," *Bioethics* 30 (2016): 511–519.

stronger. Equal consideration is compatible with certain differences in treatment in accordance with differences between the human's and the cat's interests.

Consider these and other examples of justified differential treatment together. It is generally worse to confine or kill humans than to confine or kill cats. If a situation required confining or killing members of one of these species, the cats would lose out. Ordinarily, it is problematic to treat mature humans paternalistically but not problematic to treat cats paternalistically. It is important to provide humans, but not cats, with formal education. Yet these points do *not* imply that humans have higher moral status than cats. For all of these justified differences in treatment are compatible with equal consideration, that is, with a commitment to give equal moral weight to everyone's comparable interests. The differences in justified treatment appear only because of *divergent interests* – for example, that persons have a greater stake in remaining alive than cats do, so that death harms persons more than cats.

According to views that assert *unequal consideration*, moral agents ought to attribute unequal moral weight to the comparable interests of different beings. For example, all sentient beings have an experiential welfare, including an interest in not suffering. Suppose that one has a view according to which cats have a different degree of moral status to humans. Unequal consideration would entail giving a cat's suffering less moral weight than a human's equal suffering. It would suggest, more generally, that each of the cat's interests matters less, morally, than each of the human's comparable interests, even though each has the same at stake. In this way humans have greater moral status than cats.

Unequal consideration can be conceptualized in several ways. According to one, persons deserve equal consideration whereas all other sentient beings deserve consideration that, while less than that due persons, is equal to the consideration due each other.[19] This model features two *levels* of moral status. Another way of conceiving differences in moral status features a *sliding scale* of moral status in which, say, creatures with greater overall psychological complexity deserve greater moral consideration than creatures with less psychological complexity.[20] The sliding scale would

[19] Jeff McMahan's ethical theory – which includes a "morality of respect" applying to persons and a "morality of interests" applying to all sentient beings – might be interpreted as taking this structure (*The Ethics of Killing* [Oxford: Oxford University Press, 2002]). If, however, the morality of interests as McMahan understands it assumes the form of equal consequentialist consideration, then his model approximates the one we defend later in this chapter.

[20] This sort of model is implicit in Mary Anne Warren, *Moral Status* (Oxford: Oxford University Press, 1997).

begin with the least psychologically complex of sentient creatures (perhaps a crustacean or a primitive fish) and ascend along increasing complexity and moral status before reaching a plane that represents persons' full moral status.

7.6   Against Unequal Consideration

Neutralizing Some Arguments for Unequal Consideration of Interests

One consideration that may seem to favor unequal consideration is the fact that most people apparently believe that human beings matter more than animals. Some people assert this judgment explicitly. Many imply the judgment through their acceptance of institutions that cause great harm to animals for human purposes. Animal husbandry, commerce in pets, horse racing, the use of animals in circuses, and animal research all cause extensive harm to animals for the sake of dining pleasure, entertainment, profit-making, and the advancement of human health. While the latter purpose is extremely important, the willingness to use animal subjects in ways that would be considered grossly unethical if applied to humans suggests that current animal research practices treat animals as though they had substantially lower moral status than human beings. Where the purposes for which animals are harmed are trivial (as with brutal training practices used to prepare elephants to perform tricks), the implication that animals have inferior moral status is conveyed that much more emphatically.

Despite the possible temptation of inferring from current practices and attitudes that animals *do* have less moral status, we consider this inference unfounded. Even large majorities of people are capable of making incorrect moral judgments. Indeed, considered objectively, the likelihood of error in making this judgment seems high. For one thing, people have a conflict of interest in judging about the moral status of animals: they are the ones making the judgment, yet they also stand to gain from the judgment that animals have inferior moral status due to the highly convenient implications of this thesis. Second, experience teaches us that people have a tendency to be biased against the interests of those they perceive to be very different from them.[21] Much prejudice against people of color by Caucasians, against the poor by the wealthy, against people who are

---

[21] For example, a robust literature on implicit race bias has emerged in recent decades. See, e.g., P. G. Devine, "Stereotypes and Prejudice: Their Automatic and Controlled Components," *Journal of*

regarded as "sexually deviant" by those who consider themselves sexually "normal," and the like can be understood in these terms. And if certain people can seem very different and to be members of an "out" group to other people, it is even more likely that nonhuman animals would strike human persons as being less-deserving outsiders. Indeed, we evolved as omnivores – whose diet includes meat – and therefore as animal-killers, so it seems likely that we have a natural disposition to perceive animals as "fair game" for our use. Finally, animals lack the opportunity and power to protest the way that they are treated. They do not vote, or verbally protest, or write newspaper articles explaining how badly they are treated. Unsurprisingly, their suffering is easy to ignore. For these and similar reasons, we should *not* take majority opinion on the relative moral status of humans and animals as providing grounds for the thesis that there are, in fact, differences in moral status.

We should not take majority opinion on this matter at face value. However, some people who reject the status quo of animal usage and support stronger protections for animals still hold moral views that may seem to support differences in moral status. For example, some people think that, while killing animals is often morally wrong, killing persons is, ordinarily, morally worse. One might explain this considered judgment by subsuming it under the general thesis that persons matter more than sentient nonpersons. Yet, as we noted earlier, this judgment can instead be explained by reference to the plausible thesis that death ordinarily harms persons more than it harms sentient nonpersons. So we do not regard this judgment as ultimately supporting differences in moral status.

Another challenge to equal consideration invokes judgments about general obligations of beneficence. It seems appropriate to give priority to helping humans in need over helping wild animals in need. Assume, to simplify matters, that the needy in question have no special relationship to us: the humans are not family or fellow citizens, while the animals are not under our care. That we ought to make reasonable efforts to help human beings who lack the basic necessities of life, even if they are complete strangers in other parts of the world, is clear. Yet we do not seem to have any obligation to help animals in the wild. Arguably, the priority of

Personality and Social Psychology 56 (1989): 5–18; Anthony Greenwald, Debbie McGhee, and Jordan Schwartz, "Measuring Individual Differences in Implicit Cognition: The Implicit Association Test," *Journal of Personality and Social Psychology* 74 (1998): 1464–1480; and Anthony Greenwald and Linda Krieger, "Implicit Bias: Scientific Foundations," *California Law Review* 94 (2006): 945–967.

beneficence toward humans reflects the appropriateness of unequal consideration.

We believe, to the contrary, that equal consideration is consistent with prioritizing human beings in discharging our obligations of general beneficence. Both persons and sentient animals matter. If we could reasonably expect moral agents to assist all persons and sentient animals who needed help, then doing so would be obligatory. But there is too much need in the world for any reasonable expectation that moral agents address all of it. They may be selective in deciding which important causes to support. If all of the important causes individuals address respond to humans in need, that pattern of beneficence is not objectionable. On the other hand, we reject any claim that individuals who are discharging their obligations of beneficence *must* prioritize needy humans. If an individual wants to devote time, energy, and funds to the cause of assisting marine mammals or elephants in distress, that choice would be fine. So we find no significant challenge to equal consideration here.

Challenges to Unequal Consideration

Having neutralized some considerations that might seem to favor unequal consideration, we now present three major challenges to it: (1) an appeal to logical consistency and an associated problem of relevance, (2) the dubious coherence of the two-level and sliding-scale models, and (3) the problem of nonparadigm humans.

The first argument proceeds as follows. We agree that persons enjoy equal moral status. We also agree that sentient nonpersons matter and have at least some moral status. The question is whether to extend equal consideration to them. As a matter of logic, we should grant them equal consideration *unless some relevant different between persons and sentient nonpersons justifies giving them less than equal consideration.* No candidate for a relevant difference, we submit, succeeds in justifying unequal consideration and, consequently, differences in moral status. Appeals to such characteristics as personhood, autonomy, moral agency, and membership in *Homo sapiens* all founder on the problem of relevance discussed just below.[22] Moreover, the examples of justified unequal treatment that are alleged to be inconsistent with equal consideration are best understood in

---

[22] For a detailed critique of allegedly relevant differences that would justify unequal consideration, see David DeGrazia, *Taking Animals Seriously* (Cambridge: Cambridge University Press, 1996), chap. 3.

terms of differences in degrees of harm (justifying a stronger presumption against killing adult humans than against killing animals), discretion in fulfilling obligations to help those in need (supporting a prerogative to prioritize human causes), or other factors that are consistent with equal consideration. Without a difference between persons and nonpersons that explains why the interests of one matter less than the interests of the other, we should reject the view as likely based in prohuman prejudice.

The need for a deeper explanation is highlighted in a problem of relevance. The problem, or challenge, is to explain precisely why person-hood (or any other putatively relevant characteristic) should confer higher moral status. By contrast, consider sentience and the different degrees to which different types of being can be harmed by premature death. Sentience is obviously relevant to moral status because it is the basis for subjective experiences and an experiential welfare. In this way, sentience grounds interests. Meanwhile, the plausible claim that persons ordinarily lose more from death than sentient nonpersons do is clearly relevant to the judgment that it is generally worse to kill adult humans than to kill cats. But what is the relevance of personhood to whether one's interests deserve equal consideration? If one denies that everyone deserves equal consider-ation, that claim implies that a person's suffering of some amount matters more, morally, than a cat's suffering of the same amount. By hypothesis, we are assuming that the person and cat are vulnerable to the same amount of suffering, so we cannot say (as when comparing life-interests) that the person has more at stake than the cat.

A second challenge to unequal consideration focuses on the prospects for its two major variants: the sliding-scale and two-level models. Neither appears theoretically stable. The sliding-scale model posits differences in moral status – more specifically, in how much weight one's comparable interests should receive – according to the differing degrees of psycholog-ical complexity among sentient beings. Yet if, as this model claims, persons have higher moral status than sentient nonpersons, then it is plausible that some sentient nonpersons, such as monkeys, have higher moral status than others, such as turtles. After all, monkeys are more cognitively and emo-tionally complex than turtles. If this is correct, then in order for the model to remain coherent we should also judge that persons who are more psychologically complex have higher moral status than persons who are less psychologically complex. This would mean that some human persons' interests would count more than other human persons' interests. But most of us confidently reject the notion that some human persons have higher moral status than others.

Might the two-level model of unequal consideration, which asserts equal moral status among persons, be a plausible alternative? We think not. If the greater capacities of persons justifies their having a higher moral status than nonpersons such that their comparable interests count more in consequentialist accounting, then among nonpersons the greater capacities of some of them (e.g., dogs) should justify having a higher status than others (e.g., mice). The two-level model risks collapsing into the sliding-scale model, which we have already argued is problematic. To block this move, an explanation must be given for why having some capacity or reaching some threshold of capacity makes such a difference to moral status. With no such explanation forthcoming, the view is unstable.

The third major challenge to any unequal-consideration account of moral status is the problem of nonparadigm humans. The problem will arise whatever property is supposed to confer higher moral status, be it personhood, autonomy, moral agency, the capacity for higher-level reasoning, or some other trait that most animals lack. Take, for example, the view that personhood confers higher moral status. Our conception of persons identifies them as beings with narrative identities. But many human beings who are widely thought to have full moral status do not yet have the cognitive capacities to have a narrative identity. On this view, it is not just mice, cats, dogs, and horses who will have lower moral status than human persons; it is also human infants, perhaps toddlers, and older human beings with late-stage dementia or other substantial cognitive incapacities.

How might a proponent of the view that personhood confers special moral status handle the case of ordinary infants? One natural strategy would be to claim that they enjoy special moral status on the basis of potential for personhood. However, this would imply that embryos and pre-sentient fetuses, which are also potential persons, have elevated moral status. Yet embryos and fetuses that never become conscious or sentient lack interests and therefore, we have argued, lack moral status entirely.

Appealing to potential does not satisfactorily address the problem of nonparadigm humans in the case of infants. Even if it did, this appeal could not possibly handle the case of someone – call him Fred – whose severe cognitive disability permanently prevents him from developing the capacities that would make him a person. Any unequal-consideration view that holds that cats' interests matter less than persons' comparable interests must – unless some novel solution is found – similarly judge that Fred's interests matter less than those of ordinary human adults.

A distinct strategy is to contend that social relations can ground moral status. One might claim that those who possess full moral status include not only persons but also those who enjoy special relationships with persons. Fred has full moral status, according to this view, not because he is a person – he is not – but because family members, friends and neighbors, and society confer on him the status and moral protections that ordinarily apply only to persons. In roughly this way, Mary Anne Warren has argued that moral status is a function not only of an individual's traits (e.g., sentience, personhood) but sometimes also of one's relations to others (being especially loved and protected by persons).[23] This approach might permit us to judge that all sentient humans have full moral status, whereas cats have only partial moral status.

Two major problems confront this response to the problem of nonparadigm humans. The first is conceptual. The concept of moral status attributes a kind of inherent value to certain individuals such that moral agents have obligations regarding their treatment of that individual. But inherent value *inheres* in an individual; it is based on the individual's characteristics. By contrast, relationships are not inherent to an individual; they are "external." So relationships cannot be a basis for moral status. This judgment fits with the plausible idea that a being's moral status gives moral reasons to *all moral agents* to treat that being in particular ways, whereas special relationships would provide moral reasons only to those who stand within the relationships.

Closely related to this conceptual challenge is an intuitive challenge to some implications of the present approach. Imagine a situation in which people do not have protective attitudes toward nonparadigm humans such as the severely cognitively impaired. Instead, people regard them as having only partial moral status, like a cat. The appeal to social relations as a response to the problem of nonparadigm humans implies that in this situation individuals with such impairments would have only partial moral status. If the difference in moral status between a person and a cat is judged to be large – as it is with unequal-consideration views of moral status – then humans with severe cognitive impairments would appear to be fair game for nontherapeutic, harmful research for the benefit of human persons. This is counterintuitive.[24]

---

[23] Warren, *Moral Status*, chaps. 5 and 6.
[24] There have been other recent attempts to deal with the problem of nonparadigm humans in a way that preserves a difference in moral status between humans and other animals. We find none of them promising. See, e.g., Agnieszka Jaworska and Julie Tannenbaum, "Person-Rearing Relationships as a Key to Higher Moral Status," *Ethics* 125 (2014): 242–271; and Shelly Kagan, "What's Wrong with Speciesism?," *Journal of Applied Philosophy* 33 (2016): 1–21. For replies, see David DeGrazia, "On the Moral Status of Infants and the Cognitively Disabled: A Reply to

7.7 Defense of a Qualified Equal-Consideration Account

Given the challenges to unequal consideration, we believe that the only satisfactory option is to adopt a model of moral status that grants at least equal consequentialist consideration to all sentient beings. This makes room for several approaches, prominently including (1) utilitarianism (which in its direct form does not attribute rights to anyone and in its indirect form will do so insofar as recognition of such rights promotes overall utility); (2) an equal-consideration model that attributes rights to all sentient beings, which we call "the wide rights view"; and (3) a qualified equal-consideration account of rights for persons and utilitarianism for sentient nonpersons.[25] In Chapter 3 we rejected utilitarian ethical theories on the grounds that they provide implausibly weak moral protections for persons and demand implausibly strong sacrifices of moral agents in the service of maximizing utility. We focus here on the other two theoretical options and defend the qualified equal-consideration view, while acknowledging that no view is entirely free of difficulties.

The Wide Rights View

The wide rights view asserts equal consideration for all sentient beings, but also asserts rights for all beings with moral status. On this approach, infants and severely cognitively impaired humans enjoy the full protection of moral rights in virtue of being sentient. This would include a right to adequate protection from harm, which would preclude, for example, their use in highly risky nontherapeutic research.

While this view is plausible in its implications for nonparadigm humans, it has some counterintuitive implications in extending moral rights to all sentient animals and lacks an adequate justification for doing so. The intuitive cost of this view seems especially apparent to us in the context of pest control. Imagine that you have two children and your house has been invaded by rodents who are fairly likely to carry infectious diseases. Suppose also that nonlethal methods for removing the rodents have been unsuccessful. Many people, including many who are

Jaworska and Tannenbaum," *Ethics* 124 (2014): 543–556; and David DeGrazia, "Modal Personhood and Moral Status: A Reply to Kagan's Proposal," *Journal of Applied Philosophy* 33 (2016): 22–25.

[25] In discussing this model of moral status we use "utilitarianism" (for sentient nonpersons) as shorthand for "equal consequentialist consideration," even though the view we envision does not incorporate utilitarianism's implausibly strong demand to maximize utility.

substantially in favor of animal protection, would judge it permissible to use lethal methods to remove the pests. We concur. We also believe that equal consequentialist consideration – utilitarian thinking – is a plausible framework for deciding what sorts of harms to the rodents would be justified in view of the improved household safety. Utilitarianism, we believe, could justify killing the rodents (for whom, we assume, death is a harm though much less of a harm than it typically is for persons) and some suffering if there is no way to remove or kill the pests painlessly. Yet, if the rodents had rights, this would include a right not to be sacrificed in the name of utility. So we find that in the context of pest control, utilitarianism is a more plausible guide than the wide rights view.

Another area in which the wide rights view strikes us as having dubious implications concerns our relationship to insects. Currently, we lack strong grounds for asserting that insects are sentient. But let us suppose that compelling evidence emerges for insect sentience.[26] If all sentient beings have rights, it would follow that we should take insect well-being quite seriously. I should, for example, be conflicted about whether it is permissible to kill a mosquito that lands on me. Moreover, and equally counter-intuitively, we should at present be very invested in the question of whether insects are sentient. For, if they are, then we are currently (if unintentionally) violating the rights of a huge number of beings with moral status. The commonsense judgment that we need not worry much about accidentally harming insects and about whether they are sentient suggests, the argument concludes, that if insects are sentient they nevertheless do not have rights that prohibit the trade-offs of welfare that utilitarianism permits.

One might wonder whether these intuitions regarding insects undermine not only the claim that they would have rights, if sentient, but also the claim that they would deserve equal *consequentialist* consideration. We do not think so. If it turns out that insects, or some types of insects, are sentient, their relatively primitive nervous systems make it likely that they are not *very* sentient – that is, that their capacity for feelings is relatively limited. They may be able to feel pain, for example, but it is doubtful that they would have the emotional capacity to experience great suffering – unlike persons and

---

[26] This possibility is not so far-fetched. Although, as noted earlier, the behavior of some insects suggests inability to experience pain, the overall evidence for insect sentience is mixed. For a robust argument that insects are characteristically conscious (and therefore possibly sentient), see Andrew Barron and Colin Klein, "What Insects Can Tell Us about the Origins of Consciousness," *PNAS* 113 (2016): 4900–4908.

other relatively complex animals. Moreover, we doubt that death would (nontrivially) harm creatures with such minimal sentience. Killing a mosquito would not be a significant harm to it. It seems reasonable to us to expect moral agents to refrain from harming such animals gratuitously, but it also seems reasonable not to invest great effort or resources into avoiding harm to them – or to finding out whether they are sentient and capable of being harmed. When it comes to the possibility of insect sentience, utilitarianism seems rather plausible and rights against being harmed rather implausible.

In addition to having counterintuitive implications in the contexts of pest control and our interactions with insects, the wide rights view lacks an adequate justification for extending the special protections of rights to all sentient beings. Consider sentient animals whose psychological lives are relatively simple and do not feature any significant self-awareness over time. (Perhaps crabs are such animals.) Their well-being is presumably a function of their quality of life at a given time. With little or no sense of having a future, such a creature is not really "invested" in its future, so there is apparently no basis for attributing a right to life to such a creature. Moreover, without the narrative self-awareness that we argue below grounds rights as necessary protections, it is unclear why the interests of one cannot be substituted for the interests of another. In contrast to the wide rights view, the view we defend offers a plausible foundation for the rights it ascribes to those with substantial self-awareness.

The Qualified Equal-Consideration Model: A First Approximation

A first approximation of our preferred model of moral status is "rights for persons, utilitarianism for sentient nonpersons" or "qualified equal consideration." This view affords all sentient beings equal consequentialist consideration, but affords only persons the additional protection of rights. We have argued that equal consequentialist consideration without rights is more plausible than the wide rights view in some contexts involving sentient animals such as pest control and our dealings with insects. Whether it is an adequate guide for our dealings with sentient nonpersons more generally remains to be seen. First, we need to consider qualified equal consideration's basis for claiming that persons deserve not just equal consequentialist consideration but the additional moral protection of rights.

What is so special about personhood that it grounds rights, conferring on persons stronger moral protections than those of equal consequentialist consideration? Earlier in the chapter, we characterized a person as a being with a *narrative identity* or *narrative self-awareness* – as found in typically developing human beings beyond the toddler years. On this conception, persons have substantial temporal self-awareness that allows for reflections on one's past, planning, and the understanding of one's life as comprising a sort of story with different parts.

Having a narrative identity is crucial to rights because it grounds the importance of what is sometimes called the "separateness of persons."[27] To understand this point, imagine, once again, a population of sentient non-persons whose mental lives proceed largely from moment to moment. Though sentient, each has no memory of its past or expectations for its future. For such individuals, it matters little whether some future good (or bad) experience happens to one of them or to someone else. After all, these subjects don't know the difference between these possibilities because they lack a sense of themselves as having a life, with particular projects, extending over time. They are in this way more "replaceable." Consequently, it makes sense that an ethical theory would treat such individuals as subject to trade-offs of welfare, where a greater gain to one individual justifies imposing a smaller loss on another. (Later we will consider sentient beings who lack narrative identities yet possess some nontrivial self-awareness over time. For the moment a sharp contrast is illustrative.)

Persons, on the other hand, who possess a narrative identity, have a substantial interest in the protections afforded by rights. These protections permit persons to pursue plans and projects, over considerable stretches of time, free of the insecurity that the prospect of utilitarian trade-offs can threaten. Suppose Abe's most cherished project is to start a family with his partner, nurture his children as they grow up, and enjoy family life. Abe has just become a father. But imagine that his nation's Olympic team conscripts Abe – who was a world-class rower in college but recently quit rowing – to train for the Olympics, for the good of his country and the sport. The training takes him far away from home, badly damaging his project of sustaining a certain type of family life. Here it is precisely Abe's narrative identity that engenders the longer-term interests – indeed, central life aims – that are threatened, and defeated, by violation of his autonomy rights. These and other rights (e.g., pertaining to nonmaleficence and justice) afford persons reasonable protections to live in security and pursue their dreams. The protection of rights, thus understood, is closely

---

[27] John Rawls influentially used this phrase in *A Theory of Justice* (Cambridge, MA: Harvard University Press, 1971).

connected to the special interests and vulnerabilities stemming from robust, longer-term self-awareness. Thus, personhood – construed in terms of narrative self-awareness – is a plausible ground for rights.

In this way, our view can address the problem of relevance. The relevance of personhood is its connection to longer-term interests that are often central to flourishing. These special interests mark off persons as significantly "separate" from each other and meriting special protections, which rights supply. Sentient beings who lack significant self-awareness over time have interests, but these interests do not involve longer-term investment and realization. So it makes sense, we submit, to regard these individuals as subject to consequentialist trade-offs in welfare. Thus, as a first approximation, "rights for persons, utilitarianism for sentient nonpersons."

How well does this view handle the problem of nonparadigm humans? Note, first, that the problem of paradigm humans confronting the view is relatively small. That is because, unlike the unequal-consideration views that we rejected, it embraces equal consequentialist consideration for all sentient beings. Equal consequentialist consideration is a substantial form of moral protection – essentially the protection of direct utilitarianism, which gives everyone's comparable interests equal moral weight. Although such equal consideration falls short of the protections afforded by rights, it affords far greater protections than animals have today in the research setting (which, in turn, is much more extensive than the protections of animals in industrial agriculture). For example, as we discuss below, utilitarianism will not permit the harming of mice for research purposes unless (1) the research is so promising that the expected benefits are greater than all projected costs and anticipated harm to the mice and (2) there is no alternative method that offers a better benefit/cost ratio. Considering the difficulties of successful translation from mice models to clinical medicine for humans, this utilitarian demand is actually very difficult to meet. Nevertheless, it can be met – in principle and, we believe, sometimes in practice. The problem of nonparadigm humans has been significantly reduced, but not eliminated. Let us therefore consider what the present approach can say, first, about ordinary infants and then about permanently, severely cognitively impaired individuals.

Does qualified equal consideration permit using infants for the benefit of society, say, in harmful, nontherapeutic research? Ordinary infants, although not yet persons, are expected to grow into persons. We believe this expectation provides some reason to ascribe to them the same moral status as persons. Persons have a central interest in being able to live their lives in ways that they find meaningful and satisfying (see Chapter 8). Doing so requires an ability to develop, gradually as they mature, their own values and priorities and, eventually, the opportunity to pursue their own life plans. Now suppose we treated infants as having lower moral status than persons. Although, as just discussed, they would still receive the protections afforded by equal consequentialist consideration, infants would be somewhat more available for involuntary use in the name of the common good – say, in early tests of a potential vaccine in a highly lethal epidemic. Suppose also that an infant is significantly injured in such testing, but not so much to preclude later developing into a person. Then if the effects of the injury interfere with the ability of the later person to pursue their plans and projects, then causing the injury will violate the rights grounded in their narrative identity. The interests that will ground rights in the future person now derivatively ground rights in the present infant.

In addition to this theoretical justification for ascribing moral rights to ordinary infants despite their not (yet) being persons, there are solid practical grounds for including them – as well as severely cognitively impaired humans – within the realm of legal rights-holders. The law is unlikely to operate successfully if it affords one level of protection to persons and a lower level of protection to postnatal human beings who are not yet persons. Rather than draw a line for legal purposes at the onset of personhood – which would be maddeningly difficult and contentious – the law operates better in granting rights to all (living) postnatal human beings, a *clearly demarcated* class of individuals. The amount of confusion and distress that would result if we permitted infants and toddlers, or even just infants, to be considered for risky nontherapeutic research is likely very great in anything resembling human societies as we know them today. Hence a pragmatic reason to ascribe all postnatal human beings legal rights, including rights against harms that are not balanced by compensating benefits to the rights-holder. In brief, the social benefits of assigning rights to infants are great whereas the social costs of doing so are modest to negligible. In addition, as mentioned in the previous paragraph, we believe there is a principled (not merely pragmatic) basis for attributing rights to infants.

Our response to the problem of nonparadigm humans leaves two noteworthy gaps. First, ordinary infants who are not expected to grow into persons – either because they have a terminal illness or because they will be subject to infanticide – would not be covered by our principled defense of rights for infants who are expected to become persons. Second, the pragmatic argument in favor of legal rights for all living, postnatal human beings is contingent upon a society's having sensibilities and attitudes that are best served by this sort of blanket rights-coverage. Other societies might not be so troubled by the selective conscription for the common good of severely cognitively impaired individuals or unwanted infants who are not expected to become persons. In such societies, they would not enjoy the protections of rights. This implication is a theoretical pill we have to swallow in defending the present view. It is worth stressing, however, that this pill is only slightly bitter due to the substantial protections afforded to all sentient beings by equal consequentialist consideration and our pragmatic reply to the problem of nonparadigm humans for societies like those that currently exist.

It merits emphasis that the problem of nonparadigm humans is a challenge to all models of moral status that ascribe moral status on the basis of sentience but do not assign rights to all sentient beings. The wide rights view alone escapes this problem. We have explained why we do not accept this view, though we acknowledge that there are considerations in its favor. Direct utilitarianism has the same problem of nonparadigm humans as our view has *plus a "problem of paradigm humans"*: the counterintuitive implications of this view's withholding of rights *even from persons*. Meanwhile, unequal consideration views fare *considerably worse* than our view by this measure because they afford less than equal consequentialist consideration to nonparadigm humans in implying differences in moral status between those who have their favored property (e.g., personhood, moral agency, autonomy) and those sentient individuals who lack it.

The Problem of Gradations and a Modification of Our Account

"Rights for persons, utilitarianism for sentient nonpersons" enjoys a number of theoretical strengths as an account of moral status. It embraces equal consequentialist consideration for all sentient beings, thereby improving on unequal-consideration models. It has more plausible implications than the wide rights view in the contexts of pest control and our relationship to insects (and perhaps our dealings with animals more generally). This account also offers a cogent rationale for ascribing rights, which protect against utilitarian trade-offs, to persons. Finally, it does relatively well in response to the problem of nonparadigm humans.

There remains a "problem of gradations." This challenge confronts any theory that asserts higher moral status – or, as in our account, stronger moral protections – for some beings than for others when the property that is supposed to justify the higher status or stronger protections comes in gradations. Any such theory features a mismatch between (1) a discontinuity in moral status or protections and (2) the natural continuities that underlie the putatively relevant property. For example, a traditional view of moral status might hold that all and only persons are rational and, on this basis, have moral status. This picture treats rationality as all-or-nothing. Yet it is more plausible to regard rationality as coming in gradations. So this traditional view rests on a false dichotomy between rational and nonrational beings. Although a defender of the view might select some degree of rationality that counts as just enough for moral status, such line-drawing would appear arbitrary given the gradations of rationality that characterize human beings and other cognitively complex animals.

On our account, while all sentient beings should receive equal consequentialist consideration, persons have the additional protection of rights. The increase in moral protections is justified by personhood where that is understood in terms of having a narrative identity – as found in ordinary human beings beyond the toddler years, who can think linguistically and have a sense of their own lives as constituting a sort of story. The problem is that temporal self-awareness is not all-or-nothing. Even if we judge, say, that an average two-year-old child does not yet have a narrative identity, she certainly has some temporal self-awareness, some sense of herself as a subject with a past and future, ongoing relationships, and so on. The same is true of most dogs. One possible response is to lower the bar for what counts as a person in order for these somewhat self-aware beings to qualify.[28] But this response is inadequate because it simply draws a line in a different place; a more accurate picture would display a substantial gray area rather than a line. Narrative identity is supposed to ground rights because it makes one's well-being a cross-temporal affair: one has an interest not only in immediate experiential well-being but also in protection of one's ability to pursue distinctive longer-term goals and plans. But this interest applies *to some extent* if one has *any* significant temporal self-awareness. A two-year-old toddler who is working on toilet training may want to do a "good job" today so his mother will be pleased with him

---

[28] According to one interpretation of Tom Regan's animal rights view, he is lowering the bar for personhood, although he employs the term "subjects-of-a-life," so that it includes all individuals who have some temporal self-awareness – in his estimation, at least all normal mammals one year or older (*The Case for Animal Rights* [Berkeley: University of California Press, 1983]).

when she comes home from work. Your pet dog may find a tasty bone outside and hide it in the backyard – remembering that in the past you have taken away such treats – with the intention of returning to it later when you are not present. Our account, so far, does not acknowledge the varying gradations of temporal self-awareness.

Our response is to modify qualified equal consideration. Persons, on the modified account, have rights as they have been understood so far: full-fledged rights that usually deflect appeals to utility as grounds for overriding an individual's important interests. Those sentient nonpersons who lack any significant temporal self-awareness remain covered by equal consequentialist consideration. The modification in our account, in response to the problem of gradations, is to accord *weaker rights for self-aware beings whose self-awareness falls short of a narrative identity.* These rights would vary in strength in accordance with the degree of temporal self-awareness of the beings in question (for example, elephants appear to have more self-awareness than cats). As we discussed in Chapter 3, rights have thresholds. This means that a right can be overridden by consequences that are sufficiently important. A right that is weaker is simply a right with a lower threshold, such that it is easier to justify overriding it.

As we conclude the presentation and defense of our account of moral status it will be helpful to anticipate a conceptual question: Does our account, in the end, assert differences in moral status? The answer depends on how one understands the latter phrase. If "differences in moral status" is understood to mean that some beings with moral status are entitled to less consequentialist consideration than others, then the answer is "no." If, on the other hand, attributing moral rights to only some sentient beings is understood as ascribing a higher level of moral status, then, yes, our account asserts some differences in moral status among beings who have moral status.

With this theoretical background, we proceed to examine the ethics of research with three very different scientific models: embryonic stem cells, rodents, and great apes.

7.8   Embryonic Stem-Cell Research

Stems cells have the potential to develop into many different cell types in the body.[29] In some organ systems, they provide a sort of internal repair

---

[29] For a helpful introduction to the science of stem cells, see National Institutes of Health, "Stem Cell Basics" (available at https://stemcells.nih.gov/info/basics.htm; accessed September 28, 2020).

system, dividing indefinitely to replenish other cells as long as the person or animal remains alive. For example, in the human gut and bone marrow stem cells regularly divide to repair or replace damaged tissues. In other organs, such as the heart, stem cells divide only under special conditions. Whenever a stem cell divides, each new cell has the potential either to remain a stem cell or to become a functionally more specialized cell such as a brain cell, a red blood cell, or a muscle cell.

For our purposes, we may distinguish three types of human stem cells: embryonic stem cells (ESCs), nonembryonic "adult" stem cells, and induced pluripotent stem cells (iPSCs). Adult stem cells are undifferentiated cells found throughout the body that divide to replenish dying cells and renew damaged tissues or organs. The job of adult stem cells is already relatively specialized, determined by the organ system to which they contribute. Induced pluripotent stem cells are adult cells that through deliberate intervention have been genetically reprogrammed to a functional state similar to that of embryonic stem cells. In particular, they retain some of the potential to become different types of cells – hence the term "pluripotent." Although scientists' ability to transform adult stem cells into iPSCs is a relatively recent development, they have already been used for drug development and disease modeling, and they may prove useful in transplantation medicine. What makes iPSCs special is that they are induced to recapture much of what makes embryonic stem cells unique and more scientifically and medically valuable than ordinary adult stem cells. And what makes ESCs so valuable is their potential to develop into a wide variety of cell types.

Embryonic stem cells are stem cells derived from an embryo's functionally undifferentiated inner mass cells. These stem cells are pluripotent, meaning they retain the potential to differentiate into all the cell types that make up the body. ESCs are thought to have immense therapeutic potential due to their ability to develop into and produce a virtually unlimited supply of specific needed cell types. Such diseases and conditions as diabetes, heart disease, spinal cord injury, vision and hearing impairments, Duchenne's muscular dystrophy, and Parkinson's disease may someday be treated successfully through the transplantation of cells generated from ESCs. Because ordinary adult stem cells lack this regenerative potential, and because it is unknown to what extent iPSCs may duplicate this potential, scientists regard embryonic stem cell research as an area of enormous importance.

The derivation of embryonic stem cells requires destroying a human embryo five to nine days after fertilization. If, as some people believe, embryos have full moral status – on the strength of the assumption that each of us comes into existence at conception (fertilization) and has full moral status throughout our existence – then destroying the embryo would be tantamount to intentionally killing "one of us." In that case, ESC research would seem to require the unethical violation of embryos' right to life. If, as other people believe, embryos have *partial* moral status – some but less than persons have – then ESC research may or may not be ethically permissible, depending on such factors as how one interprets the idea of their partial moral status, how much promise one ascribes to iPSC research, and the like. If, however, embryos have no moral status, then this fact would presumably pave the way for a straightforward ethical justification of ESC research.

On the view we have defended, embryos used in ESC research lack moral status. Because the developing human organism does not achieve neurological development sufficient for sentience until sometime in the third trimester of pregnancy, embryos are not sentient. Moreover, because the research embryos in question will not be implanted into a woman's uterus and permitted to develop to the point at which they would achieve sentience, they do not satisfy our criterion for moral status. They are neither sentient nor expected to become sentient. Therefore, they lack interests and moral status. In our view, there is no significant objection in principle to ESC research. Assuming its scientific and biomedical promise justifies its costs, the only significant objection we can imagine is that iPSC research is *equally* promising and has the advantage of not offending the moral sensibilities of those who believe (incorrectly, in our view) that embryos may never be destroyed for research purposes. At this time, however, it is premature to judge that iPSC research really is as promising as ESC research, so we submit that continuing the latter body of research is morally justified *at least* until we can determine the relative promise of iPSC research.

7.9   Research with Rodent Subjects

Rodents comprise a mammalian order that includes rats and mice, the vertebrates most commonly used in biomedical research, as well as hamsters, guinea pigs, and other species. It is difficult to find reliable data about the numbers of animals used in biomedical research, but according to a 2005 report by the Nuffield Council on Bioethics, globally somewhere between 50 and 100 million vertebrate animals are used each year.[30] Judging from countries where statistics on rodents are available, between

---

[30] *The Ethics of Research Involving Animals* (London: Nuffield Council on Bioethics, 2005), 7.

75 and 90 percent of these vertebrate subjects are rodents.[31] The major purposes for which rodent subjects are used are basic research into mammalian biology, the study of specific diseases and development of medicines to treat them, and safety assessment of chemicals such as household and industrial chemicals, fertilizers, herbicides, and food additives. These experiments nearly always impose nontrivial harms on their subjects, including pain, distress, injury, disease, and sacrifice at the termination of studies. Being sentient creatures, rodents have moral status. Does their moral status preclude their use in nontherapeutic research that harms them?

It is impossible to answer this question in a simple way due to uncertainty regarding three matters: the extent (if any) of rodents' temporal self-awareness, their utility as scientific models, and the scientific value of alternative models. Let us nevertheless engage the question from the standpoint of our account of moral status. For the purposes of discussion, we will assume that rodents have very little, if any, temporal self-awareness. That is, their self-awareness is insufficient to ground rights. So our analysis of the ethics of using rodents in research will be utilitarian.

The utilitarian standard sets a high bar. This may seem surprising in view of the fact that mainstream defenders of animal research often assert that the status quo enjoys the support of utilitarian thinking. They are mistaken, for several reasons.

First, as noted earlier, utilitarianism requires impartial (consequentialist) consideration of individuals' prudentially comparable interests. This means, for example, that causing fifty mice moderate pain cannot be justified unless the expected benefit from the research study – where expected benefit is a function of both the magnitude of the benefit, if it is realized, *and the probability of actually realizing it* – exceeds the disvalue of the fifty mice's moderate pain. Moreover, that the expected benefits must exceed the expected costs – including harms to animal subjects and financial expenditures – is only a necessary condition for ethical justification. The animal study in question must also offer greater expected net benefits than all reasonable alternatives. Such alternatives include the use of nonanimal methods (e.g., tissue cultures, computer models, 3D organ simulations), proceeding directly to studies with human volunteers, or forgoing the clinical research because the knowledge it seeks is not important enough to justify associated costs.

---

[31] Ibid., Appendix 2.

A second reason the utilitarian standard sets a high bar for animal research is that on the cost side of the benefit/cost reckoning we must include any harms or losses to animals incurred as a result of inadequate housing, social isolation, and other factors in addition to experimental procedures. Such costs are often substantial. Where experimental design does not require such costs (e.g., little room for moving around), they can be avoided, but often only by increasing other costs (e.g., those associated with larger enclosures). Moreover, these costs, like the financial costs, are typically known in advance and certain to occur, unlike the hoped-for benefits of animal trials.

In addition to these challenges to a utilitarian justification for research involving rodents, there is a daunting epistemological challenge: determining that rodent subjects are good models for human responses, disease, and biology. The biomedical community has generally *assumed* that rodents and other animals provide good bases for predicting human response. When this assumption has been challenged, proponents of animal research have often offered anecdotes in which animal research has been part of the pathway to important biomedical breakthroughs.[32] Of course, cherry-picking apparent successes does nothing to show the utility of animal models because, with a large number of animal trials, it is virtually guaranteed *as a matter of chance* that some will precede clinical trials that lead to important discoveries. (One can see this point by imagining coin-tossing as a basis for predicting efficacy in particular medicines: if we treat "heads" as a positive result and proceed to clinical trials on this basis, some of those trials will demonstrate efficacy, inviting the naïve impression that the coin-tossing offered successful predictions in those cases.) Moreover, even if we assume there are cases in which animal trials provide critical information, it does not simply follow that the studies were *necessary* for obtaining the information; there might have been alterative (nonanimal) routes to the same destination. There is, in fact, little rigorous scientific evidence bearing on the efficacy of animal research. What evidence exists in the form of meta-analyses or systematic reviews does not make rodent models look very impressive.[33]

[32] See, e.g., Stephen Schiffer, "The Evolutionary Basis for Animal Research," in Jeremy Garrett (ed.), *The Ethics of Animal Research* (Cambridge, MA: MIT Press, 2012), 31–49, at 38–41.
[33] See, e.g., Pablo Perel et al., "Comparison of Treatment Effects between Animal Experiments and Clinical Trials: A Systematic Review," *British Medical Journal* 334 (2007): 197–200; H. B. van der Worp et al., "Can Animal Models of Disease Reliably Inform Human Studies?," *PLOS Medicine* 7 (2010) (doi.org/10/1371/journal.pmed.1000245); Junhee Seok et al., "Genomic Responses in Mouse Models Poorly Mimic Human Inflammatory Diseases," *PNAS* 110 (2013): 3507–3512;

In view of our current state of knowledge, it is an open question whether rodents provide good models for human disease and response. Of course, the answer to this question might not be a simple "yes" or "no" that applies to all research involving rodents. Perhaps rodents provide good models for some research purposes and poor models for others. In any case, the utilitarian justification for using rodents depends on the assumption that a particular use of them (e.g., to test new drugs for heart disease) is sufficiently reliable to be part of the approach with the highest expected utility.

Meanwhile, the science of alternatives to the use of animals – including rodents – is fast developing.[34] Ironically, there has long been an expectation that alternatives to animal models be proven reliable, even though the animal models that supposedly set the benchmark were never held to this expectation. We think it is time for the biomedical community to be more scientific in advancing claims about the reliability of particular animal models, as well as nonanimal alternative methods. Moreover, from any reasonable perspective it makes sense to invest more heavily in the exploration of possible alternatives to animal research – both in order to achieve scientific and medical benefits without harming animals and because alternative methods are often faster and cheaper than animal models.

Our view of moral status implies that a great deal of rodent research is ethically unjustified. Nevertheless, it does not rule out all rodent research, some of which does not harm or pose significant risks to subjects either in experimental procedures or in conditions of housing, handling, and so forth. This is true, however, only if the subjects' basic needs are met in captivity. Laboratory studies that avoid significant risk of harm while meeting rodent subjects' basic needs might include studies that investigate their cognitive capacities and genetic studies that involve a small number of blood draws.[35]

---

and Pandora Pound and Michael Bracken, "Is Animal Research Sufficiently Evidence Based to Be a Cornerstone of Biomedical Research?," *British Medical Journal* 348 (2014) (doi:10.1136/bmj. g3387).

[34] See, e.g., National Research Council, *Toxicity Testing in the 21st Century* (Washington, DC: National Academies Press, 2007); Geoff Watts, "Alternatives to Animal Experimentation," *British Medical Journal* 334 (2007): 182–184; Francis Collins, "Reengineering Translational Science: The Time Is Right," *Science Translational Medicine* 90 (July 6, 2011): 1–6; M. Leist et al., "Consensus Report on the Future of Animal-Free Systemic Toxicity Testing," *Altex* 31 (2014): 341–356; and T. Burt et al., "Microdosing and Other Phase 0 Clinical Trials: Facilitating Translation in Drug Development," *Clinical and Translational Science* 9 (2016): 74–88.

[35] It is worth noting that three categories of animal research are easily justified on our view, though they are unlikely to involve rodents as subjects: (1) research on insentient animals, (2) nonintrusive observational studies of animals in the wild, and (3) therapeutic veterinary research, in which it is in

Our model of moral status might also justify some research uses of rodents beyond the relatively innocuous sort just described. Perhaps, for example, testing a new vaccine for a deadly infectious disease on rodents before moving to clinical trials is, in light of the strength of the rodent models and the lack of viable preclinical alternatives, the approach offering the greatest expected utility. If so, this model of moral status would permit it.

In addition to having these implications regarding the use of rodents in biomedical research, our model has an important global implication. Traditionally, there has been a presumption that animal studies should precede clinical trials involving humans, with certain exceptions (e.g., where the clinical trials pose no significant risks). Our account of moral status reverses the presumption in the case of all sentient animals: there should be a presumption *against* using such animal subjects. The burden of justification lies with those proposing to conduct a research study that is expected to harm its animal subjects.

7.10   Research Involving Great Apes

The great apes include chimpanzees, bonobos, gorillas, and orangutans. Along with dolphins, porpoises, and perhaps other cetaceans (whales), they are the most cognitively, emotionally, and socially complex nonhuman animals.[36] Some scholars have argued that great apes are actually *persons* and, accordingly, have rights to life, liberty, and freedom from torture.[37] Having defined personhood in terms of narrative self-awareness, we do not believe there is sufficient behavioral evidence to support a claim that great apes typically have this capacity, and so we will not join those who confidently assert the personhood of these animals. On the other hand, we find strong evidence that great apes are significantly *person-like*.

---

animal subjects' interest to participate. In the third category we are *not* referring to research that involves intentionally harming subjects by injuring them or giving them an infectious disease and then studying methods of treating the injury or disease. Rather, we have in mind cases in which animals who independently have health problems are entered into trials in an effort to help them while studying experimental treatments. For example, some dogs are prone to epileptic seizures. An experiment might involve two study arms in which dogs are brought into a lab by their human caretakers: one arm studying a standard therapy (the experimental control), the other arm studying a promising new therapy. In this instance, it is in the dogs' interests to enroll in the study, offering a paradigm instance of morally justified animal research.

[36] We will not discuss cetaceans further because they are rarely if ever subjects of experiments whose purpose is to advance human health. Also, we will sometimes use the term "ape" as shorthand for "great ape" (despite our exclusion of the "lesser ape" species of gibbons and siamangs).

[37] Paola Cavalieri and Peter Singer (eds.), *The Great Ape Project* (New York: St. Martin's, 1993).

One might aptly characterize them as *borderline persons*: beings who lie ambiguously between those who are clearly persons and those who are clearly not. To varying degrees, they have several traits that are closely associated with personhood, construed in terms of the capacity for narrative identity: agency, self-awareness, and sociability. The relevance of self-awareness to this capacity is obvious. In addition, agency is relevant to the extent that individuals with narrative identities have intentions and plans while sociability is relevant in that such individuals tend to see certain enduring relationships as important to their identities.

Although their agency – their capacity for intentional action – is apparent in virtually everything great apes do, it is especially evident in activities that display unusual deliberateness, reasoning, or planning. For example, chimpanzees regularly use tools, such as stems as probes for insects, moss for sponges, and rocks as nutcrackers.[38] Meanwhile, most or all ape species engage in social manipulation, including deception, of their associates in pursuit of goals.[39] Apes are also self-aware in a couple of ways. A type of bodily agential self-awareness is apparent in their carrying out of intentional actions and sequences of actions. Such self-awareness is emphatically displayed in apes' imitation of others' bodily gestures,[40] use of mirrors to investigate otherwise inaccessible markings on their own bodies,[41] and use of televised images of their arms to reach objects when (in a laboratory setting) their arms and the objects were not directly in view.[42]

Another type of self-awareness – social self-awareness, or awareness of oneself as positioned within a set of social relationships – is more directly relevant to the possibility of narrative self-awareness and is attributable on the basis of certain complex social behaviors. Chimpanzees, bonobos, and gorillas are highly social creatures. Orangutans are semi-solitary yet they engage in significant social interactions within small groups as well.

---

[38] See, e.g., W. C. McGrew, *Chimpanzee Material Culture* (Cambridge: Cambridge University Press, 1992), 44–46.

[39] See, e.g., Richard Byrne, "The Misunderstood Ape: Cognitive Skills of the Gorilla," in Anne Russon, Kim Bard, and Sue Taylor Parker (eds.), *Reaching into Thought* (Cambridge: Cambridge University Press, 1996), 111–130; Frans de Waal, *Bonobo* (Berkeley: University of California Press, 1997), 39–40; and Michael Tomasello and Josep Call, *Primate Cognition* (New York: Oxford University Press, 1997), 235–259.

[40] For a summary of the evidence, see Steven Wise, *Rattling the Cage* (Cambridge, MA: Perseus, 2000), 204–205.

[41] See Gordon Gallup, "Self-Recognition in Primates," *American Psychologist* 32 (1977): 329–338; and Karyl Swartz, Dena Sarauw, and Sian Evans, "Comparative Aspects of Mirror Self-Recognition in Great Apes," in Parker, Mitchell, and Miles, *The Mentalities of Gorillas and Orangutans*, 283–294.

[42] See Tomasello and Call, *Primate Cognition*, 52.

The social lives of great apes – especially the more social species – feature long-term relationships, dominance hierarchies, awareness of kin relation-ships, non-kin-based alliances, and the tracking of significant interactions such as fights, grooming, and altruism.[43]

What are the moral implications for the research context of the claim that great apes are borderline persons? If they are persons, they have moral rights of full strength; if they are not persons, their temporal self-awareness is nevertheless substantial enough that their corresponding rights would be similar to those of persons. We therefore suggest that the borderline personhood of great apes justifies research protections that are roughly comparable to those appropriate for young human children. The relevant comparison group, we suggest, is post-infancy children who are too immature for meaningful assent to, or dissent from, participating in research. There may even be some cases in which great ape subjects appear to grasp what involvement in a trial would entail well enough so that assent and dissent become meaningful possibilities. For example, great apes who have entered a cognitive study that involves many individual trials may, after a few trials, understand what continued participation would involve. If so, and if they indicate a clear preference not to participate on a given occasion, their nonverbal dissent should be respected. Illustrating this possibility, in the National Zoo in Washington, DC, orangutans involved in cognitive studies are given the option to join or opt out of particular trials when invited by a staff scientist's familiar hand gesture.

Even more important than considerations of assent and dissent is the matter of what harms or risks of harm great apes may permissibly undergo in research. Like human children, they should be spared from research that poses any significant risk of harm to them except in the case of therapeutic research that represents the individual animal's best veterinary option. Although strict, this standard would not entail the end of research on apes. Appropriate field studies – which involve observing animals in their natural habitats without harming or interfering with them – could con-tinue. Studies involving captive apes or apes in sanctuaries could meet this standard if the study is low-risk and their living conditions meet their basic needs and give them good lives. What would end is nontherapeutic invasive research involving great apes. The United States has already severely curtailed – and for all practical purposes terminated – such

---

[43] For helpful overviews, see Jane Goodall, *The Chimpanzees of Gombe* (Cambridge, MA: Harvard University Press, 1986); de Waal, *Bonobo*; Russon, Bard, and Parker, *Reaching into Thought*; and Parker, Mitchell, and Myles (eds.), *The Mentalities of Gorillas and Orangutans*.

research with chimpanzees.[44] The European Union has largely ended such research with great apes in general but explicitly allows for the possibility of carefully documented exceptions if necessary for preservation of an ape species or as the only viable method to fight "a life-threatening, debilitating condition endangering human beings."[45] We find the US exemption of chimpanzees an admirable step in the direction of moral progress and the EU's approach even better in covering all great apes. Our approach, based on an explicit acknowledgment of great apes' moral status, goes a bit farther than the EU in not acknowledging justified exceptions.

---

[44] See Committee on the Use of Chimpanzees in Biomedical and Behavioral Research, Institute of Medicine (now Academy of Medicine), *Chimpanzees in Biomedical and Behavioral Research* (Washington, DC: National Academies Press, 2011); National Institutes of Health, Office of the Director "Statement by NIH Director Dr. Francis Collins on the Institute of Medicine Report Addressing the Scientific Need for the Use of Chimpanzees in Research," December 15, 2011 (available at www.nih.gov/news/health/dec2011/od-15.htm); and the follow-up report, Council of Councils, National Institutes of Health, *Council of Councils Working Group on the Use of Chimpanzees in NIH-Supported Research: Report*, 2013 (available at https://dpcpsi.nih.gov/council/pdf/FNL_Report_WG_Chimpanzees.pdf).

[45] "Directive 2010/63/EU on the Protection of Animals Used for Scientific Purposes," *Official Journal of the European Union* L 276/33-276/79, adopted September 22, 2010 (available at http://eur-lex.europa.eu/legal-content/EN/TXT/?uri=CELEX:32010L0063), p. 276/35).

CHAPTER 8

Well-Being

8.1 Introduction

Value theory concerns what is good. More precisely, value theories are accounts of what things are intrinsically good and what things are intrinsically bad. *Intrinsically* means ultimately or in itself as opposed to instrumentally or as a means to something else. Value theory has various components that correspond to different sorts of things that might be thought to be good.[1] Some theorists believe that beautiful things have objective, intrinsic value, which they call aesthetic value. Others disagree, holding that beauty is subjective, residing "in the eye of the beholder." Some thinkers hold that the good includes certain moral values. For example, Shelly Kagan holds that the good includes both well-being and desert – whether individuals get what they morally deserve.[2] Brad Hooker holds that the good includes both well-being and fair distribution of benefits, involving priority to the worst-off.[3] This chapter focuses on the area of value theory that is concerned with the nature of prudential value or *well-being*.

While ethical theories offer differing guidance in relation to individual well-being, no one denies its importance. Even libertarians, who deny the existence of any obligations to promote others' well-being independent of an agent's past actions (see Chapter 6), recognize the principle of non-maleficence. As discussed in Chapter 4, this principle states that it is pro tanto wrong to harm others. Harming others, as harm is ordinarily understood, involves diminishing their well-being.

Well-being is closely related to a variety of familiar practical concepts in addition to harm. Just as harm involves diminishing well-being, *benefit*

---

[1] For an illuminating discussion, see Robert Audi, *The Good in the Right* (Princeton, NJ: Princeton University Press, 2004), chap. 4.
[2] Shelly Kagan, *The Geometry of Desert* (Oxford: Oxford University Press, 2012).
[3] Brad Hooker, *Ideal Code, Real World* (Oxford: Clarendon, 2000).

involves increasing it. A *good* or *flourishing* life for the individual who lives that life – that is, a prudentially good life – is one largely characterized by well-being. It is, in other words, a life in which one fares well more than badly, flourishes more than languishes. Both harm and benefit are connected with the concept of an individual's *interests*. An individual's well-being is a function of their interests, considered together. Indeed, we may think of each interest – for example, someone's interest in gainful employment or their interest in getting enough sleep – as a component of someone's well-being.

Unlike ethical theories or principles, value theories are not explicitly action-guiding. While they tell us what is good, they do not tell us what to do about it. Utilitarians believe that well-being (or welfare) is the only thing that is intrinsically good. They also believe that agents have an obligation to act in ways that can be expected to maximize well-being, but this latter view does not follow from their theory of the good. A moderate deontologist could agree that well-being is the only intrinsic good, but hold, as we do, that we have only a pro tanto obligation to promote well-being and that we are subject to moral constraints on promoting it such as respecting individuals' rights. So the nature of the good is one thing: the topic of value theory. What to do about the good is another thing: a topic in ethical theory.

We begin this chapter with an examination of different theories of well-being. Following a discussion of the pros and cons of subjective and objective theories, we identify three challenges that any successful theory must meet. We sketch a subjective theory of well-being that we think can meet these challenges. According to our theory, both enjoyment and the satisfaction of narrative-relevant desires are prudentially good for an individual. Suffering and the frustration of narrative-relevant desires are prudentially bad for an individual. Reality has an amplifying effect, such that enjoyment is better when its object is real and the fulfillment of desires is better when the desires are rational and informed. The chapter then proceeds to three areas of practical concern: (1) disability in relation to well-being, (2) decision-making for impaired newborns, and (3) decision-making for patients in irreversibly unconscious states.

8.2 Subjective Theories

Contemporary philosophers generally divide accounts of well-being into three categories: *mental-state theories, desire-satisfaction theories,* and *objective theories* (sometimes called *objective-list theories*).[4] We locate the first two categories under the broader heading of "subjective theories," since they understand well-being in terms of an individual's mental life (invoking one sense of "subjective") or in terms of what the individual wants (invoking another sense of "subjective").

According to mental-state theories, an individual's well-being consists in their having certain kinds of mental states or experiences. The most familiar version of this approach, *hedonism*, identifies well-being with happiness. Happiness, according to classical hedonism, consists in pleasure and the absence of pain. Importantly, the terms "pleasure" and "pain" are not restricted to *sensory* pleasures and pains.[5] The pride you experience at a loved one's graduation and the pleasing sensations of a warm bath both constitute pleasures, while the sorrow you feel upon learning of a loved one's death and the experience of stubbing a toe are both pains. So we may think of "pleasure" and "pain" as referring to the full range of pleasant or agreeable experiences and the full range of unpleasant or disagreeable experiences.

Hedonism has strengths. We generally regard pleasant experiences as making us better off and unpleasant experiences as making us worse off, other things being equal. Rewards generally consist of things that bring us some type of pleasure and punishments typically involve things that cause us some form of pain. The thesis that we are well-off to the extent that we are happy has a ring of plausibility.

Yet further reflection raises doubts about hedonism. What, after all, is pleasure? A natural answer is that pleasure is simply *the experience of feeling good*. But is this a single feeling or experience? If so, how is it distinguished from other feelings? The only experiential quality we seem able to ascribe to all pleasures is *pleasantness* – feeling good. But so many different types of experience feel good or can feel good. Maybe the term "pleasure" designates a wide variety of mental states, not just one. This conjecture seems plausible when contrasting the pleasing sensations of a warm bath to the pride felt upon achieving a major goal, to the intense sensations associated with sexual excitement, or to the quiet enjoyment of reading a good book. If pleasures comprise a variety of mental states, what do they have in common to make them all pleasures? A plausible answer refers not to the

---

[4] Derek Parfit popularized this classification, with slightly different terminology, in *Reasons and Persons* (Oxford: Clarendon, 1984), Appendix I.

[5] See Jeremy Bentham, *An Introduction to the Principles of Morals and Legislation* (Oxford: Clarendon, 1907; first published 1789), chap. V.

way they feel but to the fact that they are all *liked*, or *desired*, just for the way they feel. We might therefore understand pleasure as including all states of consciousness that are liked or desired just for the way they feel.[6]

This way of defining pleasure would enable the hedonist to explain *why* pleasure – or, more globally, happiness – should be thought to constitute well-being. The explanation is that pleasure is good for us *because we desire, prefer, or like it.*[7] For those who are attracted to the idea that each mature person's values and priorities determine what is ultimately good for them, the fact that we desire pleasure will satisfactorily explain its contribution to our well-being. But this reasoning also opens the door to another theory.

In addition to desiring pleasure, human beings want things that are *not* states of consciousness. This is the main point of Robert Nozick's "experience machine" thought-experiment.[8] Suppose you could plug into a machine that could give you any and all mental states you would like to have (varied pleasures, a sense of novelty, believing that you are achieving your life goals, and so on). For most people such a machine could not give them all they want out of life. In addition to agreeable experiences, most of us want such things as having good friends, accomplishing our ambitions, and learning about the world. And these sorts of things involve states of affairs beyond our own minds. In the case of having friends, for example, neither *believing* one has friends nor *experiencing good feelings* as a result of this belief delivers what we want: actually having friends. Mental-statism, it appears, construes well-being too narrowly.

Desire-satisfaction theories claim that we are well-off to the extent that we get what we desire. "Satisfaction" here means that what one wants to happen, happens; it does not require that one *feel* any satisfaction. This approach is subjective in the sense that each individual determines what is good for them – by desiring some things and not others. For example, if I desire to play ping-pong but not to read classic novels, then playing ping-pong contributes to my well-being but reading classic novels does not

---

[6] This is Henry Sidgwick's idea in defining pleasure as "desirable consciousness" (*The Methods of Ethics*, 7th ed. [London: Macmillan, 1907], Bk. II, chap. 3). Another option is to construe pleasure and displeasure not as types of mental states but as reflecting a *dimension* of any conscious state: the degree to which it is pleasant or unpleasant (Shelly Kagan, "The Limits of Well-Being," *Social Philosophy & Policy* 9 [1992]: 169–189). By contrast, Aristotle understood *eudaimonia*, often translated as "happiness," in terms of a particular sort of active life rather than in terms of mental states (*Nichomachean Ethics*).

[7] Here we assume that to like an experience for the way it feels involves desiring, other things being equal, that the experience continue.

[8] *Anarchy, State, and Utopia*, 42–45.

(unless instrumentally). Many philosophers, economists, and laypersons find this general approach plausible.

A challenge confronting desire-satisfaction theories is to determine *which* of an individual's desires are such that their satisfaction makes that individual better off. Not all desires can count in this way. Suppose that while traveling you make a casual acquaintance with someone who tells you she hopes to get a particular job. You form the desire that she land the job, and then you go your separate ways, and later you do not think about her. A year later, unbeknownst to you, she gets the job. Your desire has thereby been satisfied, but it is dubious that this makes you better off – even though, had you found out, you would have been pleased.[9] The problem this example reveals is that our desires can be about anything, including things far removed from our own lives. Unless restricted in some way, desire-satisfaction accounts construe well-being too broadly.

Another challenge is that desires can be misinformed or distorted. If a cult member's desires are based on systematically false beliefs, her well-being might not be promoted by satisfying those desires. If an addict's life is dominated by craving one fix after another, even to the neglect of basic necessities and formerly affirmed priorities, his current desires provide a dubious guide to his well-being. And long-term deprivation can depress expectations and, with them, desires. For example, a political prisoner might gradually lose hope of freedom and stop desiring it, yet regaining freedom would seemingly contribute to her well-being.[10] Such reflections reinforce the idea that a plausible desire-satisfaction theory must qualify the desires whose satisfaction counts in an assessment of someone's well-being.

Informed-desire (or *rational-desire*) *theories* are motivated by the idea that desires can be prudentially faulty: for example, because misinformed, contradictory, dampened by deprivation, or based on overgeneralization.[11] So an informed-desire theory focuses on ideal or hypothetical desires rather than actual desires. It asserts that one's well-being consists in the satisfaction of the desires one *would* have if one were adequately informed, logically consistent, free of prejudice, and so forth. Such a theory can avoid problems stemming from the fact that our actual desires are sometimes prudentially faulty. In order to be viable, however, an informed

---

[9] Cf. Parfit, *Reasons and Persons*, 494.
[10] Amartya Sen, "Well Being, Agency, and Freedom," *Journal of Philosophy* 82 (1985): 191.
[11] Explaining why desires based on overgeneralization would not count, R. B. Brandt proposes that only desires that would survive cognitive psychotherapy are ones whose satisfaction would make us better off (*A Theory of the Good and the Right* [Oxford: Clarendon, 1979], Part I).

desire theory must satisfy two demands. First, it must *justify* the sorts of corrections of an individual's actual desires the account will countenance. Otherwise, we might doubt that the account is actually grounding individual well-being in an individual's own priorities. Second, it must rein in the desires that count in view of the enormous range of things about which we can have desires; those that count must be sufficiently relevant to our lives.

A final challenge confronts desire-satisfaction theories however they respond to those two demands. Just as we asked what it was about pleasure that made it important to well-being, leading us to the idea of being desired, we may also ask what it is about *being desired* that makes satisfaction of a desire contribute to well-being. Some philosophers contend that the satisfaction of a desire per se doesn't contribute to well-being.[12] Consider these scenarios. Jaime has no desire to listen to hip-hop but, when music from this genre surrounds him at a party, finds that he enjoys it immensely. Kaitlin wants to learn about linguistics but, upon taking a class in the subject (satisfying her desire to learn about it), finds that it leaves her cold. The lack of desire and therefore desire-satisfaction in the hip-hop case and the presence of desire-satisfaction in the linguistics case seem irrelevant to whether Jaime and Kaitlin have beneficial experiences. Meanwhile, the presence or absence of an *enjoyable experience* seems quite relevant. Such observations seem to support mental-statism. While Jaime and Kaitlin surely have a desire for enjoyable experiences, this desire is distinct from desires to hear hip-hop and to learn about linguistics; and the absence and presence of these two desires in the cases under consideration, one might maintain, are irrelevant to our assessments of well-being.

A different line of response to the question of why the satisfaction of a desire contributes to well-being leads in another theoretical direction. Recall that satisfaction of *informed* or *rational* desires seemed more promising as an indicator of well-being than satisfaction of actual desires. One possible explanation of why we tend to believe this is that some possible objects of desire – such as friendships or achievement – seem valuable independently of whether they are actually desired by a particular person. If so, then it is the objects themselves that determine whether they are conducive to well-being, in which case desire, whether actual or

---

[12] This idea is developed in T. M. Scanlon, "Value, Desire, and Quality of Life," in Martha Nussbaum and Amartya Sen (eds.), *The Quality of Life* (Oxford: Clarendon, 1993), 185–200. See also L. W. Sumner, "Welfare, Preference, and Rationality," in R. G. Frey and Christopher Morris (eds.), *Value, Welfare, and Morality* (Cambridge: Cambridge University Press, 1993), 74–92.

hypothetical, is irrelevant. This line of reasoning leads away from desire-satisfaction accounts of well-being toward objective accounts.

8.3 Objective Theories

Objective theories of well-being claim that some conditions or activities in themselves make human life go better. A plausible list of these *intrinsic goods* might include autonomous living, deep personal relationships, understanding, aesthetic enrichment, accomplishment, enjoyment, and physical and mental functioning (or health).[13]

Whatever it includes as intrinsic goods, a plausible objective account will also include at least one intrinsic *bad*: suffering. Suffering is intrinsically negative for a subject and is not merely the absence of something good. Perhaps the same is true for some other conditions such as physical and mental dysfunction (or illness) and personal failure (the opposite of accomplishment). On the other hand, some objective theorists might regard these as simply the absence of certain intrinsic goods, an absence that often causes suffering.

An objective theory of well-being along the lines we have described makes several concessions to subjective theories. The inclusion of autonomous living leaves a lot of space to the individual to determine what is worth doing and pursuing. The inclusion of enjoyment does the same – since people enjoy different things – while also capturing the hedonist's plausible idea that experiences we like or find desirable tend to make our lives go better. Identifying suffering as something bad is also a concession to hedonism. Meanwhile, again, the approach does not present a single prescription for a good life, instead allowing for different mixes of goods for different individuals. Finally, all of these items are things that most people tend to want in their lives, at least if they are reasonably informed, and tend to find satisfying.

[13] All of these items except health and aesthetic enrichment appear in the list proposed in Griffin, *Well-Being*. For examples of objective accounts that construe health or physical and mental functioning as intrinsically – not just instrumentally – valuable for their possessor, see Amartya Sen, "Capability and Well-Being," in Martha Nussbaum and Amartya Sen (eds.), *The Quality of Life* (Oxford: Clarendon, 1993), 9–29; and Martha Nussbaum, *Women and Human Development* (Cambridge: Cambridge University Press, 2000), 70–96. Strictly speaking, Sen and Nussbaum regard *capabilities* for functioning, rather than functioning itself, as objective prudential goods, a complexity we ignore here. For examples of theorists who include aesthetic experience among objective, intrinsic goods, see John Finnis, *Natural Law and Natural Rights* (Oxford: Clarendon, 1980); and Alfonso Gomez-Lobo, *Morality and the Human Goods* (Washington, DC: Georgetown University Press, 2002).

Perhaps the greatest challenge to objective theories, even those making significant concessions to the insights of subjective accounts, is the charge that they are not flexible enough. Suppose Tushar is not interested in accomplishment. Clear in his mind about what accomplishment is, he picks several weighty and worthwhile goals, succeeds in accomplishing them, but is not impressed. Is it plausible that accomplishment is in Tushar's interests? Would he really be better off, other things being equal, if he accomplished a lot more but became somewhat less happy? Intuitions may differ here. At any rate, the challenge is for the theory to be sufficiently responsive to individual differences in temperament and proclivities.

8.4 Three Challenges for Theories of Well-Being

Given our discussion of the pros and cons of subjective and objective theories of well-being, we think there are three challenges that any plausible theory of well-being should be able to meet. Identifying these challenges will help to motivate the subjective theory we develop in the next section.

The first challenge is *to anchor judgments of well-being plausibly in an individual subject's experience or life*. Some scholars endorse an Experience Requirement: a state of affairs can affect one's well-being only if it affects one's experience. This requirement strikes some as plausible on its face – "What I don't know, can't harm me" – and has plausible implications for cases like the travel acquaintance mentioned above, in which the acquaintance's later success does not make the traveler better off. Note, further, that the Experience Requirement does not *reduce* well-being to experience or mental states, since what affects our experience (e.g., having friends) may involve states of affairs outside our minds.

If the Experience Requirement is warranted, then it poses a serious challenge to objective theories and desire-satisfaction theories, which imply that our well-being can sometimes be affected by factors that do not affect our experience. But the Experience Requirement is controversial. Suppose a hospitalized elderly man lapses into an irreversible vegetative state, surviving in this condition for several months before dying. During this time, he is maintained on a respirator and fed through an intravenous line – despite the fact that (unknown to hospital staff) he had a deeply felt, enduring preference *not* to be maintained by artificial life support in a condition of irreversible unconsciousness. Due to his unconsciousness, he does not experience this affront to his dignity. But it does affect his body.

Proponents of the Experience Requirement will deny that maintaining this patient on artificial life support harms him. Some will disagree, judging (as we do) that harm occurs despite the patient's obliviousness. Those who find the Experience Requirement too restrictive in this way may prefer an Individual Requirement: a state of affairs affects an individual's well-being only if it affects the individual – that is, their mind *or body*.[14]

Neither the Experience Requirement nor the Individual Requirement seems able to explain our judgments in other cases. Suppose Sanaa, a medical researcher near the end of her life, is searching for a way to prevent a serious childhood disease. As it happens, a vaccine she discovered proves effective, but she does not learn the good news about the clinical trials she had designed because she dies suddenly just before the news reaches her. Had the vaccine proven ineffective, her experience would have been exactly the same. Some would say that her accomplishment made her better off even though it did not affect her experience. Her life as a whole was more successful because it involved developing a vaccine that worked. Proponents of the Experience Requirement or Individual Requirement would have to disagree. They might acknowledge that her life was morally and instrumentally better than it would have been had the vaccine failed, but deny that it was better *for her*.

Consider another case that is hard to reconcile with the Experience and Individual Requirements. Someone believes herself to have a group of good friends, but, in fact, they despise her and badmouth her behind her back. Even if she never gets an inkling of their true feelings, it seems that her life goes worse for her than it would if she were enjoying genuine friendship. If effects on her experience or her body are necessary for something to go well or badly for her, this judgment is groundless.

We think that the solution to this problem is to deny the Experience and Individual Requirements and instead endorse a *Narrative Requirement*. The Narrative Requirement says that a state of affairs can affect one's well-being either by affecting her experiences and thereby her felt quality of life or, without affecting her experiences, by impacting *her life story*. An event that does not enter my experience can affect my interests only insofar as it would make sense for a story told about my life to include it. Thus, what I experience can make my life go better or worse, but so can other events, such as indignities involving my body that I would have cared greatly about, the success of people I love, the achievement of my major aims, and so forth. On the other hand, the success of the traveler's acquaintance is

---

[14] Cf. Kagan, "The Limits of Well-Being," 181–182.

still ruled out by the narrative requirement – her business is not a part of the traveler's life story. The Narrative Requirement captures the sense in which judgments about someone's well-being must be about his life, not merely someone else's, without being unduly restrictive concerning what counts as his life.[15]

We recognize that the Narrative Requirement, as just stated, is vague and requires interpretation. However, it successfully captures the cases that the Experience Requirement and the Individual Requirement cannot, while limiting the range of desires that count. Moreover, in cases in which it is hard to judge whether a particular unexperienced state of affairs affects someone's well-being (e.g., the flourishing or languishing of a grandchild to whom one is not especially close), the Narrative Requirement leaves room for the plausible judgment that, if the state of affairs does affect one's well-being, it does so *to a lesser extent* than factors that are unambiguously part of one's life story.

The second challenge for any theory of well-being is *to show appropriate deference to an individual's authority regarding what is good for them*. Our approach rests on the conviction that human beings, at least competent adults, are usually experts on what is good for them. When they make mistakes, those mistakes can generally be explained in virtue of getting the facts wrong (e.g., falsely believing that changing jobs will make them happy), reasoning erroneously (e.g., overestimating the importance of schmoozing in the quest for promotion), or acting out of weakness of will (e.g., having a drink after several sober months, against their own reflective judgment). When someone makes a mistaken judgment about whether something is good for her, it is very unusual to explain it on the grounds that she is mistaken about what is ultimately prudentially valuable for her. Competent adults generally know their own self-regarding priorities and have a sense of what they will find enjoyable, satisfying, and worthwhile that exceeds others' predictions on the matter. When they are highly confident about the worthwhileness of their aims and what will make them happy, there is little basis for challenging their judgment.

Our claim here is not merely that it would generally be inappropriate, in practice, to second-guess a competent adult's well-informed judgments about what would contribute to their well-being. We hold that no one has

---

[15] There are close parallels here with narrative identity, one sense of the term "personal identity," as discussed in Chapter 9. However, narrative identity as we construe it is essentially first-personal – that is, it concerns one's *self*-conception. By contrast, the Narrative Requirement concerns a story about someone that could be told by that person or by others who know them well.

greater authority than an autonomous chooser regarding what *constitutes* their well-being. For example, if someone loves listening to opera and finds this activity rewarding, her response to opera makes it good for her to listen to it. If, however, she has exposed herself to a fair amount of opera – thereby becoming relevantly informed about what it has to offer – yet dislikes it and doesn't find it rewarding, then her response makes it the case that listening to opera is not intrinsically good for her.

These arguments notwithstanding, one might continue to disagree with our ascribing so much authority to a mature person regarding her own well-being. We doubt that we can win over everyone who is inclined to disagree with us on this point. We find, however, that ascribing such authority about one's own well-being to a mature adult is both fairly plausible on its face – more plausible than ascribing such authority to an external source such as natural law, a deity, or a rigid conception of human nature – and that this approach has plausible implications regarding individuals' well-being in particular cases, as we hope is evident in the sections that follow.

The third challenge to any account of well-being is related to the challenge just discussed: *being appropriately flexible with respect to differences among people*. It is clear that people have different passions, engage in different projects that they consider worthwhile, and generally enjoy very different activities. We think it implausible that there is any fine-grained ranking of these activities such that, for example, one person's development of her soccer skills is better than another's development of his cooking skills. Further, people have different aptitudes and characters. We find it plausible that most of them can nonetheless flourish. For example, it seems likely that what is good for an introvert and what is good for an extrovert differs. It also seems plausible that neither is intrinsically more fortunate in virtue of being an introvert or an extrovert; that is, both can flourish in the world as humans know it. We also believe, as discussed later in this chapter, that persons with substantial physical and mental disabilities are usually able to flourish if afforded appropriate support, even if their disabilities bar them from some activities (e.g., walking, reading) that many other people consider essential to their well-being.

8.5 Sketch of a Subjective Theory of Well-Being

The preceding sections presented a dialectic featuring competing accounts of prudential value and a set of challenges that any plausible account should meet. Here we describe what we think is the most plausible theory of well-being: a subjective theory that combines aspects of hedonist and desire-satisfaction approaches.

We prefer a subjective theory for several reasons. First, as we have seen, objective theories have difficulty capturing the extent to which it seems that individuals have authority over what is in their interests, and difficulty in granting the flexibility regarding differences among individuals that seems plausible. Though it is possible to build such authority and flexibility into an objective theory, the more we do so, the less it seems that it is the objective goods listed in the theory that are guiding our judgments about well-being. For example, if our theory says that accomplishment is (for anyone) a component of well-being, then the theory can give us guidance but is not flexible enough. If it says that accomplishment is normally a component of well-being, but with exceptions for those, like Tushar, who do not seem to flourish through accomplishment, then the theory may be too indeterminate to be helpful and is so flexible that its status as an objective theory becomes questionable. Second, as we hope to show in sketching our theory, objective theories do not have obvious advantages in terms of better explaining at a fundamental level what well-being consists in or better capturing central intuitive judgments about cases.

Before we outline our preferred theory, it will help to revise the idea that the basic components of happiness are pleasure and the absence of pain.[16] Even if we understand "pleasure" and "pain" broadly to include all pleasant and unpleasant experiences, for various reasons – such as guilt, asceticism, or a desire to concentrate on something else – an individual might not welcome pleasure in certain contexts; and for various reasons – say, a desire to test one's self-control – one might welcome pain in certain contexts.

We replace the terminology of pleasure and pain with that of enjoyment and suffering. *Enjoyment* is a positive response to a whole situation – to which we may bring our values and concerns – while *suffering* is, in parallel fashion, a negative response to a whole situation.[17] Theoretical emphasis

---

[16] This move is suggested in L. W. Sumner, "Welfare, Happiness, and Pleasure," *Utilitas* 4 (1992): 199–223.

[17] Here we might be using the terms "enjoyment" and "suffering" more broadly than they are generally used. For example, we mean to include under "enjoyment" even quiet states of contentment and under "suffering" even mild states of dissatisfaction. It is worth noting, in addition, that our approach can accommodate the plausible idea that a distinctive sort of painful experience – say, spending meaningful time with a dying loved one – can contribute to one's well-being. Someone who values this activity, finding it meaningful, *prefers* it to any pleasant alternative that lacks the meaningful interaction. Here one has a desire, grounded in gritty reality, to engage

on enjoyment and suffering not only permits us to understand cases in which we disavow pleasure or welcome pain but also helps to illuminate the idea that there can be mental states that are much better than just the sensation of pleasure or much worse than the sensation of pain. For example, enjoying an hour shared with someone you love involves much more than just feeling good – it also involves valuing the experience and understanding it in the context of a long-standing relationship. It is also very plausible that what we find valuable about such moments is correspondingly greater than what we find valuable in a pleasant sensation. Thus, enjoyment and the absence of suffering are better candidates than pleasure and the absence of pain for the basic components of happiness.

With this revision, we are in a position to see that the good ideas behind traditional mental-statism and desire-satisfaction theories depend on and can reinforce one another. Critics of mental-state theories are right to point out that a life of good feeling that is not conditioned by contact with reality is not a fully flourishing life. For example, it matters that we actually have deep relationships rather than just believing we do. Relatedly, it matters that what we care about is also appropriately conditioned by reality – if we desire something only because of false beliefs or mistaken reasoning, then fulfilling that desire cannot be expected to promote our well-being.

We propose that *both* enjoyment and the satisfaction of (narrative-relevant) desires are prudentially good for an individual; suffering and the frustration of (narrative-relevant) desires are prudentially bad for an individual. Moreover, reality has an amplifying effect. Enjoyment is prudentially better when it responds to a state of affairs that actually obtains. Likewise, the fulfillment of desires is prudentially better when those desires are rational and informed. The two aspects of well-being are often united where there is felt satisfaction, which usually accompanies our getting what we want. *What unifies enjoyment and desire-satisfaction in a single coherent account of well-being is the fact that both reflect the lived, self-caring perspective of a conscious subject.* The truth in mental-statism is related to the fact that everyone cares about their quality of life, finding some experiences likable or agreeable and some experiences dislikable or disagreeable. The truth in desire-satisfaction theory is the fact that complex subjects can care about or value things, prudentially, beyond their felt quality of life. And the reason that we have to restrict the desires whose satisfaction is relevant

---

meaningfully with the dying loved one – and, as we are about to see, desire-satisfaction has a place in our theory of well-being.

to our well-being is that not all of our desires are about our own lives in the sense captured by the Narrative Requirement.

8.6 Convergence among Plausible Theories

While we have argued in favor of a specific subjective theory of well-being, it is worth noting that its verdicts for many questions in bioethics are likely to converge with those of other plausible theories. For example, earlier we described a plausible objective theory, whose list of goods included autonomous living, deep personal relationships, accomplishment, understanding, aesthetic enrichment, physical and mental functioning, and enjoyment. Such a list would be flexible, such that the well-being of different human beings would be promoted in different ways and to different degrees by the various goods. The flourishing of an intense, solitary intellectual might require more in the way of accomplishment and understanding than in the way of deep relationships; maybe lifelong partnership, for example, is not for them. These and similar observations cohere with the idea that autonomous living – steering by one's own lights – contributes to well-being. Yet for some individuals the burden of decision-making may generate so much distress that they have less of a stake in having a wide range of options than in other goods. Moreover, most of these objective goods are ordinarily tied to a subject's experience. For example, it is hard to imagine having a close friendship without the friendship affecting one's lived experience.

An objective theory with characteristics like this would converge with our subjective theory in many of its verdicts about what makes people's lives go well or badly. Some of the points of convergence that will prove most relevant to problems in bioethics are as follows.

(1) *Enjoyment and suffering will be very important to an individual's well-being on any plausible theory.* In mental-statism, we have argued, they are basic prudential goods and bads. In a plausible objective view, they will count as intrinsically good and bad, respectively, but there are other basic goods than enjoyment and maybe other basic bads than suffering.

(2) *There is a significant asymmetry between enjoyment and suffering.* Although all sentient beings, human and animal, are capable of experiencing pleasant sensations, many things that positively contribute to well-being – at least among human beings – require greater cognitive capacities than mere sentience. These include the ability to

engage in personal projects and, especially, to have meaningful relationships with other people.[18] By contrast, how much one can suffer seems less dependent on one's cognitive capacities. While greater cognitive capacities can amplify the suffering caused by pain, we think that beings incapable of finding meaning or distinctive (nonhedonistic) value in certain kinds of experiences are capable of undergoing intense pain, discomfort, or distress – and that this can be terrible for them.[19] This suggests that, for many nonhuman animals, persistent suffering in the animal's life virtually guarantees that it is not worth continuing. As we will see later, this asymmetry is also important in considering the quality of life of impaired infants.

(3) *Many of the goods of life can only be had – or can be had to a greater extent – by someone with sufficient cognitive capabilities.* On our subjective theory this follows from the earlier analysis of enjoyment. While a barely sentient creature would be able to experience pleasurable sensations, it would be unable to enjoy the rich variety of experiences and states of affairs that human life can offer. On an objective theory, many of the things that are objectively good for someone to attain – including living autonomously, deep personal relationships, many accomplishments, and understanding – require significant cognitive capacities. Note, however, that this observation is not an endorsement of intellectual snobbery. No PhD is needed to act autonomously or have close and meaningful personal relationships; nor need we think that the value of understanding relativity theory is somehow better than the knowledge acquired by gardeners, musicians, electricians, and cooks.

(4) *Mature individuals have considerable authority – when adequately informed – to determine what in in their own interests.* If someone is not misinformed about the empirical facts and is not making errors of reasoning, then we should be very hesitant to contradict her claims about what is good for her. This is clear on our subjective theory; it is a concession that we think an objective theory must make in order to be plausible. This thesis captures much of the spirit of liberal political

---

[18] Compare Nancy Rhoden, "Treatment Dilemmas for Imperiled Newborns: Why Quality of Life Counts," *Southern California Law Review* 58 (1985): 1283; and John Arras, "Toward an Ethic of Ambiguity," *Hastings Center Report* 14 (2) (1984): 25–33.

[19] Although only cognitively sophisticated beings can experience the suffering that is sometimes involved in deep shame or a sense of personal failure, we see no reason to think that these psychologically complex states involve *more intense* suffering than, say, a fox feels with a leg caught in a trap.

philosophy, and we embrace it wholeheartedly. It is also of para-
mount importance in bioethics. The mature individual's capacity to
determine her own best interests is one pillar of the doctrine of
informed consent (the other pillar being respect for autonomy
rights). It is also important in establishing that the self-regarding
priorities and values of a mature individual play a significant role in
determining whether her death, in a given set of circumstances, is
harmful to her (as discussed in Chapter 4).

(5) *Subjective and objective theories will agree on many of the specific
activities and states of affairs that are generally conducive to people's
well-being.* These likely include autonomous living, deep personal
relationships, accomplishment, understanding, aesthetic enrichment,
good physical and mental functioning, and enjoyments.[20] Subjective
and objective theories disagree on the status of these goods. For
subjective theories, the value of these goods is instrumental but, with
the exception of enjoyment, not intrinsic, whereas objective theorists
assert the intrinsic value of such goods. Despite this theoretical
disagreement, there is convergence on the prudential value – whether
instrumental or intrinsic – of these goods. This point of agreement
suggests conditions that both theories will agree tend to make people's lives go better. They include liberty and the protection of
autonomy rights, freedom of association, education and fair equality
of opportunity in the workplace, a minimum economic provision
(food, clothing, shelter, etc.), access to health care, and opportunities
for recreation and relaxation.

Having completed our theoretical exploration of well-being or prudential value, we turn to three significant areas of practical concern in which
prudential value theory proves important.

8.7　Disability in Relation to Well-Being

Both in the academic world and in broader society the nature of disability
and its relationship to human well-being or flourishing is hotly contested.
Until recently, disabilities had been almost universally assumed to be
objective defects in the physical or mental functioning of individuals.
Disability advocates have challenged this simple picture. They deny that

---

[20] We propose this list as plausible for human persons, not necessarily for other types of sentient
beings. We doubt, for example, that the absence of deep personal relationships amounts to a loss –
the absence of a relevant good – for an animal that is solitary by nature.

people with disabilities generally lead lives as bad as people without disabilities suppose and assert that insofar as their lives go worse this is substantially a result of contingent, unjust social conditions.[21] Their challenge raises the questions of what disabilities are and how bad they are for those who possess them. The answers to these questions have implications for how resources should be allocated to benefit people with disabilities, to what extent choosing or allowing disabilities for one's children should be allowed, and, more generally, how to think about disability in relation to human flourishing.

Turn first to the question of how bad disabilities are for the people who possess them. Even the way we have posed the question reveals the common assumption that physical disabilities, such as paraplegia and blindness, are prudentially *bad*. Yet many people with disabilities, even major ones, deny being frustrated with them. Indeed, some state that they are happy to be living a life characterized by their disability and that their experience with it has added something valuable to their lives.[22] If disabilities are inherently disadvantaging, what are we to make of these positive self-reports?

One response is to say that these reports result from *self-deception* and *adaptation*, which can distort people's self-assessments of well-being. People deceive themselves when they permit themselves to believe something despite compelling evidence to the contrary. A disabled person may persuade herself that she is faring as well as she would without the disability, but, it may be argued, such a self-assessment is unreliable. In cases where individuals *lose* functioning as a result of illness or accident, adaptation is common: after an initial period of frustration and a sense of loss, the individual adjusts to his new situation and reports growing satisfaction with his life. Such cases may involve a *lowering of expectations* so that one comes to have desires (say, to watch the ocean waves) that are easier to satisfy than earlier desires (say, to surf or swim in the ocean).

Data on the quality of life of people with disabilities reveal diverging evaluations by people who have them and by people who do not. For the most part people overestimate the negative effects that disability or chronic illness will have on their lives. Their misapprehensions appear to result

---

[21] In this section we use both the "people-first" terminology of "person with a disability" and the term "disabled person," which is argued to highlight the extent to which the disability experienced by people with physical or cognitive differences results from the way that the social environment has been set up.

[22] See Elizabeth Barnes, "Disability, Minority, and Difference," *Journal of Applied Philosophy* 26 (2009): 337–355, especially 341–342.

from excessive focus on the disability's specific effects on their life (e.g., how having a colostomy will affect their ability to go out in a bathing suit, but not about the many activities that would not expose their colostomy bag) and from underestimating their ability to adapt to changed circumstances.[23] However, data also suggest that at least some *acquired* disabilities have long-lasting impacts on subjective well-being.[24] Even though people with acquired disabilities generally report faring better than would be predicted by people without disabilities, on average they report lower well-being than they had before acquiring the disability.[25]

In the light of these phenomena, how should we evaluate the well-being of people with disabilities? For an objective theorist, someone's well-being must take into account not only the extent to which an individual meets their own present standards but also how those standards relate to the objective goods of human life. Accordingly, the objective theorist will maintain that major disabilities, such as blindness, deafness, paraplegia, and substantial cognitive impairment, are inherently disadvantaging and inimical to well-being. On our subjective theory of well-being, however, these conclusions do not follow. Well-being consists in reality-based enjoyment and the fulfillment of informed desires. The presence of disabilities may or may not, in individual cases, reduce well-being by these measures. We do not think that people with disabilities will, in general, be worse at identifying whether they are flourishing according to these criteria than people without disabilities. Moreover, the people living with the disabilities are clearly best placed to judge what living with them is really like.

Now, it is *possible* that people with disabilities who rate their quality of life highly are routinely self-deceived. But without good evidence in favor of this claim it seems as though we would be assuming that someone is self-deceived simply because we have assumed already that they must be worse off. Here, as elsewhere, barring evidence to the contrary, we accept that mature individuals are generally good authorities regarding their own well-being.

[23] Peter Ubel et al., "Misimagining the Unimaginable: The Disability Paradox and Health Care Decision Making," *Health Psychology* 24 (4S) (2005): S57.
[24] Richard Lucas, "Long-Term Disability Is Associated with Lasting Changes in Subjective Well-Being: Evidence from Two Nationally Representative Longitudinal Studies," *Journal of Personality and Social Psychology* 92 (2007): 717.
[25] Here we generalize over disabilities, even though the extent to which people adapt varies greatly depending on the type of disability. For example, people tend not to adapt psychologically very much to chronic pain, degenerative diseases, or schizophrenia. Psychological adaptation to stable, physical disabilities is much greater.

The phenomenon of adaptation following the acquisition of a disability is also not as problematic on our subjective theory as it might be for an objective theorist. Take the person who was once a keen swimmer but is now too physically frail to enter the ocean. Perhaps, to compensate, she takes up painting seascapes instead. Over time, she comes to enjoy painting the ocean as much as she once enjoyed swimming in it and comes to have desires related to watercolors and views, rather than exercising in the water. Provided that her enjoyment and desires are not based on mistaken beliefs or errors of reasoning, her new pastime may contribute just as much to her well-being as did her old one.

We have argued that there are good reasons to trust the evaluations of people with disabilities regarding how well their lives are going. Frequently, those evaluations rate the quality of life with a disability higher than it would be rated by someone without the disability. Nevertheless, as already noted, most people who acquire a major disability experience some enduring reduction in their subjective well-being. Perhaps, in addition, those who have *lifelong* disabilities typically, or on average, experience a lower level of well-being than those lacking such conditions. If in fact there is, typically, some disadvantage associated with disability, or at least major disabilities, what is the basis of this disadvantage? Answering this question requires us to ask what disability is.

According to the *medical model of disability*, a disability is a relatively long-lasting, biologically based condition of an individual that significantly impairs functioning in one or more ways. According to this mainstream conception, it is the person's condition itself that causes problematic functioning. Being blind, for example, is a disability because it excludes one from the important function of seeing. The *social model of disability*, by contrast, claims that disability involves a limitation or loss of opportunities to participate in valued activities or forms of community due to social or institutional barriers. According to this *disability-as-difference thesis*, so-called disabilities are really only differences in functioning from those considered normal.[26] From this perspective, such "disabilities" as dyslexia, deafness, blindness, and paraplegia are not *inherently* disadvantageous any more than being non-Caucasian is inherently disadvantageous. Disadvantages stem from the context in which the relevant conditions

---

[26] See, e.g., Union of the Physically Impaired against Segregation, *Fundamental Principles of Disability* (London: UPIAS, 1976); and Ron Amundson, "Disability, Ideology, and Quality of Life: A Bias in Biomedical Ethics," in David Wasserman, Jerome Bickenbach, and Robert Wachbroit (eds.), *Quality of Life and Human Difference* (Cambridge: Cambridge University Press, 2005), 101–124.

exist, contexts that often feature substantial discrimination and lack of consideration on the part of the "nondisabled" majority. In other words, any disadvantages that accompany the "disability" are contingent, rather than being necessary consequences of an objectively bad condition.

The case for the disability-as-difference thesis may proceed as follows. Whether a given condition is disabling depends on the context, environment, and existing social arrangements. Unless one wants to become a pilot, color-blindness is mostly ignored and not considered a disability. But if the green and red lights of traffic lights were placed in varying configurations so that color-blind people could not distinguish them, these people's ability to drive safely would be significantly impaired and they would be disabled in that regard. Dyslexia is regarded as a significant disability only where reading is expected. Before reading became part of human culture, the same condition was probably not noticed, much less considered a handicap. Deafness is considered a disability by a hearing majority that uses spoken language, but it is really only a difference – one that might not be disadvantageous in certain environments. If everyone signed instead of spoke, and texted rather than called by telephone, deafness might not seem to be a disability to the hearing majority. Indeed, if our world were filled with loud, varying noises that consistently distracted hearing individuals, hearing might count as a disability.[27]

Acceptance of the social model of disability would have significant implications. First, if disabilities are disadvantageous only because of the way the human environment has been arranged – that is, in a way that is convenient for nondisabled people without taking into account non-"normal" ways of living – then there will be a strong case in favor of removing or compensating for these disadvantages. If society makes disabled people worse off, then society has a strong obligation to correct this injustice. Second, the social model implies that people with disabilities are not people in need of "fixing." Rather than expending resources on medical interventions to remove or prevent disabilities, we should be finding ways to change the environment so that people with disabilities are able to flourish.

We find the social model to offer a helpful corrective to the naïve simplicity of the medical model: it is true that there are many socially determined ways in which people with disabilities are disadvantaged because they do not function in the same way as the majority of people.

---

[27] Cf. Robert Sparrow, "Defending Deaf Culture: The Case of Cochlear Implants," *Journal of Political Philosophy* 13 (2005): 135–152, at 138.

Examples include buildings that can be accessed only by stairs, important documents written in small print and unavailable in braille, and public lectures without signers. However, we think the social model exaggerates insofar as it claims that all disabilities are nothing more than social constructions.

We favor a more moderate *interactive model*, which construes disability as a product of the interaction between biological dysfunctions of an individual's body or mind – often called *impairments* – and the social and physical environment in which the individual lives.[28] Take a disability like blindness. Irrespective of society's choices, blindness is a physical trait that prevents normal functioning of a sort – namely, vision – that is deeply important to creatures like us. It is hard to imagine an environment in which humans would flourish but seeing would not tend to be beneficial to them. Inability to see is therefore an objective impairment in human beings, who normally see. Another example is clinical depression that is caused by an individual's natural brain chemistry (as opposed to being a response to particular events or circumstances). Depression, by its nature, causes suffering and makes enjoyment more difficult, so depression is inherently disadvantageous. To generalize, many severe disabilities prevent or impair functions that are – from the perspective of real human beings – undeniably important. These impairments, by their very nature, tend to interfere with opportunities for human well-being in the environments in which human beings live.

It is important to be clear about what does and does not follow from this interactive account of disability. It implies that at least some disabilities generally reduce the well-being of people who have them. For these disabilities, therefore, there are sometimes good reasons to develop and provide treatments for them rather than focus only on changing social and environmental factors. It also supports a presumption against permitting prospective parents to choose to create children with those disabilities when there are alternatives.[29]

On the other hand, the interactive account does not abandon the insights of the social model, which should serve as helpful correctives to common ways of thinking about disabilities. First, we understand disabilities as involving an interaction between two factors: (1) a biological

---

[28] For a helpful discussion of these models, see Wasserman et al., *Quality of Life and Human Differences*, 12–13. For a critique of the distinction between disability and impairment that is central to the interactive model, see Elizabeth Barnes, "Against Impairment: Replies to Aas, Howard, and Francis," *Philosophical Studies* 175 (2018): 1151–1162.

[29] This presumption will be challenged in some "nonidentity" cases (see Chapter 10).

impairment of a function that is valued – either in contingent social circumstances (e.g., reading) or in all realistically imaginable human circumstances (e.g., seeing) – and (2) a social context, which importantly includes attitudes toward individuals with the impairment in question and any accommodations for it. In light of the second, social factor, we suggest that prejudicial attitudes toward individuals with disabilities must be identified and countered and that accommodations should be creative and extensive. These responses will help to increase opportunities and respect for individuals with disabilities, with likely improvements to their well-being.

Second, a particular disability need not prove disadvantageous for a particular individual even if it is disadvantageous for most people who have the disability.[30] Maybe it is true, for example, that blind people experience more frustration and suffering, *on average*, than sighted people for reasons connected to their blindness. However, if a particular blind person is just as happy with his life as the average sighted person is with her life, then there is no reason to judge his well-being to be lower due to blindness. Moreover, if it is true that blind – or deaf or paraplegic – people tend to be less happy than their "nondisabled" peers, that is due in significant measure to social arrangements, institutions, and attitudes of bias and condescension that could improve. So, even if some group of persons with disabilities is less well-off *today*, that may be a contingent fact rather than a necessary consequence of their disability.[31]

8.8 Making Decisions for Impaired Newborns

Some infants are born with such severe medical complications that it may be questioned whether continued life is in their interest. In the cases in which this question is most pressing, the complications entail not simply disabilities but the prospect of substantial, enduring suffering. In such cases, parents and health care providers may have to decide whether to initiate life-extending treatments, including the artificial administration of nutrition and hydration. As discussed in Chapter 5, where someone cannot make decisions for themself and has no advance directive, as is the case with all newborns, medical treatment decisions should be guided

---

[30] Depression and chronic pain seem to be exceptions due to their directly negative impact on well-being.

[31] This point is advanced in David Wasserman, "Philosophical Issues in the Definition and Social Response to Disability," in Gary Albrecht, Katherine Seelman, and Michael Bury (eds.), *Handbook of Disability Studies* (London: Sage, 2001), 230.

by the reasonable subject standard. According to this standard, the proxy decision-maker for the child – normally a parent or parents – ought to decide on the child's behalf as the child would decide if they were a rational agent acting prudently within the constraints of morality.

The discussion in Chapter 5 noted that the reasonable subject standard differs from the best-interests standard, in part, by explicitly taking into account the interests of other parties who are affected by the proxy decision-maker's choice. In the case of a decision about whether to treat a newborn with an incurable, serious condition, two additional sets of interests are likely to be relevant. First, there are the interests of the parents, who will be responsible for looking after the child (assuming they do not give the child up for adoption). For children with severe disabilities this might entail a lifetime of caregiving. Also relevant are the interests of other members of society – especially others with serious medical needs – who are less likely to get needed treatment if the newborn is treated. All health care systems have limited resources: expending substantial resources on a newborn with a serious condition means fewer resources for others. For example, the baby might be occupying a space in a neonatal ICU that could be given to another very sick newborn with better prospects.

Although, as some of the examples that follow illustrate, we think that it can be legitimate for parents to give these other interests weight, we urge caution about when they should be allowed to do so. Very young children are completely dependent on others and unable to advocate for themselves. If parents are granted excessive discretion to refuse beneficial treatment, there is a danger that the newborn's interests will end up being inappropriately sacrificed. (Decisions about the rationing of care, where multiple parties would benefit from the scarce resources being distributed, should not be made by the parents of one of those parties, in any case.) We therefore recommend that parents not be permitted to refuse treatment for a neonate who is reasonably expected to benefit from it – except in cases in which benefit to the child is likely to be modest and the burden to the child's family is expected to be enormous. Where the child will *not* benefit from treatment, however, the interests of family and of the broader health care system provide strong reasons to withhold treatment.

This discussion indicates that in order to help parents make good decisions about the treatment of their severely sick newborn children, it is vital to assess whether a child is expected to live a life worth living if treated. In what follows, we consider a variety of incurable neonatal impairments. In each case, we ask whether it is in the interests of the infants to survive or to be given just palliative care to mitigate any suffering. Where their survival depends on medical treatment, the question is whether it is in their interests to receive such treatment. In cases in which no medical treatment is required for survival, the question is whether it is in their interest to receive food and water.[32] (We do not engage here with the additional issue of whether and when it would be permissible to actively terminate the life of a suffering infant, rather than allow the infant to die by not intervening. For discussion of the additional issues involved in euthanasia, see Chapter 4.) In several cases the expected net benefits to the child of treatment are either questionable or relatively low. We therefore consider, in addition, whether burdens to the caregivers might make it permissible to decline treatment.

Earlier we identified an asymmetry between enjoyment and suffering. Many factors that enhance well-being require greater cognitive capacities than mere sentience. These include the abilities to think of oneself as an enduring agent, to form plans and pursue them, and to have meaningful relationships with others. By contrast, how much one can suffer seems less dependent on one's cognitive capacities. Thus, we think that *very severe* cognitive disabilities can reduce an individual's capacity to benefit while still allowing them to experience substantial suffering. Where there is expected to be considerable suffering, then, this suffering is more likely to outweigh the benefits of continued life than it would in the case of an individual who is less cognitively disabled, since the latter individual is more likely to find sources of meaning and value that compensate for suffering.[33]

Anencephaly is a condition that results when the head side of the fetal neural tube fails to close, resulting in the absence of major portions of the brain, skull, and scalp. Infants with this disorder lack cerebral hemispheres, which neuroscientists generally agree are necessary for consciousness.[34] Anencephalic infants, however, are often born with a functioning brain stem, permitting certain reflexes such as spontaneous breathing and

---

[32] Our characterization of these medical conditions has benefited from three medical websites (all accessed September 28, 2020): National Institute of Neurological Disorders and Stroke, "All Disorders" (www.ninds.nih.gov/disorders/disorder_index.htm), US National Library of Medicine, "MedlinePlus: Medical Encyclopedia" (www.nlm.nih.gov/medlineplus/encyclopedia.html), and Genetics Home Reference, "Health Conditions" (http://ghr.nlm.nih.gov/BrowseConditions).

[33] Dominic Wilkinson, "Is It in the Best Interests of an Intellectually Disabled Infant to Die?," *Journal of Medical Ethics* 32 (2006): 454–459.

[34] Some neuroscientists, however, reject this view, holding that some form of consciousness is, or might be, possible for individuals lacking a cerebrum (see especially Bjorn Merker, "Consciousness without a Cerebral Cortex: A Challenge for Neuroscience and Medicine," *Behavioral and Brain Sciences* 30 [2007]: 63–81). Our discussion assumes that anencephaly precludes conscious experience or at least any sort of conscious experience that would enable a life worth continuing.

responses to sound or touch. Neurologists generally agree that such reflexive behaviors are not indications of pain or other conscious experiences, so that the capacity for sentience and higher mental life are permanently precluded. The life expectancy of such infants, even with life support, is not more than a few days or weeks – although a few cases of survival for more than a year have occurred.

How should we understand the interests of anencephalic infants? In our view, such infants have no interests at all because they are permanently bereft of consciousness. They cannot suffer any more than they can experience enjoyment. They cannot be harmed or benefited – at least in the usual senses of these terms that pertain to well-being. Being kept alive is therefore neither in their interests nor contrary to them. This entails that there is no morally important reason to provide life-supporting medical treatment (except perhaps to give parents a little time to come to terms with their child's condition). Given that there are weighty reasons against expending scarce medical resources on individuals who receive no benefit from them, the morally best decision for parents and clinicians is not to treat these infants.

Tay-Sachs disease is a genetic disorder in which infants, after apparently normal development for several months, begin a relentless physical and mental decline.[35] Afflicted individuals become blind, deaf, and unable to swallow. Muscles atrophy, leading to paralysis. Neurological symptoms include seizures and the onset of dementia. Children with Tay-Sachs may need a feeding tube. Most die by age four from recurring lung infections. Treatment is solely aimed at relieving symptoms, such as by using medication to prevent seizures and relax muscles.

Overall, we think that infants who live out their lives with Tay-Sachs do not experience enough good to outweigh the bad in their lives. Unlike normally developing children who are increasingly able to interact with their environment and the people around them, these infants become less and less able to access such goods. Moreover, there is clearly a great deal of suffering that accompanies the relentless decline in nervous system functioning.

However, because of the delay before symptoms of Tay-Sachs appear, the question of whether and how to treat newborns with the condition is challenging. The first months of life will not be bad for the infant, which suggests that it would be in her interests to live through those at least. It is

[35] A rare form of Tay-Sachs occurs in patients in their twenties or early thirties. We discuss only the more common, juvenile condition.

only because she is destined to suffer so much later that dying immediately after birth would be preferable. How much she will suffer later depends on both how effective symptomatic management will be and what options are available for assisting the death of young children. An additional complicating factor is the interests of the child's parents. It is not just that providing care for a medically complicated child is more burdensome than caring for other children – this might be true but primarily argues in favor of giving such parents much greater support. It is also the awful experience for the parent of raising and loving a child who is destined to die so young and in such a terrible manner. One could scarcely blame a parent who wanted to avoid such a fate.

Given the amount of suffering for the child and parents involved in seeing Tay-Sachs disease through its natural course, we think that the option of ending the child's life at birth should be available. Depending on one's views on the correct policy regarding euthanasia, this might entail interventions to end the newborn's life directly or the withholding of nutrition and hydration and providing comfort care. Moreover, if there will be no further opportunity to end the child's life when she has declined to the point that the suffering outweighs other prudential goods, it would be better to choose death as a newborn than wait until the child is three or four and suffers respiratory arrest.

Lesch–Nyhan syndrome (LNS) is an inherited disorder involving over-production of uric acid. Symptoms include severe gout, poor muscle control, and developmental delay. Few children with this disease learn to walk and many have severe difficulty with speech. Beginning in the second year, compulsive self-mutilating behaviors emerge, such as lip- and finger-biting and head banging. Symptoms also include severe kidney dysfunc-tion and neurological symptoms such as grimacing and writhing that are similar to those found in persons with Huntington's disease. Individuals with LNS usually die of renal failure in their first or second decade of life, though some survive well into adulthood.

LNS is clearly associated with a great deal of suffering. The physical symptoms are painful. The inability to walk and communication difficul-ties present serious impediments to many of the activities that make human lives go well. The self-mutilating behaviors are injurious to health, interfere still further with the patient being able to do as they want, and are highly aversive experiences – LNS patients do not welcome these behaviors but view them as alien. No one would deny that this is a tragic condition.

Is LNS so bad that it is better to die than to live with it? Despite some uncertainty on this matter, we think it probably is not. Three consider-ations are crucial to drawing this conclusion.

First, LNS is frequently described as involving substantial intellectual disability and consequently lower prospects for flourishing.[36] However, the data on cognitive impairment that seem to support this picture might reflect the challenges of administering standardized tests to this patient population, who have communication difficulties, tend to recalcitrant behavior, and cannot be schooled in standard ways. A survey of caregivers of forty-two LNS patients concluded that:

> Only 1 boy appears to have any significant generalized cognitive impairment. The patients' memory for both recent and past events is excellent, their emotional life has a normal range of reactions and is appropriate; they have good concentration, are capable of abstract reasoning, have good self-awareness, and are highly social.[37]

A later study suggested a picture lying somewhere between the claim of pervasive intellectual disability and the alternative just quoted: "intellectual levels ranged from moderate mental retardation to low average intelligence, with some common patterns of strength and weakness."[38] Based on these findings, and despite some empirical uncertainty about LNS in relation to cognitive disability, it seems reasonable to assume that in general people with LNS are capable of enjoying many things, including meaningful personal relationships.

A second crucial consideration in our thinking about this condition is that the self-mutilating behaviors that evoke such consternation in commentators on LNS can be managed to a substantial extent. At its simplest this management involves the use of restraints. It should be emphasized that people with LNS welcome receiving these restraints when they feel an urge to self-harm coming on.

Third, given that people with LNS frequently reach a point at which they can have reasonable understanding of their condition, we should respect their own views about whether their lives are worth living. We do not know of any studies that asked people with LNS so directly about their views on their lives, but suicidal behavior does not seem to be common. That suggests that people with LNS generally want to continue their lives, and we doubt there are compelling reasons to second-guess their apparent judgments that their lives are worth continuing.

---

[36] See, e.g., Wilkinson, "Is It in the Best Interests of an Intellectually Disabled Infant to Die?," 456.
[37] Lowell Anderson, Monique Ernst, and Susan Davis, "Cognitive Abilities of Patients with Lesch-Nyhan Disease," *Journal of Autism and Developmental Disorders* 22 (1992): 189–203, at 189.
[38] See Wendy Matthews, Anita Solan, and Gabor Barabas, "Cognitive Functioning in Lesch-Nyhan Syndrome," *Developmental Medicine and Child Neurology* 37 (1995): 715–722.

At the same time, the interests of parental caregivers are also morally important. Parents might find the prospect of raising a child with this syndrome, even with optimal support, overwhelmingly burdensome, especially considering the significant chance of losing the child in their first decade or two. Such a judgment would be understandable and might justify a decision to bring about the death of an infant diagnosed with LNS (unless there is a realistic prospect of transferring the child to adoptive parents who are well prepared to assume the burdens of care). Moreover, if parents made such a decision, any harm that death would entail for the infant would be significantly discounted due to his very weak psychological connections over time (see Chapter 4's discussion of our "gradualist" account of the harm of death). If, however, such an infant grows into a person, with the associated rights against harm and much stronger psychological connections to his future self, this would cease to be a permissible option for the parents to choose.

Juvenile Batten disease, an inherited disorder of the nervous system, is another condition that features a postinfancy onset. Indeed, its onset is sufficiently late that afflicted children are likely to be aware of their profound loss of capacities. Symptoms usually appear around age five or six, with vision problems or seizures. Vision loss advances rapidly, eventually resulting in blindness. After the initial symptoms appear, children with this disease experience developmental regression – losing previously acquired skills such as the ability to speak in complete sentences and motor skills such as the ability to walk or sit. They also develop bodily stiffness and slow movements. Affected children may have epilepsy, heart problems, mood disorders, and behavioral problems. Most people with juvenile Batten disease live into their twenties.

Given the relatively late onset of juvenile Batten disease, afflicted individuals typically have a significant segment of healthy childhood. After symptoms begin to appear, cognitive and physical decline is relentless and, with some aspects of health such as vision, rapid. What makes this disease especially devastating is that its victims experience life as ordinary-functioning, healthy children before undergoing the loss of their powers and health. The decline occurs late enough in childhood for the children to be aware of their deterioration. And most endure their condition for many years.

As with LNS, however, the tragic nature of the disease should not lead us to the conclusion that it is better to die at birth than to live a life with juvenile Batten disease. Even during the child's decline, most of the time their life will be worth living. After all, even if we judge blindness or the inability to walk to be bad for someone, these conditions are entirely compatible with a life worth living. Likewise, with most mood disorders and other cognitive problems that people with juvenile Batten disease experience; very rarely would we judge that someone's depression is so bad that their life is not worth continuing. In considering these matters, those of us who are relatively healthy might assume that life with this condition is intolerable – because it is so much worse than our status quo – but fail to grasp that those who have this condition may regard living with it as preferable to not living at all.

At the same time, like LNS, juvenile Batten might be a condition in which burdens to caregivers are so great as to justify a parental prerogative not to preserve the life of an infant with this condition – despite the likelihood that the child would have several years of worthwhile life. We have in mind not only the burdens of providing direct care to an afflicted child as their symptoms become more severe, but also the emotional burden of losing a child in late childhood or adolescence. We find it reasonable that these costs to caregivers overturn the usual presumption that, if a child is likely to have a life worth living (even if it is a short life), the only reasonable option is to try to preserve that life. As with LNS, however, we note the possibility that the availability of capable adoptive parents might undermine any such prerogative of the biological parents.

The final condition we will consider is *Down syndrome* (or Trisomy 21), a condition caused by an extra chromosome 21. Individuals with Down syndrome have below average cognitive ability. About half of affected children are born with a heart defect and sometimes there are digestive abnormalities, such as blockage of the intestine. Individuals with Down syndrome also have an increased risk of gastroesophageal reflux (a backflow of stomach acids), celiac disease, hypothyroidism, and hearing and vision problems.

The severity of cognitive impairment and most of the physical problems that sometimes accompany the former are difficult, if not impossible, to forecast after an infant with Down syndrome has been born. Nevertheless, children, adolescents, and adults with Down syndrome – at least when supported appropriately – generally appear to have happy lives with significant personal relationships and often continual employment as adults. They are often among the highest-functioning of cognitively disabled persons.

Even if it is obvious that a diagnosis of Down does not justify over-turning the ordinary presumption that survival is in a newborn's interests, what about Down plus a significant physical dysfunction? Suppose a baby with Down syndrome is born with an immediately detectable heart defect or intestinal blockage. Normally, these anomalies can be easily corrected by surgery, so their presence along with the cognitive impairment of Down provides no serious reason to question the usual presumption in favor of preserving neonatal life. In several high-profile US cases in the 1970s and early 1980s, parents and medical personnel reasoned differently, allowing infants with Down syndrome who had life-threatening but surgically correctable defects to die from nontreatment. These decisions were seriously wrong.

8.9   Irreversibly Unconscious Patients

The previous section included a discussion of anencephalic infants, whose condition (neurologists generally assume) makes them permanently incapable of conscious experience. There are several other conditions – besides the temporary periods of dreamless sleep that we regularly undergo – that render an individual temporarily or permanently unconscious. *Coma* is a state in which one appears to be asleep and, except for spontaneous breathing, may appear to casual observation to be dead. Usually, within a few weeks, a comatose patient (1) awakens into consciousness, (2) dies in virtue of meeting legal criteria for *brain death* (in which all significant brain functions, including those necessary for spontaneous breathing, are irretrievably lost), or (3) enters a so-called *vegetative state*. In vegetative states, there is an absence of responsiveness and awareness due to overwhelming cerebral dysfunction but sufficient function in the brainstem to permit sleep-wake cycles – and therefore a sort of unconscious "wakefulness" – as well as a host of reflexes including yawning, swallowing, and eye tracking. The apparent wakefulness and reflex movements of vegetative patients sometimes induce observers to believe that the patients have some subjective awareness or consciousness. However, the absence of cerebral function appears to preclude this possibility. Matters are complicated by the fact that it is sometimes difficult to distinguish vegetative states from *minimally conscious states*, which patients can enter when they partially recover from vegetative states or comas. In minimally conscious states, patients have some conscious experience but are still too neurologically compromised to produce unambiguously purposeful or conscious behaviors.

The term *persistent vegetative state* (PVS) is a source of some confusion. According to standard medical usage in the United States and many other countries, a diagnosis of PVS – based on various neurological and other tests – indicates that due to extensive and apparently irreversible brain damage, a patient is highly unlikely ever to regain consciousness. Informal guidelines permit making this diagnosis once a patient has been in a vegetative state for four weeks with no indications of recovery. Occasionally, such diagnoses prove incorrect when a patient emerges from the vegetative state into consciousness.

For the purposes of our discussion, we will introduce a technical term: *irreversibly unconscious state* (IUS). We will use this term to refer to any medical state about which competent neurologists would judge that recovery of consciousness is, for all practical purposes, impossible. Thus, IUS includes, along with anencephaly, PVS or coma where expert opinion states that there is no realistic possibility of the patient's regaining consciousness.[39]

Family and medical personnel must decide whether to terminate life support for IUS patients. According to the commonly accepted hierarchy of medical decision-making standards, in cases in which informed consent is impossible, proxy decision-makers should follow a valid advance directive if one exists and applies to the case at hand. If not, they should attempt to apply the substituted judgment standard by determining on the basis of available evidence what the patient would have wanted in the present medical circumstance. If there is insufficient evidence to support a substituted judgment, then caregivers should apply the best-interests standard.

In Chapter 5, we argued for several modifications to this hierarchy. First, filling out an advance directive or appointing a surrogate decision-maker constitutes an exercise of someone's autonomy. There are good reasons to respect those decisions. Deciding on someone's behalf using a substituted judgment standard, however, does not involve the patient exercising their autonomy at all. Insofar as the substituted judgment standard is warranted, it is because what people would want is often a good guide to what is in their interests. This follows directly from our theory of well-being. Second, the best-interests standard does not capture all the considerations that are relevant to deciding on someone else's

---

[39] In this discussion we assume that the legal standards for the determination of death remain as they are today. Accordingly, we assume that an individual who is irreversibly unconscious yet maintains cardiopulmonary function or at least some brain function is alive. In Chapter 9 we argue that the higher-brain standard of death – according to which one who has irreversibly lost the capacity for consciousness is dead – is as reasonable as the cardiopulmonary and whole-brain standards. We do not infer from this that changing current laws is necessarily optimal; an alternative is to retain current laws and liberalize certain practices traditionally associated with a determination of death such as vital organ procurement and unilateral discontinuation of life support.

behalf, since sometimes the interests of others are morally relevant. Instead, where someone has not given instructions on how they should be treated, a proxy decision-maker should adopt a reasonable subject standard and ask: What would be in the patient's interests within the constraints of morality?

What can our theory of well-being tell us about an IUS patient's interests? IUS patients cannot have experiences, either now or in the future. This has led theorists who accept the Experience Requirement to judge that an IUS patient has no interests, in which case there is no reason to maintain them on life support.[40] As Allen Buchanan and Dan Brock put it, "the best interest principle does not apply to beings who have no capacity for consciousness and whose good can never matter to them."[41]

We rejected the Experience Requirement in favor of a theory that includes the satisfaction of informed, narrative-relevant desires as one aspect of well-being. Because people often have desires regarding what will happen to them in a state of irreversible unconsciousness, and these desires might be important enough for their satisfaction or frustration to affect their life stories, this suggests that IUS patients sometimes have interests.[42] In some cases, then, remaining on life support is either in the interests of or contrary to the interests of an IUS patient. How should a proxy decision-maker then decide what to do?

To begin, note that the extent to which a patient's interests can be affected by her treatment while in an IUS is very limited. The patient cannot suffer, nor can she enjoy anything. Moreover, because the majority of people's desires are intimately linked to experiences that they could have, none of these desires can be fulfilled or frustrated by what happens to her when permanently unconscious.

---

[40] Here we set aside the possibility of justified continuation of life support for a limited time in order to give loved ones an opportunity to say goodbye to the patient while the patient is alive.

[41] "Deciding for Others: Competency," *Milbank Quarterly* 64 (supp. 2) (1986): 67–80, at 73.

[42] Some commentators thought this was true of Nancy Cruzan, the American PVS patient whose parents fought for removing her feeding tube, arguing that some of Cruzan's prior statements expressed a desire not to live in PVS. In response to this case, the US Supreme Court recognized for the first time a right to refuse unwanted medical treatment while also judging that the state of Missouri (where Cruzan resided) did not violate her constitutional rights by applying a "clear and convincing" standard of evidence for determining what she would have wanted. See United States Supreme Court, *Cruzan v. Director, Missouri Department of Health*, in *United States [Supreme Court] Reports* 497, 1990: 261–357. For a commentary that rejects the "clear and convincing" standard as overly strict, see John Arras, "Beyond *Cruzan*: Individual Rights, Family Autonomy, and the Persistent Vegetative State," *Journal of the American Geriatric Society* 39 (1991): 1018–1024.

Nevertheless, it is useful to consider desires someone may have that could be relevant to her treatment while in an IUS. These are most likely to be desires relating to her body, to specific interventions that might be used on her, and to other people. Regarding her body, she might be concerned about the "indignities" involved in continued care, such as emaciation, highly contorted postures, permanent incontinence, and compromised privacy. These concerns are amplified for patients for whom resuscitation will be attempted if they experience cardiac arrest. Such resuscitation can be quite violent. On the other hand, she might care about the continued biological life of her body and want it to be prolonged as long as possible. Someone might care about specific medical interventions – for example, she might not want cardiopulmonary resuscitation, artificial respiration, and other "aggressive" life support, but still want artificial nutrition and hydration as well as antibiotics as needed. Regarding other people, one might think that such a patient can continue deep personal relationships, but such relationships would be so one-sided – with the patient completely unaware of them – that we cannot plausibly ascribe much of a contribution to the patient's well-being on the basis of such relationships. She might still care a great deal about the well-being of the people close to her; for example, she might want them not to see her waste away or be burdened by medical decision-making, or she might want them at her bedside.

After weighing up whether continuing on life support is in the IUS patient's interests, a decision must be made about what to do. If there is reason to think that maintaining life-support measures would be contrary to the patient's interests, then the decision is straightforward: these measures should be discontinued. If there is no evidence to suggest that she would have wanted to remain on life support, we think it is also best to remove her from it. For most people, there are likely to be desires that will be thwarted either way. A judgment about whether remaining on life support is in someone's interests is therefore very difficult to make. But there are also additional reasons for taking her off life support relating to the opportunity costs of using scarce medical resources. Where we are unsure either way about the patient's interests, these additional reasons should be sufficient to provide a verdict about what to do. In this regard, it is worth recalling how restricted the possible interests are that can be affected in an IUS. It does not take as much to outweigh them as it would to outweigh the interests of someone who was expected to regain consciousness.

If, on the other hand, there is good evidence that a patient in an IUS would prefer to remain alive, then this provides a consideration in favor of maintaining her on life support. In this case the question of how to proceed is much more challenging. In most cases, we think the presumption should be to withdraw life-support measures from irreversibly unconscious patients. The factual basis of this prerogative is concerns about resource allocation and the reasonable assumption that better use can be made of a health care institution's resources and personnel. The moral basis of this presumption becomes apparent when we remember the proviso of the reasonable subject standard, which calls for making medical decisions as the patient would make if acting prudently *within the constraints of morality*. In this context, the constraints of morality include responsible use of health care resources.

CHAPTER 9

Personal Identity Theory

9.1 Introduction

In everyday human life, the identification of persons is so commonplace and straightforward that it might seem odd to suggest that personal identity could be the subject of intense scholarly debate. Many social interactions require us to know who the other person in the interaction is. Usually, we have no trouble identifying family members, friends, colleagues, and acquaintances. In our internal psychological lives, each of us presupposes that our memories feature us – not someone else – as their subject and that it is us – not someone else – who will carry out the actions we plan. In moral and legal contexts, we assume that if someone did something culpably wrong at some past time, it is that person who bears primary responsibility for the action. Marriages and other human relationships presuppose the continuing existence of the individuals who occupy the relevant positions in the relationships even if their characteristics change significantly over time. Each person is distinct and persons typically live for many years. We are so familiar with such facts and so adept at identifying and reidentifying persons in everyday life that these phenomena may seem unworthy of investigation.

Yet in some situations personal identity is uncertain. A victim of amnesia may know neither who he is nor the experiences his past contained. An individual in the late stages of progressive dementia may strike others as not being the person they knew before. Meanwhile, the demented individual may feel no connection to her distant past and have no plans for the future. Even in cases that are free of medical pathology, some aspects of our existence might provoke questions about identity. For example, you might wonder when you came into existence. Did you exist as a fetus before it had any mental life? Might you, on the other end of life, continue to exist after losing the capacity for consciousness? The answers to such questions are far from obvious.

As these reflections suggest, questions about personal identity intersect with issues in bioethics. In the bioethics literature, personal identity theory has animated discussions concerning the authority of advance directives, the definition of death, the ethics of human enhancement, and the "nonidentity problem" (as discussed in Chapter 10). Considerations of personal identity have also played a role – sometimes only implicitly – in debates about such topics as abortion and embryo research, preimplantation genetic diagnosis and embryo selection, and prenatal genetic manipulation.

In this chapter, we explore four approaches to personal identity as philosophers have usually understood this concept – that is, in terms of so-called *numerical* identity: person-based accounts, a biological account, a mind-based account, and a social account. In exploring person-based accounts, we introduce the distinct concept of *narrative* identity, which involves a person's self-conception or self-told story about herself and her life. The chief upshots of our theoretical investigation are, first, that person-based accounts and the social account are implausible accounts of numerical identity and, second, that the mind-based and biological accounts are *both* plausible. This motivates a pluralistic approach to personal identity in the sense that policies and practices should be consistent with both accounts.

With these theoretical resources, we turn to three areas of application. In the first, we neutralize some concerns about human enhancement through biomedical means. In the second, we investigate and ultimately vindicate the authority of advance directives in cases of severe dementia. Finally, we take up the controversy over the definition of death and associated questions about unilateral discontinuation of life support and vital organ procurement. We find that proper resolution of these issues turns primarily on practical considerations other than the nature of death. The overarching lesson of our practical investigations *deflates* the role of personal identity theory in bioethics. Contrary to the claims of numerous bioethicists who have invoked personal identity, after we have narrowed down the theoretical options to genuinely plausible accounts, the latter do not have far-reaching implications in bioethics.

9.2 Person-Based Accounts and Their Difficulties

Dating back at least to the pre-Socratics in the West, philosophers have wondered about the fact that objects of ordinary experience can change over time yet continue to exist. A diary may change gradually – its pages becoming more yellow, the binding less sturdy – yet common sense suggests that one object, the diary, persists through the changes. On the other hand, truly radical change may end an object's existence, for example, when the diary is burned to ashes. Some changes, apparently, are compatible with the persistence of a particular object, while other changes are not.[1] Identity in this sense is called *numerical identity*.

What are the criteria of identity for beings like us, that is, human persons? In Chapter 7, we conceptualized persons as *beings with narrative identities – relatively complex understandings of themselves as persisting over time and as having an implicit life story*. Thus, while many mammals and birds may display a degree of rationality and some awareness of themselves as persisting over time, few if any nonhuman animals possess a narrative identity. We assume that most human beings have acquired a narrative identity and therefore qualify as persons by the age of three or four.

Narrative identity constitutes a second sense of the term "personal identity." Whereas numerical identity concerns criteria for persistence over time, narrative identity concerns an individual's self-conception: their implicit autobiography, most central values, and identifications with particular persons, activities, and roles. This is the sense of identity that is at risk of falling apart in an identity crisis.[2] When an adult undergoing a mid-life crisis or a confused adolescent asks, "Who am I?" they are typically not suffering from amnesia or for any other reason trying to work out their numerical identity. Rather, they are trying to get their bearings about how to "define" themselves, what is most important to them, and what self-image should guide them through major life decisions. In this way, narrative identity straightforwardly involves an individual's psychology. It therefore varies with each individual insofar as each has a distinct self-conception.

Our personhood is so central to our lives that we might find it natural to assume that we are *essentially* persons – that we literally cannot exist at any time without being persons at that time. We may call this thesis *person*

---

[1] Criteria of identity for a particular object *over time* involve persistence conditions. But criteria of identity also determine whether a particular object *would exist in counterfactual situations* – a matter of "trans-world identity." For example, assuming a particular copy of a book was made from a particular stock of paper, could that very same copy have existed despite being made from a different stock of paper? Could you have come into existence as the result of the fertilization of a different sperm and egg cell than those that were actually involved in your history? For a classic discussion of trans-world identity, see Saul Kripke, *Naming and Necessity* (Cambridge, MA: Harvard University Press, 1970). This chapter focuses on persistence conditions rather than conditions for trans-world identity – except in discussing genetic interventions on gametes or embryos that might affect who comes into being.

[2] For an excellent exposition of narrative identity, see Marya Schechtman, *The Constitution of Selves* (Ithaca, NY: Cornell University Press, 1996).

essentialism. If person essentialism is true, then our numerical identity consists in the continuing existence of a being with a narrative identity, suggesting that we come into existence as such beings and persist as long we maintain our narrative identities. Reflection suggests that this view cannot be correct. Even though it is debatable precisely when one of us comes into being, it seems obvious that we existed by the time of our birth. Yet person essentialism implies that we did not come into existence until the emergence of a narrative identity at around age three or four. Even if we adopted some other conception of personhood within the Lockean tradition, which invoked a trait such as rationality or self-awareness, person essentialism would implausibly entail that none of us existed as a newborn infant (since newborns clearly lack such traits). The infant would have to be someone else, a predecessor rather than oneself at an early age. This "newborn problem" suggests that person essentialism is untenable.[3]

Another possible problem with person essentialism concerns the other end of life, when our cognitive capacities may diminish gradually rather than suddenly. If person essentialism is true, then a person who is undergoing the progressive cognitive decline associated with Alzheimer's disease would go out of existence whenever narrative capacity is lost during the cognitive decline. Yet, at this time, a sentient or conscious human patient continues to live.[4] Perhaps some will accept the implication that they could go out of existence during the gradual cognitive decline despite the continuing existence of a sentient individual. But many will find this very difficult to believe. They would judge that it would be reasonable for someone in the early stages of progressive dementia to *fear* (for their own sake) reaching the late stages, implying the judgment that they would *still exist* in the late stages of dementia. For those who think along these lines, person essentialism is unacceptable not only due to the newborn problem but also due to the "dementia problem."

9.3 The Biological Account

According to the biological account, human persons are most fundamentally living human animals (or organisms).[5] The idea that we are fundamentally animals has the attraction of cohering with a world view

---

[3] David DeGrazia, *Human Identity and Bioethics* (Cambridge: Cambridge University Press, 2005), chap. 2.

[4] This point is explored in Jeff McMahan, *The Ethics of Killing* (New York: Oxford University Press, 2002), 47–48.

[5] For the preeminent defense of this position, see Eric Olson, *The Human Animal* (New York: Oxford University Press, 1997).

according to which we are part of the natural world. In contrast to person-based accounts, the biological account implies that our existence and persistence conditions are biological, not psychological. Thus, we come into existence either at conception or shortly thereafter (when integration of embryonic parts makes spontaneous twinning impossible[6]), and we go out of existence when the human animal dies.[7] Within biological approaches there is debate about what counts as dying. Some argue that total brain failure is sufficient for a human being's death and others that irreversible loss of circulatory-respiratory function is also necessary. We examine these possibilities in a later section.

Proponents of the biological account tend to emphasize the difference between the metaphysical issue of our numerical identity and such value-based questions as what is most important in human life. When we come into existence is one thing; when we have moral status and a life worth continuing is another. Even if each of us lacks moral status as a pre-sentient fetus, as many bioethicists (including us) assert, it would not follow that we did not *exist* as such fetuses. Similarly, when we die is a matter of the termination of biological life. But it might be possible to lose everything that we value in our lives before dying – for example, if consciousness is necessary for the things that we value. From the perspective of the biological account, it appears that psychological accounts of identity – both person-based accounts and the mind-based account to be discussed next – may be motivated, in part, by a conflation of two distinct issues: our identity and, to use Parfit's phrase, "what matters in survival."[8]

The biological account vindicates the claim that we are fundamentally animals while avoiding some questionable implications of other views. First, it avoids the implausible implication of person essentialism that we did not exist as infants. It also avoids the implication that a person would go out of existence during the gradual cognitive decline associated with progressive dementia despite the fact that a conscious patient would remain. Further, by stating that human persons *are* animals, it identifies the relationship between human persons and the animals associated with

---

[6] Before significant integration exists among embryonic cells and while twinning remains possible, a particular human organism has yet to be uniquely individuated. One early embryo might yield one being of our kind, a human organism, or it might yield two.

[7] This assumption is common among personal identity theorists. However, there are dissenters. For example, W. R. Carter argues that we are essentially animals but not necessarily living animals, so we continue to exist as dead animals – corpses – so long as the remains constitute a single object ("Will I Be a Dead Person?," *Philosophy and Phenomenological Research* 59 [1999]: 167–171).

[8] Derek Parfit, *Reasons and Persons* (Oxford: Clarendon, 1984), Part III.

them more straightforwardly and – some may think – more plausibly than the mind essentialism we discuss in the next section. Some might also find it an advantage of the biological account that it conceptualizes human death in biological terms, whereas mind-based accounts of personal identity understand human death as the loss of some psychological capacity – despite the fact that life and death are, first and foremost, biological phenomena.

Nevertheless, the biological view faces challenges. The most significant challenge, we think, concerns the hypothetical cerebrum-transplant case. In this thought-experiment, Alfred's body remains alive while his cerebrum (the large outer portion of the brain in which the contents of mental life are realized and encoded) is surgically extracted and transplanted, still fully functional, into the head of Bill, whose own cerebrum had been removed while his body remained alive.[9] There are now both a living, but mindless, human organism associated with Alfred's body and a person associated with Bill's body. That person's mental life is continuous with presurgery Alfred's mental life: the same values and life plans as Alfred had along with his apparent presurgical memories. Following the transplant, where is the individual known as Alfred? Many have the intuition that Alfred has moved, along with his mental life, to Bill's body. Yet the biological view suggests that, because Alfred is essentially a living human animal, he remains alive albeit mindless in his original body – so that the person in Bill's body is *wrong* in believing himself to be Alfred.

While this counterintuitive result challenges the biological view, the challenge is not decisive. For one thing, in the cases that confront us *in everyday life* the biological view has very plausible implications: we track the existence and persistence of human persons in ways that are consistent with the biological understanding of numerical identity. Second, one might argue that the common intuitive reaction that Alfred moves with his cerebrum into Bill's body is a result of overgeneralization from ordinary cases. In all cases with which we are familiar, continuity of a mental life with particular memories, values, and plans coincides with continuity of a particular human person. However, that may be because, in familiar cases, continuity of mental life has always *also* tracked a continuing biological life. In responding to the cerebrum-transplant case, in which the contents of a mental life are separated from the individual's body and realized in a

---

[9] If brain parts in addition to the cerebrum are, in fact, implicated in the encoding and realization of the contents of a person's mental life, the thought-experiment may be modified to include those brain parts in the transplant.

different body, we might overgeneralize from familiar cases if we judge that the individual must go with the contents of his earlier mental life. Instead, we might think that Alfred remains with his still-living body, especially if his cerebrum, lodged in an entirely different body, generates a personality and mental life that (contrary to the thought-experiment) are significantly different from those associated with Alfred. In our judgment, the biological approach to personal identity remains a contender.

9.4 A Mind-Based Account

According to the mind-based account of personal identity, human persons are essentially beings with minds.[10] The relevant sense of "mind" here is broad and inclusive; it is sufficient for having a mind in this sense that one has the capacity for any conscious states – any subjective experience – whatsoever. Such *mind essentialism* claims in effect that we are essentially conscious or sentient beings.[11] We come into existence whenever the developing human organism first possesses a mind and we continue to exist for as long as that organism has a mind. More specifically, this approach implies that we come into being as late fetuses, whenever sentience emerges (see Chapter 10), and that we go out of existence at the irreversible loss of the capacity for consciousness. So the mind-based account avoids the newborn problem that undermines person essentialism: the implausible implication that we come into existence postnatally. It also avoids the dementia problem associated with person essentialism: the implication that one goes out of existence at some point during the cognitive decline associated with progressive dementia, prior to the onset of irreversible unconsciousness. A further strength of this account is that it avoids the cerebrum-transplant intuition that challenges the biological account by plausibly implying that Alfred would go with his cerebrum – and mind – into Bill's body. But the mind-based account faces a substantial challenge.

The challenge is to provide a satisfactory explanation of the relationship between the "minded being" – that is, one of us – and the closely associated human organism. According to the mind-based view, a human organism comes into existence at conception (or perhaps shortly afterward,

---

[10] This account is developed in McMahan, *The Ethics of Killing*, chap. 1.

[11] Sentient beings have the capacity to experience feelings such as pain or pleasure. In principle, there could be minded beings that could experience only conscious states that were not feelings, but as far as we know all actual animals, including humans, who have minds experience feelings and are therefore sentient.

as explained earlier), gradually develops in utero, and then, when the fetus becomes sentient, one of us comes into being. At the other end of life, if the human organism enters an irreversibly unconscious state before dying, the minded being goes out of existence although the human organism lives on. So what is the relationship between one of us and the longer-living human organism?

According to the mind-based view, you are not identical to a human animal because the two of you have different persistence conditions: The animal can exist at times when you do not. Thus, the mind-based view implies that, strictly speaking, we are not animals but rather their minds. And what are minds? Most philosophers and scientists today have a naturalistic understanding of minds as inseparable from brains. If we assume, along these lines, that minds are equivalent to brains – or, more precisely, those parts of functioning brains in which conscious states are realized – then, according to the mind-based view, *we* are parts of functioning brains.[12] So the answer to the question of how we relate to the human organisms associated with us is that each of us is *part of* such an organism, which came into existence before we did (since the organism existed before developing a brain) and may outlive us (if our brains irreversibly cease to function while the organism remains alive). Yet this cannot be the whole story: brain parts can continue to exist after irreversibly losing the capacity to function. This suggests that we cannot simply be those brain parts, but must be – or be closely associated with – those brain parts *when they are functional*.

Perhaps, then, we – as minds – are *realized* in functioning brains. But what does this realization consist in? One might hold that we are immaterial substances that are intimately related to our working brains.[13] But substance dualism is deeply problematic. For example, it leaves the nature of causal interactions between an immaterial mind and the material brain completely mysterious.[14] Another possible suggestion, exploiting an

---

[12] See McMahan, *The Ethics of Killing*, chap. 1.

[13] See, especially, Rene Descartes, *Meditations on First Philosophy* (1641).

[14] Another major difficulty with substance dualism, which is rarely noted, involves what happens to consciousness in "split brain" patients. As a treatment for severe epilepsy, certain patients have had their corpus callosa (singular: collosum) – neural connections joining the two cerebral hemispheres – severed. Under experimental conditions it becomes clear that the surgery has caused the conscious life of each patient to divide into two independent spheres of consciousness – in brief, has caused one mind to divide into two (see R. W. Sperry, "Hemisphere Deconnection and Unity in Conscious Awareness," *American Psychologist* 23 [1968]: 723–733). But, according to substance dualism, the mind is an *immaterial* substance. Why would severing connections between two cerebral hemispheres have the effect of dividing one

analogy with computers, is that we are like the software that permits the hardware of the brain to operate. But this would imply that we are abstract beings that are incapable of existing concretely without an underlying physical substrate – just as a particular shape has no concrete existence without things that possess the shape. The analogy to software also suggests that each of us, as a mind, could enable mental life in an indefinite number of human bodies just as Windows software can enable an indefinite number of computers to operate. The analogy to software seems unpromising.

A more promising variant of mind essentialism asserts that each of us is *constituted* by a human organism. The idea of constitution may be understood with the example of a bronze statue. Once a hunk of bronze is sculpted into the shape of a statue, the statue exists and is constituted by its material substrate, the hunk of bronze. The hunk of bronze exists before the statue does, may outlast the statue if the latter is melted down, and coincides or overlaps with the statue when it has the shape of a statue. In brief, the hunk of bronze constitutes the bronze statue when and only when the hunk has the relevant shape. Similarly, according to the present suggestion, one of us is constituted by a human animal when and only when the animal has the capacity for consciousness. Perhaps the constitution thesis offers a plausible answer to the question of the relationship between one of us and the associated human animal. In any case it is clear that the mind-based account, like the biological account, is a contender among theories of personal identity.

9.5   A Social Account

One further theoretical approach deserves our attention. This account is a variant of person essentialism, but, by construing numerical identity in partly social terms, it may be able to sidestep the newborn problem and the dementia problem we described above.[15]

On this social account, the lives of persons feature a cluster of properties and relations that ordinarily support each other. A paradigmatic human life features a characteristic developmental trajectory that can be understood in terms of typical human traits and capacities, activities and social

immaterial substance into two? And is an immaterial substance even a plausible candidate for something that can divide?

[15] For a recent elaboration of this general approach, see Marya Schechtman, *Staying Alive* (Oxford: Oxford University Press, 2014). See also Hilde Lindemann Nelson, *Damaged Identities, Narrative Repair* (Ithaca, NY: Cornell University Press, 2001), chap. 3.

relations, and status within a community of persons.[16] Most human persons come into being as a member of a particular family; develop into individuals who can speak, socially interact, plan, and play; and are recognized as members of a community and various smaller social groups. They continue to mature physically before beginning a gradual physical decline, which continues until they die in relatively old age. While these general features are *characteristic* of the lives of human persons, on this account, they are not all strictly *necessary* for a human to qualify as a person. Someone might, for example, suffer from cognitive disabilities that prevent some human-typical forms of psychological and social life. Nevertheless, if she has several of the other person-characteristic traits and is an *identifiable locus of social interaction within a community of persons*, then she is a person.[17] Thus, on this account, our numerical identity is a function of having and sustaining the life of a person, which means existing and persisting as an identifiable locus of social interaction.

This account integrates narrative identity into its account of numerical identity. It does so by way of two assertions: (1) that we are essentially persons and that persons are *characteristically*, though not necessarily, individuals who possess self-narratives and (2) that the relevant sorts of narratives are not only *internal* to an individual person – as suggested by the term "self-narrative" – but also *social* in that other persons' understandings of one's life (e.g., "This boy is the son of so-and-so") are part of one's broader personal narrative. An important implication is that your existence begins long before you are able to construct a self-narrative. In our society it begins no later than birth, when one becomes a locus of social interaction and the subject of a personal narrative (commenced by other individuals). And your existence may continue after you have lost narrative capacity, say, due to advanced dementia. The narrating work, in this case, would be continued by family members, hospital staff, and the state, all of whom continue to regard you as a living member of a family (someone to visit and talk to, for example) and of the broader community (someone who maintains the legal status of a person). According to the social account, then, the severely demented patient persists as a person until the time of what is socially recognized as death.

The social account avoids the implication of standard versions of person essentialism that we never existed as newborns. It also plausibly allows that we could survive into a dementia that destroyed our narrative capacity and ability to plan. Moreover, it offers a possible response to the problem of

---

[16] Schechtman, *Staying Alive*, chap. 5.   [17] Ibid.

nonparadigm humans (as discussed in Chapter 7): by implying that newborns and the severely demented are persons, it implies that they have full moral status.

Despite such attractions we find this novel account of personal identity inadequate. Consider its basis for assigning moral status. In the case of an infant or deeply demented human being, who lacks their own narrative capacity, the view permits other individuals to recognize the individual as a person, to do the "narrating work" for them so to speak, thereby socially conferring personhood on the individual. We do not believe that moral status can depend on social recognition or special relationships. As discussed in Chapter 7, the concept of moral status attributes a type of inherent value to individuals such that moral agents have obligations regarding their treatment of those individuals. But inherent value must be *inherent*, resting on the valuable entity's characteristics. By contrast, relationships are "external" to an individual rather than inherent. So relationships cannot be a basis for moral status. This judgment fits with the plausible idea that a being's moral status gives moral reasons to *all moral agents* to treat that being in particular ways, whereas special relationships would provide moral reasons only to those who stand within the relationships. In addition to this conceptual point, there is a substantive moral concern: social recognition, by depending on the perceptions and perhaps choices of others, seems too unstable and contingent to be a plausible basis for moral status.

In addition, social recognition is implausibly unstable as a basis for numerical identity. Consider a society that did *not* regard newborn infants as persons and members of the community. On the conception of numerical (and narrative) identity that understands it as constituted by one's self-conception and others' social recognition there would be no grounding for newborns' numerical identity. This implies, implausibly, that in the imagined society those newborns who survive and later "grow into" persons with narrative capacity did not actually exist as newborns. That is, in such a society, it would be true of children who are persons that they had not existed as newborns, who were instead numerically distinct predecessors. So the newborn problem would apply to human beings in such a society.

Personhood, numerical identity, and moral status must rest on the properties of individuals, not on their relationships to others or on social recognition more generally. The social account of numerical identity fails to meet this requirement. So, despite its apparent advantages, we do not consider it a viable contender among accounts of numerical identity.

9.6   Our Approach to Personal Identity

As previously noted, we reject person-based accounts of numerical identity. Standard person-based accounts have deeply counterintuitive implications about our identity as found in the newborn problem and the dementia problem. We also reject the social account, a variant of the person-based approach, since it makes some individuals' personhood and moral status – and, in some possible societies, even their existence as newborns – depend on social recognition and special relationships.

Our discussion of the biological view, according to which we are essentially living human animals, noted several advantages over person-based accounts and no fatal weaknesses. We reached a similar verdict for the mind-based approach, according to which human persons are essentially beings with the capacity for consciousness. Therefore, as far as numerical identity is concerned, our approach is pluralistic: we regard both the mind-based account and the biological account as reasonable options, so our policies and practices should be as consistent as possible with each. On either account, we are essentially living beings – assuming, as we do, that we must be alive in order to have a mind.[18] Meanwhile, we regard narrative identity as closely connected with much of what human persons care about in their lives. That is because we care about – even if not *only* about – our existence as persons; and in our view persons are beings with narrative capacity and an (internal) narrative identity.

9.7   Personal Identity and Human Enhancement

Background

Human enhancement through biomedical means has received ample scholarly attention in recent decades. There is a substantial literature on such topics as cosmetic surgery, the pharmacological enhancement of cognition and mood, doping in athletics, and genetic enhancement.[19] There is even a literature on "moral bioenhancement," the aim of which is to improve, through biomedical means, moral capacities such as those

---

[18] This may not be true for advanced forms of artificial intelligence, but "we" here refers to human persons.

[19] Helpful introductions to biomedical enhancement include Erik Parens (ed.), *Enhancing Human Traits* (Washington, DC: Georgetown University Press, 1998); and Julian Savulescu and Nick Bostrom (eds.), *Human Enhancement* (Oxford: Oxford University Press, 2009).

for sympathy and fairness.[20] The focus in this section is a particular set of concerns about biomedical enhancements *in relation to personal identity*.

Before turning to those concerns, it is worth noting the range of ways in which enhancement is understood. Many scholarly discussions of biomedical enhancement define it by way of contrast with medical treatment or therapy: enhancements are interventions designed to improve human form or function without responding to genuine medical need.[21] So treatment endeavors to restore health or normal functioning, in keeping with the traditional objectives of medicine, whereas enhancement aims to take an individual beyond what is needed for health or normal functioning. The medication modafinil, for example, is used to treat the sleep disorder narcolepsy, but it can also be used to enhance academic performance by reducing the (normal) need for sleep and improving cognitive focus. Defining enhancement by contrasting it with treatment invites concerns about whether enhancement lies beyond the proper scope of medicine.

Some authors, however, doubt that the distinction between promoting health and normal functioning and seeking to transcend these standards has any fundamental importance. Accordingly, they define enhancement independently of any contrast with therapy. For example, Allen Buchanan conceptualizes enhancement as any deliberate intervention that aims to improve an existing capacity or create a new capacity in a human being.[22] This broad definition includes such nonbiomedical enhancements as education and athletic training. Our purposes do not require deciding between traditional and nontraditional definitions of enhancement, for the interventions that are likely to provoke concerns about personal identity – concerns about a kind of death or loss of oneself – are also likely to satisfy any reasonable definition of enhancement.

Concerns about Numerical Identity

Substantial, deliberate endeavors to improve oneself – which we may call *enhancement projects* – appear to be connected with personal identity because they concern who someone is or who they want to become. The fact that Dasha's greatest dream is to become a highly accomplished writer

---

[20] For a helpful introduction, see Thomas Douglas, "The Morality of Moral Neuroenhancement," in Jens Clausen and Neil Levy (eds.), *Handbook of Neuroethics* (Dordrecht: Springer, 2015), 1227–1249.

[21] See, e.g., Eric Juengst, "What Does 'Enhancement' Mean?," in Parens (ed.), *Enhancing Human Traits*, 25–43.

[22] Allen Buchanan, *Beyond Humanity?* (New York: Oxford University Press, 2011), 23.

says much about who she is – that is, what sort of person – and concerns the sort of individual she wants to become. In some sense, then, Dasha's enhancement project involves her identity. But what sense of identity is at issue? Some scholars suggest that numerical identity is sometimes implicated. Walter Glannon, for example, expresses this thesis in the context of discussing genetic therapy:

> [G]ene therapy designed to correct or treat a cognitive or affective disorder would be more likely [than gene therapy with no direct effects on mental life] to alter one's identity. The manipulation of the relevant neurotransmitters or regions of the brain that generate and support mental life would directly affect the very nature of the mental states definitive of personhood and personal identity through time.[23]

Glannon applies this contention about identity to already-existing persons and not merely to fetuses and newborns. His reasoning would extend from therapy to enhancements with similarly far-reaching effects on one's mental life.

But the contention that enhancing an already-existing person's mental characteristics might result in a numerically distinct person is deeply implausible. Consider the implications of various contending accounts of numerical identity. If the biological account is correct, then the contention is obviously false, because a single human animal persists through the improvements of mental life. The contention is also false according to the mind-based account because a single embodied capacity for consciousness survives the changes associated with the enhancement project. Indeed, the contention is dubious even if one shares Glannon's assumption of person essentialism.[24] For the post-enhancement person will presumably *remember* pre-enhancement life, suggesting continuity of one and the same person-constituting mental life. Furthermore, most of the individual's attitudes and intentions are likely to survive the enhancement. In sum, there is no reason to think that enhancing an existing person's mental abilities would affect numerical identity. Apparently, Glannon has reasoned as follows: he intuitively appreciates that a substantial enhancement of mental characteristics would occasion a significant change in *narrative* identity, the person's self-conception; but, failing to distinguish the two types of identity, he fallaciously infers a change in numerical identity.[25]

---

[23] Walter Glannon, *Genes and Future People* (Boulder, CO: Westview, 2001), 81–82.
[24] Ibid., 25.
[25] In later work Glannon avoids this conflation (see *Bioethics and the Brain* [New York: Oxford University Press, 2007], 113–114).

Although a *person's* enhancement project will not alter their numerical identity, the enhancement of a human organism or of its constituent biological material *at a sufficiently early stage* could affect numerical identity. The timing would be sufficiently early if it occurred prior to the origination (the coming into being) of one of us. When – at what stage of development – one of us originates depends on what we essentially are. To focus our investigation, let's consider deliberately induced genetic changes with the intention of improving the cognitive capacities of the resulting individuals. If the mind-based account of numerical identity is correct, then we are essentially minded beings and come into being when the capacity for consciousness emerges – that is, sometime in the later months of pregnancy when the human organism becomes sentient. In this case, genetic interventions for the purpose of cognitive enhancement would affect identity if they occurred before the onset of sentience and the emergence of a minded being.[26] It seems plausible to judge that identity would be affected: an individual would originate who is numerically distinct from the one who would have originated had the genetic enhancement not taken place. Rather than affecting numerical identity by ending the existence of one of us, this sort of enhancement would determine that a different being comes into existence. Now, if the biological account is correct, then in order to affect numerical identity, a genetic enhancement would have to occur at an earlier stage (so that it precedes the origination of one of us). If we come into existence at conception, the critical changes would have to occur in the gametes prior to fertilization; if we come into being somewhat later – say, when the primitive streak forms and spontaneous twinning is precluded – then the critical changes could occur in the early embryo.

These reflections suggest that certain types of enhancement could affect numerical identity so long as they introduce a significant change – such as a nontrivial change in cognitive capacities – that would alter the "nature" of the individual who comes into existence. Does this observation suggest that some enhancements are morally troubling for reasons pertaining to identity? Emphasizing that we are still focusing on numerical identity, we answer negatively. That is because determining *which* particular human individual comes into existence is not a morally weighty matter (setting

---

[26] Here we make the simplifying assumption that the genetic intervention succeeds in making a change to someone's genome that will, in fact, have some significant effect on their mental life. It is debatable whether making a genetic (pre-origination) change that induced no significant change should count as affecting the numerical identity of the individual who comes into being.

aside cases in which such a choice is expected to have a substantial negative impact on quality of life).[27] One might think otherwise, holding that an individual who would have come into being were it not for the genetic enhancement of the pre-origination gametes, embryo, or fetus would be "cheated" out of existence and thereby wronged. But, surely, prior to the origination of one of us, there is no being with moral status. No such being can be cheated in any significant sense any more than potential persons who are never conceived – say, because two prospective parents decide not to attempt pregnancy – can be cheated. In the present set of cases, interventions that bring about enhancements affect numerical identity in a morally innocuous way.[28]

Concerns about Narrative Identity

Despite the concerns expressed by various commentators,[29] biomedical enhancements either do not affect numerical identity or do so in a morally innocuous way. At the same time, enhancements are likely to affect narrative identity because an agent embarking on an enhancement project intends to change themselves and their life in a way that matters to them. Perhaps some such changes raise significant moral issues. If so, they apply only to persons, who have narrative identities, and not to embryos, fetuses, or infants, who do not.

In ordinary cases, it would seem that self-chosen enhancements that affect one's sense of self and thereby narrative identity would be morally unproblematic – especially when we limit consideration to identity-related moral concerns – so long as the enhancements are genuinely *self*-chosen or pursued autonomously. For example, a young woman who is a talented but uncultivated athlete might decide (autonomously) to lift weights, improve her diet, and train intensely in her sport in order to become an outstanding athlete. Success in this enhancement project is likely to change

---

[27] See our discussion of the "nonidentity problem" in Chapter 10.

[28] An issue we have not considered here (because it does not focus on identity) is the concern of some disability advocates that preimplantation and prenatal genetic manipulations and genetic diagnosis – whether with therapeutic or enhancement-based intent – may express a devaluation of persons with disabilities. See, e.g., Adrienne Asch, "Reproductive Technology and Disability," in Sherrill Cohen and Nadine Taub (eds.), *Reproductive Laws for the 1990s* (Clifton, NJ: Humana, 1989), 69–124. We believe that use of such genetic technologies need not express any disrespectful message. For elaboration, see David DeGrazia, *Creation Ethics* (New York: Oxford University Press, 2012), 102–106.

[29] For further examples of such concerns, see Carl Elliott, *A Philosophical Disease* (New York: Routledge, 1999), 28–29; and President's Council on Bioethics, *Beyond Therapy* (Washington, DC: PCB, 2003), 300.

her sense of herself in a way that is important to her. But this feature of her endeavor does not make it morally problematic. Suppose her enhancement project used some sort of genetic intervention to bring about a greater capacity for growing muscle. Although the genetic means to her end would introduce some important ethical considerations – including concerns about safety and fair play – it would not introduce new identity-related concerns. Whether her means are traditional ones or exotic genetic means, her enhancement project will affect her narrative identity, but there seems to be nothing inherently objectionable about doing so.

In a provocative discussion, Farah Focquaert and Maartje Schermer argue that some types of moral enhancement – the attempt to improve an individual's moral capacities – could raise serious issues in connection with narrative identity.[30] The concerns they raise could also apply to other types of enhancement projects and to therapeutic interventions that use similar means to their respective enhancements. Among the means to moral enhancement, Focquaert and Schermer distinguish (1) direct interventions, which affect the brain directly and thereby indirectly affect the individual's way of thinking (e.g., deep brain stimulation) and (2) indirect interventions, which directly affect the agent's way of thinking, thereby indirectly affecting her brain (e.g., cognitive psychotherapy). They suggest that the direct/indirect distinction is important insofar as it tracks a distinction between relatively active and relatively passive roles of the agent. Someone who participates in psychotherapy, for example, is active in processing ideas and changing ways of thinking, whereas the recipient of deep brain stimulation assumes a considerably more passive role. Direct means and a correspondingly passive role for the individual might induce abrupt, profound psychological changes with little connection to her life story, threatening the coherence of her narrative identity. Additionally, the authors argue, there is the greater possibility of major changes in personality that go unnoticed by the enhanced individual, resulting in a kind of self-blindness and inauthenticity. Such disruptions in narrative identity or self-awareness, the authors imply, are likely to diminish the well-being of the individuals in question.

We agree with Focquaert and Schermer that moral enhancement might sometimes lead to harmful disruptions in narrative identity. At the same time, we find their response to the possibilities of such outcomes

---

[30] Farah Focquaert and Maartje Schermer, "Moral Enhancement: Do Means Matter Morally?," *Neuroethics* 8 (2015): 139–151.

satisfactory.[31] As the authors propose, where direct interventions aimed at enhancement are involved, the individuals in question should undergo a very robust informed consent process that explores the possibilities of disrupted narrative identity or self-blindness. Moreover, during the intervention (if it is undertaken in steps and communication between the steps is feasible) and following it, the individuals should receive counseling that serves to minimize these possibilities. Such autonomy-promoting measures, we think, reduce the reasons for concern to tolerable levels – both by lowering the risks of narrative-identity-related harm and by increasing awareness of any residual risks so that individuals may accept or reject them in a well-informed manner.

9.8   The Authority of Advance Directives in Cases of Severe Dementia

Background

Advance directives are exceptionally important instruments for medical decision-making. They permit competent adult patients to provide instructions regarding their medical care in the event that they lose decision-making capacity in the future.[32] In this way, advance directives allow the patient's proxy decision-makers and medical personnel to respect the patient's autonomy even though the patient lacks the capacity for autonomous choice at the time decisions are needed. It is sometimes said that advance directives facilitate respect for *precedent* autonomy – the autonomy one had during a prior period of time.

One concern about the employment of advance directives is that in certain cases in which a patient undergoes massive psychological change, the individual who exists following the change might be a different person than the one who earlier completed the directive. If there is in fact a disruption of numerical identity, there is substantial reason to challenge the authority of the directive in question, since an advance directive applies only to the individual who authored it. This is the "someone else problem" of advance directives.[33]

---

[31] Ibid., 147–148.

[32] They also permit such patients to designate proxy decision-makers in the event of losing decision-making capacity. But a proxy decision-maker needs some basis for deciding on behalf of the incompetent patient. Instructional advance directives supply such a basis, so our discussion focuses on this type of advance directive.

[33] David DeGrazia, "Advance Directives, Dementia, and 'the Someone Else Problem,'" *Bioethics* 13 (1999): 373–391. See also DeGrazia, *Human Identity and Bioethics*, chap. 5.

Dementia comes in various forms, including Alzheimer's disease, vascular dementia, substance-induced persisting dementia, HIV-related dementia, and dementias caused by head trauma, Parkinson's disease, and Huntington's disease. The various forms of dementia share the following features:

1. Memory impairment
2. One or more of the following: (a) language disturbance, (b) impaired ability to carry out motor activities despite intact motor function, (c) failure to recognize objects despite intact sensory functioning, (d) disturbed executive functioning (planning, organizing, sequencing, etc.)
3. As a result of the above symptoms, significant impairment in social or occupational functioning that represents a substantial decline from the patient's baseline of functioning.[34]

Here we focus on Alzheimer's disease, which features a fairly characteristic pattern of decline. In mild or early-stage Alzheimer's, symptoms are relatively subtle. For example, a patient may experience mild memory loss and feel unusually disorganized at times. Moderate or middle-stage Alzheimer's is characterized by more obvious symptoms such as frequent lapses in memory, losing valued objects, and more pronounced difficulty in performing tasks like bill-paying and planning a trip. Severe or late-stage Alzheimer's, by contrast, features profound loss of capacity. A patient might be nearly or entirely unable to speak, to perform activities of daily living such as getting dressed and self-feeding, and to recognize loved ones.

The Someone Else Problem and Numerical Identity

Suppose that Mary, at age sixty, is familiar with several cases of Alzheimer's disease in her extended family. After reading up on the disease, she thinks carefully about the possibility of succumbing to it and how she would want her life to go. Her conclusion is that, in view of the value she puts on intellectual pursuits and personal independence, she would not want to live for very long in a state of conscious obliviousness. Mary completes an advance directive that calls for withholding life-extending medical

---

[34] This summary draws from the American Psychological Association, *Diagnostic Criteria from DSM-IV* (Washington, DC: APA, 1994), 85–93. In the current, fifth edition of the *Diagnostic and Statistical Manual of Mental Disorders* (*DSM-5*), the term "dementia" is deemphasized while the various dementias are clustered – together with delirium, amnesia, and various other conditions – under the umbrella of "Major Neurocognitive Impairment" (Washington, DC: APA, 2013).

interventions, including artificial nutrition and hydration as well as anti-biotics, in the event that she becomes incapable of (1) performing any activities of daily living (dressing, bathing, walking, toileting, etc.) and (2) recognizing loved ones. After a few years of "mild cognitive impairment," Mary is diagnosed with early-stage Alzheimer's disease at the age of sixty-five. The dementia progresses over the next ten years with the result that at age seventy-five Mary is severely demented and resides in a nursing home. She is now unable to perform independently any activities of daily living and shows no indications of recognizing loved ones. Nevertheless, she does not appear to be suffering. Indeed, she seems to enjoy being dressed, fed, wheeled around in her wheelchair, and spoken to by staff and visitors.

When Mary contracts pneumonia, which would ordinarily call for antibiotics, the nursing home staff consult her advance directive and revisit its instructions. A dispute erupts among the staff. Some believe that the directive straightforwardly applies and should be followed: no antibiotics, with the predictable result that Mary will die within days. Other staff members stress that the patient, who appears to have a relatively pleasant existence, is so psychologically cut off from the time of authoring the advance directive that it should no longer apply. She seems to have independent interests that favor life-extending antibiotic treatment. Who is right?

An advance directive is supposed to apply to decisions regarding medical care for the individual who completed the directive. Various commentators have suggested that a severely demented patient is not the individual who, while competent, expressed their medical preferences through the directive. Consequently, the advance directive should not apply. Some of these authors claim that the severely demented individual is *a different person* from the person who completed the directive.[35] Others, who regard persons as beings with the capacity for *relatively complex* forms of consciousness, have judged that someone with (sufficiently) severe dementia is not a person at all.[36] A and B cannot be the same person if B is not even a person. Given our analysis of personhood, we agree that a severely demented individual like Mary-at-75 is not a person and so cannot be a different person. But perhaps the nonperson is, in virtue of that fact, "someone else" from the competent individual who preceded her.

[35] See, e.g., Rebecca Dresser, "Life, Death, and Incompetent Patients: Conceptual Infirmities and Hidden Values in the Law," *Arizona Law Review* 28 (1986): 373–405.

[36] See, e.g., Allen Buchanan, "Advance Directives and the Personal Identity Problem," *Philosophy and Public Affairs* 17 (1988): 277–302.

The reasoning, applied to the present case, may be reconstructed this way:

1. Mary-at-60 (who is competent) is a person.
2. Mary-at-75 (who is very severely demented) is not a person. Therefore:
3. Mary-at-75 is *numerically distinct from* Mary-at-60.

This reasoning is fallacious. The conclusion about numerical distinctness does not follow from premises (1) and (2). In order to infer the conclusion, one needs another premise: that Mary is *essentially* a person, so that the individual who completed the advance directive cannot exist at any time without being a person at that time. But the only reason to assume that Mary is essentially a person would be the general thesis of person essentialism, which earlier we found to be deeply implausible. What *is* plausible is that Mary existed for many years as a person but may survive for a time as a nonperson after losing traits such as narrative capacity.

Our pluralistic approach to numerical identity regards both the mind-based account and the biological account as plausible. Both vindicate the central metaphysical assumption underlying the presumed authority of advance directives in cases of severe dementia: that the author of the advance directive is numerically identical to – is the same individual as – the severely demented patient to whom the directive apparently applies. The mind-based account reaches the verdict because Mary-at-60 retains her basic capacity for consciousness throughout the cognitive decline leading to the condition of Mary-at-75. The biological account reaches this result because Mary-at-60 and Mary-at-75 are one and the same living animal. So the earlier advance directive applies to the older Mary. If there is any significant reason for doubting its authority, the reason will not concern numerical identity.

What about Narrative Identity?

In considering the possibility that personal identity theory challenges the authority of advance directives in certain cases, we have focused on numerical identity. With this focus, it appears that the someone else problem is misconceived. But *narrative* identity can challenge the authority of advance directives in a distinct way.

Consider Mary. While her numerical identity is maintained throughout the ravages of dementia, her narrative identity is disrupted. Mary's sense of herself as the protagonist of her self-narrative is entirely absent at age seventy-five. She is at most very weakly psychologically connected to the life of the person who completed the directive, a past she does not remember at all. Although, strictly speaking, Mary has persisted into her present state, she has in an important sense become someone other than the earlier Mary. While the relevant sense of distinctness here is qualitative, not numerical, it captures a profound sort of qualitative change: the termination of one's self-narrative. Moreover, the loss of narrative capacity not only entails that she is no longer a person, as we have conceptualized personhood; it is precisely what destroys her awareness of being the same individual as Mary from the past. Such disruption of narrative identity, one might argue, threatens the authority of the earlier advance directive *just as if* the earlier person and present demented individual were numerically distinct. For all practical purposes, they might as well be distinct because the present patient is psychologically cut off from her past. We should not assume that the interests of deeply demented Mary are the same as those of the younger, competent Mary; nor should we assume that the younger person had authority to make decisions for the later demented woman who neither remembers nor cares about the values and priorities of the woman who completed the directive. Mary at age seventy-five has her own, relatively simple interests in states and activities that give her enjoyment – and these interests call for staying alive.

Despite some initial intuitive appeal, the narrative identity–based challenge to the authority of advance directives is problematic. In claiming disruption of narrative identity, the argument views identity *retrospectively* from the standpoint of the demented or irreversibly unconscious individual, rather than prospectively from the standpoint of the earlier person. The prospective standpoint is no less important. Individuals who actively contemplate the possibility of becoming severely demented or irreversibly unconscious and take these possibilities into account in completing advance directives presumably *identify*, in some sense, with such future possible stages of themselves and care about their fate during those stages. In the case of Mary, it is clear that the patient identifies in a relevant way with her possible future, deeply demented self because she realizes she might *become – transform into – such an individual* and decides that she does not want to live for long if that transformation occurs.

One might challenge the idea that the person who completes an advance directive and anticipates the possibility of severe dementia identifies with the later individual in any sense of "identification" richer than bare acknowledgment of numerical identity. One might, accordingly, deny that this very weak identification is enough to give the person authority over her later self. In response, we suggest distinguishing and examining the implications of two senses of narrative identity.

Bearing in mind that any sort of narrative identity presupposes numerical identity, we may distinguish strong and weak narrative identity.[37] *Strong* narrative identity involves one's continued existence with significant psychological unity and the capacity for appreciating one's unfolding narrative. Given our conception of personhood, it also involves one's continuing existence *as a person*. Strong narrative identity does not obtain between Mary-at-60 and Mary-at-75, because the latter clearly lacks narrative capacity. Now consider *weak* narrative identity: the relationship between a person at a particular time and possible future stages of herself that she (at that earlier time) consciously acknowledges as part of her life and cares about prudentially. Weak narrative identity obtains between Mary-at-60 and Mary-at-75. For Mary, at age sixty, completed an advance directive after carefully considering the possibility of becoming deeply demented and decided that she would not prefer to persist for long in such a state.

We contend that it would be unreasonable to require strong narrative identity as a condition for recognizing an advance directive's authority. After all, while Mary-at-60 is only weakly narratively identical to Mary-at-75, no other individual has a stronger claim of being identical to Mary-at-75.[38] Moreover, the very purpose of advance directives is to permit individuals to authorize, prospectively, the provision or withholding of certain kinds of medical treatment at a later time when they are incapacitated. A requirement of strong narrative identity would invalidate all use of advance directives when patients have lost narrative capacity. Such a radical revision to current practice and restriction in the scope of individual autonomy rights would require a powerful rationale. We do not believe any such rationale has been advanced.

We conclude that, contrary to some authors,[39] considerations of personal identity pose no significant threat to the presumptive authority of advance directives in cases featuring severe dementia.

---

[37] We borrow the distinction from DeGrazia, *Human Identity and Bioethics*, chap. 5.

[38] Thanks to David Benatar for suggesting this argument.

[39] See, e.g., Allen Buchanan and Dan Brock, *Deciding for Others* (Cambridge: Cambridge University Press, 1989), chap. 3; Rebecca Dresser, "Advance Directives, Self-Determination, and Personal Identity," in Chris Hacker, Ray Mosely, and Dorothy Vawter (eds.), *Advance Directives in Medicine* (New York: Praeger, 1989), 155–170; Jeffrey Blustein, "Choosing for Others as Continuing a Life Story: The Problem of Personal Identity Revisited," *Journal of Law, Medicine, and Ethics* 27 (1999): 20–31; and Mark Kuczewski, "Whose Will Is It Anyway? A Discussion of Advance Directives, Personal Identity, and Consensus in Medical Ethics," *Bioethics* 8 (1994): 27–48. Interestingly, while these authors incorrectly assert that cases of severe dementia feature a disruption of numerical identity, each ultimately vindicates the authority of advance directives.

9.9 The Definition and Determination of Human Death

Background

For the most part, questions about the definition and determination of human death did not get much public attention until well into the twentieth century.[40] Sufficient destruction of the brain, including the brain stem, ensured respiratory failure, which led quickly to terminal cardiac arrest. Conversely, prolonged cardiopulmonary failure led inevitably to total, irreversible loss of brain function. After the invention of mechanical respirators in the 1950s, however, it became possible for a previously lethal extent of brain damage to coexist with cardiopulmonary function, which sustained the functioning of other organs. Was a patient in this condition alive or dead? In the 1960s widespread dissemination of such technologies as respirators and defibrillators to restore cardiac function underscored the possibility of separating cardiopulmonary and neurological functioning. While these developments cleared conceptual space for a debate over the nature of human death, other developments motivated the debate in more practical terms.

Two developments are especially noteworthy. First, soaring medical expenditures and a limited supply of beds in intensive care units (ICUs) provoked concerns about prolonged, possibly futile treatment of patients who presented some but not all of the traditionally recognized markers of death. If the patient were dead, it would be permissible to discontinue life support and remove them from an ICU bed. Second, the evolving techniques of organ transplantation motivated physicians not to delay unnecessarily in determining that a patient had died. Moreover, if physicians were permitted to remove organs from patients whose cardiopulmonary function was sustained by respirators yet who were judged to be dead by neurological criteria, the well-perfused organs would be more likely to benefit recipients. Removing vital organs as quickly as possible, and with organs in the best condition possible, would improve the prospect of saving other patients' lives. But removing vital organs from living patients would cause them to die, violating laws against homicide as well as the commonly accepted moral rule prohibiting the intentional killing of innocent human beings (see Chapter 4).

---

[40] For a historical discussion, see M. Pernick, "Brain Death in a Cultural Context: The Reconstruction of Death, 1967–1981," in Stuart Youngner, Robert Arnold, and Renie Shapiro (eds.), *The Definition of Death* (Baltimore, MD: Johns Hopkins University Press, 1999), 3–33.

These developments set the stage for a landmark 1968 Harvard Medical School committee report, which supported a whole-brain standard of death.[41] A 1981 US President's Commission report, *Defining Death*, recommended the Uniform Definition of Death Act (UDDA), which incorporated the whole-brain standard of death alongside the traditional cardiopulmonary standard.[42] The UDDA states that "an individual who has sustained either (1) irreversible cessation of circulatory and respiratory functions or (2) irreversible cessation of all functions of the entire brain, including the brainstem, is dead."[43] Current law in the United States incorporates both standards of death, with most states adopting the UDDA, while others have embraced similar language. The United Kingdom and Canada both use a brainstem standard, which has virtually the same practical consequences as a whole-brain standard but requires fewer clinical tests.[44] Most countries around the world have accepted the whole-brain standard or the brainstem standard either by themselves or alongside the cardiopulmonary standard.[45]

This legislative consensus, however, has not prevented physicians, lawyers, philosophers, and others from defending a variety of significantly different views about the nature of human death. These views often invoke, explicitly or implicitly, accounts of our numerical identity. Understanding and contributing to the ongoing debate requires understanding the implications of these competing accounts.

Implications of the Biological Account

The biological account of our numerical identity asserts that human persons are essentially living human animals and *not* essentially persons or even minded beings. Therefore, just as we came into existence prior to becoming conscious, we might continue to exist after irreversibly losing our mental lives. According to the organismic definition of death, which coheres with the biological account of our numerical identity, death

---

[41] Ad Hoc Committee of the Harvard Medical School, "A Definition of Irreversible Coma – Report of the Ad Hoc Committee of Harvard Medical School to Examine the Definition of Brain Death," *JAMA* 205 (1968): 337–340.

[42] President's Commission for the Study of Ethical Problems in Medicine and Biomedical and Behavioral Research, *Defining Death* (Washington, DC: Government Printing Office, 1981).

[43] Ibid., 119.

[44] Andrew McGee and Dale Gardiner, "Differences in the Definition of Brain Death and Their Legal Impact on Intensive Care Practice," *Anaesthesia* 74 (2019): 569–572. For elaboration on the brainstem standard, see Christopher Pallis, "On the Brainstem Criterion of Death," in Youngner, Arnold, and Shapiro (eds.), *The Definition of Death*, 93–100.

[45] Eelco Wijdicks, "Brain Death Worldwide: Accepted Fact but No Global Consensus on Diagnostic Criteria," *Neurology* 58 (2002): 20–25.

involves the termination of biological life. Like other organisms, we die when the organism stops functioning as a more or less integrated unit. Whereas a living creature is a dynamic entity that extracts energy from the environment to maintain its own structure and functioning, death yields an inert piece (or pieces) of matter subject to disintegration and decay. In the case of humans, like other animals and plants, death involves the irreversible loss of integrated bodily functioning. While this organismic definition of death is relatively clear, its proper translation into a standard for the determination of human death is disputed.

According to the traditional *cardiopulmonary standard*, human death is the irreversible cessation of circulatory and respiratory function. According to the *whole-brain standard*, human death is the irreversible cessation of functioning of the entire brain, including the brain stem. Proponents of each standard generally maintain that only *it* correctly specifies an organismic definition of death for the case of human beings.[46]

The difference between assisted and unassisted respiration is crucial in distinguishing these two standards. A mechanical respirator can enable a "brain-dead" patient – a patient whose entire brain is nonfunctional – to breathe and thereby sustain cardiac function. Yet such a patient is incapable of unassisted or spontaneous respiration. On the cardiopulmonary standard, such a patient counts as alive as long as breathing and circulation occur, no matter how they occur. But such a patient is dead according to the whole-brain standard. At the same time, this standard judges that a patient who is irreversibly unconscious yet retains some measure of brain-stem function is alive.

Reviewing a few points of neurology may help to clarify the two standards' distinct clinical implications. The human brain includes what might be called the "higher brain" – consisting of the cerebrum, the primary vehicle of consciousness, and the cerebellum, which enables the control and coordination of voluntary muscle movements – and the "lower brain" or brainstem. The brainstem includes the medulla, which controls spontaneous respiration, and the reticular activating system, a sort of on/off switch that makes consciousness possible without affecting its contents. Whole-brain death involves loss of function in both the higher brain and brainstem. In what is called a *persistent vegetative state* (PVS), while damage

---

[46] See, e.g., the arguments of Lawrence Becker ("Human Being: The Boundaries of the Concept," *Philosophy and Public Affairs* 4 [1975]: 334–359), who defends the traditional standard, and those of James Bernat, Charles Culver, and Bernard Gert ("On the Definition and Criterion of Death," *Annals of Internal Medicine* [94]: 398–394), who defend the whole-brain standard.

to the higher brain causes irreversible unconsciousness, a largely functional brainstem permits some or all of the following: spontaneous respiration and heartbeat, sleep and wake cycles (but without consciousness), eye movements and pupillary reactions to light, and such reflexes as swallowing and coughing. A patient in *irreversible coma*, by contrast, never appears to be awake due to a damaged reticular activating system but remains capable of unassisted breathing. The ability to breathe spontaneously in either PVS or irreversible coma – as well as the sleep/wake cycles and reflexes present in PVS – presents the impression that patients in these conditions are alive. Both the whole-brain and the cardiopulmonary standards affirm this judgment.

What considerations might favor one standard over the other? To begin, why did proponents of the whole-brain standard propose a departure from the traditional cardiopulmonary standard? There were two main reasons. The first was straightforwardly practical: the whole-brain standard would permit extraction of vital organs while a patient maintained cardiopulmonary function with mechanical assistance, meaning more viable organs would be available for transplant. Although it may seem strange that a criterion of human death could be motivated by the good consequences that would result from its acceptance, the seminal report by the Harvard Medical School committee contained no philosophical or conceptual justification at all for its recommendation of the whole-brain standard. By contrast, the later President's Commission report did offer such a justification – one that connected the organismic definition of death to the whole-brain standard by way of the thesis that the human brain is the *primary integrator* of overall bodily functioning. Accordingly, the argument goes, only loss of function of the entire brain is necessary and sufficient for human death. Life involves the integrated functioning of the whole organism. While circulation and respiration are centrally important, so are hormonal regulation, maintenance of body temperature, and various other functions – including consciousness in humans and many other animals. A central integrator – the brain – permits the integration of these vital functions.

Although the whole-brain standard has been recognized in jurisdictions around the world, it has always had detractors and has recently faced especially vigorous counterarguments. Some traditionalists never accepted the whole-brain standard, rejecting its practical advantages as irrelevant to the nature of death and maintaining that cardiopulmonary function, no matter how it is sustained, entails the continuation of life.[47] Most of the

---

[47] See, e.g., Hans Jonas, "Against the Stream: Comments on the Definition and Redefinition of Death," in Hans Jonas, *Philosophical Essays* (Chicago: University of Chicago Press, 1974), 132–140.

intense recent pushback against the standard, by contrast, has appealed to empirical evidence that lack of brain function is not sufficient for the irreversible collapse of integrated bodily functioning. Many of the human body's integrated functions, according to this challenge, are not mediated by the brain and can persist in individuals who satisfy whole-brain criteria for death by standard clinical tests. These functions include homeostasis, detoxification of cellular waste, assimilation of nutrients, wound healing, fighting infections, and hormonal stress responses to unanesthetized incisions; in a few cases, brain-dead bodies have even matured sexually, grown, or gestated a living fetus.[48]

Champions of the whole-brain standard have replied to this and other challenges.[49] Rather than entering into the details of those replies or adjudicating between the two sides, we simply note that we find both the cardiopulmonary standard and the whole-brain standard reasonable specifications of the organismic definition of death – which, as stated earlier, is consonant with the biological account of our numerical identity. We therefore find the UDDA, which states that a human being has died upon satisfying either standard (whichever applies first), a sensible compromise from the standpoint of a biological understanding of human life, identity, and death. But consideration of a more progressive standard, discussed in the next section, will take us in a more radically pluralistic direction.

Implications of the Mind-Based Account

The mind-based account of identity asserts that human persons are essentially beings with the capacity for consciousness. This view implies that each of us came into existence when the developing fetus first became sentient and began to have subjective experiences such as tactile and auditory experiences. On the other side of human life, the mind-based view implies that we die – and go out of existence – upon the irreversible loss of the capacity for consciousness. This implication of the mind-based view of identity is known as the *higher-brain standard* of human death. No jurisdiction in the world has yet adopted this standard.

---

[48] D. A. Shewmon, "The Brain and Somatic Integration: Insights into the Standard Biological Rationale for Equating 'Brain Death' with Death," *Journal of Medicine and Philosophy* 26 (2001): 457–478.

[49] See, e.g., James Bernat, "A Defense of the Whole-Brain Concept of Death," *Hastings Center Report* 28 (1998): 14–23; and President's Council on Bioethics (PCB), *Controversies in the Determination of Death* (Washington, DC: PCB, 2008).

One common argument against the higher-brain standard appeals to the nearly irresistible intuition that a human body that can breathe unassisted is alive. Surely, the argument goes, if someone falls into an irreversible unconscious state but continues to breathe spontaneously, that individual cannot be dead. Indeed, it would seem grotesque to cremate or bury a breathing body even if it were irreversibly unconscious.

In response to this challenge, the mind-based account can assert that in cases of this sort there are in fact two deaths: the death of the person or minded being, who dies upon irreversibly losing their capacity for consciousness, and the death of the human organism that constituted them. In cases of the present sort, the person dies before the organism does. The organism, though still breathing, is insentient and lacks moral status. For this reason, it would not wrong the person whose body it was to cremate or bury the breathing body. Of course, since doing so would probably strike most people as grotesque, that would be sufficient reason to ensure that the body died too before cremation or burial.

Just as we find the mind-based account of our numerical identity fairly plausible, as discussed earlier, we believe that the higher-brain standard of death deserves a place next to the cardiopulmonary and whole-brain standards as among those criteria for human death that it is reasonable to believe.

Living with Pluralism about Standards of Death

Our view of numerical identity, which finds the biological and mind-based accounts about equally reasonable, leaves us with full-fledged pluralism regarding the three leading standards of human death.

Where does our pluralism leave us in terms of practical guidance? We believe it invites a reconsideration of the presumed practical significance of death. Earlier we noted that the modern debate over the nature of human death was driven both by technological advances that made it possible to separate cardiopulmonary and neurological function and by certain practical concerns. Let us revisit the latter. Clarity on the appropriate standard for death was supposed to help physicians decide whether it would be permissible (1) to discontinue life support for patients whose cardiopulmonary function was maintained artificially and (2) to harvest vital organs from the same class of patients (given their prior consent). We believe that affirmative answers to these questions may be justified *independently* of whether the patients are dead. So we recommend detaching the ethics of universal discontinuation of life support and of organ transplantation from the determination of death. Both practices can be justified without any assumption that the patients in question have died.

Unilateral withdrawal of medical life support from patients who have entered an irreversible unconscious state (IUS) is justified on the basis of resource constraints and the near-impossibility of benefiting them in such a state. Patients who will never again return to consciousness cannot enjoy life or derive satisfaction from anything in it. The only way they can derive benefit is if some aim of theirs is satisfied despite their lack of awareness. Very few important aims can be satisfied by being kept on life support. We therefore think that it would be excessively demanding to expect hospitals and nursing homes to continue to dedicate their resources to preserving the lives of individuals who are irreversibly unconscious. In our view, it does not matter whether or not the patients have died according to the traditional or whole-brain standard of death (although they will necessarily have satisfied the higher-brain standard). Other considerations justify unilateral withdrawal of life support.

In parallel fashion, the harvesting of vital organs for transplant is justified by ethical considerations other than whether or not the patients have died. It is justified by the prior valid consent of the patient to donate upon reaching a particular medical condition (e.g., an IUS, whole-brain death) and by the fact that, from the standpoint of this patient's values, continuing existence is less important than donating vital organs. In brief, donation is justified by respect for autonomy rights and is not prohibited by nonmaleficence.[50]

What is the upshot of our approach for laws concerning the determination of death? Two broad possibilities suggest themselves. One possibility is to leave current laws for determining death as they are, even if they fail to acknowledge the higher-brain standard as a reasonable option. If these laws remain in place, then it is certain practices that have been traditionally associated with death – unilateral withdrawal of life support, organ donation, and perhaps others – that should be extricated from the need for determinations of death. For example, the extraction of vital organs from still-living patients causes them to die, violating laws against homicide. Open practice of such organ procurement may therefore require modification of these laws. A second, more radical possibility would be to change laws about death in a pluralistic direction. For example, one standard – say, the whole-brain criterion – might serve as a legal default,

---

[50] Cf. Franklin Miller and Robert Truog, "Rethinking the Ethics of Vital Organ Donations," *Hastings Center Report* 38 (6) (2008): 38–46.

from which competent individuals could depart in selecting a different standard for themselves or for their legal dependents. In effect, the standard for your death would become a matter of your choice (within the reasonable options we have discussed). While moving in this radical, pluralistic direction might have unique advantages insofar as people might consider what constitutes their own death a highly personal matter, one worth troubling over, this move would also be costly in terms of the multiplicity of laws that would have to change and would no doubt prove confusing to many people. Given the recognition that death has less practical importance than we have traditionally assumed, it might be preferable to limit our changes to modifying practices such as those we have discussed.

CHAPTER 10

Creating Human Beings

10.1 Introduction

It is a momentous thing to bring a new human being into the world. Conception, pregnancy, childbirth, and parenting are all loaded with cultural significance and are the source of a great deal of the value people find in their lives. They inspire joy, anxiety, disagreement, and debate like few other topics. They also implicate medicine and ethics.

We begin our discussion in this chapter by examining whether there is a right to procreate. We derive a negative right to procreative autonomy from the rights of autonomous agents to control their own bodies. Like other autonomy rights, these rights are limited in scope by potential negative effects on others. Nevertheless, this right would permit the use of a wide range of procreative technologies. A positive right to procreative autonomy would constitute a claim to assistance with procreation. We argue that people's interests in procreating may ground claims to assistance on the basis of justice, but they have no special weight compared with other interests and so do not qualify as positive rights.

From procreative autonomy we turn to the ethics of making decisions that affect which humans come into being (or come to term). These divide into two categories: fixed-identity and identity-determining decisions. Fixed-identity decisions occur when someone chooses whether or not to bring a specific individual into the world. For example, a decision to terminate a pregnancy in the first trimester because the fetus has Down syndrome is a decision not to allow a specific fetus to develop and be born. The most fundamental question in fixed-identity cases is whether and when abortion is ethically permissible. Many other important bioethical questions concerning fetuses cannot be answered until the answer to that question is settled. We argue that pre-sentient fetuses are not harmed by death and so it is not wrongful for someone to exercise their right to control their body and terminate a pregnancy. Once sentience emerges – which is probably no earlier than twenty-eight weeks gestational age – it is plausible that death harms the fetus. However, due to the fetus's weak psychological connections to its possible future, the harm of death is relatively small. Terminating even a late-stage pregnancy can therefore be justified when there is a morally important reason to do so.

Identity-determining decisions occur when someone's choice affects which of several possible individuals will come into existence. For example, a couple might attempt to get pregnant now or – concerned about an outbreak of an infectious disease that might damage a fetus – wait until the end of the summer. The sperm and egg that would be part of conception now will not be the same sperm and egg that would be involved in a conception a few months hence. The decision of whether or not to delay determines which of two possible individuals will later exist. Identity-determining cases are difficult when the individuals who could come to exist differ substantially in their expected quality of life or well-being. Many philosophers judge that it would be wrong to bring into existence someone whose life would go worse than that of another individual who could be brought into existence instead. But it is hard to make sense of this judgment once we note that there is no one whose actual life is made worse. We argue that in at least a subset of these "non-identity" cases, it is not wrong to cause the existence of someone whose life will go worse than that of another possible individual.

Finally, we apply our theoretical conclusions regarding fixed-identity and identity-determining decisions to two practical issues: the use of medical technologies to select the sex of one's child and public health measures in the context of a Zika virus outbreak.

The discussion here, as elsewhere in the book, is selective. We omit important strands of argument, such as alternative defenses of the permissibility of abortion. We also omit some cutting-edge topics in bioethics that relate to procreation, such as enhancement and gene editing (although Chapter 9 takes up aspects of these two topics). Perhaps more significantly, this chapter engages *population ethics*: the ethics of making decisions that affect who will come into existence and how many individuals will come into existence. The boundaries of population ethics do not end with the human species. Our actions affect which nonhuman animals exist, too, such as via our food choices or habitat destruction. Though we think these issues are tremendously important, we set them aside here for lack of space.[1]

---

[1] For some recent discussion, see Sue Donaldson and Will Kymlicka, *Zoopolis* (New York: Oxford University Press, 2011); and Lori Gruen, *Ethics and Animals* (New York: Cambridge University Press, 2011), chap. 6.

10.2 Procreative Autonomy

Control over whether and how one creates new human beings is immensely important to almost everyone. Those who wish to have sexual relationships without procreating need ready access to contraception. Those who wish to procreate and parent may need assistance in conceiving, bearing, and rearing a child. Do all these people have a right to access what they need? We argue here that persons have a negative right to procreative autonomy, that their interests in procreation do not ground any special claim to assistance, but the value of parenting may support assistance in being parents.[2]

The Right to Procreative Autonomy

As we discussed in Chapter 3, rights typically function to protect important interests. But to justify saying that some person P has a right to X, it is not sufficient to show that she has an important interest in X. It is also necessary to show that a right is *necessary to protect* P's interest in X and that it is *P's* interest in X that merits protection (rather than, say, someone else's equally strong interest in X).[3] Thus, the existence of a right to procreative autonomy does not simply follow from the important interests such a right would support.

Start with the question of whether there is a negative right to procreative autonomy. Such a right would consist in a claim against others not to interfere with a person's procreative actions. We think that a prima facie negative right to procreative autonomy is entailed by other rights that autonomous agents have.[4] In particular, autonomous agents have a right to bodily integrity, which gives a person the right to control what happens to their body.[5] This right includes the power to consent to sex with another autonomous individual. In typical cases it would be wrongful for others to

---

[2] Similar ideas to those we discuss under the label of "procreative autonomy" are discussed by others under the labels of "reproductive liberty," a "right to procreate," and "procreative liberty." See, respectively, John Harris, "Reproductive Liberty, Disease, and Disability," *Reproductive Biomedicine Online* 10 (2005): 13–16; Sarah Conly, "The Right to Procreation: Merits and Limits," *American Philosophical Quarterly* 42 (2005): 105–115; and John Robertson, *Children of Choice* (Princeton, NJ: Princeton University Press, 1996). We are not drawing fine distinctions among these terms.

[3] These conditions correspond to the *existence* and *entitlement* theories underlying a putative right. See Joseph Millum, *The Moral Foundations of Parenthood* (New York: Oxford University Press, 2018), 16–17.

[4] This chapter does not consider the issue of procreative acts by nonautonomous individuals.

[5] See Chapter 5.

interfere with their having sex. The right also includes the right to refuse medical interventions or other bodily intrusions. So, if sex leads to pregnancy, the pregnant individual has the right to carry the pregnancy to term without interference by others. Thus, in paradigmatic cases of procreation, the acts involved fall clearly within the scope of the broader right to bodily integrity.

What about assisted reproduction where medical professionals are involved in helping an individual to become pregnant, such as through fertility-enhancing drugs or in vitro fertilization (IVF)? These methods comprise medical procedures that autonomous individuals are also generally thought to have the power to consent to or refuse. There is nothing different in kind about the medical procedures involved in assisted reproduction than the procedures involved in other medical care that also require consent.

The negative right to procreative autonomy as we have derived it is prima facie because its scope is restricted in the same way as with other autonomy rights: it does not extend to actions that wrong others, including by violating their rights against being harmed. It follows that questions of who, if anyone, is wronged by procreative acts are crucial to determining whether there are any grounds for restricting them. When considering whether an individual should be permitted to use some novel means of procreating, those who would restrict access must first show that there is a victim.

Deriving a negative right to procreative autonomy from widely accepted autonomy rights has important implications for debates about assisted reproductive technology (ART). It implies, for example, that people should be free to make use of fertility-enhancing drugs, IVF, and the like. Moreover, these results follow without our having to endorse anything special about procreation per se.[6]

The question of whether there is something particularly important about procreating is, however, relevant to assessing claims for a positive right to assistance with procreation. Understood as just one way that someone can exercise their bodily autonomy, there is no reason to provide them with additional resources in order to procreate. But, for example, a couple who is struggling to conceive may not be able to afford IVF

---

[6] Other arguments for a liberty right to access ART generally involve a great deal of argument intended to establish the importance of procreation. See, e.g., John Robertson, "Liberalism and the Limits of Procreative Liberty: A Response to My Critics," *Washington & Lee Law Review* 52 (1995): 233–267, at 235.

themselves. Should the state subsidize the treatment? Likewise, there are infertile couples who cannot conceive even with existing medical technology. Should government research agencies support research into infertility in the same way as they might support research into dengue fever or lung cancer?

A number of writers have argued that procreation is special. One possibility is that there is something especially valuable in the genetic or biological connection between a parent and the child created by them. Certainly, many people seem to think that genetic relationships are important. However, efforts to justify such views have not been persuasive.[7] The desire to make a child that resembles me – in looks or personality – seems too trivial, if not narcissistic. The desires to pass on my genes or continue my lineage likewise seem to put an implausible degree of weight on the importance of genetic connections.[8] Given the value of persons, there is surely something very morally weighty involved in bringing a person into existence. But whether the act of procreation has *positive* value presumably then depends on the fate of the person so created. Consequently, many writers are skeptical that humans have a strong interest in genetic or biological reproduction in itself. Instead, it is argued, procreation and gestation are "valuable largely because of the opportunity it gives people to parent a child (i.e., to be 'rearers')."[9] We endorse this view.

The final possible ground for a positive claim to assistance with procreation, then, is that people have an interest in becoming parents, where this is understood as a social relationship between parents and their children. For many people, parenting is a central life project and a source of a great deal of meaning. Through it they create and maintain a family while assisting a child through their development.[10] The intimate relationship that (good) parents have with their children is both valuable and unique.[11] For some individuals, then, it is plausible that their lives would go much

[7] See Tina Rulli, "Preferring a Genetically-Related Child," *Journal of Moral Philosophy* 13 (2016): 669–698, for an overview of various grounds for preferring a genetically related child and arguments against them in the context of a duty to adopt rather than procreate. Rulli allows a possible exception for those who powerfully desire to experience pregnancy.
[8] For reasons to distrust our intuitions about the importance of genetic connections, see Joseph Millum, "How Do We Acquire Parental Rights?," *Social Theory and Practice* 36 (2010): 112–132, at 125–128.
[9] Andrew Botterell and Carolyn McLeod, "Can a Right to Reproduce Justify the Status Quo on Parental Licensing?," in Sarah Hannan, Samantha Brennan, and Richard Vernon (eds.), *Permissible Progeny* (New York: Oxford University Press, 2015), 184–207.
[10] Millum, *Moral Foundations of Parenthood*, 50–53.
[11] Harry Brighouse and Adam Swift, "Parents' Rights and the Value of the Family," *Ethics* 117 (2006): 80–108.

worse if they were unable to parent. Such powerful interests in parenting could ground correspondingly powerful claims to assistance with becoming parents, such as through subsidizing access to ART.

To this proposal it might be objected that one need not procreate in order to parent. Adoptive parents are just as much parents of their children, and rearing a genetically unrelated child is no less valuable than rearing one's offspring.[12] In a large number of countries, there are many children in need of parenting. For example, the US Department of Health and Human Services reported 437,000 children in the foster care system in 2016, of whom 118,000 were waiting to be adopted.[13] These children in foster care are in need of loving, stable families and would benefit enormously from adoption. Crucially, they already exist. The children who might be created through ART, on the other hand, do not yet exist and their needs will matter morally only if they do come to exist. Consequently, given a choice between creating a new child (whether through ART or a more traditional method) and parenting a child who already exists and needs a stable family, some philosophers think we have an ethical obligation to choose the latter.[14]

Were there a surplus of healthy babies in need of adoption, we think this argument would be compelling. However, matters on the ground are more complicated. For the most part, the children in foster care waiting to be adopted are not infants. For example, in the United States the average age of children waiting to be adopted is 7.7 years, and only 4 percent are under one year of age. Though children who are adopted later do generally recover to a large extent from the negative effects of early deprivation, they are still less likely to form secure attachment relationships with their new parents.[15] Moreover, many of these children are medically complicated

---

[12] There might be differences in specific ways in which parenting an adopted child is valuable for the parents (Tina Rulli, "The Unique Value of Adoption," in Francoise Baylis and Carolyn McLeod [eds.], *Family-Making* [Oxford: Oxford University Press, 2014]).

[13] US Department of Health and Human Services, Administration for Children and Families, *The AFCARS Report* (2017) (available at www.acf.hhs.gov/sites/default/files/cb/afcarsreport24.pdf). Statistics Canada reports 28,030 foster children under fourteen years (Statistics Canada, *Portrait of Children's Family Life in Canada in 2016*; available at www12.statcan.gc.ca/census-recensement/index-eng.cfm). The UK Department of Education reports 72,670 "looked-after" children in England in 2017, of whom only 4,350 were adopted (www.gov.uk/government/collections/statistics-looked-after-children).

[14] See, e.g., Daniel Friedrich, "A Duty to Adopt?," *Journal of Applied Philosophy* 30 (2013): 25–39.

[15] See Linda Van den Dries et al., "Fostering Security? A Meta-analysis of Attachment in Adopted Children," *Children and Youth Services Review* 31 (2009): 410–421; and M. H. Van Ijzendoorn and F. Juffer, "Adoption as Intervention: Meta-analytic Evidence for Massive Catch-up and Plasticity in Physical, Socio-emotional, and Cognitive Development," *Journal of Child Psychology and Psychiatry* 47 (2006): 1228–1245. According to van Ijzendoorn and Juffer the evidence does not suggest

and so will require greater care than healthy children would. Adopting from foster care generally means missing out on one's child's early years, and parenting such a child is likely to be harder than average. We therefore think that it is not *ethically required* that prospective parents adopt such children, rather than procreate, even if it would be better to do so.

Meanwhile, private domestic adoptions and international adoptions are more likely to involve a healthy infant. However, domestic supply is exceeded by the number of parents looking to adopt, and children adopted from developing countries are frequently not those in great need of new families.[16] Thus, other prospective adoptees – the healthy infants that many would-be parents ideally want – are likely to find parents in any case. There is therefore no duty to adopt them rather than procreate either.

Two caveats are in order here regarding our conclusions. First, while we believe that many individuals have a morally important interest in procreating in order to parent, this conclusion depends on the nonideal circumstances that prevail in the high-income countries with which we are familiar. In the United States and United Kingdom, for example, more just and efficient systems for finding permanent families for foster children might involve placing children for adoption at younger ages. So, it might currently be supererogatory for individuals to adopt instead of procreating, but it does not follow that government entities are off the hook. Given how important it is for a child to have a stable family environment, governments should do everything they can to find good parents for needy children, including providing incentives to possible adopters.

Second, the conclusions we have drawn so far regarding a right to procreative autonomy require the assumption that it is permissible to procreate in the first place. Though it is commonly thought that creating children is ethically permissible, even praiseworthy, this view has been challenged. One challenge is based on environmental degradation. More children means more consumption, which will accelerate climate change

---

substantial differences between adopted and nonadopted (birth family) peers in behavioral problems, even for children adopted older than one year.

[16] Data on the number of US couples looking to adopt are hard to obtain, but it apparently exceeds the number of babies given up for adoption at birth (see, e.g., Jeff Katz, "Adoption's Numbers Mystery," *Washington Post*, November 8, 2008; available at www.washingtonpost.com/wp-dyn/content/article/2008/11/07/AR2008110702807.html). For a popular exposé of the international adoption industry, see E. J. Graff, "The Lie We Love," *Foreign Policy*, October 6, 2009 (available at http://foreignpolicy.com/2009/10/06/the-lie-we-love/). It may well be that many children in poorer countries would benefit enormously from adoption, but it does not follow that those children can be readily identified by foreign would-be adopters.

and other effects of the overuse of the earth's resources.[17] Another is based on the interests of the people who would be brought into existence. For example, David Benatar thinks that it is wrongful to bring people into existence because of the suffering that they will predictably undergo without having had any say in the matter of coming into existence.[18]

Procreative Autonomy and Public Policy

We have argued that individuals have a negative autonomy right to procreate derived from other autonomy rights they have to control their own bodies. This establishes a right against interference with attempts to procreate, including attempts that involve the help of (consenting) others. The desire to *procreate* does not, we have argued, have special weight, even though people may have a strong interest in *parenting* that grounds claims to assistance on the basis of distributive justice. What do these points of theory tell us about public policy concerning reproduction?

First, the right against interference with procreative acts implies a presumption in favor of allowing people to avail themselves of assistance with procreation. The burden of justification falls on those who would ban some practice or technology, not on those who want to use it. Even when evidence is provided that some form of assisted procreation is harming or otherwise wronging others, it does not follow automatically that it should be prohibited. Regulation that protects potential victims but still allows others as much freedom as possible should be attempted first. For example, a woman may act as a surrogate by agreeing to become pregnant on another's behalf. This may involve artificial insemination of the surrogate or IVF. The legality of paying surrogates for their services and the enforceability of surrogacy contracts varies by jurisdiction. Some critics argue that commercial surrogacy contracts are exploitative. This would be the sort of consideration that could count against the presumption of allowing people to procreate via surrogate mothers. But even if it were shown that commercial surrogacy contracts are often exploitative, it would be better to regulate them to prevent exploitative terms than to ban the practice outright.[19] Later in this chapter, we examine sex selection in some detail.

---

[17] Thomas Young, "Overconsumption and Procreation: Are They Morally Equivalent?," *Journal of Applied Philosophy* (2001): 183–192.

[18] David Benatar and David Wasserman, *Debating Procreation* (New York: Oxford University Press, 2015).

[19] For critical discussion, see Stephen Wilkinson, "The Exploitation Argument against Commercial Surrogacy," *Bioethics* 17 (2003): 169–187.

This is another practice that some commentators have argued should be prohibited on the basis of anticipated social costs.[20]

Second, the bioethics literature, understandably, focuses more on questions relating to novel procreative practices and technologies than on ones whose permissibility is settled. Reproductive cloning and three-parent babies are much more exciting and controversial than whether people should have access to condoms. But emphasis on the ethics of novel means of exercising procreative autonomy might give the impression that these are the most important issues for public policy. We think this is typically mistaken. *Many more people are affected – and affected more negatively – by the failure of states to protect aspects of their reproductive autonomy that are mostly uncontested by ethicists.* For example, in 2017 an estimated 142 million women worldwide who were married or in a union had an unmet need for family planning.[21] Most women in low-income countries have not heard of emergency contraception, and providers frequently have negative attitudes toward it, even where emergency contraceptive products are available.[22] Gender power disparities mean that many women and girls are not able to control the circumstances under which they have sexual relations, exposing them to unwanted pregnancies and infectious disease.[23] When thinking about how state resources should be allocated to protect people's autonomy rights, these are the rights in greatest need of protection.[24]

---

[20] Some writers have argued that procreation itself typically burdens society so people should not be subsidized in procreating and parenting – doing so is like subsidizing an expensive hobby (see, e.g., R. S. Taylor, "Children as Projects and Persons: A Liberal Antinomy," *Social Theory and Practice* 35 [2009]: 555–576). However, procreation may also be providing benefits to other members of society. After all, we rely on the next generation to work to produce the goods that everyone will consume (S. Olsaretti, "Children as Public Goods?," *Philosophy and Public Affairs* 41 [2013]: 226–258). Whether adding an additional individual to the population is a net gain or a net cost will be very dependent on details of the social context, including a society's economy and what other potential procreators will do.

[21] United Nations, Department of Economic and Social Affairs, Population Division (2017), *World Family Planning 2017 – Highlights* (ST/ESA/SER.A/414).

[22] Elizabeth Westley et al., "A Review of Global Access to Emergency Contraception," *International Journal of Gynecology & Obstetrics* 123 (2013): 4–6.

[23] Geeta Rao Gupta, "How Men's Power over Women Fuels the HIV Epidemic: It Limits Women's Ability to Control Sexual Interactions," *British Medical Journal* 324 (2002): 183–184.

[24] It is sometimes thought that resource allocation issues are irrelevant to negative rights because they only impose duties on others not to interfere. This is mistaken. In order for negative rights – including rights to bodily integrity and procreative autonomy – to be meaningful, they must be protected. To protect such rights effectively requires enforcement by the state. For example, an individual's right to bodily integrity will be effective only if there are laws against assault, and police and courts who enforce those laws. But to protect rights requires resources; for example, police must be paid and legal processes must be accessible and efficient. For extensive argument for and illustration of this point, see Henry Shue, *Basic Rights* (Princeton, NJ: Princeton University Press, 1996).

Similar points apply to the positive claim to assistance with becoming a parent. We accept that this interest is morally weighty, such that it matters from the point of view of distributive justice. But in thinking about, for example, whether the state should subsidize IVF for infertile couples, we must consider what other claims there are to the resources that IVF requires. For many women around the world, access to complex artificial reproductive technologies is not the aspect of reproductive control that is most vital to their flourishing. Rather, access to birth control, safe abortion, antenatal care, and the like are more urgent needs, not to mention – from the perspective of allocating scarce resources – cheaper ways to provide important benefits.

To sum up, there is a presumption in favor of permitting people to use new reproductive practices and technologies. Moreover, people's interests in procreation matter from the point of view of distributive justice. However, in our nonideal world, there are likely to be higher priorities for spending money on reproductive autonomy. These priorities should not be forgotten, even though much of the debate in bioethics over procreation focuses on novel and often expensive reproductive technologies.

10.3   Evaluating Creation

We have defended a negative right to procreative autonomy. However, that right is limited by actions that wrong others. The main effects of procreative decisions concern the children who might be brought into the world. In this section we analyze possible wrongs to them under the labels of *fixed-identity decisions* and *identity-determining decisions*. Recall that fixed-identity decisions about procreation occur when someone chooses whether or not to bring a specific individual into the (postnatal) world. Can it be permissible to kill a fetus? Is it permissible to destroy an embryo created in vitro or to allow it to die? Identity-determining decisions occur when an agent's actions affect which individual will come into existence. Can such decisions be wrongful, even if the individual created was not harmed?

Fixed-Identity Decisions

Questions about whether it is permissible to damage or destroy individual human zygotes, embryos, and fetuses arise with regard to an array of ethical and policy issues. The most salient of these concerns the permissibility of terminating a pregnancy. But whether, when, and for what reasons women and girls should be permitted to utilize abortion services – or have them subsidized – is only one important issue.[25] Consider, for example, embryonic stem-cell research (an issue we discuss in Chapter 7). This research is potentially very valuable, but it involves the destruction of human embryos. Or consider couples who use IVF and freeze embryos that are not ultimately implanted. Is it ethically permissible for couples or fertility clinics to discard the unused embryos?[26]

The most plausible reason for thinking that it is generally wrong to kill a fetus is that killing the fetus harms a being with moral status.[27] As discussed in Chapter 7, if an individual has moral status, this means that others have obligations regarding their treatment of her that are based on her interests. In Chapter 7, we argued that only beings who are sentient at some point in time have interests and therefore moral status. A fetus that dies early in pregnancy – before the point at which it could be sentient – will never be sentient and so, on our account, lacks moral status. Our account of moral status makes the permissibility of aborting pre-sentient fetuses a relatively straightforward matter.

Suppose, though, that someone doubted this view of moral status and claimed that the fact that *the fetus would very likely become sentient if allowed to develop normally* is sufficient for moral status. They would say the *potential* of the fetus was sufficient for moral status. For surplus embryos from IVF this might not matter – unless adopted for gestation, they would not otherwise develop into sentient beings. However, for a fetus that is currently being gestated it would. At least after the first few weeks of gestation (when rates of spontaneous abortion are high) the development of that fetus may be expected to proceed unless some intervention ends it.

Nevertheless, we think that even this more expansive view of moral status would not imply that killing pre-sentient fetuses is wrongful. This is because prior to sentience a fetus is not harmed by death; that is, the pre-sentient fetus does not have an interest in continued life. In Chapter 4, we

---

[25] We recognize that a trans male or gender nonconforming person might become pregnant and our conclusions in this section would apply to those persons too. We generally talk of *women* (or *women and girls*) in this context because of the heavily gendered nature of many discussions and policy decisions.

[26] Ellen McCarthy, "Fertility Treatments Give Birth to Dilemma for Parents," *The Guardian*, May 23, 2015 (available at www.theguardian.com/science/2015/may/23/fertility-technology-unused-sperm-eggs).

[27] For convenience, we use the term "fetus" to refer to all stages of human prenatal development.

defended a gradualist view of what makes death bad for an individual. We argued that death is bad in virtue of what it deprives the decedent of, but in order for an individual to be deprived of future goods by dying, there needs to be some psychological connection between her present state and the goods that are lost.

No matter what we might think about the moral status of the fetus, it is clear that there are no psychological connections between the pre-sentient fetus and its future self. There are no such connections because the fetus does not yet have psychological states. Non-sentient fetuses are not psychologically connected to the goods of which death deprives them. Hence, we believe, they are not harmed by death.[28] Nor would killing a pre-sentient fetus violate the fetus's rights. In Chapter 7, we argued that a creature must be more cognitively complex than merely being sentient – having at least some nontrivial temporal self-awareness – in order to have rights. It follows that pre-sentient fetuses do not have rights.

Turn now to sentient fetuses. Sentience, at least in the form of the ability to feel pain, probably appears around twenty-eight weeks gestational age.[29] It is at least possible that a fetus becomes sentient some weeks before then.[30] Given our current understanding of the physiology underlying pain, however, it is not possible that sentience begins earlier than twenty weeks gestational age.[31]

Since they are not yet persons (and if they die will not develop into persons) in the sense we describe in Chapter 7, even sentient fetuses lack rights. Abortion therefore does not violate a right to life. But sentient fetuses do have interests that matter morally. It would be wrong to gratuitously inflict pain on a third-trimester fetus, for example. Would it be wrong to kill such a fetus? Clearly, killing a fetus that would develop into a person typically deprives it of a great deal of valuable life. However, the psychological links between the current fetus and its future life are very weak. It cannot matter much, if at all, to the fetus whether it misses out on

---

[28] For a more extended argument along similar lines, see David DeGrazia, *Creation Ethics* (New York: Oxford University Press, 2012), 34–35. DeGrazia's argument shows a central problem for Don Marquis's celebrated argument against abortion ("Why Abortion Is Immoral," *Journal of Philosophy* 86 [1989]: 183–202). In brief, Marquis argues that killing a person is wrongful because it deprives one of a valuable future. Since fetuses that are allowed to develop normally have a similar future – a "future like ours" – it is likewise wrong to kill even a presentient fetus. The argument fails if we adopt a gradualist account of what makes death bad for an individual.

[29] Susan Lee et al., "Fetal Pain: A Systematic Multidisciplinary Review of the Evidence," *JAMA* 294 (2005): 947–954.

[30] E. C. Brugger, "The Problem of Fetal Pain and Abortion: Towards an Ethical Consensus for Appropriate Behavior," *Kennedy Institute of Ethics Journal* 22 (2012): 263–387.

[31] See Lee et al., "Fetal Pain."

this future life. Thus, even for a sentient fetus, death is nowhere near the harm that it is for an older child or a young adult.

The foregoing discussion has some clear implications for the ethics of abortion. Prior to twenty weeks gestational age fetuses are not harmed by death. Assuming that the only considerations a pregnant woman needs to take into account concern the interests of the fetus, it is not even pro tanto wrong to terminate a pregnancy at this stage. After twenty weeks, it is possible that the fetus is sentient and can be harmed by death. Abortion will then be justified only when there is a sufficient moral reason in favor of it. Since the likelihood of fetal sentience and possibly the strength of a fetus's psychological connections to its future increase over the course of development after twenty weeks of gestation, it is morally preferable to abort earlier rather than later where possible. The moral reasons given to justify an abortion need to be weightier the greater the gestational age beyond twenty weeks.[32]

What sorts of reasons might justify inflicting the harm of death on a sentient fetus? Mere convenience would not be enough. Late-stage abortions are not generally sought for reasons of convenience, though.[33] Parenting a child is a life-changing and time-consuming project. Suppose a woman becomes pregnant, does not think that she could bear to give up a child for adoption, but believes that raising a child would interfere with other valuable life goals. This might be sufficient justification. Likewise, for fetuses who are expected to have severe congenital conditions requiring a lot of additional care, we think it plausible that the additional burden on parents would be sufficient to justify a third trimester abortion, even for people who otherwise would want to become parents. Unsurprisingly, we also judge that serious risks to the life or well-being of the mother would be sufficient to justify even a late abortion.[34]

Our discussion so far has focused on the individual decision of a woman deciding whether to terminate her pregnancy. However, it also has

---

[32] Here we have ignored a second common line of argument in favor of the permissibility of abortion. That line of argument – made popular by Judith Jarvis Thomson – starts from the premise that persons have strong rights to decide what happens to their bodies, so a pregnant woman would have no duty to continue a pregnancy even if the fetus were already a person. See Thomson, "A Defense of Abortion," *Philosophy & Public Affairs* 1 (1971): 47–66; and David Boonin, *A Defense of Abortion* (New York: Cambridge University Press, 2003). For critical assessment of this argument, see DeGrazia, *Creation Ethics*, 39–43.

[33] For example, only 1.4 percent of abortions carried out in England and Wales take place after nineteen weeks (Roger Ingham et al., "Reasons for Second Trimester Abortions in England and Wales," *Reproductive Health Matters* 16 [supp. 31] [2008]: 18–29).

[34] In this category we include the trauma of carrying to term a pregnancy resulting from rape.

important implications for other actors, including clinicians and the state. We briefly describe some of them here, though space does not permit a full ethical analysis.

First, safe abortions require some interaction with clinicians, whether to prescribe abortifacient drugs or to carry out surgical procedures. Some clinicians who have strong views about the morality of abortion may not want to be involved in providing abortion services. They may even consider it wrongful to refer patients to other providers who would be willing to assist with abortions, since this would make them complicit in acts they believe to be wrong. There are ongoing debates in several countries about whether clinicians have the right to refuse to provide certain medical services and what governments should do in response to such conscientious objectors.[35] On the other side, clinicians in countries with restrictive abortion laws face dilemmas about how to help patients who seek termination of pregnancy. Suppose that the law permits a second trimester abortion in case of a threat to the woman's health. Should a physician interpret this exception so loosely that they essentially allow abortion on demand, even though they knows that this is not the intended interpretation of the law?

Second, there is the issue of what legal limits, if any, states should impose on access to abortion services, and whether access to abortion should be subsidized by the public health system. In general, where an act does not harm or wrong anyone, there is a presumption in favor of allowing it.[36] This implies that it should be permissible for someone to obtain an abortion for any reason up to at least twenty weeks gestational age. After that time, we acknowledged the possibility that the fetus could be harmed by death (and probably is harmed by death after twenty-eight weeks gestational age). This harm to the fetus provides the sort of reason that might ground legal restrictions. Consistent with this idea, there are restrictions on late abortions even in countries with quite liberal abortion laws. For example, in the United Kingdom, abortions after twenty-four weeks are permitted only if "necessary to prevent grave permanent injury to the physical or mental health of the pregnant woman," if continuation of pregnancy increases the risk of the woman's death, or if there is a "substantial risk" that the fetus will be severely disabled.[37]

---

[35] See, e.g., Carolyn McLeod and Jocelyn Downie, "Let Conscience Be Their Guide? Conscientious Refusals in Health Care," *Bioethics* 28 (2014): ii–iv, and the various articles in this special issue.
[36] See Chapter 5's discussion of the harm principle.   [37] The Abortion Act 1967, Section 1(1).

Although our arguments do support an ethical difference between decisions to abort, say, a first-trimester fetus versus a third-trimester fetus, we are less sanguine about marking this difference through a legal prohibition. This is because of the range of reasons we think could justify terminating even a late-stage pregnancy. They include judgments about what burden bringing a pregnancy to term would place on the pregnant woman. It would be very hard for someone other than that woman to make these judgments reliably. This does not rule out alternative ways to treat later terminations as more weighty decisions, such as offering counseling services for individuals contemplating abortion or mandating a more comprehensive informed consent process.

Turn now to public subsidy of abortion services. Here we see no difference between how the public health system should treat abortion and how it should treat other forms of birth control and medical treatments for pregnant women. Providing access to safe termination of pregnancy – wherever the line is drawn for when that is permitted – promotes the well-being of women by giving them control over important aspects of their bodies, including promoting reproductive autonomy, preventing the risks of illegal abortions, and avoiding the negative effects on health and other aspects of well-being of bringing an unwanted pregnancy to term.

Finally, on the flip side, the harm to late-stage fetuses who die or are injured provides a further reason in favor of providing health care interventions that benefit the fetus. For example, it supports the provision of prenatal care to reduce the risk of stillbirth.[38] According to our arguments, stillbirth is bad not only for the woman but also for the fetus.[39]

Identity-Determining Decisions: The Nonidentity Problem

Suppose that a couple is considering procreation in the midst of an infectious disease outbreak. The woman currently has the disease, which involves minimal symptoms for her but would cause any child she gestated to have a developmental disability involving mild cognitive impairment and episodic pain. In three months, the woman will have cleared the infection from her system. Any child conceived after that point could be expected not to have the disabling condition. Should the couple stop using

---

[38] The World Health Organization (WHO) defines a stillbirth as "a baby born with no signs of life at or after 28 weeks' gestation" (www.who.int/maternal_child_adolescent/epidemiology/stillbirth/en/).

[39] Alexander Heazell et al., "Stillbirths: Economic and Psychosocial Consequences," *Lancet* 387 (2016): 604–616.

contraception now, as originally planned, or wait three months before attempting to conceive?

Many couples might choose to delay for their own sake. They might want to avoid the additional burdens involved in raising a child with developmental problems. Policy-makers might recommend delaying pregnancy for the sake of societal benefits, such as reduced burden on the health care system. This policy goal might support increased subsidies for contraception, for example. But even if the couple would be happy to parent a cognitively disabled child and had the resources to do so well, many people believe that it would be morally wrong to choose to conceive now instead of waiting.[40] This moral judgment is puzzling.

The puzzle is this. If the couple would be doing something wrong by having a child with cognitive and pain-causing disabilities, whom would they wrong? Assume that the child with disabilities has a life that is nevertheless well worth living. It then seems odd to say that they would wrong that child. If they delayed pregnancy, then that child would not exist: if the couple conceived in three months, a different sperm would fuse with a different ovum and produce a different child. This is the *nonidentity problem*: there seems to be a wrongful action but there does not seem to be a *victim* of the wrong. (The term "nonidentity" is used because the individual who comes into existence with the developmental disability is not identical to – is not the same individual as – the individual who would have come into existence had the couple delayed pregnancy.)

The nonidentity problem arises whenever an agent makes a choice that affects which individuals come into existence where those who come into existence following one choice are expected to have lives that are significantly worse than the different individuals who would come into existence following a different choice.[41] It will arise, for example, if a woman receiving IVF decides to implant an embryo with a deleterious congenital condition rather than one without it. It also arises at the population level. For example, consider the effects of human activity on the climate. The massive emissions of greenhouse gases are rapidly changing the earth's climate. Without dramatic action to curtail emissions soon, large areas of

---

[40] Compare the more idealized cases in Dan Brock, "The Non-identity Problem and Genetic Harms: The Case of Wrongful Handicaps," *Bioethics* 9 (1995): 269–275, at 270; and Derek Parfit, *Reasons and Persons* (Oxford: Clarendon, 1984), chap. 16.

[41] This problem was first examined systematically in Parfit, *Reasons and Persons*, Part IV. For a good overview of strategies for addressing this problem, see M. A. Roberts, "The Nonidentity Problem," in Edward Zalta (ed.), *Stanford Encyclopedia of Philosophy* (Winter 2015 edition; available at https://plato.stanford.edu/entries/nonidentity-problem/).

the earth will become much more hostile to human and other life.[42] The resulting large-scale migration, conflicts over water, and other negative impacts are likely to make the lives of people living in fifty or a hundred years much worse. If we do nothing, then it seems that we wrong future generations. They will – and probably should – blame us for failing to change our lifestyles to protect the climate. However, dramatically reducing emissions of greenhouse gases would involve many people changing their behavior. Small changes such as how they get to work (e.g., taking a bus rather than driving) may easily lead to significant changes (e.g., whom they meet and with whom they ultimately procreate). At the very least, behavioral changes associated with more environmentally responsible lifestyles would likely affect the timing of procreative actions. Even a small difference in when two people conceive is likely to change which sperm fertilizes the ovum. And this, plausibly, is sufficient to change the identity of the person who is conceived. But then it appears that making the changes needed to avoid catastrophic climate change will also, within a small number of generations, change which people come to exist. If these future generations will have lives worth living even given the damage to the climate, then how can they complain that we did them wrong? After all, without climate change, they would not exist at all.[43]

Note that nonidentity cases are not usually cases of "wrongful life." Wrongful life cases arise when procreative decisions lead predictably to someone's quality of life being so bad that, for their sake, they should not have been brought into existence at all. This might apply to a child with a congenital condition such as Tay-Sachs disease, which was expected to cause so much suffering that the bad in her life would outweigh the good. A woman might discover through testing early in pregnancy that she is carrying a fetus with Tay-Sachs. If she judged that she ought to terminate the pregnancy, we can make sense of this judgment on the basis of the interests of the future child.[44] Not so for most nonidentity cases, where existing with some predictable disadvantage nevertheless involves a life well worth living, such as in cases involving Down syndrome.[45]

---

[42] Intergovernmental Panel on Climate Change, *Global Warming of 1.5° C* (2018) (available at www.ipcc.ch).

[43] Cf. Parfit's depletion case (*Reasons and Persons*, chap. 16, sect. 123).   [44] See Chapter 8.

[45] For some discussion of "wrongful life" suits and the associated philosophical issues, see Joel Feinberg, "Wrongful Life and the Counterfactual Element in Harming," *Social Philosophy and Policy* 4 (1986): 145–178; and Seana Shiffrin, "Wrongful Life, Procreative Responsibility, and the Significance of Harm," *Legal Theory* 5 (1999): 117–148.

The nonidentity problem has spawned a large philosophical literature. Here, we sketch some of the main ways in which philosophers have attempted to amend their moral theories to address the nonidentity problem.[46] We then describe one proposed solution that we find promising and sketch its implications for bioethics.

The nonidentity problem arises out of three plausible but conflicting moral judgments. First, there are no victimless wrongs: if an action is wrong, then there must be some individual who is wronged. Second, if the only way that someone could come to exist involves their having some sort of welfare-reducing feature, they are not wronged by being brought into existence (provided that their life is worth living). The child whose parents could not have created her without a congenital condition causing chronic pain is not wronged by being born, provided that her life is worth living overall. Third, the acts described in the nonidentity cases we outlined are wrongful acts.

One solution to the problem is to deny that there are no victimless wrongs. On one version of this solution, we should adopt an "impersonal" morality, such as a utilitarian theory that requires agents to maximize the amount of well-being in the world, independent of who exists. This sort of view can explain very well why the couple should delay attempting to get pregnant and why people living now should take dramatic actions to reduce climate change. In both cases, the total well-being in the world will probably be greater.

Adopting an impersonal morality would solve the nonidentity problem. However, impersonal moralities tend to entail other moral judgments that are at least as implausible as the ones that they help us avoid. For example, it is widely held that killing another person is very wrong in most cases. It would be very wrong for a couple to kill an innocent, healthy twenty-year-old waiting in the bus line. It is also widely held that a decision not to procreate is not wrong in most cases. It would not be wrong for the couple to use contraception to avoid having a baby, even if their baby would likely have a flourishing life. But on a wholly impersonal morality, the act of removing a flourishing life from the world is, all else equal, no worse than the act of omitting to add a flourishing life. The utilitarian view that requires agents to maximize total well-being – an impersonal morality – will regard the two acts as equivalent if their effect on well-being is the same. This seems clearly mistaken. Further, the reason it is mistaken seems

---

[46] Space precludes a comprehensive overview here. For longer discussions on which we draw here, see DeGrazia, *Creation Ethics*, 176–186; and Roberts, "The Nonidentity Problem."

to be that the murder would violate the rights of the twenty-year-old and deprive him of a valuable future, whereas not procreating would not affect any actual person. Intuitions that what makes certain acts wrong is their effects on specific victims are strongly held.

A compromise would be to adopt a mixed view, such that there can be acts that are wrong because they affect specific individuals and acts that are wrong just in virtue of their impersonal effects.[47] Such a view could explain the wrong in nonidentity cases because it would still be wrong, at least in some situations, to act in ways that produce worse outcomes, even when there is no victim of the wrongdoing.

The challenge for mixed views is to say exactly how impersonal effects matter. If a mixed view says that impersonal effects are just as important as personal effects, then it is likely to face similar problems to the ones facing wholly impersonal views. If impersonal effects matter less than personal effects, then some of those problems are reduced. Such a view could say that while it is good to create a child who will live a flourishing life, it is morally much more important to avoid harming a person who already exists. However, taking this route has its own challenges. There will be situations where the negative outcomes of two actions are similar but one affects who will come to exist and one does not. On a mixed view like the one we are considering, the identity-determining action should be taken, because its negative effects will not be as wrongful. So, for example, if we had the choice, it would be better to pollute the environment in ways that affect who comes to exist rather than in ways that do not, even when the outcomes for those who come to exist are the same. The Zika virus case we describe in Section 10.5 has this structure. We offer one possible way to address this challenge there.

A third response to the nonidentity problem is to bite the bullet and reject the judgment that there is any wrong done in nonidentity cases.[48] All wrongs do indeed need a victim, and we do not need to cite mysterious impersonal effects or duties to maximize the amount of well-being in the universe. Our intuitive responses to the cases, one might argue, simply reflect the fact that we have trouble keeping in mind the difference in identity between the individuals who could exist. In cases where a couple could create a child now who could not exist without a condition that somewhat reduced her welfare, procreating does not wrong the child.

---

[47] Cf. DeGrazia, *Creation Ethics*, 184–185.
[48] David Boonin, *The Nonidentity Problem and the Ethics of Future People* (Oxford: Oxford University Press, 2014).

Since, on this view, there is no moral requirement to increase the total well-being in the universe, there is still no wrong done if the couple could have created a completely different child who would predictably fare better.

The greatest challenge for this bullet-biting response is how to deal with the effects of our actions on future generations. As described above, the many small actions that would be taken by people who currently exist in order to avoid the worst effects of human-made climate change will likely affect which people come into existence in future generations. It seems highly implausible that this means continuing to degrade and pollute the environment will not wrong them.

Our preferred solution to the nonidentity problem bites the bullet on a subset of nonidentity cases while arguing that other cases are not true nonidentity cases because there are victims. In addition, we think it is plausible that impersonal effects matter morally, though to a substantially lesser degree than do effects that impact specific individuals. A world with less suffering is morally better than a world with more suffering, all else being equal. And the fact that one state of affairs is morally better than another gives moral agents a reason to choose it. However, this reason is relatively weak when there is no victim or beneficiary of an agent's choice.

Our solution draws on ideas developed by Melinda Roberts.[49] Roberts distinguishes two types of nonidentity case: *genetic* and *expectational*. In genetic cases, "the agent had, prior to conception, *no ability whatsoever* to make things better for the child than they in fact are."[50] The delayed conception case is a genetic case: there is no way for the couple to create *this* child without the increased risk of developmental disability.[51] By contrast, in the expectational form of the nonidentity problem, "the agent has some slight chance – some slight *expectation* – of making things better for at least some future person."[52] The climate change case is an example of this: for any individual living 100 years in the future on an inhospitable planet it is very unlikely that she would have existed if humans had not polluted the planet as they did. Very unlikely, but not impossible, since nothing about polluting versus not polluting rules out the possibility that a particular future egg and sperm will join in either case.

---

[49] For a clear statement of her view, see Melinda Roberts and David Wasserman, "Dividing and Conquering the Nonidentity Problem," in S. Matthew Liao and Collin O'Neil (eds.), *Current Controversies in Bioethics* (New York: Routledge, 2017), 81–98.
[50] Ibid., 83.   [51] Note that Roberts uses the term "genetic" to refer to origins, not to genes.
[52] Roberts and Wasserman, "Dividing and Conquering the Nonidentity Problem," 83.

In genetic cases, Roberts believes that voluntarily creating a person who will have a flawed but worthwhile existence and whom the agent could not have created without the flaw need not be wrongful. We agree. Provided that third parties are not harmed or unduly burdened, then other members of society have no cause for complaint. And provided that the agent had some nontrivial reason for creating someone who has lower expected well-being than someone else she could have created, this can justify not making the world as good as she could have. As just noted, while we think that impersonal effects do matter, these impersonal effects do not have substantial moral weight.

To illustrate, return to the couple deciding whether to delay conception in order to avoid having a child with a developmental disability. Suppose that it would take a year for the woman to clear the infection and that women in her family have a history of early menopause – she is concerned that in a year's time she may be unable to conceive. This, it seems to us, would be sufficient reason to justify not delaying: they would not be introducing avoidable suffering to the world for a trivial reason.

On the other hand, suppose instead that the couple decide not to delay simply because they do not want to take an additional trip to pick up contraception. This would seem to fail to take seriously enough the challenges that a child born with a serious condition would experience. We could therefore criticize the couple for not taking into account the impersonal effects of their actions, such as the amount of well-being or suffering that they cause. Not delaying conception out of laziness would lead to a world with less expected well-being for no good reason.[53]

It does not seem overly counterintuitive to us that caring parents who accept having a child with a welfare-reducing disability do not act wrongly by bringing her into existence. Cases involving future generations are a different matter. It seems bizarre to think that future generations who have to struggle with the effects of climate change will not have been wronged by our twenty-first century neglect. Here, Roberts's distinction between the genetic and expectational forms of the nonidentity problems is crucial.

Consider one individual, Ahmed, living a life worth living 100 years from now on an Earth damaged by irresponsible earlier choices regarding the climate. Should he wish that we had not made such choices because then *he* would be living a better life? Presumably not: the chances that

---

[53] David Wasserman contends that the attitude of would-be parents toward their future child is also relevant to this assessment ("The Nonidentity Problem, Disability, and the Role Morality of Prospective Parents," *Ethics* 116 [2005]: 132–152).

Ahmed would have been born in the alternative timeline in which we reversed our irresponsible habits are very small indeed. This is why it might seem odd to say that Ahmed is harmed by the effects of our earlier choices.

But now consider the same question from the perspective of agents in the present. Suppose we are deciding whether to dramatically reduce emissions of greenhouse gases a century before the age of Ahmed. (It is, of course, implausible that we could collectively make a single choice of this kind, but imagining this possibility helps to simplify the thought experiment without affecting the moral lesson.) What are the chances that Ahmed, or any other specific possible individual, will exist in 100 years? They are very small in both possible futures. But, as far as we know, he might exist in either. Which future should we prefer for possible person Ahmed? Presumably, we should prefer the future in which he exists in a more hospitable world to the future in which he exists in a much less hospitable world. Both are unlikely – as far as we know they are equally unlikely – but Ahmed is much worse off in one than in the other.[54] His expected well-being is therefore lower under one choice than the other. This, we contend, provides the comparison that allows us to say that Ahmed is wronged if we make the irresponsible choice and he comes to exist. Ahmed, of course, is not special in this regard. For any possible person whose existence is – as far as we know – equally likely at the point of choosing whether to pollute, we can compare their lives in a polluting and a nonpolluting future. Each time, the expected well-being of that person is lower in the polluting future. Thus, whoever comes to exist on a polluting planet will be in a position to complain that they were wronged by our earlier actions.

To summarize, some procreative or other types of choices are identity-determining, in that there was no way the agent could have created a person without that person suffering from some well-being-diminishing condition. Even though they could have created someone else with higher well-being, they generally will not have acted wrongly, provided that their procreative decision was not arbitrary or based on trivial reasons. In other cases, which initially appeared equally identity-determining, the person suffering from diminished well-being actually might have existed otherwise and the action that caused the diminished well-being did not make that person's existence any more likely. In those cases, acting in the way that leads to diminished well-being wrongs the person who comes to exist.

[54] See Roberts and Wasserman, "Dividing and Conquering the Nonidentity Problem," 89–91, for a more extensive argument to this effect.

We have now extended our bioethical theory to encompass the ethics of creating human beings. Some of the practical upshot of our theoretical work becomes apparent as we apply it to two areas of bioethical interest: sex selection and reproductive decisions in the face of the Zika virus.

10.4   Sex Selection

Many couples who procreate care about the sex of their child. Some may fervently want to have a girl or to have a boy. We now have medical technologies that would allow them to make this happen. Prior to conception, sperm-sorting techniques can be used to increase the proportion of sperm carrying either X or Y chromosomes that are used in intrauterine insemination.[55] Prior to implantation using IVF, it is possible to select only embryos of one sex or the other. Post-conception, it is now possible to detect the sex of a fetus after seven weeks gestational age using noninvasive prenatal testing. Once the sex has been ascertained, elective abortion could be used to screen against children of the undesired sex.[56]

There are different reasons for which procreators might want to select the sex of their offspring. Some of these are medical. For example, Duchenne muscular dystrophy (DMD) is an X-linked recessive genetic disorder that causes severe suffering and premature death in males. A woman who thought she was a carrier of the mutated gene might want to select for a female child in order to avoid having a boy who suffered from DMD. Most commentators agree that avoiding serious hereditary diseases is sufficient justification for sex-selective procedures. They disagree regarding cases in which prospective parents wish to select the sex of their child, but do not anticipate that a child of the undesired sex would have a serious sex-linked health condition. For example, in many countries a large proportion of people have preferences for families with at least one son and one daughter.[57] In others, cultural preferences for sons are so strong that the sex ratio has been dramatically skewed by sex-selective abortions,

---

[55] Ethics Committee of the American Society for Reproductive Medicine, "Use of Reproductive Technology for Sex Selection for Nonmedical Reasons," *Fertility and Sterility* 103 (2015): 1418–1422.

[56] In some countries, sex selection may also take the form of infanticide, either by directly killing (usually) female babies or through neglect. Since we regard these practices as obviously very wrong, we do not discuss them here.

[57] See F. Arnold, "Gender Preferences for Children," *Demographic and Health Surveys Comparative Studies* 23 (1997): 1–56; and Karsten Hank and Hans-Peter Kohler, "Gender Preferences for Children in Europe: Empirical Results from 17 FFS Countries," *Demographic Research* 2 (2000; available at www.jstor.org/stable/26347999).

infanticide, and the mistreatment or neglect of female children. At birth, the natural ratio of male to female children is approximately 105:100.[58] In China, in 2017 it was estimated to be 115:100.[59] Similarly skewed sex ratios are found in many Indian states, countries in central Asia, and (until recently) South Korea.[60]

Regulations regarding sex selection tend to distinguish "medical" from "social" reasons. A 2009 analysis identified thirty-six countries with laws or policies on sex selection. Five of them, including South Korea, prohibited sex selection for any reason, and thirty-one, including China and India, prohibited it for "social" or "nonmedical" reasons.[61] Are such restrictions ethically justified? And would someone who used medical technologies to increase the chances of conceiving a child of a specific sex be acting wrongly?

Earlier in this chapter we argued for a general presumption in favor of permitting people to use reproductive technologies – the negative right to procreative autonomy. Restrictions on this liberty require justification. Absent such justification, individuals should be permitted to avail themselves of methods for choosing the sex of their child whether for medical reasons or because of their personal preferences.[62]

One possible justification for restricting sex-selective procedures is that sex selection would harm or otherwise wrong the child.[63] It has been suggested, for example, that the flow cytometry method of sperm sorting might pose safety risks.[64] The challenge for such justifications is that they seem to run afoul of the nonidentity problem. Sperm sorting affects which child comes into existence, and so it is hard to see how that child has been

[58] Fengqing Chao et al., "Systematic Assessment of the Sex Ratio at Birth for All Countries and Estimation of National Imbalances and Regional Reference Levels," *Proceedings of the National Academy of Sciences* 116 (2019): 9303–9311.

[59] World Economic Forum, *The Global Gender Gap Report 2018* (available at www.weforum.org/reports).

[60] Woojin Chung and Monica Das Gupta, "Why Is Son Preference Declining in South Korea?" (World Bank Policy Research Working Paper, 2007; available at https://ssrn.com/abstract=1020841).

[61] Marcy Darnovsky, "Countries with Laws or Policies on Sex Selection," *Center for Genetics and Society* (2009).

[62] John Harris, "Sex Selection and Regulated Hatred," *Journal of Medical Ethics* 31 (2005): 291–294.

[63] For discussion of other ethical objections raised against sex selection, see ESHRE Task Force on Ethics and Law 20, "Sex Selection for Non-medical Reasons," *Human Reproduction* 28 (2013): 1448–1454, at 2013; Ruth Macklin, "The Ethics of Sex Selection and Family Balancing," *Seminars in Reproductive Medicine* 28 (2010): 315–321; David McCarthy, "Why Sex Selection Should Be Legal," *Journal of Medical Ethics* 27 (2001): 302–307; and Julian Savulescu and Edgar Dahl, "Sex Selection and Preimplantation Diagnosis: A Response to the Ethics Committee of the American Society of Reproductive Medicine," *Human Reproduction* 15 (2000): 1879–1880.

[64] ESHRE Task Force, "Sex Selection for Non-medical Reasons."

harmed by the procedure given the reasonable presumption that they have a life worth living. Note that this same point applies to allowing sex selection on the basis of medical benefits to the child. When a female child is conceived instead of a male child in order to avoid an X-linked disorder, there is no individual who benefits by avoiding the disorder. Creating someone who will suffer less is better than creating someone who will suffer more, but we should not confuse this with saving any specific individual from suffering. Similar points about nonidentity have been raised to counter the view that sex selection should be prohibited because it constitutes sex discrimination.[65] Someone might prefer a male or a female child for sexist reasons, but choosing the sex does not seem to discriminate against any actual individuals.

A distinct objection argues that would-be parents who opt for sex selection for nonmedical reasons violate a parental duty. Rosalind McDougall argues that because children's characteristics are unpredictable, virtuous parents would exhibit acceptance toward their child.[66] A parent who would reject a child of the undesired sex fails to display this virtue, even if she in fact has a child of the sex she prefers. Similarly, Peter Herissone-Kelly argues that "proper parental love" is love that a parent would offer to "any incumbent" of the role of *their child*.[67] Parents should not choose their children, since: "Under such circumstances, B's nature does not enjoy the independence from A's will that is a necessary condition of A's authentically loving him."[68]

Both arguments advance claims about the appropriate attitudes of parents. But both, we think, rely on dubious empirical assertions. McDougall claims that parents who attempt to have a child of one sex and end up with another will reject that child. However, in conception, as in other endeavors, trying for one outcome does not preclude acceptance of the actual result. Virtuous athletes try to win but accept it if they lose. Likewise, parents who try to raise their child to be sporty are still able to accept her when she prefers a book to a racquet. It seems perfectly possible that a parent could love any child they have while still trying to make the

---

[65] Macklin, "The Ethics of Sex Selection and Family Balancing," 317–318.

[66] Rosalind McDougall, "Acting Parentally: An Argument against Sex Selection," *Journal of Medical Ethics* 31 (2005): 601–605.

[67] See Peter Herissone-Kelly, "Parental Love and the Ethics of Sex Selection," *Cambridge Quarterly of Healthcare Ethics* 16 (2007): 326–335; and Peter Herissone-Kelly, "The 'Parental Love' Objection to Nonmedical Sex Selection: Deepening the Argument," *Cambridge Quarterly of Healthcare Ethics* 16 (2007): 446–455.

[68] Herissone-Kelly, "Parental Love and the Ethics of Sex Selection," 334.

actual incumbent fit their preferences. We can, for example, make clear sense of the person who says, "I'm going to bring my son up to be sporty and assertive: it would be so painful to love a child who was weak and got bullied." And we do not regard adoptive parents who chose a child similar to them in race, of a specific sex, or with (or without) a disability as somehow disqualified from authentically loving their child.

At the individual level, then, there do not seem to be good reasons to prohibit sex selection. Two questions remain. First, should public resources be used to provide people with the means to select the sex of their child? In most cases, we think the claim to assistance will be weak when would-be parents are acting on personal preferences for the sex of their child – a case would have to be made for why this sort of preference could ground a claim to scarce health care funds. On the other hand, when sex selection would reduce the chances of creating a child with a serious health condition, there are good reasons for public resources to be spent on it. After all, it is those same public resources that will be used to treat the health condition, and reducing the amount of suffering in the world is a morally valuable goal.

The second question is how policy-makers should take into account the wider social effects of permitting or restricting the use of sex-selective technologies. Here we think much depends on the specific social context. There likely can be situations in which harm to others is sufficient to outweigh the value of procreative autonomy. For example, in countries where the sex ratio is heavily skewed, there are concerns about the social unrest that may result from the millions of men who will remain unmarried (given the value placed on marrying and having children).[69] There might therefore be good reasons to restrict access to sex-selective technologies in these countries. Such considerations would not support restrictions in other countries, like most European countries, in which current sex preferences do not seem likely to skew the sex ratio.

10.5 Zika and the Nonidentity Problem

During 2015 and 2016 a Zika virus epidemic spread across Latin America and the Caribbean. Zika virus had previously been documented in only a few cases and was not considered a serious disease. It causes mild fever, joint pain, and rashes in about 20 percent of people infected. Zika virus is primarily transmitted by mosquito bites (though sexual transmission also

[69] Xinran Xue, "The Worldwide War on Baby Girls," *The Economist* (March 4, 2010): 77–80.

occurs). The warm temperatures and high rainfall of 2015 and 2016 were conducive to the spread of the virus, and tens of thousands of people were infected in Brazil and other South American countries. With the higher numbers of people infected, additional health effects of infection became apparent. In adults, a small fraction of people developed Guillain-Barré syndrome – a serious neurological disorder in which the body's immune system attacks the peripheral nervous system, sometimes causing extensive paralysis. Zika infection also affected some of the babies of infected pregnant women, causing congenital Zika syndrome (CZS) – a serious condition characterized by brain malformations, including microcephaly (small head size as a result of improper brain development).[70]

Due to the increased risk of microcephaly and other effects on fetal development, several countries recommended that women who were planning to become pregnant delay doing so.[71] Outbreaks were expected to be limited in duration and people who became infected would likely develop immunity to the virus. Thus, delaying pregnancy by even a few months would substantially reduce the probability of giving birth to a child with CZS. These recommendations were criticized on the grounds that they placed responsibility for avoiding Zika infection on women living in countries where access to contraception was limited and more than 50 percent of pregnancies were unplanned.[72] But even for women with access to birth control and effective control over their reproductive lives, the recommendations generate an ethical conundrum by implicating the nonidentity problem.

In fact, this situation is very similar to the scenario we described in introducing the nonidentity problem. If a couple delayed conceiving during an outbreak, then they would reduce the probability that any child they created would have CZS. But, as we have seen, this would be a different child than the one they would have created during the outbreak. Any child born with CZS could not have been helped by such a delay.

The added complication in this case is that other measures could be taken to protect a fetus from the Zika virus. For example, mosquito control measures – such as indoor residual spraying, removal of breeding

---

[70] World Health Organization, "One Year into the Zika Outbreak: How an Obscure Disease Became a Global Health Emergency" (Geneva: WHO, May 5, 2016) (available at www.who.int/emergencies/zika-virus/articles/one-year-outbreak/en/).

[71] *BBC News*, "Zika Virus Triggers Pregnancy Delay Calls" (January 23, 2016) (available at www.bbc.com/news/world-latin-america-35388842).

[72] Charlotte Alter, "Why Latin American Women Can't Follow the Zika Advice to Avoid Pregnancy," *Time* (January 28, 2016) (available at https://time.com/4197318/).

sites, and individual use of insect repellants – would reduce the chances of a pregnant woman getting infected with Zika virus to begin with. Though there are no current vaccines or treatments available, research into Zika virus is underway, and such medical interventions may become available in the future. Individuals and governments have – or may have in the near future – methods to protect children who will come to exist.

Two types of decision-maker can be helpfully distinguished for the purposes of ethical analysis: individuals who are considering having a child and policy-makers deciding how to address a public health problem.

From the point of view of an individual woman or couple, our view on the nonidentity problem applies in a straightforward manner. All else being equal, they should choose to delay rather than conceive, since that will lead to the creation of a child with higher expected well-being. However, as we noted in our discussion above, all else may not be equal. If the couple have a nontrivial reason to press on with trying to conceive, then that may be sufficient to justify doing so. They cannot wrong the child they create by choosing to procreate now rather than later. Either way, means permitting, they should take steps to reduce risks to the fetus they actually conceive.

From the point of view of a policy-maker, matters are different. Resources for health care and public health are limited, so hard allocation decisions must be made. Resources spent on providing and promoting contraception cannot be spent on eliminating mosquito breeding sites and spraying insecticides. Does the nonidentity problem affect such allocation decisions?

To see why it might, consider two possible public health interventions.[73] In the first, the government allocates its Zika funds to mosquito control measures. Where effective, these protect pregnant women and thereby fetuses who would otherwise have developed CZS. In the second intervention, the government allocates the same funds to providing at-risk individuals with contraception. Where effective, this delays conception and leads to the creation of individuals who do not have CZS instead of the creation of individuals who do have CZS. Suppose, for the sake of discussion, that the cost and impact on the number of cases of CZS are the same for each intervention.[74] If the government should care more about

---

[73] This scenario is based on one discussed in Keyur Doolabh et al., "Zika, Contraception, and the Non-identity Problem," *Developing World Bioethics* 17 (2017): 173–204.

[74] If they differed, we would still want to know the cost-effectiveness of each and so we would still want to know if we should evaluate one differently than the other on the basis of nonidentity concerns.

helping individuals who will exist than about "helpfully" changing which individuals will come to exist, then it should prefer the mosquito control measures. Indeed, even if the mosquito control measures are (somewhat) more expensive or less effective, this view would still imply that the government should prefer those measures.

Despite our views on the individual case, when it comes to the policy matter of allocating societal resources, we think that policy-makers should evaluate the two interventions in the same way. This is because the *claims* that individuals will have on societal resources are the same in both scenarios. Take a fetus that would develop CZS without the mosquito control intervention. The loss of well-being to the child into whom the fetus will develop grounds a claim to resources to prevent that loss. Equally, for those children who do get CZS, they will have a claim to resources to help treat their condition. The basis for the claim is the same, even though, given existing technologies, preventing CZS is much more cost-effective than treating its effects. Now consider a child born with CZS because her parents did not have access to contraception and so could not delay conception. That child will have the same claim to societal resources to treat her condition. In this case, the government could avoid having to expend scarce resources on treatment by preventing children who need treatment from coming into existence – that is, by providing access to contraception. From the point of view of a government deciding how to allocate scarce societal resources, the two interventions can be treated the same.

Concluding Thoughts

This book has covered a lot of ground. We began with the development of our theory of bioethics at a very abstract level. It is an ethical theory that recognizes two fundamental values – well-being and respect for rights-holders – along with a formal principle of equal consideration. At this level, it is easy to state, but it is not immediately obvious how to apply it to problems in bioethics. Much of the book has therefore involved specifying the theory at a level of detail that allows us to apply it to real-world questions. Given that well-being is a fundamental value, we need to know what well-being consists in, what it is to harm and to benefit someone, and who has a welfare that matters morally. Given that respect for rights-holders is a fundamental value, we need to know who has rights, what they are rights to, and so forth. Development and application of the theory go hand-in-hand.

Specifying the theory at a level of detail that allows it to be applied has led to our consideration of a wide range of topics in clinical ethics, research ethics, and health policy. Among others, in clinical ethics, we examined medical assistance-in-dying, proxy decision-making, treatment decisions for impaired newborns, advance directives for dementia patients, and the nature of death. In research ethics, we addressed permissible risk levels in pediatric research, embryonic stem-cell research, and research with rodents and great apes. As for health policy, applications of our theory included explorations of pharmaceutical marketing, access to health care, intellectual property laws, and sex selection.

Beyond these developed applications, there remain many important questions in bioethics that we have not covered. These include questions relating to the role morality of clinicians, medicalization and the classification of disease, race and racism in medicine, numerous issues concerning the design of clinical trials and the provision of benefits to research participants and communities, how public health systems should allocate scarce resources for care and research, and the proper scope of health care.

Nor is this list exhaustive, as a glance at the table of contents of any of the many bioethics journals will show.

Our coverage of issues in contemporary bioethics is incomplete. Moreover, our conclusions regarding the issues that we do cover are often controversial: we do not attempt to represent a consensus view. What, then, one might ask, should a reader make of all this theorizing?

Our goal is neither to be complete nor to have the final word. It is more modest than that. We aim for sufficient clarity in the presentation of our theory and how we developed it that it can help readers in their own thinking about bioethics. Where they disagree, we hope that it will be clear where the disagreement lies and what underlies it. That recognition will help them to develop their views on the basis of rigorous, well-informed argumentation. Where they find the theory plausible, we hope that it will be clear how to apply it to the specific questions in bioethics that the reader finds pressing and unresolved. That may illuminate those questions. Our theory of bioethics is a tool whose value will depend on how it is used.

Recommended Further Readings

Bioethics

Beauchamp, Tom, and James Childress, *Principles of Biomedical Ethics*, 8th ed. (New York: Oxford University Press, 2019).

O'Neill, Onora, *Autonomy and Trust in Bioethics* (Cambridge: Cambridge University Press, 2002).

Steinbock, Bonnie (ed.), *The Oxford Handbook of Bioethics* (New York: Oxford University Press, 2007).

Sugarman, Jeremy, and Daniel Sulmasy (eds.), *Methods in Medical Ethics*, 2nd ed. (Washington, DC: Georgetown University Press, 2010).

Veatch, Robert, *A Theory of Medical Ethics* (New York: Basic Books, 1981).

Moral Philosophy

Griffin, James, *Well-Being* (Oxford: Clarendon, 1986).

Hooker, Brad, *Ideal Code, Real World* (Oxford: Clarendon, 2000).

Kamm, Frances, *Intricate Ethics: Rights, Responsibilities, and Permissible Harm* (New York: Oxford University Press, 2007).

Parfit, Derek, *Reasons and Persons* (Oxford: Clarendon, 1984).

Singer, Peter, *Practical Ethics*, 3rd ed. (Cambridge: Cambridge University Press, 2011).

Political and Legal Philosophy

Appiah, K. Anthony, and Amy Guttman, *Color Conscious: The Political Morality of Race* (Princeton, NJ: Princeton University Press, 1996).

Brock, Gillian, *Global Justice* (Oxford: Oxford University Press, 2009).

Feinberg, Joel, *Harm to Others* (New York: Oxford University Press, 1984).

Kymlicka, Will, *Contemporary Political Philosophy*, 2nd ed. (Oxford: Oxford University Press, 2002).

Nozick, Robert, *Anarchy, State, and Utopia* (New York: Basic Books, 1974).

Nussbaum, Martha, *Frontiers of Justice: Disability, Nationality, Species Membership* (Cambridge, MA: Belknap Press, 2006).

Rawls, John, *A Theory of Justice* (Cambridge, MA: Harvard University Press, 1971).

Sandel, Michael, *Justice: What's the Right Thing to Do?* (New York: Farrar, Straus and Giroux, 2009).

Topics in Bioethics and Philosophy

Benatar, David, and David Wasserman, *Debating Procreation* (New York: Oxford University Press, 2015).

Buchanan, Allen, and Dan Brock, *Deciding for Others* (New York: Cambridge University Press, 1989).

DeGrazia, David, *Taking Animals Seriously: Mental Life and Moral Status* (New York: Cambridge University Press, 1996).

   Human Identity and Bioethics (New York: Cambridge University Press, 2005).

Faden, Ruth, and Tom Beauchamp, *A History and Theory of Informed Consent* (New York: Oxford University Press, 1986).

McMahan, Jeff, *The Ethics of Killing* (Oxford: Oxford University Press, 2002).

Millum, Joseph, *The Moral Foundations of Parenthood* (New York: Oxford University Press, 2018).

Norheim, Ole, Ezekiel Emanuel, and Joseph Millum (eds.), *Global Health Priority-Setting* (New York: Oxford University Press, 2019).

Olson, Eric, *The Human Animal: Personal Identity without Psychology* (New York: Oxford University Press, 1997).

Schechtman, Marya, *Staying Alive: Personal Identity, Practical Concerns, and the Unity of a Life* (New York: Oxford University Press, 2014).

Sumner, L. W., *Assisted Death* (Oxford: Clarendon, 2011).

Warren, Mary Anne, *Moral Status* (Oxford: Oxford University Press, 1997).

Wertheimer, Alan, *Coercion* (Hoboken, NJ: John Wiley & Sons, 1987).

Index

For EU product safety concerns, contact us at Calle de José Abascal, 56–1°,
28003 Madrid, Spain or eugpsr@cambridge.org.

www.ingramcontent.com/pod-product-compliance
Ingram Content Group UK Ltd.
Pitfield, Milton Keynes, MK11 3LW, UK
UKHW020359140625
459647UK00020B/2560